EDUCATION REFORM

EDUCATION REFORM

Making Sense of It All

Edited by

SAMUEL B. BACHARACH

Cornell University

Allyn and Bacon
Boston   London   Sydney   Toronto

Copyright © 1990 by Allyn and Bacon
A Division of Simon & Schuster, Inc.
160 Gould Street
Needham Heights, Massachusetts 02194

Library of Congress Cataloging-in-Publication Data

Education reform: making sense of it all / edited by Samuel B.
    Bacharach.
        p.   cm.
    Includes bibliographical references.
    ISBN 0–205–11957–3
        1. Education—United States—Aims and objectives.
    2. Educational planning—United States.   3. Education—United
    States—Evaluation.
    I. Bacharach, Samuel B.
    LA217.R393   1990
    370′.973—dc20   89–35939
                                                                         CIP

Printed in the United States of America
10 9 8 7 6 5 4 3 2 1 93 92 91 90

Contents

Foreword

Governor Bill Clinton of Arkansas

W<small>HEN</small> *A Nation at Risk* burst on the national scene like a firestorm in early 1983, feelings about public education and its problems that a large majority of Americans had held for some time began to surface.

All over the United States, and especially in the South, the poorest and least educated part of the country, people began to respond. Even before *A Nation at Risk*, Florida and Mississippi had enacted major reform programs supported by tax increases for schools.

Since then, there has been a substantial effort to upgrade education in almost every state: to increase the number of courses schools have to offer and the number students must take; to reduce class size in the early grades; to increase opportunities for gifted students; to provide more computers; to test students more; to evaluate teachers more effectively; and, in many states, to reward outstanding performance by schools, students, and teachers.

In almost every state, the schools are doing a better job and students are learning more. In my state, enrollment over the past five years is up by 300 percent in advanced math, 270 percent in foreign languages, and 330 percent in computer science. The college-going rate is up by 15 percent, and the dropout rate is the lowest in the South.

Still, American students' scores are behind those of most other countries' students on science and math exams. Our dropout rates are far higher than those of all our competitors, as are our rates of infant mortality, teen pregnancy, and drug abuse. Because our school year is so short, our high school graduates have two to three years' less knowledge than their counterparts in other countries. That explains in part the stunning findings of the recent Grant Commission that the earnings of high school graduates under age 25 are 28 percent less than they were 15 years ago.

We have to measure ourselves by international standards. By those standards, we're not doing very well. Unless we do better, our ability to compete in the world economy will be severely damaged.

Samuel Bacharach has gathered here an outstanding collection of essays on the state of education reform in the United States. Professor Bacharach provides a needed perspective on the "second wave" of reform in which we currently find ourselves. The reader will find deeply insightful writings on the movement through a discussion of the federalism of the reform effort, as well as essays on school choice, values, effective teaching methods, and the never-ending debate over how our children should learn. Dr. Bacharach's concluding essay offers a perceptive analysis of the five themes of reform.

Like most others, I have my own ideas of what steps we should be taking to ensure that the accomplishments of the first wave of reform are not short-lived. The United States must continue its efforts to upgrade its educational system. First, like modern corporations, our schools need restructuring, with goals set from the top but more decisions made at the grassroots school level. That means reducing bureaucracy, paperwork, and unnecessary layers of management. It means pushing more decisions down to the school level. To do that, we have to do a better job of selecting, training, and supporting local school teachers. We have to do more to get teachers involved in decision making, including issues of curriculum and school organization.

Second, we have to pay teachers more. Our schools will only be as good as our teachers are, and present pay levels just aren't competitive with those in other professions, especially after the first few years on the job.

Third, we have to increase the number of our high school graduates who go on to college or other postsecondary education. Our competitors in Europe and Japan, with a much longer school year, have had about two years' more learning than U.S. students by the time they finish high school.

Fourth, we have to do a better job of keeping kids in school, and keeping them free of drugs, teen pregnancy, and other problems.

Fifth, we have to develop ways to teach our students to be better problem solvers as well as to master more information. That's what it takes to make it in our competitive, technologically complex world.

Sixth, we have to make sure our education efforts include measures of accountability by strengthening our ability to ensure that schools are meeting the standards fully.

The nation has come a long way since we began these efforts in 1983. That is why, although we still have much to do, I remain optimistic. I have seen how much we can accomplish when we really care about the future of our children.

Our education system is still at risk. The risk, now, is that we'll fail to follow through after coming so far.

Foreword

Governor Thomas H. Kean of New Jersey

SAM BACHARACH DESERVES our thanks for collecting these essays under one title. They represent the thoughtful opinions of some of this country's most respected experts on virtually every important topic of educational reform. This book should prove to be an important asset as we struggle to come to grips with how best to improve our schools. It will be particularly valuable to that important group of participants who are now largely unheard in discussions of educational reform: our teachers in training. Here they can find the seminal arguments that may very well determine their futures in—or out of—education.

In organizing these essays into six of the most important issues facing the education establishment and its constituents, Professor Bacharach enables both the newcomer and the old hand to arrive at (or reconsider) his or her opinions on how our schools should be run.

A single thread runs throughout virtually all of these proposals and discussions of how best to prepare our schools and our students for the challenges of the twenty-first century. That common but unstated denominator is the crying need for *leadership* on every level and in every interest group.

It is important to differentiate between "being the boss" and being a leader. If I risk offending those in traditional leadership positions, at least this single shoe will pinch many feet equally.

Being the boss implies a fairly arbitrary allocation of power. In essence, being the boss allows you to tell other people what to do. Being a leader, on the other hand, is much harder; it involves having a clear sense of what needs to be done and the ability to convince usually skeptical followers to choose for themselves the path you suggest, as opposed to ordering them down it. The difference, in effect, is between confrontation and persuasion.

As you read the chapters of this book, notice that—no matter which side of the issue the author takes, or even which issue is in question—a basic assumption common to all of them is that leadership is the sine qua non at every level of action, from the Oval Office to the principal's office, from the school board meeting room to the individual teacher's classroom.

Professor Bacharach begins his summary chapter with the observation that words and ideas are often bandied about too loosely when we discuss educational reform. Each player takes on a bit of the attitude of Humpty Dumpty in Lewis Carroll's *Through the Looking Glass:* "When *I* use a word it means just what I choose it to mean—neither more nor less." Because such posturing only clouds the waters of fruitful debate, let me briefly explain what *I* consider to be the fundamental elements of leadership.

Leadership requires *vision*—the ability to question established and entrenched traditions in light of the bigger picture, as well as a clear sense of what that bigger picture is. It requires *experience*—a proven track record that inspires trust in those one would have follow.

But vision and experience are candles under a bushel barrel unless one also has the ability to communicate vividly that bigger picture and to inspire those one would lead. Also essential is *power*, not to wield arbitrarily, but (as the old joke goes) to get the mule's attention—also, to give others confidence that one's efforts will be effective.

Finally, true leadership takes *time*. A desert thunderstorm strikes with a flash and a roar, releasing all its water and energy at once. But the flashes quickly fade, and the water is mostly lost in runoff. Effective leadership takes the time to allow efforts and skills the chance to sink in, as opposed to the flash-flood phenomenon of high-visibility attempts at quick fixes. It takes the time to allow others to consider and embrace one's proposals, to win over those committed to different agendas. Time, however, is no excuse for inaction. If we are to turn deserts into gardens, it is not enough to wait for the rain. We must take action and irrigate.

Vision, experience, and the skills to convey them are developed from within. But what about power and time? These must be granted by others, whether one is a kindergarten teacher or a member of Congress. This is precisely my point about leadership: It comes from the consent of those who would be led. It comes, in other words, through cooperation, not confrontation. And it comes from keeping sight of the ultimate goal of education: to prepare our children for their future.

If my definition of leadership or my description of the challenges presented in these chapters makes true education reform seem daunting, take heart. Improving our schools *should* be a difficult, drawn-out process— it is the most important issue facing us as a nation. No other issue demands the direct involvement of every single person in the country; no other issue will so directly affect this country's economic, moral, cultural, and intellectual future. Quite literally, our children *are* our future.

As all the participants in this difficult process become more aware of the implications of this seemingly obvious fact, their pointing fingers will, one hopes, turn away from each other and toward the path to a greater tomorrow.

Acknowledgments

THIS BOOK REFLECTS years of commitment to the improvement of education. Each of the contributors has been actively involved in trying to rethink our attitudes toward education, restructure the framework of education, and better understand the educational process. It is for this reason that I want to thank each of the contributors who gave their time to write a thoughtful essay for this book.

During this two-year process, I have been assisted by many individuals. My colleagues in Ithaca at Organizational Analysis and Practice (OAP), including Stephen Mitchell, Scott Bauer, Joseph Shedd, Rose Malanowski, and Thomas Corcoran, have been the primary source for many of my thoughts about education reform. Indeed, their applied work in such areas as evaluations, compensation, school-site management, and career development gave me the benefit of first-hand experience with the reform movement. Working as one of their active consultants in the field gave me an opportunity to visit districts throughout the country and made clear to me how widespread this movement is. Ultimately, it is practitioners like my colleagues at OAP who make the difference.

Peter Kachris, superintendent of Orleans-Niagara BOCES, has been a constant source of intellectual support. Frank Masters, while serving as the research director of the National Education Association, opened doors often closed to academics. My colleague Sharon Conley at the University of Arizona strongly supported this project throughout. Cecil Miskel at the University of Michigan, Rod Ogawa and Steve Bossert at the University of Utah, and Bruce Cooper at Fordham University have all been of great assistance throughout this project.

Bryan Mundell helped considerably with the difficult task of putting together thirty-two different essays into a coherent framework, and Anna Mundell kept the process, paperwork, and people from falling apart in disorder. Mylan Jaixen at Allyn and Bacon has been supportive from beginning to end, as has his entire staff, especially Terry Williams. Lori Van xvi *Acknowledgments*

Etta, my secretary at OAP, took on the administrative responsibility of coordinating the difficult logistics of such a volume. Tim Schmidle also gave generously of his time to fine-tune the volume. Alex Green was a supportive friend on this project, as he has been on other projects.

Many of the chapters in this book originally appeared, some of them in slightly different form, in two issues that I edited for *Educational Administration Quarterly*, Volume 24, Numbers 3 (August) and 4 (November) 1988. These articles, copyright © 1988 by the University Council for Educational Administration, are reprinted by permission of the authors and Sage Publications, Inc.

I will always be grateful to my three good friends Fred, Carol, and Bosch, who provided humorous nonacademic escapes during this entire period.

Finally, I want to thank Moe Rhine, who introduced me to the field of educational administration.

Samuel B. Bacharach

Contributing Authors

Michael W. Apple is professor in the Departments of Curriculum and Instruction and Educational Policy Studies at the University of Wisconsin at Madison. His research interests are the relationships of political, economic, and cultural power and education. His recent publications are *Education and Power*, 1986, and *Teachers and Texts*, 1988 (both Routledge & Kegan Paul).

Jann Azumi is a management specialist in the Newark, New Jersey, public school system and a former member of the board of education in the city in which she resides. Her research interests include organizational structure and processes, organizational change, and teacher reward systems. She has recently published "Selecting and Rewarding Master Teachers: What Teachers in One District Think," co-authored with James L. Larman (*The Elementary School Journal*, November 1987).

Samuel B. Bacharach is professor of organizational behavior and education administration at Cornell University. He is also currently a senior research consultant with Organizational Analysis Practice, Ithaca, New York. In education, he has written on such topics as merit pay, school administrative evaluation and school-based management. Among his books are *Power and Politics in Organizations, Bargaining Power Tactics and Outcomes, Paying for Better Teaching: Merit Pay and Its Alternatives*, and an edited volume titled *Organizational Behavior in Schools and School Districts*. He is currently completing a volume on education reform and is the author of the forthcoming book *Organizational Behavior: The Science of Analysis and the Art of Synthesis*.

John H. Bishop is associate professor of personnel and human resource studies at the ILR School, Cornell University. His research interests include the hiring, training, and promotion of workers and the impact of educational quality on the nation's productivity and competitiveness; the competencies required to get and keep jobs; and the effectiveness of different educational and training institutions. Professor Bishop has written numerous articles and books on youth employment, job training, and the economics of poverty. He has testified before congressional committees on economic growth, employment, and revenue sharing.

William Lowe Boyd is professor of education at Pennsylvania State University. His research interests are educational policy and politics, and organizational behavior. He was co-editor of *Educational Policy in Australia and America: Comparative Perspectives* and *The Politics of Excellence and Choice in Education* (both Falmer Press, 1988).

Ernest L. Boyer is president of the Carnegie Foundation for the Advancement of Teaching, Princeton, New Jersey. Two of his recent publications are *College: The Undergraduate Experience in America*, 1987, and *High School: A Report on Secondary Education in America*, 1983 (both Harper & Row).

Edwin M. Bridges is professor of education at Stanford University and is also director of the Prospective Principals' Program. Author of *Managing the Incompetent Teacher* and *The Incompetent Teacher*, he has lectured on the problem of teacher incompetence in both the United States and the People's Republic of China. Professor Bridges has also served as consultant to local school districts, universities, associations for school administrators, and various international organizations including the World Health Organization and the World Bank.

Sharon C. Conley is assistant professor in the Department of Educational Administration at the University of Arizona, Tucson. Her research interests include organizational behavior in school districts, career development, and job design. One of her most recent publications is "Holmes Group Report: Standards, Hierarchies, and Management," co-authored with Samuel B. Bacharach (*Teachers College Record*, Spring 1987).

Bruce S. Cooper is associate professor of education administration and policy at the Fordham University School of Education, New York. He was senior lecturer and visiting scholar at the Institute of Education, University of London, 1986–1988, where he examined the progress of Tory school reforms, particularly efforts to decentralize and "privatize" education. His research has focused on school politics and policy and reform in public and private schools. His recent books include *Magnet Schools* and *The Separation of Church and Child*, with Tom Vitullo-Martin; forthcoming, with Denis Doyle, is *Federal Aid to the Disadvantaged: What Future for Chapter 1?*

Larry Cuban is professor of education in the School of Education at Stanford University, Stanford, California. His research interests are history of instruction (K–12 and university), urban schools (policymaking, administration, instruction, and curriculum), and leadership. His recent publications include *The Managerial Imperative: The Practice of Leadership in Schools* (State University of New York Press, 1988) and *How Teachers Taught* (Longman, 1984).

Denis Doyle, currently senior research fellow at the Hudson Institute, is a recognized authority on education policy both in the United States and abroad. He has written widely about education for scholarly and popular audiences, including the recently published *Winning the Brain Race: A Bold Plan to Make Our Schools Competitive,* with David T. Kearns, chief executive officer of the Xerox Corporation. Mr. Doyle has held several posts in government service and has been a consultant to many organizations, including the Ford Foundation, the Institute for Educational Leadership, and the Xerox Corporation.

Mary Hatwood Futrell is past president of the National Education Association, Washington, D.C. Her research includes site-based decision making and equal educational opportunities for children. Her most recent articles include "Selecting and Compensating Mentor Teachers: A Win-Win Scenario" (*Theory into Practice,* Summer 1988); "Public Schools and Four-Year-Olds" (*American Psychologist,* March 1987); and "Equity in Education: An Economic and Moral Imperative" (*Proceedings of the American Association of Colleges of Teacher Education,* Spring 1987).

Lynette Diamond Glasman is a private consultant in the field of program evaluation. Her research includes program evaluation, cognitive development, and educational psychology.

Naftaly S. Glasman is professor in the Graduate School of Education, University of California at Santa Barbara. He researches evaluation in decision making. His most recent publications are *Evaluation-Based Leadership: School Administration in Contemporary Perspective* (State University of New York Press, 1986) and *Evaluation in Decision Making: The Case of School Administration* (Kluwer Academic Publishers, 1988).

Emil J. Haller is professor in the Department of Education at Cornell University in Ithaca, New York. His research includes social class, race and ability grouping, and rural education. Two of his most recent publications are *The Ethics of School Administration* (Teachers College Press, 1988) and *An Introduction to Educational Administration* (Longman, 1986).

Willis D. Hawley is dean of Peabody College and professor of education and political science at Vanderbilt University in Nashville, Tennessee. His research includes teacher education, school reform, urban politics, organizational change, and educational policy. His most recent publications are *Good Schools* (1984) and *The Politics of Government of Reorganization* (1988).

Bill Honig is currently the California Superintendent of Public Instruction. He is a former teacher, administrator, and member of the California State Board of Education. His most recent publications are *Last Chance for Our Children: How You Can Help Save Our Schools* (Addison-Wesley) and *Handbook for Planning an Effective Reading Program* (4th printing, California State Department of Education, 1983).

Charles T. Kerchner is associate professor at the Claremont Graduate School, Claremont, California. His research includes educational politics and governance, human resource management, and organizational development. His most recent publications are *The Politics of Excellence and Choice in Education*, co-authored with William L. Boyd, and *The Changing Idea of a Teachers' Union*, co-authored with Douglas Mitchell (both Falmer Press, 1988).

Michael W. Kirst is professor of education and chair of administration and policy analysis in the School of Education at Stanford University, Stanford, California. He is also co-director of Policy Analysis for California Education. His research interests are the politics of education, and federal and state policy analysis. His most recent books include *Who Controls Our Schools* (W. H. Freeman) and *Schools in Conflict* (McCutchan).

Daniel Koretz is senior social scientist with the Rand Corporation in Washington, D.C. Dr. Koretz's research interests are educational assessment and indicators, educational accountability, mathematics and science education, and education of the disadvantaged. Two of his most recent publications are *Trends in Educational Achievement* (Congressional Budget Office, 1986) and *Educational Achievement: Explanations and Implications of Recent Trends* (Congressional Budget Office, 1987).

Betty Malen is an associate professor in the Department of Educational Administration at the University of Utah. She received her Ph.D. from the University of Minnesota and joined the faculty of the University of Utah in 1984. Her main interests are in educational policy and politics. At present she is studying school-based management and mechanisms of participative decision making as strategies in the reform movement.

Carl Marburger is one of three senior associates responsible to a board of directors for the operation of the National Committee for Citizens in Education (NCCE). Prior to coming to NCCE, he was commissioner of education for the State of New Jersey, and has also been a public schoolteacher and administrator. Long a practitioner of democratic decision making, he brings his passion and enthusiasm to the process called school-based management.

Marcello Medina, Jr., is assistant professor in the Program of Educational Administration at the University of Arizona. His research interests are Hispanics and school reform, longitudinal effects of bilingual education programs, and state policymaking and bilingual education. His recent publications are "Passing Arizona's Bilingual Education Legislation: A Case Study in the Management of Policy Symbols" (*Educational Policy*, 1988) and "Academic Achievement as Influenced by Bilingual Instruction for Spanish-Dominant Mexican American Children" (*Hispanic Journal of Behavioral Sciences*, 1985).

Mary Haywood Metz is associate professor of educational policy studies at the University of Wisconsin at Madison. Her broad research includes the organizational life of schools, including teachers' working lives, authority and control in schools, and the organizational and political processes surrounding desegregation. Two of her most recent publications are *The Context and Character of Three Magnet Schools* (Routledge & Kegan Paul, 1986) and *Classrooms and Corridors: The Crisis of Authority in Desegregated Secondary Schools* (University of California Press, 1978).

David H. Monk is associate professor in the Department of Education at Cornell University in Ithaca, New York. His research includes economic aspects of educational administration. His most recent publications include *Educational Finance: An Economic Approach* (Random House, in press) and *Micro-Level School Finance: Issues and Implications for Policy*, edited with Julie Underwood (Ballinger, 1988).

Rodney Muth is a professor of educational administration and chairperson of the Department of Personnel Services at Wichita State University in Wichita, Kansas, and formerly was a school board member in New Jersey. His research interests include power, leadership, educational governance and reform, and policy analysis and problem-solving models. Among his recent publications are "The Decision Seminar: A Problem-Solving Technique for School Administrators" (*Planning and Changing*, Spring 1987); "Balance the Power: Schooling Loses When Either the Board or the Superintendent Always Wins," co-authored with Vincent Beni and Bruce Cooper (*American School Board Journal*, August 1988); and "Harold Dwight Lasswell: A Biographical Profile," in *Harold D. Lasswell: An Annotated Bibliography* by Rodney Muth, Mary Finley, and Marcia Muth (Kluwer Academic Publishers, 1989).

Rodney T. Ogawa is an associate professor in the Department of Educational Administration at the University of Utah. He received his Ph.D. from the Ohio State University in 1979 and completed a year of postdoctoral study at Stanford University. Professor Ogawa's main interests are the application of organizational theory and the study of administrative leadership in educational settings. Currently he is engaged in an examination of school-based management and participative decision making as reform strategies.

A. Harry Passow is Jacob H. Schiff Professor of Education at Teachers College, Columbia University, New York City. His research interests are urban education, education of the gifted, and school reform. His most recent publications are "Present and Future Directions in School Reform," in *Restructuring Schooling for Quality Education: A New Reform Agenda,* edited by T. Sergiovanni (Allyn and Bacon, 1989) and "Curriculum and Instruction: Reactions," in *Education for Whom?* edited by B. I. Williams, P. A. Richmond, and B. J. Mason (Chapel Hill, N.C.: Research and Evaluation Associates, 1987).

Robert B. Reich teaches courses in law, political economy, and public management at Harvard's John F. Kennedy School of Government. His current research focuses on the government's role in helping a national economy adjust to changes in world markets and on the relationships between law and industrial structure. While in government, Mr. Reich served as director of policy planning for the Federal Trade Commission (1976–1981); assistant to the U.S. Solicitor General (1974–1976); and law clerk to Judge Frank M. Coffin, chief judge of the U.S. Court of Appeals for the First Circuit (1973–1974). As a Rhodes Scholar, Mr. Reich studied economics at Oxford University from 1968 to 1970; thereafter he received his J.D. from Yale University. Mr. Reich is the author of *The Next American Frontier* (1983) and *Tales of a New America* (1987), co-author of *Minding America's Business* (1982) and *New Deals: The Chrysler Revival and the American System* (1985), and the editor of *The Power of Public Ideas* (1987). He has published numerous articles on regulation, economic policy, and public administration.

Richard L. Schwab is an associate professor of education at the University of New Hampshire and is director of field experiences in their Five-Year Education Program. His current research interests are in the areas of occupational stress, personnel evaluation and extended teacher education programs. Professor Schwab's academic accomplishments include publications in major journals in teacher education and educational administration and a book, *Teach Them Well: An Introduction to Education* (Harper & Row), co-authored with George Madaus and Thomas Kellegham. He is also the associate editor of the *Journal of Personnel Evaluation.*

Albert Shanker is president of the American Federation of Teachers AFL-CIO. His research includes how students learn, redesigning schools to accommodate student learning, and professionalizing the teaching profession. He has had numerous articles published in the *Harvard Educational Review, Teachers College Record,* and *Phi Delta Kappan.* Shanker also writes a weekly column for the *New York Times.*

Joseph B. Shedd is director of the Educational Systems Division, Organizational Analysis and Practices, Inc., in Ithaca, New York. His most recent publications are "The Work Environment and School Reform," co-authored with Samuel B. Bacharach and Scott C. Bauer (*Teachers College Record,* Winter 1986), and "A Career Developmental Framework for Evaluating Teachers as Decision Makers," co-authored with Samuel B. Bacharach and Sharon C. Conley (*Journal of Personnel Evaluation in Education,* September 1987). His research includes teacher participation in school/district decision making, teacher compensation and career development systems, management of school systems, and the changing character of white-collar unions.

Jonas F. Soltis is William Heard Kilpatrick Professor of Philosophy and Education at Teachers College, Columbia University, New York. His research interests are philosophy of education, professional ethics, and philosophy of educational research. His recent publications are *The Ethics of School Administration* (Teachers College Press, 1988), co-authored with K. Strike and E. Haller, and *Reforming Teacher Education* (Teachers College Press, 1987), as editor.

Gary Sykes is an assistant professor in the Department of Educational Administration at Michigan State University in East Lansing. His research includes the areas of policy and research on teaching, teacher education, and school reform. He has published "Establishing a Professional Culture for Teachers," co-authored with Kathleen Devaney, in *Building a Professional Culture in Schools,* edited by A. Lieberman (Teachers College Press, 1988); "Reckoning with the Spectre," (*Educational Research,* August–September 1987); and "Professionalism and Teaching: A Cautionary Perspective" (edited by L. Weis, H. Petrie, and P. Altbach, in press).

Adam Urbanski is president of the Rochester (New York) Teachers Association and vice-president of the American Federation of Teachers (AFT). A former teacher at the high school and college level, Dr. Urbanski is now an active proponent of change in the education industry. Dr. Urbanski served on AFT's Task Force on the Future of Education and was a recipient of the Phi Delta Kappa Leadership in Education Award (Rochester chapter, 1983). He is a member of the National Board for Professional Teaching Standards and was recently named to the board of directors of the National Center for Education and the Economy.

Laura A. Wagner is manager of the Intersegmental Teaching Improvement Projects in the California State Department of Education. She is responsible for working with the various postsecondary institutions and other state agencies to support collaborative teacher preparation programs, new teacher induction efforts, and the assessment of teachers for state licensure.

Arthur E. Wise is director of the Rand Corporation's Center for the Study of the Teaching Profession in Washington, D.C. He is best known as the author of *Rich Schools, Poor Schools*, the 1968 book that conceived the idea of school finance equalization lawsuits. His 1979 book, *Legislated Learning*, underscores the importance of teacher professionalism, school-based management, and local control of the schools. As a consultant to President Jimmy Carter's Reorganization Project, Dr. Wise helped to create the U.S. Department of Education.

Education Reform: Making Sense of It All

SAMUEL B. BACHARACH

O<small>N THE SUBJECT</small> of the social responsibility of the federal government, U.S. history is described as dialectical at best and fickle at worst. We protest that the government is doing too little to reinforce the social fabric of our society, pointing to such problems as homelessness as evidence of indifference on the part of our federal government. But no sooner does the government act on these issues than we complain about bureaucracy, socialism, and the intrusion of the state into our homes.

Federal urban policies from the Johnson to the Nixon administration are testimony to the search for the appropriate level of federal intervention. During this period, more was written about the role of centralization and decentralization in the delivery of social services than in any period before or since. We struggle for appropriate terms to describe the policy that will miraculously create a balance between the demands of Roosevelt liberals and libertarians. In the broadest sense, the traditional debate has been between the macro politics of centralization and the micro politics of local control.

What implications does this dialectic have for American public education? To understand this, it may be helpful to reconceptualize the reform movement from a simple macro–micro continuum to a living, growing "tree."

THE *ROOTS* OF REFORM: CYCLES OF HISTORY IN PUBLIC EDUCATION

Perhaps the current reform movement is rooted in some underlying philosophical dialectic that is basic to the American "way of life." In Chapter

1

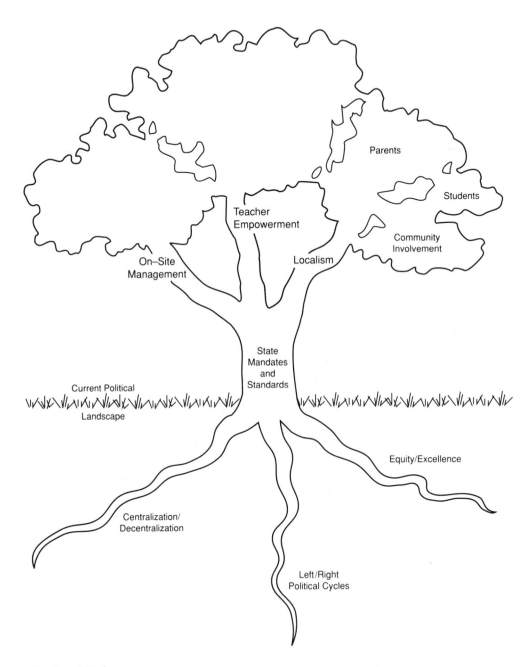

Roots of Reform

11, Cuban suggests that the twin themes of *equity* and *excellence* keep returning to haunt every other generation of reformers. *Equity* can be described as the pressure to make each school responsive to the *particular needs of its community constituency*, whereas *excellence* can be described as the pressure to ensure that the *general needs of the country* are being met. Advocates of equity work to tailor each school to its specific students' needs in order to ensure that all students have an opportunity to make it in society. Excellence advocates work to prepare students to be good citizens and to ensure that the system produces enough students with the skills to keep society functioning.

The dilemmas of the Reagan administration illustrate perfectly the interesting parallel that exists between the *equity versus excellence* cycle and the *macro centralization versus micro localism* dialectic. As Passow (Chapter 1) and Kirst (Chapter 2) point out, the Reagan administration came into office by seizing control of the agenda of reform through intensive advocacy of the criteria of *excellence.* To ensure that schools everywhere adopted their program of "excellence," they advocated uniform standards of teaching and testing—clearly a macro centralism approach. At the same time, this mania for standardization of curriculum and content could not be implemented from the federal level without enormous federal expenditures on education—expenditures that were anathema to Reagan's ideological platform. Indeed, the problem may have been the fundamental inconsistency between Reagan's agenda and his Jeffersonian micro localist style.

THE *TRUNK* OF REFORM: STATE MANDATES ABOUT STRUCTURE AND GOALS

So how was general excellence to be implemented without the local pluralist process diverting the reform movement toward *particular* local goals? In retrospect, the solution arrived at seems only natural: Use the federal Department of Education as a bully pulpit to encourage the various *state* governments to centralize at their level. Encourage the states to set boundaries on the proliferation of "alternative curricula" and to get everyone "back to basics." Statehouses across the country were only too happy to take the driver's seat, setting standards and passing laws with the effect of removing local and teacher discretion. This *centralizing* action could actually be sold to the public as a *decentralizing* part of Reagan's New Federalism, and thus not inconsistent with the Reagan style.

Thus, the first wave of reform placed the issues of *accountability* and *achievement* as its highest priorities. Accountability generally referred to teachers. Specifically, teachers were held accountable for students' achievement as measured on state-level standardized tests. Teachers were removed from the curriculum decision-making process, then blamed if their students did not learn what the state told them to teach. The hue and cry for merit pay best captures the flavor of the first wave because merit pay proposals are directed at teachers and allow state legislators to avoid taking responsibility for the mess that we are in.

Yet merit pay never really caught on in the United States, and not for lack of trying. Governors soon realized that education reform would go nowhere without the active cooperation of teachers, and teachers were adamantly opposed to merit pay, which they saw as divisive to their new-found bargaining unity. In the political horsetrading that followed the first wave of reform, merit pay was sacrificed in exchange for a general tightening up of curriculum and content that allowed governors and legislators to report to the public that they were taking action. The general effect was to put pressure on teachers, especially those seen as responsible for the poor performance of students. The message to these teachers was: Shape up or ship out.

But what about the majority of teachers who were already performing to the best of their ability? State governments could set goals, raise minimum standards, and demand accountability, but the first wave of centralization could not actually improve the quality of teaching. In fact, many have argued that the first wave prescriptions actually damaged the quality of teaching by further limiting teachers' discretion and increasing their already heavy load of paperwork. The point is that implementation of successful reform was practically impossible at the state level.

THE *BRANCHES* OF REFORM: A SECOND WAVE OF LOCALISM AND TEACHERISM

A tidal wave of education reform has swept the country, having manifested itself as a myriad of state-level initiatives, laws, tests, procedures, and conditions for funding. The general idea of the reformers of the first wave seemed to be to prune some of the longer and more superfluous branches of our education tree. The media were full of horror stories of illiterate high school graduates who spent their days studying basket weaving or sitcom analysis. If the curriculum could be cleaned up of such resource-diverting activities, these reformers argued, then teachers and students would go back to the basics.

Yet such an approach was self-limiting. Once the states had imposed more restrictive core course requirements, where was the reform movement to go? As mentioned before, it soon became clear that the next step in improving our children's education was actually to improve the quality of teaching, which the first wave's *structural* approaches could not do.

At the same time, it was recognized that mandating tougher minimum standards was counterproductive for those students who were not succeeding in staying in school even under the old, looser standards. In fact, some argued that tougher standards would actually cause the already excessive dropout rate to increase, as students at the margin realized that they would have to work harder to obtain a diploma. How was this paradox to be resolved?

What was clearly needed was more flexibility and diversity in the system than state leadership could provide. Forward-thinking state governors recognized the need for many different branches and styles of reform, each one serving the unique needs of the particular community in which it was implemented. It followed naturally that the best fit between reform packages and communities was with *reform packages developed at the district and school-site level.*

While this was going on, the *teachers' unions* were clamoring to get involved in the reform movement. After having been portrayed as obstructionist special interests by antiunion politicians and parts of the media, the teachers were particularly eager to become productively involved in the reform movement. After all, it was reasoned, who else could better customize reform for a particular school than those who already make the crucial classroom decisions about how the material is learned? Out of this, the *teacher empowerment* movement was born, emphasizing such issues as professionalization, collegiality, shared decision making, and consensus management.

THE *LEAVES* OF REFORM: INVOLVING PARENTS AND STUDENTS

One of the problematic elements of the current reform movement is the fact that many sociologists believe that the problem of unsuccessful schools is a reflection of much larger societal problems. Schools in our society are simply not designed and equipped to handle such pervasive phenomena as one-parent families, two-income families where neither parent has enough time for the children, latchkey households, the use of TV as a babysitter, language problems of children from minority subcultures, the widespread use of drugs, and the violence that accompanies the drug markets.

Since parents currently have little choice about which school their children attend, they see themselves as powerless to effect real change in their children's schools. Therefore, they seldom avail themselves of existing opportunities for participation in the school program. If the PTA is just a group of cheerleaders for the current school or district administration, why should they waste their precious time going to meetings?

The *public choice* movement is based on the premise that if parents and children have the opportunity to choose their school within a public district, they are in a position to "vote with their feet" unless administrators listen and respond to their complaints. This *public empowerment* forces the public schools to compete with each other to develop a *school mission* that the public accepts as valuable. The development of this mission should in turn spur the development of such norms as collegiality among teachers and a sense of shared ownership among all the stakeholders—students, parents, teachers, and administrators (see Chapter 21 by Cooper and Chapter 22 by Urbanski). With any luck, this should encourage the development of links between the school and the wider community, which may be a prerequisite to the joint amelioration of school and societal problems.

UNIT ONE

An Overview of Education Reform

These three chapters provide a representative sample of the kinds of questions raised in what can loosely be called the reform movement. The questions are chronologically organized into two general waves of reform. This wave metaphor probably came from the "tidal wave of reform" that was claimed to be sweeping the nation after the Nation at Risk *report was released in 1983.*

The first wave can probably best be identified as an intensification *of the current system, which has evolved over decades. Rather than changing the fundamental nature of the education system, this process aims* to make the students work harder *(Kirst, Chapter 2). The mechanism for this is summarized as* legislation, regulation, *and* mandate *by the states of* higher standards *and* tougher course requirements *(Passow, Chapter 1).*

What resulted from the first wave? Kirst suggests that, as we might expect, the outcomes of the intensification *were primarily* quantitative. *He suggests that there has been* more money for

7

teachers' salaries; more *students signing up for core courses like math, science, history, and English; and* more *hours or days spent in school.*

Unfortunately, this tidying up quickly ran into several major obstacles. First, taxpayers wanted to know what they were getting for the much larger sums of money that were being spent on education. In Chapter 3, Boyer points out that our systems of measurement and evaluation have lagged behind what is needed, making it difficult to give taxpayers an unambiguous answer.

Second, teachers perceived the new standardization as having the result of "deskilling" them, resulting in loss of face and power in the classroom. In fact, many of the mandates, like competency testing and merit pay, are easily read as blaming teachers for the problems. The resulting teacher frustration could very easily cause political gridlock, since it is impossible to visualize a successful reform movement without the cooperation of teachers (Passow).

Third, Passow correctly sees the state-directed reforms as providing a sort of skeleton of reform that can only be fleshed out by individual school boards and schools. Such things as course content, teacher recruitment and training, and organizational culture can only be addressed at the local level.

These latter two problems were soon apparent. In fact, the second wave could even be seen as a reaction to the first wave. If the first wave emphasized a sort of centralization of power to the statehouse level, then governors soon recognized the limits of their ability to implement the changes that they mandated. Perhaps because of this, the Governors Conference emphasized the triple theme of achievement, assessment, *and* accountability. *The governors suggested issuing a state report card to measure local progress in implementing reform, then tying state money to the results of these efforts. In effect, they were simply tossing the ball back to the states, but with a warning that they would be watching closely this time.*

A parallel theme was seen in the Carnegie and Holmes reports. Both of these panels looked at education reform from the point of view of the teacher, with the recognition that teaching needed to be restructured toward professionalism (giving teachers more freedom *to use their judgment, but also making them more* accountable *for the results). Perhaps this will help to create a climate of "contagious enthusiasm for learning" among both teachers and students (Boyer).*

Will these two waves result in lasting changes? Kirst suggests three necessary conditions for lasting reform:

1. Structural or organizational change
2. Easy monitoring of results
3. The creation of a powerful constituency for reform

Without putting it in those terms, Boyer deals with those very issues. He talks about structural changes in the school day (adjusting it to new family and work patterns) and in the content of schooling (making it more applicable to today's world). He talks about the fact that we need better testing in order to monitor the results of reform. Finally, he talks about improving teachers' working conditions, which would have the effect of creating a powerful constituency for change.

In summary, the first section of this book discusses the first wave of reform as the standardization and centralization of goal-setting authority at the state level, with the second wave (a reaction to the first) being a decentralization of implementation authority back to the local level.

1

How It Happened, Wave by Wave

Whither (or Wither?) School Reform?
A. HARRY PASSOW

T OWARD THE END of 1983, the Education Commission of the States Task Force observed: "Hardly a month has passed without the release of a major report by a prestigious group of citizens concerned about the nature of American education" (p. 1). The 1983 report of the National Commission on Excellence in Education, *A Nation at Risk,* had put the theme that was common to most of these reports, most dramatically: "Our once unchallenged preeminence in commerce, industry, science, and technological innovations is being overtaken by competitors throughout the world" (p. 5). Since the 1983 Report of the Committee on Secondary School Studies (Committee of Ten), various reports have regularly criticized some aspect(s) of American education and urged reform, but not since the orbiting of Sputnik a quarter of a century earlier had there been such a frenetic outpouring of school reform activities. Sputnik contributed directly to the passage of the National Defense Education Act of 1958—certainly one of the most significant pieces of federal legislation affecting schools and colleges ever passed—and scores of projects at national, state, and local levels focused on strengthening curricula (especially in, but not limited to, the sciences, mathematics, and foreign languages), upgrading the quality of teachers and teaching, and developing new instructional resources and materials.

By May 1984, the U.S. Department of Education observed that the reports issued in 1983 had "created a tidal wave of school reform which promises to renew American education" with an "extraordinary array of initiatives under discussion and underway" (p. 11). Although the report described these initiatives as diverse and comprehensive, it also described state leadership as "one of the hallmarks of this reform effort" that "also saw a quantum increase in the variety of public school activities involving leaders of the university, corporate, and foundation communities"(p. 17).

REFORM BY LEGISLATION, REGULATION, AND MANDATE

Two years after *A Nation Responds* (1984), a survey by the Education Commission of the States reported that if this extensive state reform activity were reduced to its least common denominator, the two unifying themes were clearly "more rigorous academic standards for students and more recognition and higher standards for teachers" (Pipho, 1986, p. K5). Pipho also noted that almost all states had enacted sweeping legislative mandates, some through single laws that sometimes numbered 100 pages or more in length and others through reform packages of several bills. In addition, state boards of education were also mandating changes through alterations in rules and regulations.

Begun before *A Nation at Risk*, California's school reforms may illustrate a number of state efforts, although they are probably more extensive and comprehensive than those of most other states. California's SB 813 provided the legislative authority for school reform. In its study of *Conditions of Education in California, 1985–1986,* the PACE (Policy Analysis for California Education, 1986, p. 3) group described what it called the "structural changes" that the reform efforts had brought about, changes including

> creation of model curriculum standards, increased enrollment in academic courses, longer days (six periods in every high school) and longer school years (180 days), participation in the Mentor Teacher Program, certification of administrators in skills for teacher evaluation, creation of new administrator training centers, development of additional and more rigorous assessment tests, and publication of 28 quality indicators for each local school district.

A year later in its 1986–1987 analysis, PACE (1987, p. 3) pointed out that these kinds of changes were relatively straightforward. For example, the state could easily mandate increased mathematics and science requirements, but

> determining the content of those courses, selecting adequate textbooks, purchasing appropriate materials, recruiting qualified teachers, training

teachers in the necessary skills, changing the district policies and school structure to nurture the teaching of those courses, and ensuring that new courses produced improved student learning is a long-term complicated process, the existence and success of which are not assured by structural changes alone. . . .

PACE argued that full and effective implementation of the goals of reform—"better curriculum, improved teaching, successful schools, and rising student knowledge and ability to think"—requires changes in teachers' attitudes and skills, in administrators' expertise, and in school organization and culture, all of which are difficult, time consuming to produce, and dependent upon local enthusiasm, commitment and effort.

The bottom line, PACE asserted, was that if "the hopes of educational reform and improvement" were to be realized, the locus of action and responsibility had to shift from the state level to the local level—to the "persons who actually manage and deliver educational services to students"(p. 3).

Since 1983, there have been numerous report cards on reform activity—few based on the kind of analysis of the PACE group. A fall 1985 survey of state-level education reform actions by Kemmerer and Wagner (1985) concluded that, in general, "the states have concentrated on low cost, high visibility activities," with those kinds of initiatives that are more "likely to produce significant improvements in student performance" receiving much more limited support (p. 1). A number of other observers of the current school reform scene recognize a tidal wave of activity but are not convinced that significant reform has resulted. As Chance (1986, p. 2) put it:

> The reforms are seen as both significant and superficial. Skepticism over their relevance, precision, and persistence underlies metaphorical references to band-aids, furniture rearrangements and additional coats of paint. (One) analyst argues that "if the reforms do not affect who is teaching and what is going on in the classroom, they can hardly be considered reforms. . . . improvements, maybe, but to call it reform is to misuse the vocabulary."

In the chair's summary of a 1986 report from the National Governors' Association titled *Time for Results,* Governor Alexander (1986, p. 7) reaffirmed the governors' readiness to provide "the leadership needed to get results on the hard issues that confront the better schools movement . . . (and) to lead the second wave of reform in American public education." Alexander (pp. 3–4) pointed out, however, that he wanted it clearly understood that he and his fellow governors would not "bargain away minimum standards that some states are now setting" but that they had "learned that real excellence can't be imposed from the distance. *Governors* don't create excellent schools; *communities*—local school leaders, teachers, parents, and citizens—do." The recommendations of the Governors' Association were understandably the kind that are "legislatable" and for which *schools* could be held accountable on the improved "state report card" that is currently being considered. This theme of "achievement, assessment, and accountability . . . (as the) fundamental principles of educational reform" has also been stressed by Secretary of Education William Bennett (1987, p. 3).

TEACHERS AND EDUCATIONAL REFORM

There is a growing concern among some educators that state legislation and mandates increasing school and teacher accountability for student achievement—the current mode for reform—are, in reality, contributing to the "fragmentation of teachers, curricula and teaching." For example, McNeil (1987, pp. 6–7) found in a study of magnet schools in one school district that reforms meant to upgrade quality of instruction had an opposite effect: "By applying standardized, reductive formulas to content and pedagogy, (the reforms) undermine the integration of teacher, student and subject; they unintentionally (or so one hopes) set in motion a de-skilling not present in the pre-reform days of the magnet school." State-mandated stress on achievement, assessment, and accountability led teachers to report "a real loss of power and in some ways a loss of face" as well as a "further distancing of the teacher as a person and as subject matter expert from the discourse of the classroom" (p. 7). Rather than perceiving the student assessment program as a way of bringing equity of educational quality to the district's children, the teachers viewed it as taking away their chief areas of discretion and authority and reducing their professional teaching role. Sizer (1985, p. 23) has warned that many reformers "confuse standardization with standards. . . . We trivialize the process of learning by oversimplifying it; and by the oversimplification represented by mandated standard practice, we lessen the potential of teachers."

Ravitch (1985, p. 19) asserts that "educational reform movements have taken teachers for granted and treated them as classroom furniture rather than as thinking, possibly disputatious human beings." Similarly, the report from the Carnegie Forum on Education and the Economy (1986, p. 26) observed that many of the best teachers now staffing schools "are immensely frustrated—to the point of cynicism"—seeing reform activities bringing about very little change in those things that directly affect teaching and learning, bureaucratic structures within which they work becoming even more rigid, and opportunities for exercising professional judgment increasingly limited. They believe, the report noted, "that teachers are being made to pay the price for reform, and many do not believe that the current conception will lead to real gains for students" (p. 26). The Carnegie report further warned of "a real danger now of political gridlock, a situation in which those who would improve the schools from the outside are met by teachers on the inside who, because they distrust policymakers' motives and disapprove of their methods, will prevent further progress" (p. 26). What we now need, the Carnegie report declared, is a fundamental redesign and restructuring of the teaching force and the schools in order "to provide a professional environment for teaching, freeing teachers to decide how best to meet state and local goals for children but holding them accountable for student progress"(p. 26).

Another report by the consortium of school of education deans called The Holmes Group (1986) argued that in dealing with the problems of public education "simple remedies abound," many "aimed at teachers: Institute merit pay; eliminate teacher education; test teachers to make sure they know eighth grade facts" (p. 3). The Holmes Group set five goals for its member schools and colleges of education: (a) strengthen the liberal arts foundation of teachers, (b) restructure the teaching profession to recognize differences in teachers' knowledge, skills, and commitment, (c) raise the standards for entering teaching, (d) strengthen the connections between the schools and the teacher-preparing institutions, and (e) make schools better places for teachers to work and learn.

FROM STATE LEVEL TO LOCAL LEVEL

The "first wave" of reform efforts consisted mainly of state-level legislation, regulation, and mandates that were somehow to be implemented at the local or district levels. Sedlak and his colleagues (1986) see this approach as basically flawed:

> Reformers have attempted to change public education from the top down with mandates to address a particular problem; with rules, procedures, and standards generated to facilitate goal attainment, and with monitoring and evaluation to assess progress. What has been missing has been an appreciation of how such programs would actually affect the daily lives of students and teachers.(p.185)

Two conflicting trends seem to have emerged from the recent school reform activities. On one hand, there has been a marked shift from local to state control, a growing legalization of the educational process, and an increase in state monitoring and accounting activity. On the other hand, there has been an increasing recognition of the need for local building and district involvement in all aspects of school reform and school improvement. Goodlad (1987, p. 215) believes that there has been a dramatic change in perceptions of teachers' roles in school improvement since 1983 when

a "narrowing in the scope of their decision making . . . went almost unnoticed in the policy arena." He asks whether it is "overly cynical to suggest
that those who confidently invaded the culture of the school and the ecology of the system as a whole in order to put things right began to realize
the complexity of the problems and the political wisdom of transferring
the improvement to teachers."

In the recent report entitled *Results in Education: 1987*, the members
of the National Governors' Association (1987) were not yet satisfied with
the quality of education in their states. The report noted that "state initiatives in the early part of the decade focused on raising performance standards and providing resources to achieve higher levels of performance,"
but "these steps have not completed the education improvement task facing
us"(p.1). The governors declared that "states will have to assume larger
responsibilities for setting educational goals and defining outcome standards"while, at the same time, stimulating local inventiveness. Increased
educational productivity and the professionalization of teaching would
require new school structures that allowed "more varied instructional arrangements, greater collegial interaction among teachers, and greater teacher
involvement in decision making" (p.3). The governors urged the development of a "more useful and sophisticated assessment system. . . . De-
regulating educational practices and holding educators accountable for
results requires the capacity to accurately measure the results we want"
(p.3).

WHITHER (OR WITHER?) SCHOOL REFORM?

Whither school reform? Will it really happen or will reform efforts wither
and die as they seem to have done so often in the past? The history of
school reform might well lead us to conclude that "these efforts, too, will
pass in short order." For instance, three decades ago, the post-Sputnik
period ushered in what has since become known as the Era of Curriculum
Innovation. The National Defense Education Act of 1958 provided funds
initially for (a) upgrading the teaching of science, mathematics, and foreign
languages through content revision, development of instructional materials, and training/retraining of teachers; (b) improved guidance and counseling services; (c) special programs for the disadvantaged; and (d) upgrading
libraries and media centers. The National Science Foundation increased its
support for projects to improve curricula and materials in mathematics and
science. Foundations invested heavily in projects to upgrade instruction.
Soon projects and programs in practically every subject area resulted in
new curricula, instructional resources, organization, technology, teacher
training, and staff deployment patterns.

Silberman (1970) observed 10 years later, in *Crisis in the Classroom: The*

Remaking of American Education, that "the reform movement [of the 1960's] had produced innumerable changes, and yet the schools themselves are largely unchanged" (p. 50). A study by the Ford Foundation (1972) of its 1960–1970 Comprehensive School Improvement Program, which involved $30 million in grants to some 25 projects, found few lasting changes. The report speculated whether the "CSIP's original design would have been much more effective if only the relative tranquility of the early 1960s had continued" (p. 42). Whether that tranquility was real or not, clearly neither the nation nor its schools have enjoyed much of it in recent years.

Most of the 1973–1975 reports urging school reform in the secondary schools began with criticisms of the schools as unchanging and immutable institutions. More recently, Myron Lieberman asserted that inherent weaknesses in the reform movement—for example, many special interest groups that block reform for their own reasons, no one person or group being responsible for making reform work, inertia in the education profession, legal obstacles such as tenure laws—resulted in its being "dead on arrival" (in Pipho, 1986, p. K6). Ann Lieberman and Rosenholtz (1987), on the other hand, conclude that the staff and the culture of a school are simultaneously both the major barriers to reform and the major bridge to improvement and change.

About a year after the flood of reports appeared, Cross (1984) concluded somewhat pessimistically but, in retrospect, accurately:

> The curriculum will be tidied up, goals will be articulated, standardized tests will control transitions from one level of schooling to another, prospective teachers will study a core of common learnings, and the teacher education curriculum will be restructured to include certain experiences in specified sequences. There is not much evidence that the current mania for tidiness will produce orderly schools in which students and teachers pursue learning with the contagious enthusiasm that is so essential for excellence. (p. 69)

Five years after the current school reform "movement" began, the states may have taken the tidying-up process about which Cross wrote as far as legislation and regulation can take it. Goodlad (1987) has argued "that mandating ways to improve pupil achievement is at best futile and at worst dangerous, especially as we come to know more about such phenomena"(p. 9). To some extent, the leading advocates of change by state mandate through legislation and regulation, the National Governors' Association, appear to be recognizing this. Speaking for his fellow governors, Kean (1987) urged that they "help reinvent the school for modern times. For all that we have changed in educational policy, most schools still operate as they have for generations" (p.6). The governors (National Governors' Association, 1987) now seem to agree that states will need to be more aggressive in carefully setting educational goals and defining outcome standards, in order to leave decisions about how to accomplish state goals to professionals at the building level. Setting standards is not enough, though. Greater flexibility at the local level needs to be accompanied by effective approaches for state intervention in local districts that are unable to meet reasonable educational goals. (p. 2)

Shifting to the local district and the individual building as the unit for change and reform has proven, as has long been known, a complex and difficult process. Louis (1986) has argued that

> under the right circumstances, change orchestrated at the school level has a significant chance of making a difference. . . . Our best bet for improving schools lies not with fine-tuning state reforms (although some of these are, of course, necessary) but with stimulating individual schools to change and providing them with appropriate assistance. A number of studies suggest that both process assistance (help in guiding the school's progress through the change programs) and specialized training (to provide staff with new skills) are needed to implement significant change. (p. 34)

The 1986 Carnegie Forum on Education and the Economy report called for restructuring the schools to provide a professional environment; restructuring the nature of the teaching force; revising the recruitment, education, and induction of teachers; making salaries and career opportunities market competitive; relating incentives to schoolwide performance; and providing the technology, services, and staff needed for teacher productivity. Some reviewers see this report as a prototype for the "second wave of reform," a blueprint for stimulating change at the local level by involving those persons who deliver education and schooling. For others, those proposals are a blueprint for chaos and conflict. Professionalization of teaching, empowerment of teachers, teacher leadership and involvement in decision making, restructuring the conditions for teaching and school governance—all these issues are confounded by issues of power and control.

Recognizing "the crucial function of the teacher" is but a first step in orchestrating change at the building level. Understanding how all of the players—teachers, principals, other professionals and nonprofessionals, parents, community leaders, businesses and industry, and others—function and relate to each other in the reform process is a much more complex matter that cannot be dealt with by rhetoric alone. Some schools and school systems are dealing with these critical issues as they work to bring about change. Others are simply reacting to state mandates and implementing them at minimal compliance levels. A few schools and school systems are dealing with these issues of power and control in a systematic fashion, but they tend to be exceptions at this time.

As the current reform movement—never monolithic despite some common rhetoric and recommendations—develops, moving from a first wave to a second wave and perhaps beyond, some hard questions will be asked with more and more insistence. Some of these will concern purposes of education and schooling: Do schools exist to increase the nation's productivity or for other equally important personal and social goals? Will the reforms advocated really prepare all Americans for the twenty-first century or are they simply the "basics" of the past? Can the schools achieve equity and excellence without significant changes in the nature and structure of society? Will the curriculum, instructional strategies, and services of the past century be appropriate for the next?

In sum, school reform is an ongoing process and needs to be recognized as such. The current reform efforts appear to be widespread, multilevel, diverse. They are resulting in changes—some significant and others (most?) superficial. In the view of some observers, they are aimed at the relatively easy problems and avoid the difficult ones—the problems that result from changes in the demographics of society and school. The reform movement is not likely to wither but, if past history is any guide, at some point reform efforts will change direction once again. Just studying the differences between the analyses of the problems and recommended solutions in the reports of the 1970s and those of the 1980s is in itself enlightening.

REFERENCES

Alexander, L. (1986). Chairman's summary. In National Governors' Association, *Time for results*. Washington, DC: National Governors' Association.

Bennett, W. J. (1987, April 5). *Is the education reform movement being hijacked?* Unpublished paper presented to the 40th Anniversary National Seminar of the Education Writers' Association in San Francisco, CA.

Carnegie Forum on Education and the Economy. (1986). *A nation prepared: Teachers for the 21sth century*. Report of the Task Force on Teaching as a Profession. New York.

Chance, W. (1986). " . . . the best of educations": *Reforming America's public schools in the 1980s*. Washington, DC: John D. and Catherine T. MacArthur Foundation.

Committee on Secondary School Studies. (1983). *Report of the committee on secondary school studies (Committee of Ten)*. Washington, DC: U.S. Government Printing Office.

Cross, K.P. (1984). The rising tide of school reform reports. *Phi Delta Kappan, 66*(3), 167–172.

Education Commission of the States Task Force on Education for Economic Growth. (1983). *Action for excellence*. Denver, CO: Education Commission of the States.

Ford Foundation. (1972). *A foundation goes to school.* New York: Ford Foundation.

Goodlad, J. I. (1987). Toward a healthy ecosystem. In J. Goodlad (Ed.), *The ecology of school renewal*(pp. 210–221). 86th Yearbook, Part I, National Society for the Study of Education. Chicago: University of Chicago Press.

The Holmes Group. (1986). *Tomorrow's teachers.* East Lansing, MI: The Holmes Group.

Kean, T. J. (1987). Foreword. In *Results in Education* (pp. v–ix). Washington, DC: National Governors' Association.

Kemmerer, F., & Wagner, A. P. (1985). A report card: Education reform in the states. In *National education reform and New York State: A report card* (pp. 1–50). Albany, NY: State University of New York.

Lieberman, A., & Rosenholtz, S. (1987). The road to school improvement: Barriers and bridges. In J. Goodlad (Ed.), *The ecology of school renewal* (pp. 79–98). 86th Yearbook, Part I, National Society for the Study of Education. Chicago: University of Chicago Press.

Louis, K. S. (1986). Reforming secondary schools: A critique and an agenda for administrators. *Educational Leadership, 44*(1), 33–36.

McNeil, L. M. (1987, April). *The cooptation of the curriculum.* Paper presented at the annual meeting of the American Educational Research Association in Washington, DC.

National Commission on Excellence in Education. (1983). *A nation at risk: The imperative for educational reform.* Washington, DC: U.S. Government Printing Office.

National Governors' Association. (1987). *Results in education: 1987.* Washington, DC.

Pipho, C. (1986). States move closer to reality. *Phi Delta Kappan, 68*(4), K1–K8.

PACE. Policy Analysis for California Education. (1986). *Conditions of education in California, 1985–86.* Berkeley: Policy Analysis for California Education.

Policy Analysis for California Education. (1987). *Conditions of education in California, 1986–87.* Berkeley, CA: Policy Analysis for California Education.

Ravitch, D. (1985). *The schools we deserve.* New York: Basic Books.

Sedlak, M. W., Wheeler, C. W., Pullin, D.C., & Cusick, P. A. (1986). *Selling students short: Classroom bargains and academic reform in the American high school.* New York: Teachers College Press.

Silberman, C. E. (1970). *Crisis in the classroom: The remaking of American education.* New York: Random House.

Sizer, T. R. (1985). Common sense. *Educational Leadership, 42*(6): 21–22.

U.S. Department of Education. (1984). *A nation responds: Recent efforts to improve education.* Washington, DC: U.S. Government Printing Office.

2

The Crash of the
First Wave

Recent State Education Reform
in the United States:
Looking Backward and Forward
MICHAEL W. KIRST

THE FIRST WAVE of school reform has crashed upon the education beach, but are other waves now forming out at sea?

The year 1983 is generally regarded as the beginning of the current cycle of state education reform. The *Nation At Risk* report was released that year, but many states had sponsored education legislation before the report came out. The last states to engage in legislation on education—Washington, Indiana, and Iowa—joined in 1987. The spread of this reform is very impressive, and its consistency in concept qualifies it as one of the hallmarks in state policymaking. The 1986 report of the National Governors' Association demonstrates the reform's impressive diffusion and breadth. It is now appropriate to look backward and forward because states have completed their initial statutes based on the 1983 reform concepts. Will there be a second wave or is the momentum spent?

ASSUMPTIONS OF REFORM

Some key assumptions underlie the first wave. There is a presumed linkage between international and interstate economic competition and education. An educated work force is considered crucial to higher productivity and adaptability to rapidly changing markets. Economic competition includes both highly technical personnel and the average worker who could once get by with repetitive manufacturing routines. For example, the Japanese are reputed to have the best bottom academic quartile in the world. The education linkage with economic growth maintains its hold on public opinion in 1988, and "competitiveness" is a cliché in Washington and state capitals. This continued interest in education by top-level politicians augurs well for a second round of reform after 1987.

A second key assumption underlying state statutes from 1983 to 1987 is that education does not need to be fundamentally changed, but the existing delivery system can be intensified to meet the economic challenge. The proposal by Ted Sizer (1984) to drastically reorganize secondary schools or the one by Coons and Sugarman (1983) favoring vouchers found scant support in state capitals. Rather, the key variable in 1983 was thought to be a more rigorous curriculum. As one legislator told me, "Let's make the little buggers work harder."

This assumption posits that more time on more difficult academic content is beneficial and that *all* students can meet the increased academic expectations. The curriculum can be narrowed and vocational education pruned without much increase in dropouts, the reformers contend. Values can be taught through direct instruction but need to be woven throughout the curricular subjects. Both states and localities have centralized and aligned curriculum for greater uniformity but also to emphasize somewhat higher-order skills. Politicians assume that students learn the subject they study in school; for example, students who take French know more French than those who do not. The high school was top priority because achievement scores had not increased at the secondary level commensurate with elementary test gains in the 1975–1983 period.

A start has been made on improving teachers through some traditional devices, such as increased teacher preparation and university entrance requirements, as well as recycling differentiated staffing in a new guise of career ladders. There is real concern in many states about their ability to attract and retain teachers and numerous attempts to increase staff development as well as pay. But before the first wave of reform was half over, a 1986 forum sponsored by the Carnegie Corporation termed the 1983–1986 changes "cosmetic" and called for a drastically "restructured" and "professionalized" work force. The Carnegie Forum recommended a new national standards board, with a completely new concept of teacher assessments, a greater voice for teachers in running schools, and "lead teachers" who are similar to British headmasters.

OUTCOMES FROM THE FIRST WAVE

In many ways, state politicians got what they wanted, because the quantities of education increased substantially:

1. Expenditures after inflation increased by 25% in three years. Not all of this money went to new reforms because many states needed to restore cutbacks made during the recession of the early 1980s. Moreover, reform did not cause all or most of the expenditure increase because the crucial influence was the 1983–1986 national economic growth (Odden, 1987).
2. Entry-level teacher salaries increased by an equivalent amount. For example, California's minimum increased from $15,000 to almost $22,000 in 1987, and more teachers reentered the work force after stepping out for a while.
3. High school course-taking patterns changed significantly, with much more emphasis on math, science, foreign language, and world history and much less enrollment in vocational education and electives such as photography. These changes were particularly dramatic in California, where vocational education enrollments declined by 15 percent and science and math enrollments increased by 15 percent in four years.
4. There was a slight extension of school time in states that had five- or six-period days, but no major change in the summer vacation. The 180-day school year and summer vacation appear deeply embedded in the American culture.
5. There was no measurable increase in dropouts, in part, because the dropout statistics are so unreliable. At this juncture, state politicians cannot be convinced of an increasing dropout rate based on any hard evidence.
6. Teacher career ladders are in place in a few states and have created a constituency of teachers who benefit from the higher pay that will prevent major surgery in the ladder concept in the short run.
7. Curricular alignment has produced new state course content guides and matching tests that are having an impact on local policy.
8. Many state achievement tests are up slightly, although this may be unrelated to reform.

RESULTS FROM A CALIFORNIA STUDY

Beneath these quantitative changes, there is little evaluation of whether qualitative changes have resulted. However, Allan Odden led a California PACE study of a group of schools with large increases in test scores and student enrollment in academic courses. Though not a representative sample, their achievement suggests the qualitative changes that can occur in

schools that improved dramatically in quantitative indicators. Each researcher spent about 15 days at a school site or at district headquarters
tracing the aggregate and cumulative impact of the 1983 reform law (Odden
& Marsh, 1987).

In these 17 California schools, districts increased high school graduation requirements, upgraded curriculum standards, lengthened the school
day and year, purchased new and better textbooks, administered new and
tougher state tests, created a new cadre of mentor teachers, raised teacher
salaries, and expanded accountability by developing quality indicators—
all between 1983 and 1987. These actions constitute the core of education
reform implementation using the intensification strategy. The near-term
effect of SB 813 is that students are taking more academically demanding
courses.

Districts generally are involved in upgrading course content. None
of the schools studied had "watered down" the overall content in the
courses. The local perception is that new state money had significant impact
in providing resources for implementing the more rigorous, academic program; but given how California's law was financed, it is difficult to trace
precise financial impacts. However, the strategy of linking new state money
to local reform has helped. Local educators feel that the funding increases
of the past four years have been positive, have improved teacher morale,
and have helped school districts to do things they wanted to do. Continued
funding, and perhaps continued funding increases by the state, are required to continue reform and improvement momentum, they feel.

Improving schools as institutions is definitely on the local agenda,
and considerable progress has been made. The state—through statewide
Model Curriculum Standards, State Curriculum Frameworks, and CAP
tests—and local districts—through a variety of efforts generally called "curriculum alignment"—have played a key role in defining the "technical
core" of curriculum at the school site. There is both a complementarity
among state, district, and school roles and strong interrelationships between appropriate top-down and bottom-up roles and functions.

State tests do "drive" local curriculum. While the old state tests produced a curriculum focused on basic skills, the new tests, especially the
eighth-grade test, are stimulating a local curriculum with more subjects
(e.g., science), and greater attention to problem solving.

The district is also an important actor in local school reform. While
education improvement occurs school by school, the appropriate unit for
analyzing the local site improvement process is the school district, since
the district can play several crucial and important roles in the site improvement process. This study, fortunately, includes data on both district and
school roles as well as state roles and actions.

Reform tended to be initiated in a district office top-down manner,
but initial unhappiness with this aspect of the process has waned. There
is more district centralization of curriculum development and textbook

selection, but site teachers and administrators participate intensively. Districts and schools seem to be "teaming" in ongoing reform development and implementation. Instruction-oriented superintendents are principal players in reform initiation in most districts and schools.

Most secondary schools can change old course offerings and implement more traditional, academic courses fairly easily and quickly; such changes seem to be initial response to California's reform law and other recent stimuli for reform. Some reasons are that these changes require few new skills for teachers. Furthermore, most secondary school teachers would prefer to teach more academic courses than "general track" courses or even many of the electives. They have been trained to teach academic courses and do not need additional training or help to begin teaching more of them.

It is much more difficult to change the nature of pedagogy or the general nature of the curriculum—for example, introducing the problem-solving skills proposed in the new state mathematics and science curriculum frameworks. It is even more difficult to get a greater degree of new types of pedagogical emphases into the curriculum such as higher-level thinking skills, critical thinking skills, and statistical inference. Odden and Marsh found less progress on these types of improvements because of inadequate resources and assistance for teachers.

Very few states have appropriated significant money to evaluate omnibus reform bills that include as many as 80 separate initiatives that interact with each other in complex ways. Consequently, we must speculate about a second wave without a clear grasp of what happened in the first, beyond some obvious quantitative changes. More in-depth case studies are needed that include representative samples of schools.

LOOKING FOR THE SECOND WAVE OF REFORM

As of late 1989, the surf looks very flat despite a few ripples in major newspapers about restructuring, professionalism, and at-risk youth. About half the state economies are not growing because of depressed prices for oil, farming, and other commodities. Stagnant economies will not provide the kind of fiscal dividends for state treasuries that helped in 1983 after the recovery from the 1980–1982 recession. Another problem is the lack of consensus, clarity, or enthusiasm for any new concept similar to the 1983 symbols of academic excellence and standards. The Carnegie Forum featured "teacher professionalism" as a rallying cry, but the teacher empowerment recommendations have frightened off the school boards and administrators. The concept of school "restructuring" is unclear to state politicians and not likely to provide a committed constituency or an emotive symbol. The Carnegie-backed national standards board for teacher certification faces a long period of test development (perhaps three more years) before any experienced teacher can even be considered.

Other contenders for the second wave, such as middle or elementary school reform, are not building support at the political grass-roots level. The concern about at-risk youth has resulted in a few token dropout and preschool programs, but nothing very substantial or widespread has appeared yet. Indeed, the large expenditure built up from 1983–1986 (about 25 percent after inflation) cannot continue indefinitely. There are cycles to school finance that correlate roughly with periods of economic growth or recession. The slower growth in the U.S. economy during 1989 is not an optimal time for major new and costly reforms. But the at-risk youth issue remains linked in many state policymakers' minds with economic competitiveness and is building momentum.

STRATEGIES FOR FUTURE REFORM

When the time is propitious for a second wave of reform, several alternative strategies are possible.

Intensifying the existing service delivery system. More of the 1983 priorities would be emphasized such as academic courses, staff development, and a revamped curriculum that stresses higher-order skills. However, this approach leaves the basic structure of schooling unchanged, while curriculum alignment becomes even more centralized, the number of crossrole teams to help implementation increases, and long-term staff development to help teachers implement higher-order skills rises.

Professionalism. The recommendations of the Carnegie Task Force are encompassed here, including the "restructuring of schools" to include more teacher decision making, peer review of teacher effectiveness, and an end to the 50-minute, six-period lockstep school day.

A subpart of professionalism is the *technology* strategy whereby major increases in computers, VCRs, and other electronic devices would drastically revamp the teacher's role. Technology would also enable us to reconfigure the teaching force to use more aides with fewer, but much more highly paid, professionals to manage the technology.

Output performance strategy. This approach would stress state payment for results based on an index of indicators that includes tests plus several other relevant outcomes. Some feasibility issues concern the precision of the output measures and how to link financial aid formulas to increases or decreases of an index that included dropouts, achievement, attendance, course-taking patterns, and others. The output strategy would focus on the school site as the unit for financial aid distribution rather than the school district. Florida has a program entitled "merit schools" that allows local districts to establish different performance criteria.

An employer-driven strategy. This strategy would apply primarily to secondary education and would feature specialized vocational schools (e.g., Aviation High in New York) with close linkages to the needs of employers. The California experiment in Peninsula Academies is another manifestation of this philosophy combined with a revamped Regional Occupational Center approach. The key component is part-time work that involves business as a partner in the student's academic preparation at the work site.

A consumer-driven strategy. This potentially radical change includes a broad-based voucher system, vouchers only for particular groups such as the disadvantaged in low-performing schools, and expanded choice *within* the public system, including eliminating all boundaries beween public school districts.

An analysis of these options should focus on which mix of strategies is optimal for which types of pupils. In general, the top two-thirds of the achievement band can benefit from the intensification strategy because changing the content that these pupils study can result in enhanced academic attainment. The technology strategy could be part of the intensification effort, as could a state-merit schools program that pays for results. Obviously, enhanced professionalism would help make any of these strategies more effective.

But the bottom one-third of the achievement band needs drastic change in the current delivery system and an overall attack on out-of-school influences that inhibit school attainment. Such approaches might include expanded choice and closer linkages with employers to impart work skills. Moreover, my forthcoming report on the conditions of children in California will highlight the need to improve and coordinate such things as children's health, attitudes, child-care, income support, and protective services if we are to make a major impact on at-risk youth. The schools cannot provide all these integrated services, but they can do a better job at brokerage for individual children who are particularly at risk. Out-of-school influences are crucial to improving performance in school, and new integrated service delivery systems could be a part of this effort. Some Chief State School Officers have proposed an individualized teaching and learning plan (ITLP) for at-risk youth based on the IEP for special education students, including linkages among schools and other service delivery agencies.

Ironically, it is the lowest one-third of school achievers who are the most threatened by the impending changes in the labor market. According to the Department of Labor, the average level of education needed for the lowest-level jobs is rising. The labor market appears to be providing sufficient supplies of highly skilled labor and engineers. The at-risk youth are needed to fill many jobs that require more than repetitive low-skill operations. The inner city at-risk youth may need such approaches as residential schools or a coordinated service delivery system that exists almost nowhere today between public and private agencies.

Reforms that last usually involve (a) structural or organizational change, (b) easy monitoring, and (c) creation of a powerful and lasting constituency (Kirst & Meister, 1985). The academic excellence reformers, for example, generated more math and science courses and used media and emotional appeals to create a constituency (e.g., "rising tide of mediocrity"). The teacher professionalism strategy, so far, lacks a passionately committed constituency. The Carnegie Forum for a new national teacher standards board includes leaders from three crucial sectors—state government, industry, and teacher unions. But teachers are attracted to some parts of it, such as increased decision-making power, while feeling uncertain about national tests and peer review for tenure or dismissal. School boards and administrators want to change collective bargaining procedures and contracts as part of "professionalism."

State policymakers are not clear what "restructured" schools would look like or what the appropriate state role is in stimulating this type of second reform wave. In short, as of 1988, the teacher professionalism movement needs more clarity on concept and a more cohesive constituency before it can build up a great deal of momentum. The Carnegie National Board of Professional Teaching Standards, however, is a three- to five-year effort, and it is too early to predict its impact. Massachusetts will fund some experiments called "Carnegie schools" that may help define the concept, and the new teacher assessment models being developed by the Carnegie Foundation promise to have a major impact on teacher education and teacher evaluation.

The Holmes Group of leading research universities, using a self-study approach, may also bring about significant changes in teacher preparation, but Holmes relies on the political influence of education deans and has no power base outside the schools of education. Not many deans are major players in state politics, nor do they have much influence over the liberal arts faculties. Some quotes from an *Education Week* article reveal why the National Education Association is cautious about "teacher professionalism," as articulated by reformers (Olson & Rodman, 1987, p. 1). Gary Sykes of Michigan State noted that, compared to the AFT, the NEA is "a much larger, more bureaucratic, and more entrenched organization that has a whole set of complex procedures, and that relies much more on grassroots democratic decision making"(p. 20).

John N. Dornan, president and executive director of the Public School Forum of North Carolina and a former state executive director within the NEA, stressed that in the past "many of the NEA's fears about unworkable systems or systems that would start and not be funded have in fact been borne out"(p. 21).

An NEA staff member admitted, "Over all, the teachers' perspective on education reform is that it is teacher bashing" and conceded that the NEA's positions "are really reflective of the very defensive . . . besieged kind of attitude of a lot of teachers"(p. 21).

In sum, there is no major new initiative to change the status of most experienced teachers in the near term. The national election, however, may produce some new ideas because all candidates are giving a great deal of attention to education. So far the national presidential debates have not clarified what the specific federal role can and should be in the second wave of reform.

Vouchers have never been voted on in any state, and federal tuition tax credits were defeated during the Reagan presidency. Consequently, it is hard to see choice as a major reform at this juncture. The period of 1986–1988 appears to be one of digesting the reforms from an earlier era.

The future of education reform depends primarily on the growth of the American economy and how this growth is distributed among the various states. Without continued economic impetus, state governments will focus more on efficiency, performance incentives, and evaluation of the 1983–1987 changes. For instance, the National Governors' Association 1986 report states that "the governors are ready for some old-fashioned horse trading. We'll regulate less, if schools and school districts will produce better results"(p. 3). But this new reform thrust by the governors will also be difficult. Chester Finn (1987) observes:

> To oversimplify just a bit, governors were asking educators for a commitment to results. What they got instead from most spokesmen was, "Thanks for noticing education; we're willing to sit down and talk with you about your ideas."(p. 315)

Consequently, education remains a priority issue for politicians, but they are searching for a specific set of initiatives that would be similar in scope to the 1983–1986 reform wave.

NOTE

Author's Note: I acknowledge the assistance of Allan Odden, University of Southern California, and James Guthrie, University of California at Berkeley, in the middle portions of this chapter. They created sections on the PACE/ACE and reform strategies as part of our mutual work on PACE.

REFERENCES

Carnegie Corporation. (1986). *A nation prepared: Teachers for the 21st century.* New York.

Coons, J., & Sugarman, S. (1983). *Education by choice.* Berkeley: University of California.

Finn, C. (1987). Governing education. *Educational Policy, 1*(3), 35.

Kirst, M., & Meister, G. (1985). Turbulence in American secondary schools: What reforms last? *Curriculum Inquiry, 15*(2), 169–186.

National Commission on Excellence in Education. (1983). *A nation at risk: The imperative for educational reform.* Washington, DC: U.S. Department of Education.

National Governors' Association. (1986). *Time for results.* Washington, DC: National Governors' Association.

Odden, A. (1987, April). *The economics of financing educational excellence.* Paper presented at the annual meeting of the American Educational Research Association, Washington, DC.

Odden, A., & Marsh, D. (1987). *How state education reform can improve secondary schools.* Berkeley: Policy Analysis for California Education.

Olson, L., & Rodman, B. (1987, November 4). Seeking profession's "soul." *Education Week 7*(9), pp. 1, 20–21.

PACE. Policy Analysis for California Education (PACE). (1987). *Conditions of education in California, 1986–87.* Berkeley.

Sizer, T. (1984). *Horace's compromise: The dilemma of the American high school.* Boston: Houghton Mifflin.

3

What to Teach, How to Teach It, and to Whom

The New Agenda for the Nation's Schools

ERNEST L. BOYER

O UR NATION IS at risk," declared a National Commission on Excellence in Education five years ago. The report began with a dark assessment: "If an unfriendly foreign power had attempted to impose on America the mediocre educational performance that exists today, we might well have viewed it as an act of war. As it stands, we have allowed this to happen to ourselves."

In the ensuing months, more reports appeared. Among them were *High School*, the Carnegie Foundation's report on secondary education in the United States, and, this year, *College*, our report on undergraduate education in America. These reports are now part of a burgeoning education literature on how American education may have wandered off course in its efforts to satisfy all of the demands of the society it serves.

Despite the hyperbole of some of these reports, they address real problems and identify needs for new policies to improve school and college performance. As educators and the general public discussed the reports, the recommendations gradually found their way into education policy and practice. School boards and college trustees looked more closely at the facilities and programs under their jurisdictions. Parents became better informed about issues in American schools and colleges and guided the education choices of their sons and daughters with more understanding.

Soon after the reports were issued, 30 governors named state commissions on school reform. High school graduation requirements have been raised; teacher training has improved; certification procedures have been tightened, and teacher salaries have gone up twice the inflation rate. Above all, there has been a turnaround in the public attitude toward teachers and the teaching profession.

We have made progress. We are still the nation of Thomas Jefferson, who said, "Education is the anvil on which democracy is forged," and we are willing to respond quickly and generously when we find it in trouble. So I propose two cheers for the recent push for school renewal in the nation.

But rejoicing should be muted. The school reform movement has not confronted adequately some of the harsh realities encountered by school officials and faculty members.

In some city schools, for example, 4 out of 10 students are absent on any given day. How is excellence possible when students are not even in the school building?

Almost half of the Mexican-American and Puerto Rican students who enroll in public schools drop out before they are awarded a diploma. In Philadelphia, the dropout rate is 38 percent, in Boston, 43 percent. In 1984, over half of the students in Chicago failed to graduate; of those who did, only one-third were reading at the twelfth-grade level. In 1987, the Cleveland public schools did not have a single semifinalist in the National Merit Scholarship competition. Boston and Detroit each had only *one* high school with semifinalists.

The breakup of families, communities wrenched by crime, lack of money, and the loss of good teachers—all of these "outside" realities threaten to overwhelm our most troubled schools. Requiring a failing student in an urban ghetto to take another unit in math or foreign language without a better climate or better teaching is like raising a hurdle without giving more coaching to someone who has already stumbled.

By the year 2000, one of every three pupils in American public schools will be nonwhite. Already headed toward the educational system is a group of children who will be poorer, more ethnically and linguistically diverse, and more handicapped in ways that will surely affect their schooling. Clearly, unless we deepen our commitment, the crisis in urban education will also deepen. An aging white population will be more reluctant to provide support, and the gap between the haves and the have-nots in education will widen. What we might find in our major cities is a kind of educational Third World. And it is precisely in these schools that the battle of American education will be won or lost.

So far, most of the education reforms have focused on the regulatory parts of school renewal. It is now time to apply to the reform movement a test of quality that takes us to the very heart of public education.

I

The first test to be applied is this: *Will we teach students what they really need to know?*

No amount of rhetoric can conceal that in most states the K–12 curriculum lacks both quality and coherence. We have added Carnegie units to our graduation requirements, but we have failed to ask, "What's behind the label?" We say "science," but what science? History? Yes, but what history? The last and most influential commission to consider what history should be taught in school issued its report in 1926. "English" can mean anything from Shakespeare to oral reading. Tomorrow's curriculum surely must be something more than the minimalist, fragmentation of information and the disconnected courses that exist today.

The next question is *Where do we begin?* The first curriculum priority is that all students must become proficient in the written and the spoken word. On this point, everyone agrees. What we cannot agree upon, it seems, is the *level* of literacy to be attained. Will we settle for the embarrassingly elementary vocabulary tests now required in some states—even at the college level? Is *that* what it means to be linguistically proficient?

Recently, the National Assessment of Educational Progress reported that most young adults in the United States are literate by UNESCO standards—they can read words in passages appropriate to their age. The study also found, however, that more than 40 percent of those surveyed had trouble drawing meaning from the message. There was word recognition but not sufficient insight or understanding.

What this nation urgently needs are citizens who can think critically, listen with discernment, and communicate with power and precision. Such empowerment should begin the first day of school. The early years are transcendentally the most important. If this nation would give as much status to first-grade teachers as we give to full professors, that one act alone would bring quality to public education.

I propose that every school district organize what might be called *The Basic School*, a nongraded unit that would include kindergarten through grade 4. In the Basic School, children, from the very first, would be speaking, writing, reading, talking about words, listening to stories, building a rich vocabulary, and creating a climate foreign language people call "the saturation method." The goal would be to assure that every child—by grade 4—would become linguistically empowered.

We also urge in our report, *High School*, that schools give priority to writing, since it is through clear writing that the skills of clear thinking can be taught. We propose that writing be taught in every class from kindergarten to grade 12. We also recommend that every high school senior be asked to write a paper on a consequential topic. After 12 years of formal education, students should be able to express themselves with clarity and coherence, integrate ideas, and state their conclusions with cogency.

Finally, it is urgently important to teach students that language is a sacred trust. We hear a lot of talk these days about teaching values in the public schools. I'm not sure this worthy goal can be accomplished with a separate course in morality or ethics. I *am* convinced, however, that teaching values is determined, ultimately, by the truth people put in their own words—and in the words of others. If the Iran hearings taught us anything at all, they taught us that good communication means not just clarity of expression, but *integrity* as well.

Beyond language, all students—through a study of history, literature, geography, civics, and the arts—should achieve "cultural literacy," to use E. D. Hirsch's helpful formulation. They also should become familiar with languages and traditions other than our own. Several years ago, 40 percent of the community college students surveyed in California could not locate either Iran or El Salvador on a map. During our study of the American high school, we discovered that only two states require students to complete a course in non-Western studies. And three years ago, in a survey of 5,000 undergraduates, we learned that over 30 percent of today's college students said they had "nothing in common" with people in underdeveloped countries. *Nothing* in common with less-privileged human beings?

Dr. Lewis Thomas, former chancellor of the Sloan-Kettering Cancer Center in New York, said on one occasion, "If this century does not slip forever through our fingers, it will be because learning will have directed us away from our splintered dumbness and helped us focus on our common goals—both national and global as well."

As we approach the year 2000, students also must discover their connections to the natural world and, through science, understand the interdependent nature of our planet. Today, we live in a world that is ecologically imperiled. The protective ozone layer is endangered. Our shorelines are polluted. The tropical rain forests are being depleted at the rate of 100,000 square kilometers every year. Yet, for far too many years, students' knowledge of nature and its resources has gone about as far as the refrigerator door and the light switch on the wall. Not all students are budding scientists, to be sure. But becoming a responsible citizen in the twenty-first century means becoming scientifically literate and understanding more fully the interdependent world in which we live.

What we seek, then, is a core curriculum that focuses on cultural literacy that is global as well as national, on science literacy with an ecological perspective, and on language study that includes the mastery of symbols, clear thinking, and integrity. What students need, in short, is a solid course of study that relates content to the realities of life.

II

Now, I would like to say a word about teachers. Thus far, teacher reform has focused primarily on salaries, testing, merit pay, and on a bold plan for national teacher certification—a proposal I applaud. I am convinced, however, that even with these crucial and creative moves, teaching will remain imperiled, not because standards are too low, but because poor working conditions continue to discourage even the ablest from entering the profession.

For most of their working days, teachers are alone with their students. They have little interaction with parents or even with other teachers. At the Carnegie Foundation, we surveyed 22,000 teachers from coast to coast, and found that, among high school teachers, over 90 percent say lack of parental support is a problem at their school.

Even more disturbing, we found that teachers are not involved in key professional decisions. We discovered, for example, that nearly one-third say they have no role in shaping the curriculum they are asked to teach. Over 50 percent do not participate in designing their own in-service programs. A total of 70 percent are not asked to help shape retention policies at their schools. More than 50 percent of all high school teachers are not even involved in determining which students should be tracked into special classes. Apparently this critical decision is something that is just "imposed." And then we wonder why good students do not go into teaching!

There are poor teachers, to be sure. For the reform movement to succeed, the teaching profession must monitor itself vigorously. This nation simply will not endlessly support mediocrity in the classroom.

It is also true, however, that no profession is made healthy by focusing only on what is bad. Teacher accountability is absolutely crucial. But in the days ahead, if we hope to attract and hold outstanding teachers in the classroom, the reform movement must increasingly focus on the three Rs of teacher excellence: *recruitment, recognition,* and *renewal.*

To attract and hold outstanding teachers, we need a teacher excellence fund in every school to help teachers implement good ideas. We need a travel fund to encourage teachers to stay abreast of new ideas. If continuing education is important for doctors and lawyers, it is doubly critical for those who teach the coming generation.

We need federal leadership as well. Thirty years ago, in response to Sputnik, President Dwight D. Eisenhower proposed the National Defense Education Act, a dramatic move that sent a powerful signal to the nation. I recommend a 1990 version of Eisenhower's NDEA, a legislative package that would, among other things, vigorously expand the Talented Teachers Act, a program that gives scholarships to top high school students who agree to teach in public schools. After all, we send volunteers overseas. Why not also send our gifted students to teach the rural poor and the disadvantaged in our inner cities? The new act would also provide a massive program of federally funded summer fellowships for teachers.

Above all, we need more teacher recognition. Perhaps here we can borrow something from the Japanese. In that culture the teacher is held in very high regard. For the Japanese the term *sensei*—teacher—is a title of great honor. In America we say, "He or she is *just* a teacher."

The time has come for the leaders of this nation to be as concerned about getting outstanding teachers into the classrooms as they are about getting weapons into space.

III

Next is the pressing question: "Will we effectively evaluate results?" On this point the reform movement deserves a barely passing grade. When it comes to testing and evaluation, educators have, for years, been playing blindman's bluff. They have criticized almost every test that has been proposed while failing to develop useful yardsticks of their own.

When I was Commissioner of Education, the "minimum competency testing" movement was in full swing. On their own initiative, 34 states mandated testing to find out what was happening to students in the school. This grass-roots movement should have been a warning about accountability. With all the talk about school renewal, we are still far too ignorant about how to measure the results. The nation's taxpayers will not continue to invest $140 billion every year in public education without hard evidence that the investment is paying off. If good evaluation instruments are not devised, almost anything will be used to judge the effectiveness of schools.

Thus far, in many states, we have been measuring what matters least, and in the process we run the risk of trivializing the push for school reform. Already, the SAT has become—inappropriately—a report card on public education, and many of our tests focus only on the recall of isolated facts. What we need today is a national nongovernmental panel organized, perhaps, by the chief state school officers, the Education Commission of the States, and the six major regional accrediting associations. The proposed panel, which might be called The Commission on Tomorrow's Schools, would monitor national assessment efforts and develop a model program to be used optionally by each state.

What might such a program include? First, an assessment of basic language and computation in the elementary grades to verify that students have mastered the tools of learning; second, a battery of general education examinations at the secondary level to evaluate student knowledge in such areas as science, civics, literature, history, and geography; third, an assessment of the high-order aptitudes: for example, aesthetic sensitivity, creativity, and problem solving; finally, a senior writing program that demonstrates students' capacity to think critically and integrate ideas.

Evaluating human beings is a difficult task. Still, I am convinced progress can and must be made. In his insightful book, *Frames of Mind*, Howard Gardner reminds us that beyond verbal intelligence, children have other intelligences ranging from aesthetic to mathematical. Currently, Gardner is working on portfolios for assessment in the arts, an experiment that may prove useful in other areas as well.

In the end, what we measure will determine what we teach. Shaping a comprehensive program of assessment—one that enriches rather than trivializes the goals of education—may well be the most urgent and essential challenge the reform movement now confronts.

IV

Finally, will the reform movement reach all students, and not just the privileged few?

In 1647—129 years before the Revolution—the Massachusetts Bay Colony passed a law requiring that every town or village of 50 or more souls hire a schoolmaster to teach the children to read and write. From the very first, this nation has understood that education and democracy are inextricably interlocked. Now, it would be almost an embarrassment to ask: "Which students will be served?" Today, everyone agrees that excellence in education must mean excellence for *all*.

But the reform movement is not working out that way. The harsh truth is that while "advantaged" schools are getting better, others remain deeply troubled. There is still an enormous gap between rhetoric and results.

Clearly, many of the nation's schools still are in deep crisis, and yet we accept this failure as a way of life. It is significant, for example, that 21 percent of today's teachers believe that schools cannot expect to graduate more than 75 percent of those enrolled. Still more sobering, about 30 percent of urban high school teachers feel this way.

If snow were piling up on city streets, if we had heaps of garbage on the curbs, if a health epidemic was striking one-fourth of our children in this country, the president, governors, and mayors would declare a national emergency. They would bring together all appropriate officials in a round-the-clock crisis session, and no one would be dismissed until an appropriate plan of action had been shaped. But when students' lives are wasted, when thousands of our children leave school educationally and socially unprepared, public officials do not act with the sense of urgency—and persistence—the emergency requires.

The very language of the school reform movement tells a revealing story. We hear much talk these days about "model schools" and "magnet schools" and "essential schools." The focus is on a handful of privileged institutions that are "showcased," as educators like to say. This strategy, which might best be described as "excellence by exception," benefits the "lighthouse" institutions, while the rest struggle on their own.

The United States, if it is to remain an economically vital nation, cannot tolerate a system that divides the winners from the losers. We must affirm that all children, even those from the most difficult backgrounds, will have available to them the conditions to ensure that they will academically and socially succeed. The goal must be quality for all.

Here, then, is my conclusion. Since 1983, we have had one of the most sustained and consequential periods of school renewal in the nation's history. But if we stop now, the movement will have failed. To succeed, we must

- identify a core of common knowledge that recalls the past, anticipates the future, and helps students apply what they have learned to the realities of life;
- give priority to the teacher, focusing on recruitment, recognition, and renewal;
- find better ways to measure student progress; and
- above all, we must confront the crisis of the disadvantaged.

When all is said and done, the reform movement must be measured not by what happens to students in our privileged schools, but by what happens to the rural poor and to neglected children in the inner city.

James Agee wrote on one occasion that "in every child who is born, under no matter what circumstances, the potentiality of the human race is born again." That audacious vision is what the education reform movement is all about.

UNIT TWO

Actors in Reform

The chapters in this unit were included to give the reader an idea of the complexity of this issue. Starting with the federal perspective and working down to the school site level, the role of actors in the reform movement are discussed by people involved in policymaking or re-search at that level. *This is more than just an elaboration of Unit One's conclusion about the standardization and centralization of goal setting and the decentralization of implementation responsibility. It demonstrates that effective reform requires the* integration *of efforts at many different levels.*

Could fifty thousand masons build a skyscraper? How about fifty thousand heavy-equipment operators? Fifty thousand engineers? Could any combination of the above build a skyscraper without at least one financier and at least one architect? Constructing a system to educate millions of children is probably a more daunting challenge than building a skyscraper. At least physical building materials obey known and quantifiable laws! What we in the education reform movement are dealing with are unpredictable, diverse, and constantly changing interest groups, *each with its own ideological and role agenda.*

By looking at how each group of participants is reacting to the tidal wave of education reform, the reader should gain a better under-standing of the constraints to action *that are already built into the system. We have a huge, unwieldy system of decentralized public ed-ucation, with political power groups at each level vying to define and control the reform agenda. The problem is that implementation of new goals* at any level *requires the active cooperation of all other levels. Successful implementation of reform is thus dependent on the current actors.*

To return to the skyscraper metaphor, a developer who wants to build a new type of skyscraper must first consider federal, state, local, and union conditions, as well as the market conditions for the space that he seeks to rent out. Next, he must negotiate compromises that are satisfactory to all major groups. In education, it is even harder, because there is no single office or institution that is respon-sible for the overall outcome. Instead, different levels and groups are held responsible for different outcomes—but it is not always clear to whom they are responsible.

Despite the different perspectives expressed in these six chap-ters, some common threads emerge. The "Toyota problem" (Boyd, Chapter 4) seems to continue to exert strong pressures for more than just rhetoric at the federal level. Almost everyone agrees that more federal resources will be necessary in raising educational performance in poor and minority areas. As mentioned in Unit One, the state governments now recognize that the state role should be to set goals, measure performance, and coordinate resources, while letting local districts and communities decide how best to achieve these goals, and granting teachers the autonomy and flexibility to implement the state and local plan (Honig, Chapter 5).

At the district level, Muth and Azumi (Chapter 6) believe that the local school board is being neglected as a potential instrument of change. They point out that most funding is generated at the district level, and voters will spend more money only if they feel they have a voice in the process. A large number of these voters are parents, and Marburger (Chapter 7) claims that their involvement in education is crucial to the success of their children. He presents some ideas for encouraging that involvement, and concludes that school-based management is the "best mechanism available to involve parents in the affairs of the schools" (Marburger, p. 90).

Another important interest group is made up of teachers, who are very often unionized. Shedd (Chapter 8) discusses the fact that the bargaining process is tending to involve teachers more in decision making. If this increased participation results in teachers gaining a better understanding and acceptance of the goals, then it will probably help in goal implementation. Although Malen and Ogawa (Chapter 9) doubt the real effectiveness of participatory structures for both teachers and parents, even Honig (at the state level) calls for more flexibility and autonomy (i.e., professionalism) for classroom teachers.

To sum up, each level or interest group has its own agenda, but these agendas do not entirely conflict with one another. Improving the system is in everyone's interest, and each group tends to fight hardest about those issues most dear to it, leaving some room for compromise on the peripheral issues (those that overlap). The very diffuse nature of the system, then, does not necessarily prevent reform.

4

The National Level: Reagan and the Bully Pulpit

How to Reform Schools without Half Trying: Secrets of the Reagan Administration
WILLIAM LOWE BOYD

Sɪɴᴄᴇ 1983, American public schools have been experiencing the most sustained and far-reaching reform effort in modern times. Leadership from the Reagan administration galvanized this national effort to improve school performance in pursuit of excellence and economic growth. Yet, unlike previous administrations, this administration mobilized reform with a minimum of federal expenditures and no direct intervention into state and local educational affairs. How the Reagan administration has managed to reform schools "without half trying," and the strengths and weaknesses of its strategy in producing enduring reforms, are the subjects of this paper.

It has long been recognized that reforming schools is very difficult, for they are remarkably resistant to change. The perennial problems of schools and the traditional methods of teaching persist despite decades of efforts to alter them. Changing schools is like punching a pillow. They absorb innovative thrusts and soon resume their original shape. Indeed, innovations often disappear quickly, leaving scarcely a trace behind (Cuban, 1979).

Thus the amount of change that the Reagan administration has prompted in school affairs is truly extraordinary. Michael Usdan, president of the Institute for Educational Leadership, has been quoted as saying that it would have taken 30 years to enact, through regular education channels, the wave of reforms many states adopted in the past three years (November 7, 1986, as quoted in *Johnstown Tribune-Democrat*, p. 2A). How has all of this been accomplished?

If we compare the Reagan administration's approach to that of its predecessors, the contrast is striking. The Great Society programs of the Lyndon B. Johnson administration made public education a central feature of dramatic federal programs for social reform. For the first time, the federal government intervened strongly in elementary and secondary education. Such programs as compensatory education and school desegregation got big bucks and major federal enforcement. Yet, by the end of the 1960s, there was a strong sense that these programs weren't working very well. Many wondered, as one evaluation study of the time asked, "Should we give up or try harder?" (Rivlin & Timpane, 1975).

ORIGINS OF THE *NATION AT RISK* CRISIS

Remarkably, rather than trying harder, as most federal administrations following Lyndon Johnson endeavored to do, within their fiscal and political constraints, the Reagan administration hit upon a strategy for reforming schools "without half trying." I say "hit upon" purposely, because President Reagan began inauspiciously in the education domain. Soon after being inaugurated as president he commented that he wasn't sure that the federal government had any legitimate function in education. Technically, he was right. Education is not even mentioned in the Constitution and, consequently, is a function reserved to the states.

Yet, since World War II, the federal government has become increasingly involved in education because of the strong connections between education and national defense, welfare, civil rights, and social justice, all of which are very much in the Constitution. Nevertheless, Reagan began by denying that his administration had an important federal role to play in education.

But what has been called the "Toyota problem" was closing in on the president. America was losing its technological and productivity edge to foreign competitors, notably the Japanese. The American economy and balance of trade were suffering.

Many observers felt that to preserve our standard of living we had to substantially improve our system of schooling to meet this technological and economic challenge. Reagan concurred, but he maintained that this was a problem for state and local governments to solve, not the federal government. Still, criticism was mounting, and many felt that the federal government should be doing something about the emerging crisis. Wasn't this situation similar to the Sputnik crisis in 1957 that threatened national security and prompted passage of the National Defense Education Act? It seemed almost—to coin a phrase—that the "nation was at risk."

Predictably, the Democrats called for major federal aid for the schools and introduced several ambitious bills along these lines. What was Reagan to do? Major federal intervention was antithetical to his New Federalism. But things were heating up, and he was on the defensive. Then, in a masterful political stroke, Reagan turned the tables on his opponents.

In an address at Seton Hall University in the spring of 1983, Reagan said the answer to the educational problems was to demand excellence and improve the quality of teaching. The way to do this, he said, was to use merit pay so that teachers would be rewarded for outstanding performance.

The commonsense appeal of merit pay was extraordinarily powerful. Who could be against rewarding excellence? The teachers' unions, that's who. Even now, the National Education Association, the largest teachers' union, still basically opposes it ("NEA Official Predicts," 1986). But, under the shrewd leadership of Albert Shanker, the American Federation of Teachers moved almost at once to a more conciliatory stance, positioning itself well in the face of political winds that blew strongly in favor of merit pay, though many of its rank and file continue to oppose it ("Teachers Found Skeptical," 1986).

The views espoused by Reagan in his Seton Hall address echoed the findings of the extraordinarily influential report of the federally appointed National Commission on Excellence in Education. The belief that we need to demand and reward better performance from both teachers and students is at the heart of the commission's report, *A Nation at Risk: The Imperative for Educational Reform*. The report, released in April 1983, argues that these goals could be accomplished best by state and local government, not by federal intervention. As Linda McNeil (1985) has noted, by successfully selling this argument, the Reagan administration was able

> to preempt Democratic candidates' call for increased aid to education. To balance this preemptive policy issue, the Reagan administration had to seize on education as an issue without alienating its usual constituency for decreased federal support of social and educational welfare. The solution was to endorse the commission report on public schools while tossing the responsibility back to the states. (p. 183)

THE STRATEGY AND POLITICS OF REFORM

But how was Reagan able to sell the idea that the states should take on this problem themselves? What set all this state-level reform activity in motion? In a nutshell, it was an astute combination of politics and leadership. Reagan and his two Secretaries of Education—first, Terrel H. Bell and then, especially, William J. Bennett—have made masterful use of their high offices as "bully pulpits" from which to sermonize about what needs to be done to improve our public schools (Jung & Kirst, 1986). With very little more than effective use of rhetoric and symbols and their ability to command attention from the media, they have reshaped the semantics and agenda of American educational policy (Clark & Astuto, 1986; Jung & Kirst, 1986).

As Richard Jung and Michael Kirst (1986) emphasize, launching the Commission on Excellence and its *Nation at Risk* report cost the federal government very little. But because of the report's powerful rhetoric— describing "a rising tide of mediocrity" and claiming it would have been seen as "an act of war" if an unfriendly power had imposed our educational system on us—the report captured the attention of the media and the public. Above all, the state governors, particularly the southern governors, picked up the *Nation at Risk* agenda. They saw the connection between improved schooling and improving a state's economy. Schooling, for the first time, became a hot and profitable political issue, one linked to the creation of jobs.

For just one example of how this worked, and how the *Nation at Risk* rhetoric has influenced developments, we can look at Pennsylvania. There, Governor Richard L. Thornburgh called his educational reform package *Turning the Tide* and, at the end of his tenure, issued a report that declared in its title: *The Tide Is Turning* (1986).

Let us consider more closely how the Reagan administration has exerted influential leadership. First, it has produced a dramatic reversal in the semantics, goals, and means of federal education policy. As David Clark and Terry Astuto (1986) have documented, a systematic program of policies and pronouncements has produced a 180-degree shift in emphasis away from the values that guided federal policy in the 1970s: from equity to excellence, from needs and access to ability and selectivity, from regulations and enforcement to deregulation, from the common school to parental choice and institutional competition, and from social and welfare concerns to economic and productivity concerns.

One of the great successes in the pursuit of educational excellence has been the introduction of statewide performance standards where few existed before, either for students or teachers. As Denis Doyle and Chester Finn, Jr. (1984) note, "In the past, one has had to look long and hard for serious statewide standards of individual performance" (p. 84). In this respect, one of the most influential federal initiatives was the introduction of the controversial "Wall Chart" comparing student performance in the 50 states. Initially, many state leaders complained bitterly about what they viewed as unfair and inappropriate comparisons. But ultimately, the Council of Chief State School Officers accepted the idea that performance comparisons were here to stay and agreed to collaborate on the venture.

Finally, if Terrel Bell seemed to get a lot of publicity for his ideas, it was nothing compared to the performance of his successor as Secretary of Education, William Bennett. Under Bennett, the use of the bully pulpit became an art form. Indeed, his performance has been so exceptional that a lengthy article in the *Chronicle of Higher Education* analyzed how he orchestrated this remarkable public relations "blitz" (Wilson, 1986).

PROBLEMS IN THE REFORM MOVEMENT

Undeniably, the successes of the Reagan administration's inexpensive strategy are impressive. But, as with many strategies, it also has weaknesses that are becoming increasingly evident. On the one hand, the Reagan administration unquestionably deserves high marks for mobilizing the "excellence" reform movement and for encouraging energetic state leadership—a great accomplishment and one likely to have very positive and lasting effects. But on the other hand, this approach suffers from two acute and fundamental weaknesses: the excessive emphasis on external, "top-down" reform measures and the gross neglect of the federal responsibility to provide leadership and funding to alleviate the dire educational problems of the disadvantaged, many of whom are concentrated in large urban school systems now on the brink of disaster.

On the first point, as James Guthrie (1986, p. 306) notes, "fundamental components of the reform strategy seem to be painfully at odds with the dynamics of organizational revitalization." The emphasis of the national commission reports, as Paula Silver (1986, p. 140) observed, "is on changing the schools from *without* by mandating changes in the requirements, procedures, position titles, and/or accountability processes of schools." But, as she noted, this approach generally neglects the *internal* workings of schools and what we've learned from the "effective schools" movement. Instead, "the new state 'initiatives' address such factors as length of school day, course title requirements, certification procedures, . . . and the rituals of supervising instruction" (Silver, 1986, pp. 140–141; italics added). Thus some reform policies are helpful and highly visible but leave untouched much of what goes on in schools; other policies attempt to alter behavior in schools but do not come to grips with the essential underlying organizational dynamics (Clark, 1985b).

Another serious weakness in the reform effort is that the major education professional groups have been against nearly all of the reforms following the *Nation at Risk* report. In a review of case studies of seven of the leading "reform" states, Allan Odden (1986) concluded that "the lack of enthusiasm of the education community and outright opposition by elements within the community to nearly all of the proposed education reforms is a consistent theme" (p. 4).

This opposition by the key institutional interest groups makes the progress of the current reform movement all the more remarkable. However, as Odden notes, state politicians have insisted that more dollars for education would be forthcoming *only* in exchange for acceptance of reforms. Indeed, in Texas, the "Rambo" reformer par excellence, H. Ross Perot, used as his slogan, "Millions for reform, but not one dime for the status quo" (Plank, 1986).

Educators object to the reform movement largely because of the character of the reforms selected and the manner in which they have been implemented. Generally speaking, powerful actors outside the educational system have enacted "top-down" reforms, and frequently these reforms have been forced onto unwilling teachers. This approach shows no sensitivity to the "bottom-up" realities of organizational change and implementation in human services organizations (Elmore, 1983). Further, it ignores the need for a fundamental restructuring of the career and incentive systems of teachers and school administrators so that real change and improvement in the performance of the public schools are possible.

In reforming organizations, as in art, it's just as Stephen Sondheim said in his song, "Putting It Together": "The art of art is putting it together. . . . Having just the vision's no solution, everything depends on execution." Thus we have to have a sophisticated plan for *systemic* organizational change if we're going to translate vision into reality, and this is precisely where the reform-through-rhetoric approach of the "bully pulpit" gets into trouble. By themselves, exhortations and mandates will never be enough to produce fundamental and lasting change.

For despite the administration's extensive ballyhoo and touting of the sweeping reforms being launched and successfully implemented across the states, the truth is that there may be less real reform occurring than meets the eye. For instance, research to date suggests that, in many cases, teachers and their unions are successfully resisting such reforms as merit pay and career ladders. This phenomenon has been especially well documented in Utah—a state generally thought to be strong on educational reform—by Betty Malen and Ann Hart (1987). More broadly, a national opinion survey in 1986 underscored the divergence in views between teachers and the leaders of the reform movement—governors, education school deans, and union leaders ("Teachers Found Skeptical," 1986).

Significantly, one of the most vulnerable points about the strategy of reforming schools through rhetoric has also been one of its great selling points—namely, promoting change "on the cheap" by arguing that federal dollars aren't needed. Consistent with this theme, Secretary Bennett told

Congress in January 1987 that more homework and more third graders who can read—not more federal dollars for schools—are what the nation's education system most needs.

Here, however, recent developments, emphasizing such problems as the critical needs of urban areas and "at risk" minorities, indicate that a shift of opinion is underway. As the social and political mood of the country changes, Reagan's "bully pulpit" advocates are finding themselves increasingly on the receiving end of the rhetorical war.

In one of the more colorful developments, for example, *To Secure the Blessings of Liberty*, a commission report prepared for the American Association of State Colleges and Universities and chaired by former Secretary Bell, said, in November 1986, that the United States was in grave danger unless it sharply increased spending on its schools and colleges ("Bell Panel's Plan," 1986). The report called for a domestic Marshall Plan to nearly double the number of college-educated adults by the turn of the century, and it excoriated cutbacks on spending for remedial programs: "Public officials who propose budget reductions in education at a time when the republic is handicapped by the burden of an under-educated populace are unthinkingly abetting an act of national suicide" (p. 7). In addition, the report claimed that the real value of federal aid to students had dropped 25 percent since Reagan took office in 1981.

Not surprisingly, William Bennett and his associates reacted strongly against the report. They called it "silly, overblown rhetoric" and suggested Terrel Bell was a "turncoat" for attacking the very administration he had served ("Bell Panel's Plan," 1986). The great irony, of course, is that they were merely being subjected to the same sort of rhetoric they've been using for their own purposes all along. Increasingly, they find themselves facing the point of view voiced by Representative Jim Wright of Texas: "While it may be true that you can't solve these problems simply by throwing money at them, you surely can't solve them simply by throwing words at them" (Olson, 1987, p. 23).

CONCLUSION

Fortunately, there may be a happy ending to this story. Efforts are underway to replace rhetorical reform with more substantive programs aimed at transforming both the fundamental characteristics of public schools and the teaching profession. Part of this effort includes an increasing recognition of the need to ameliorate the monopoly performance problems of our public schools by promoting parental choice among them (Chubb & Moe, 1986; Clark, 1985a; Doyle & Finn, 1984; *Time for Results*, 1986). To revitalize the performance and career and incentive structures for teachers and school administrators we must break up the complacent, consumer-insensitive monopoly that public schools have over most of their clients. This can be done by fostering curriculum variety and differentiation among public schools, and then permitting competition among them for clients (Clark, 1985a).

At the forefront of the so-called "second" wave of reform are the efforts of the Carnegie Forum, the Holmes Group, and the National Governors' Association. The influential reports of these three groups— *A Nation Prepared: Teachers for the 21st Century* (1986); *Tomorrow's Teachers* (1986); and *Time for Results: The Governors' 1991 Report on Education* (1986)—represent a comprehensive and far-reaching agenda for the reform and revitalization of America's public schools. Significantly, the three groups recognize that they need to work together as a coalition for effective reform. In a large sense, of course, this collaboration represents a victory for the federal leadership embodied in the "half-trying" approach because nonfederal actors have taken on this responsibility.

On the other hand, as the Bell report and numerous others have argued, greater federal funding will be essential in meeting critical national education needs. Economically and politically, the federal government is much abler than cities and states to redistribute resources vitally needed to aid disadvantaged groups. As Paul Peterson (1981) has shown, cities and states can do very little of this because it weakens their economic position in the ongoing competition for productive residents and businesses.

Although the stock market problems and the federal budget deficit constrain federal funding, there is mounting concern about the need for policies that will promote U.S. economic "competitiveness." Revelations about such matters as the continuing poor mathematics performance of American students, when compared to those of other nations, are likely to bolster the view that improved educational achievement is imperative for better economic performance in this technological age. Just as the Sputnik crisis generated the National Defense Education Act of 1958, it is probable—as the "Reagan revolution" runs down—that a more substantive federal role in meeting the current crisis will yet be forthcoming.

Finally, the case for optimism about the long-range success of the second wave of the reform movement is bolstered by recent research on federal policy innovations of the recent past. This research suggests that, despite initial resistance and setbacks, reforms may succeed over the long haul if advocates persist and manage to gain legitimacy and acceptance (Peterson, Rabe, & Wong, 1986). Too often, we have prematurely judged the success of new programs or policies. Early evaluations frequently highlight the confusion and inefficiency of initial efforts at implementation. But as programs mature and external advocates maintain their support and encouragement, the fidelity and commitment of local implementation can grow very substantially (Jung & Kirst, 1986; Peterson et al., 1986).

As we move from the easy victories of the "half-trying" approach to the more difficult challenges before us, the great hope of the second wave of reform is to release the constructive potential of the teaching profession. By restructuring schools and altering career lines, incentives, and relationships among teachers, schools administrators, students, and parents, we can enhance both the professionalism of teaching and the quality of education. But an enormous amount of work and successful negotiation will be required to achieve these goals. For instance, authority relationships between teachers and school administrators will have to be renegotiated. Another unresolved problem, in the quest for greater professionalism and empowerment of teachers, lies in the countervailing trend toward greater "standardization" and bureaucratization of the curriculum through the movement for curriculum alignment and testing now sweeping across the states (Kirst, 1987). Only when all of these hurdles have been cleared will substance indeed have replaced rhetoric in school reform.

NOTE

This article is revised from a commentary published as "Rhetoric and Symbolic Politics: President Reagan's School-Reform Agenda," *Education Week*, March 18, 1987, pp. 28, 21.

REFERENCES

Bell Panel's plan seeks to halve school-dropout rate. (1986, November 19). *Education Week*, p. 7.

Carnegie Forum on Education and the Economy. (1986). *A nation prepared: Teachers for the 21st century*. Report of the Task Force on Teaching as a Profession. New York: Carnegie Corporation of New York.

Chubb, J. E., & Moe, T. M. (1986). No school is an island: Politics, markets, and education. *Brookings Review, 4*, 21–28.

Clark, B. R. (1985a, February). The high school and the university: What went wrong in America, Part I. *Phi Delta Kappan*, 391–397.

Clark, B. R. (1985b, March). The high school and the university: What went wrong in America, Part 2. *Phi Delta Kappan*, 472–475.

Clark, D., & Astuto, T. (1986, October). The significance and permanence of changes in federal education policy. *Educational Researcher*, pp. 4–13.

Cuban, L. (1979). Determinants of curriculum change and stability, 1870–1970. In J. Schaffarzirk & G. Sykes (Eds.), *Value conflicts and curriculum issues*. Berkeley, CA: McCutchan.

Doyle, D. P., & Finn. C. E., Jr. (1984). American schools and the future of local control. *Public Interest, 77*, 77–95.

Elmore, R. F. (1983). Complexity and control: What legislators and administrators can do about implementing public policy. In L. S. Shulman & G. Sykes (Eds.), *Handbook of teaching and policy*. New York: Longman.

Guthrie, J. W. (1986, December). School-based management: The next needed education reform. *Phi Delta Kappan.*

The Holmes Group. (1986). *Tomorrow's teachers.* East Lansing, MI: The Holmes Group.

Jung, R., & Kirst, M. (1986). Beyond mutual adaptation, into the bully pulpit: Recent research on the federal role in education. *Educational Administration Quarterly, 22*(1), 80–109.

Kirst, M. W. (1987, April). Curricular leadership at the state level: What is the new focus? *NASSP Bulletin,* pp. 8–14.

Malen, B., & Hart, A. W. (1987). Career ladder reform: A multi-level analysis of initial efforts. *Educational Evaluation and Policy Analysis, 9*(1), 9–23.

McNeil, L. (1985). Teacher culture and the irony of school reform. In P. G. Altbach et al. (Eds.), *Excellence in education: Perspectives on policy and practice.* Buffalo, NY: Prometheus.

National Commission on Excellence in Education. (1983). *A nation at risk: The imperative for educational reform.* Washington, DC: U.S. Department of Education.

NEA official predicts demise of merit pay, career ladders. (1986, October 31). *Johnstown Tribune-Democrat.*

Odden, A. (1986). When votes and dollars mingle: A first analysis of state reforms. *Politics of Education Bulletin, 13*(2), 3–8.

Olson, L. (1987, March 4). Governors anticipate major role for education in work initiative. *Education Week,* p. 23.

Peterson, P. E. (1981). *City limits.* Chicago: University of Chicago Press.

Peterson, P. E., Rabe, B. G., & Wong, K. K. (1986). *When federalism works.* Washington, DC: Brookings Institution.

Plank, D. N. (1986). The ayes of Texas: Rhetoric, reality, and school reform. *Politics of Education Bulletin, 13*(2), 13–16.

Rivlin, A., & Timpane, M. (Eds.). (1975). *Planned variation in education: Should we give up or try harder?* Washington, DC: Brookings Institution.

Silver, P. F. (1986). Review of organizational environments: Ritual and rationality. *Educational Administration Quarterly, 22*(2), 140.

Teachers found skeptical about impact of reforms. (1986, November 19). *Education Week,* pp. 6, 18.

The tide is turning: A progress report on the agenda for excellence in Pennsylvania public schools. (1986, October). Harrisburg: Pennsylvania Department of Education.

Time for results: The governors' 1991 report on education. (1986). Washington, DC: National Governors' Association.

Wilson, R. (1986, December 10). A finely tuned public-relations effort keeps Bennett in the public eye. *Chronicle of Higher Education,* pp. 16–18.

5

The State Level: The View from California

The Key to Reform: Sustaining and Expanding upon Initial Success
BILL HONIG

Educational reform is more than just a collection of random improvements. True educational reform is the creation of a new or renewed identity in the school environment and student productivity. All too often the reform recommendations, such as those included in *A Nation at Risk*, are treated like a shopping list instead of a road map to be carefully studied before selecting a course toward a specific destination. Parents and educators share equally in educational reform but address it in different ways, given their relative contexts and vantage points in the system. However, the local school and district are the most critical points on the implementation map, for real change occurs at the school and classroom level when teachers and students interact together in new, more productive ways.

It is my purpose in this article to (a) describe the route California is taking to reform, (b) present evidence that change has and is occurring, and (c) identify where continued work needs to be done.

BACKGROUND

Several movements coalesced in the early 1980s to create the impetus for the California educational reform movement. A variety of personal experiences led to my candidacy for Superintendent of Public Instruction. Initially, as a classroom teacher in the Hunter's Point section of San Francisco, and subsequently, as a school district administrator, it became increasingly clear that what California lacked was a vision of what students ought to learn or a comprehensive approach to their education. This viewpoint was confirmed as I traveled around the state as a state board member. A clearly stated vision of the kind of education our children needed, and how the various organizations and individuals in the educational system could work together to ensure that students received that education, was definitely called for. These issues became the springboard for my 1982 campaign for Superintendent of Public Instruction, for discussions with members of the business community, and for the development of a legislative reform package, Senate Bill 813, authored in 1983 by Assemblywoman Teresa Hughes and State Senator Gary Hart. During the ensuing years, we have worked with parents, teachers, and business leaders to refine that vision, describe it in curricular standards, and measure student learning in a variety of assessment tools.

We began with a rationale for why California's students need to learn more for economic, civic, cultural, and personal reasons. California's future—and the nation's—depends on educating more students at higher levels. The growing trade deficit and economic indicators suggest that American workers are not competing successfully with their foreign peers. Large segments of our labor force are undereducated and ill-equipped to manage the changes in our occupational structure and international economy. At the same time, fewer and fewer of our citizens are voting or taking an active role in communities and government at all levels. The reform agenda in California is intended to begin dealing with these issues and to help California's students be better prepared to enter the work force and to participate as citizens of the democracy. At the same time, we need to do a better job of connecting students to our culture. Otherwise, we are depriving them of true choice and opportunity and of the ability to develop their human potential.

I have written elsewhere about the strategy we used to develop broad commitment to our goals for educational improvement (Honig, 1985). However, before moving to a discussion of our strategic plan for implementing that vision, I will summarize its basic tenets:

1. Schools have a responsibility to prepare students for the workplace. The job market is changing in fundamental ways; American competition in the international marketplace will be based, not upon our industrial

output, but upon our leadership ability in the information revolution. We must have a well-educated labor force that can use information effectively, make thoughtful decisions, and change careers as technological advances dictate.

2. Schools have a responsibility to help students develop as citizens. Periodic bursts of patriotic spirit are all to the good; but in addition to a spirit of loyalty to our democratic traditions, we need to educate students to be creative, independent thinkers, able and willing to participate in the decision-making responsibilities of citizenship in a democracy.

3. Schools need to help the individual realize his or her potential. By cultivating the whole person, schools support the acquisition of knowledge, skills and moral and ethical perspectives that make our society a better place to live and that help the individual appreciate, value, and contribute to the broader culture.

The evidence suggests that a traditional academic curriculum is the best vehicle for helping students achieve success in adult life (Bloom, 1987; Finn & Ravitch, 1987; Hirsch, 1987). English, history, a foreign language, mathematics, science, the fine arts, and human development form the central foundation from which young people build specialized knowledge and skill to become productive workers, citizens, and cultural "consumers."

An education grounded in the academic disciplines has the potential to provide a quality education for all children, regardless of socioeconomic background, race, or aspirations. Although at the outset some critics argued that the curriculum that we advocate best served the white, middle-class, college-bound student, it is now clear that just the opposite is true. Watering down the course of study, expecting less of some students based upon their background or prior experience with English, and disrupting the educational process with successive pullout programs compromise the integrity of the educational process itself and may be the most serious disadvantage for poor and minority students.

WHAT WE'VE ACCOMPLISHED

A lot has been accomplished since the 1983 educational reform legislation provided the resources to initiate implementation of our reform agenda. Student achievement scores are up; more students are enrolling in rigorous academic courses; student enrollment in mathematics, English, science, history, foreign languages, and fine arts has steadily increased; and student performance on the California Assessment Program (CAP) reflects achievement gains in reading and mathematics. Larger numbers of students are taking the SAT and advanced placement tests and are scoring at higher levels (California State Department of Education, 1987). Although it is difficult to tie specific policies to changes in course enrollments or other reforms, the general program of higher standards, greater school account-ability, and improvements in student performance have proceeded hand in hand.

Nor is this all of the evidence that Senate Bill 813 reforms are beginning to show results in California schools. As early as 1985, the California Tax Foundation documented that, in response to reform legislation, a majority of school districts had raised graduation requirements, increased instruc-tional time, chosen to participate in the mentor teacher program, and were moving toward implementation of State Board of Education graduation standards (Kaye, 1985). Then in 1985, 1986, and 1987, the Policy Analysis for California Education (PACE) research group documented substantial school and district program change in response to SB 813 reforms. The Stanford and University of California researchers note:

> In short, the major SB 813 policies were (by 1987) at the advanced stages of implementation in nearly all schools studied and seemed to be ac-complishing the goals of California's 1983 education reforms. High school graduation requirements were greater, and academic standards for stu-dents were tougher. Student enrollments in traditional academic courses had risen substantially. The courses themselves covered substantively sound subject matter content, the texts used had expanded and deeper content, and teachers were more skilled in both managing the classroom and delivering instruction. Administrators were more skilled in super-vising and evaluating teachers. Student test scores in basic skills had risen to the highest in recent years. School climates were better, teach-ers' sense of professional efficacy was up, and administrators were more able to develop and implement a new vision of a good district and excellent school. If these local education reforms had eroded in quality during the 1970s, it seems that they had returned to traditional notions of excellence during the past four years, with SB 813 generally being a positive influence. (PACE, 1987a, p.9)

The level of funding for education is an issue in 1980s California. Proposition 4 limits future spending by state and local governments to an inflation and population growth formula. Because of this limit, California school funding on a per pupil basis will continue to shrink, increasing the gap between California and other industrialized states. Many people feel that this limit will interfere with future educational reform efforts. On the other hand, California voters reaffirmed their commitment to the spending limit initiative in the June 1988 election. Until a change is made, California will have to live within this limit.

Financial resources to support local change were, and are, important, but money alone doesn't improve student achievement. Further, no single set of conditions is responsible for improved student performance. Rather, implementation of a thoughtful combination of initiatives, set in motion simultaneously, will provide a flexible framework of standards, resources, and accountability measures to help local school people make the necessary changes.

We began by getting consensus on the vision—the purposes of schooling and what we wanted all students to know and be able to do. We then identified the key actors and leverage points in the educational system where new (or renewed) action could "make a difference" in the kind of educational experience students received. As discussed below, we adopted new standards for textbooks and aligned our state testing system to match the expectations defined in higher graduation requirements and model curriculum standards (see Table 5.1).

Core Curriculum

SB 813 increased high school graduation requirements, and the state board adopted model high school graduation standards, urging local school districts to expect more of students. In addition to increased requirements in

Table 5.1   Leverage Points for Implementing a More Rigorous Curriculum for All Students

The What	*The How*
Core curriculum	Higher graduation requirements State board graduation standards New textbook standards
Aligned texts, tests, and curriculum	Grades 9–12 model curriculum standards Matched elementary guidelines Aligned curriculum frameworks Revised CAP tests
Comprehensive accountability package	Strengthened student assessment Performance reports linked with local quality indicators Blended program review/WASC accreditation
Teacher professionalism	Mentor teacher program Higher beginning teacher salaries Staff development for novice and experienced teachers
School site leadership	Administrator training centers
District leadership	Categorical program coordination Articulation of curriculum, instruction, and assessment

English, mathematics, science, social studies, foreign languages, fine arts, and physical education, the legislature added a required semester of economics.

Simultaneously, the three public segments of higher education (California State University [CSU], University of California, and the Community Colleges) committed themselves to the joint development of competency statements in the core curriculum areas. New admission requirements were adopted at CSU and the University of California revised its "A-F" course sequence requirements.

Aligned Texts, Tests, and Curriculum

To support these new requirements, the State Department of Education developed Model Curriculum Standards in each of the subject areas for grades 9–12. The standards outline curricular targets, based upon a consensus within the educational community of what knowledge is of most worth. Guidelines for K–8 curriculum, again written by classroom teachers and intended to help build toward the 9–12 curriculum standards, have also been published.

The State Board of Education developed new standards for textbook adoption, working intensively with publishers to ensure that the new adoptions reflect the content and critical thinking expectations outlined in the Model Curriculum Standards. Concurrently, the State Department of Education and county offices of education realigned the development of state frameworks, county courses of study, and technical assistance strategies to support district textbook adoption and staff development processes.

Comprehensive Accountability Package

A sound assessment system is essential to monitoring and stimulating academic growth. Since 1983, California's student testing program has been significantly revised to place greater emphasis on its ability to assess higher order reasoning and knowledge in the subject areas required for high school graduation. CAP scores have improved since 1985–1986. In response to numerous calls from the research community (Cooper, 1977; J. Gray, personal communication, December 16, 1985), the test implemented a direct assessment of student writing for eighth grade in 1987 (to be expanded to grade 12 in 1988). In addition to providing important data about student writing ability, the assessment provided an important staff development experience for teachers.

Student achievement scores are only one measure of system performance, and over the past four years, the state has developed and implemented an accountability program that recognizes schools that make significant progress. Other quality indicators include increased enrollments in selected academic courses, improved statewide test scores, reduced dropout rates, and increased performed of the college-bound on SAT and advanced placement exams. Each school's performance report may include a local section that provides information on local indicators such as number of books read, homework assigned, and use of direct writing assignments.

Reflecting the focus on local, school site change, California has also invested heavily in upgrading our school accreditation standards. In co-operation with the Western Association of Schools and Colleges (WASC), high schools have the option to participate in a self-study and program quality review as part of their accreditation process. Quality criteria targeted to subjects and grade levels are applied by both internal and external review teams to an analysis of a school's program.

The Golden State Examination was initiated to recognize and provide an incentive for students taking academic courses required for college admission. Implemented first in 1987, these assessments are designed to be end-of-course examinations that embody statewide achievement standards. In 1988, over 41,000 students were locally recognized by school and community leaders and will receive citations on their diplomas and transcripts for performance on this voluntary assessment.

Teacher Professionalism

Textbooks and curriculum materials are inherently dry stuff without the richness of good teaching. Although California currently has many well-qualified classroom teachers, the rate of new knowledge production, increased pupil enrollments, and the changing demography of the state's students make it essential that we strengthen teacher preparation, professional development opportunities, and systems for encouraging and rewarding excellence in teaching.

To strengthen teacher preparation, we are jointly implementing an intersegmental budget proposal that funds collaborative district and higher education participation in training prospective teachers and supporting them during their first years in the classroom. This work is coordinated with that of the National Board for Professional Teaching Standards, the National Governors' Association, and other state education agencies who are developing state-level candidate-based assessment and support systems for new teachers.

In addition to these efforts for new teachers, we are giving high priority to professional development for current staff. Two types of staff development initiatives have driven our professional development in recent years. First, the state has supported curriculum-based methods training with colleges, universities, and county offices of education. These intensive curriculum institutes provide teachers with opportunities to review the contents of the new curricula and collaboratively develop approaches to teaching it. The California Writing Project, California Mathematics Project, and California Literature Project serve as models for effective staff development. Teachers learn the contents of the curricular-instructional approach in research-based, intensive settings, which are followed by local support services conducted by fellow teachers.

In a second approach, the California Mentor Teacher Program provides both a staff development resource for new and experienced teachers and recognizes those so selected as "exemplary teachers." In that sense, it introduces a career ladder into the occupation. At the same time, because mentors provide staff development and curriculum services as part of their responsibilities, the program is providing support for new teachers and occasions for experienced teachers to work together on instructional issues. This program has the potential to create a more collegial school environment and foster increased teacher and student productivity (Hanson, Shulman & Bird, 1985).

School Site Leadership

Another leverage point in implementing our reform efforts is based on the recognition that, without administrative leadership, opportunities for teachers to improve in their teaching and take leadership roles are a hollow promise. The principal's instructional leadership role has been well documented elsewhere (Blum et al., 1987; Bossert, Dwyer, Rowan, & Lee, 1982). Knowledge of the curriculum, student learning progress, and instructional priorities are as critical for administrative attention as resource allocation and community relationships (Mortimore & Sammons, 1987).

The development of these instructional skills has been the focus of training offered to 2,000 school administrators through the state-sponsored California School Leadership Academy. The Academy helps prospective and practicing administrators learn to balance knowledge of textbooks, curriculum, instruction, student assessment, program evaluation, and staff development with their traditional roles in resource allocation, facilities planning, and public relations (Schainker & Roberts, 1987). This is no easy set of tasks, as the diverse and competing demands made upon school principals frequently take their attention away from instructional issues.

District Leadership

The district, represented by its superintendent and the local governing board, also has a pivotal leadership role (Hallinger & Murphy, 1982). A superintendent who talks about specific curricular goals for students and focuses on instructional issues gives a very different message to parents and educators than one who attends only to resource allocation and facilities. Over the past five years, districts have engaged various resources to encourage site-level implementation of reform, including

- better articulation of the various categorical program services in support of a common core curriculum for all students,
- increased capacity for site-level decision making about school improvement activities,
- financial incentives to increase the instructional day and year,
- partnerships to encourage schools to work with other social service agencies to encourage school safety and reduce violence and vandalism, and
- improvement in school district capacity to finance facilities improvements.

Space precludes a full discussion of these components of our comprehensive approach to reform. Suffice to say, however, that they are much more than a list of programs and priorities to be implemented. Rather, they are the resource capacity to realize the curricular and instructional improvements already discussed. For instance, better articulation of the various categorical programs combined with a rigorous academic curriculum and the support of an effective drug prevention program can help at-risk students in the middle grades to succeed.

In sum, both qualitative and quantitative evidence suggest that California students, teachers, and administrators have accomplished a great deal in implementing the reforms set in motion five years ago. Through a broad public consensus on the knowledge that is of most worth, we established a vision (goals) and then proceeded to provide a framework (quality standards), opportunity (time and flexibility), and support (recognition and resources) for local school people to engage in change efforts that reflect the local context. But our task is not completed.

WHAT IS NEEDED TO SUSTAIN THE REFORMS?

At this point we need to consolidate the reform efforts to (a) strengthen standards for individual and institutional accountability, (b) grant teachers greater autonomy and flexibility within a professionally accountable environment, and (c) shift the emphasis to support greater improvements in the academic performance of Black and Hispanic students.

Black and Hispanic students have lower graduation rates from high school than white students, lower participation rates in postsecondary education, and lower per capita incomes within the economy at large (Smith, 1987). Despite recent improvements in academic achievement (College Entrance Examination Board, 1987), Black and Hispanic students in California continue to be underrepresented in advanced course enrollments and in completing the course patterns necessary for admission to higher education (PACE, 1987b). It is, thus, imperative that we focus special resources on helping all students in California succeed in a rigorous academic program.

To do so, we must make wholesale, structural efforts to assist low-income and minority students. The most important lesson to be learned from past efforts is that programs to assist these students cannot be treated as add-ons or pilot initiatives. Institutional barriers such as teacher and administrator attitudes, low teacher expectations, differential and discriminatory curricula, and indifference must be dealt with.

Low income and minority students need to have access to and spend more time with the rigorous core curriculum. Too often, efforts to meet the "special needs" of low-income and minority students have resulted in remedial and pullout courses that provide less access to a common base of knowledge. Teachers, school administrators, and other school staff need to assume roles that create an environment of fairness, responsiveness, and high academic expectations for success so that each student can fully reach his or her potential. Classroom teachers need to use a variety of instructional strategies to meet the diverse needs of the student population and to ensure that minority students succeed in academically challenging educational programs.

As Ann Lieberman (1986) has pointed out, "Schools are complex organizations; we therefore need complex ways of thinking about them" (p. vii). Shifting the emphasis to provide a more coordinated approach to improving the academic performance of our at-risk youth will require focused efforts at the classroom, school, and district levels. And a single approach won't work. Rather, we need to initiate the simultaneous "loose-tight" properties derived from management research (Peters & Waterman, 1982). This means that we provide clearly defined goals, enough accountability so that we can measure progress, and sufficient flexibility, autonomy, time, and resources that the teachers and students can realize these goals.

Expanded assessments of individual student knowledge and production skills will provide diagnostic information for student improvement and inform the public about our institutional progress toward improved student achievement. California currently leads the nation in our comprehensive assessment of student knowledge of basic and higher-order thinking skills. At the same time, the assessment system needs to become more performance based to actually measure what students can do. With the exception of writing, most items don't assess production skills. Given the multiple audiences for data on educational outcomes, we need to design assessments that measure the student's ability to apply knowledge and supply individual achievement scores. We also need performance standards so that we can predict the likelihood of student success with later grade curricular expectations or use of knowledge in the work force.

This is no easy task. It means moving beyond current multiple-choice assessments of discrete skills to assessment of knowledge and skill in applied settings. It also entails developing new scaling metrics to better set and describe performance standards. In short, these changes will entail a major revolution in the testing industry. The British have made some progress in the area of student performance assessment (Bock & Mislevy, 1987; Burstall, 1986), but translating this work to the large-scale testing of millions of students at many grade levels will take time and resources.

However, it will be worth the effort, because a truly comprehensive educational assessment system will allow us to provide the autonomy and flexibility at the school site for teachers and administrators to tailor their educational program to meet students' instructional needs. In addition to providing comprehensive data on student performance, data in such an assessment system will provide measures of organizational performance. Armed with performance specifications for academic excellence at a given school, incentives for implementation, and rewards and sanctions for performance, we can then grant teachers the autonomy called for in the arguments for "increased professionalism" and "participatory school management."

Increasing teacher professionalism will require a multifaceted strategy to recruit, train, certify, compensate, and provide better working conditions for classroom teachers. The performance, character, and commitment of our teachers determine in large part the quality of education our children receive. Professionalizing the teaching work force in California is a central policy issue (PACE, 1987b). We are working both locally and nationally with teachers, administrators, higher education faculty, and members of the legislature to develop a collaborative approach to the continued strengthening of teacher preparation, licensure, and support. Our work reflects the recently completed study of *Staff Development in California* (Little et al. 1987), which calls for a more comprehensive and consistent policy orientation toward professional development for classroom teachers. Such a system will build upon our School Improvement model, use curriculum-based training and regional delivery systems, and provide more opportunities for teacher decision making.

Top priority will be given to recruiting well-qualified high school and college students, particularly minority students, to consider teaching as a career. The combined effects of enrollment growth, retirements, more attractive career alternatives, and demographic changes in the population of California's public schools argue for focused effort to provide all individuals—but particularly minority persons—with information, academic counseling, grants, loans, and other institutional supports to encourage them to pursue a career in teaching.

We must first improve the undergraduate education of all students. As numerous reports attest, the proliferation of courses and program options at the undergraduate collegiate level has resulted in a lack of balance in many undergraduate baccalaureate programs and, for prospective educators, a lack of substantive preparation in the arts and sciences (Boyer, 1987). At the same time, many in the higher education community consider teaching the route for those who are not successful in the arts and sciences curricula. Thus would-be teachers are taught to "cope" rather than to excel and in turn receive "watered-down" content courses.

Improving teacher preparation cuts across the undergraduate program, the teacher preparation program, and the transition between higher education and entry into the classroom. We must provide institutional and organizational supports for prospective teachers to have early field experiences, student teach with recognized master teachers, and receive guidance and assistance during their induction into the classroom (Griffin & Millies, 1987; Ishler & Kester, 1987). At the same time, teacher candidates need to demonstrate mastery of their subject area and the ability to teach it before we grant them a teaching credential (Haertel, 1987).

Making teaching more of a profession is the central mission of the National Board for Professional Teaching Standards. The board has commissioned research on teacher performance assessment and will eventually issue certificates to teachers who demonstrate that they meet prescribed standards of knowledge and ability (Shulman, 1986). National board certification is a central piece, but it is only one element in making teaching more of a profession. Other long-range goals include changing the occupational climate of schools to make them more professional environments for teachers, increasing teacher salaries, providing more organizational time for teachers to interact with one another on professional issues, and supplying opportunities for teachers to take leadership roles, if they choose.

In such an environment, we can "restructure" how schools are organized to give teachers greater control over the curriculum and professional issues and to shift the emphasis from "what works for all students" to "what works for the students in this school." Greater accountability for teachers will necessarily accompany greater responsibiliy and autonomy. Improving instructional programs depends in part on our ability to use special programs to enhance the overall vision. Articulating the plethora of categorical programs to ensure that all students have opportunities to participate in the regular program makes programmatic "good sense." However, how we do so will differ school by school based upon student learning needs and the necessity to serve targeted students in the most effective manner.

CONCLUSION

In sum, we have accomplished a great deal, but a great deal remains to be done. We have made a good start at defining what students should know and be able to do. Students are taking more rigorous courses, and both state and national measures indicate that they are doing better. An aligned system of textbooks, curricular standards, staff development, and assessment requirements have contributed to these changes. We need to continue focusing attention on these leverage points and put resources into developing professional judgment of student and organizational performance. With a stronger accountability system, we can then encourage greater autonomy and flexibility for staff at the site level to participate actively in programmatic decision making.

Simultaneously, we must broaden and consolidate the various elements in our educational reform strategies. Greater participation of minority and at-risk students in academically rigorous courses and focused attention on improved training, pay, status and working conditions for classroom teachers are central to sustaining our reform initiatives.

So, in answer to the question "Reform: change or rhetoric?" the answer must be, "Both," because both are needed. We need the rhetoric to serve as a catalyst for change. At the same time, we have evidence that students are learning more and that the reforms of the past five years are making a difference, though no one strategy can take the credit. The rhetoric of reform provides a symbolic catalyst for continually renewing the discussion of "What should our schools be about?" and "How can we best organize to meet the diverse needs of our students and teaching professionals?" As evidenced by numerous reports, change can and does occur when local educators get the right mix of vision, opportunity, resources, and support. The test for policymakers is whether they can sustain the momentum and respond to the challenges that lie ahead.

NOTE

Author's Note: Laura Wagner, California State Department of Education, participated in the preparation of this article.

REFERENCES

Bloom, A. (1987). *The closing of the American mind: How higher education has failed democracy and impoverished the souls of today's students.* Chicago: University of Chicago Press.

Blum, R., Butler, J., & Olson, N. (1987). Leadership for excellence: Research-based training for principals. *Educational Leadership, 45*(1).

Bock, R. D., & Mislevy, R. J. (1987). Comprehensive educational assessment for the states: The duplex design. Los Angeles: University of California, School of Education, Center for Student Testing, Evaluation, and Standards.

Bossert, S., Dwyer, D. C., Rowan, B., & Lee, G. V. (1982). The instructional management role of the principal. *Educational Administration Quarterly, 18*(3), 34–64.

Boyer, E. (1987). *College: The undergraduate experience in America.* New York: Harper & Row.

Burstall, C. (1986). *Innovative forms of assessment: A United Kingdom perspective.* Report of the National Foundation for Educational Research in England and Wales.

California State Department of Education. (1987). *Performance report for California schools.* Sacramento.

College Entrance Examination Board. (1987). *1987 Scholastic Aptitude Testing results.* Princeton, NJ: Educational Testing Service.

Cooper, C., & Odell, L. (1977). *Evaluating writing.* Urbana, IL: National Council of Teachers of English.

Finn, C. E., & Ravitch, D. (1987). *What do our 17-year olds know?* New York: Harper & Row.

Griffin G. A., & Millies, S. (1987). *The first years of teaching: Background papers and a proposal.* Springfield: Illinois State Department of Education.

Grossman, P., Kirst, M., Negash, W., & Schmidt-Posner, J. (1985). *Curricular change in California comprehensive high schools: 1982–83 to 1984–85.* Berkeley: University of California, Policy Analysis for California Education (PACE).

Haertel, E. (1987). *Teacher licensure issues in California.* Washington, DC: Council of Chief State School Officers.

Hallinger, P., & Murphy, J. (1982). The superintendent's role in promoting structional leadership. *Administrator's Notebook, 30*(6).

Hanson, S., Shulman, J., & Bird, T. (1985). *California mentor teacher program case studies: Implementation in medium and large school districts.* San Francisco: Far West Laboratory for Educational Research and Development.

Hirsch, E. D. (1987). *Cultural literacy.* Boston: Houghton Mifflin.

Honig, B. (1985). *Last chance for our children.* Reading, MA: Addison-Wesley.

Hughes, T., & Hart, G. (1983). *Senate bill 813: Omnibus educational reform.* Sacramento: California State Legislature.

Ishler, P., & Kester, R. (1987). Professional organizations and teacher induction: Initiatives and positions. In D. M. Brooks (Ed.), *Teacher induction: A new beginning* (pp. 61–69). Reston, VA: Association of Teacher Educators.

Kaye, L. (1985). *Making the grade? Assessing school district progress on SB 813.* Sacramento: California Tax Foundation.

Lieberman, A. (Ed.). (1986). *Rethinking school improvement.* New York: Teachers College Press.

Little, J., Gerritz, W. H., Stern, D. S., Guthrie, J. W., Kirst, M. W., & Marsh, D. D. (1987). *Staff development in California.* San Francisco/Berkeley: Far West Laboratory for Educational Research and Development/Policy Analysis for California Education.

Mortimore, P., & Sammons, P. (1987). New evidence on effective elementary schools. *Educational Leadership, 45*(1).

Peters, T.J., & Waterman, R. H. (1982). *In search of excellence: Lessons from America's best-run companies.* New York: Harper & Row.

PACE. Policy Analysis for California Education. (1987a). *Aggregated-cumulative effects of Senate Bill 813.* Berkeley: University of California.

PACE. Policy Analysis for California Education. (1987b). *Conditions of education in California, 1986–87* (p. 5). Berkeley: University of California.

PACE. Policy Analysis for California Education. (1988). *Conditions of education in California* (p. 6). Berkeley: University of California.

Schainker, S., & Roberts, L. (1987). Helping principals overcome on-the-job obstacles to learning. *Educational Leadership, 45*(1).

Shulman, L. (1986). Those who understand: Knowledge growth in teaching. *Educational Researcher, 15,* 4–14.

Smith, G.P. (1987). *The effects of competency testing on the supply of minority teachers.* Washington, DC: Council of Chief State School Officers.

6

The District Level: Involving School Boards in Reform

School Boards and School Reform

RODNEY MUTH

JANN AZUMI

ALTHOUGH MORE THAN 15,000 boards of education determine educational policy for millions of students and staff nationwide, little attention has been paid to the role of school boards in achieving reform in American education. Apart from time-honored reflections (Campbell, Cunningham, Nystrand, & Usdan, 1985; Haller & Strike, 1986; Knezevich, 1975), only intermittent and fragmentary attention has been paid to the role of boards of education. What attention exists has been more "how to" than "why for," as is illustrated by any recent issue of the *American School Board Journal* or of the many state school board publications. Except for occasional flurries of interest (Cistone, 1975; Institute for Educational Leadership, 1986; Ziegler, 1975, 1980), one might assume that the role of boards of education is too inchoate or inconsequential for extended research efforts.

Yet, in a time of potentially dramatic change—vouchers, declining enrollments, tuition tax credits, merit pay, private versus public schools, master teachers, effective schools, teacher empowerment, and the like—focusing on the role of boards of education in school reform is not only appropriate but vital. To date, recommendations about school reform (cf.

Boyd & Kerchner, 1988; Haskins & MacRae, 1988; Joyce, Hersh, & McKibbin, 1983; Lieberman, 1986)—which range from the exhaustive (Kyle, 1985) to the naive (Glazer, 1984)—only tangentially attend to the role of school boards. Even reports that examine management issues tend to concentrate solely on the role of the superintendent (Schlechty, 1985). On the rare occasions when boards of education are mentioned, they generally are exhorted to "do what's best." But "what's best" may be quite unclear.

Further, traditional myths about school boards may limit their contributions to educational improvement efforts. One myth, that school boards are nonpolitical, isolates them from mainstream political processes and justifies their exclusion from most reform planning. Two other myths—that school boards represent overall community interests (when they quite often represent much narrower individual or group interests) and that they exercise local control (when state and other mandates severely constrain their discretion)—tend to compound public confusion about school boards.

Misunderstandings about the role of boards of education are not surprising, for relatively few people clearly understand how most levels of government work. Nevertheless, understanding the role of school boards is particularly important for researchers and policymakers during this time of change. If boards of education continue to be ignored, they are increasingly likely to impede rather than facilitate school reform.

BACKGROUND

Boards of education set policy for local schools, and the long—and jealously guarded—tradition of local lay control claims to serve the public interest and manage local affairs competently. But now the question of who controls or is responsible for the outcomes of public education is not so clear. The rise of the superintendency, the proliferation of state and federal mandates, and the growth of unionism have done much to lessen school board control and to cloud accountability.

Local control is embedded in historical precedent, but the authority of local boards has been constantly eroded almost since their institution. The Massachusetts School Ordinance of 1642 asserted the supremacy of the state while delegating responsibility for disseminating its values to local citizens. In those days, municipal "townsmen" were responsible for levying taxes, providing school "houses," hiring teachers, and determining wages, standards, and the school calendar. Not until 1727 in Boston were school and community affairs separated; the Boston Visiting Committee, a subcommittee of selectmen, was assigned to visit schools and report about their condition. In time, more and more responsibilities were delegated to such committees. These evolved into today's familiar "school committees" (trustees, boards of directors, commissioners, inspectors, or boards).

At each step in their evolution, however, what school boards could and could not do has been circumscribed—by federal laws and regulations, court decisions, state legislative measures, and state department of education mandates. Today, board members rate mandated programs (for which they often feel hard pressed to pay) as one of their two or three most difficult problems.[1]

Although state mandates and minimum standards, which vary widely from state to state, have set floors for the education of "average" and "special" children, board discretion still permits broad interpretation of how—and sometimes whether—many programs are implemented. Consequently, curricular and other reform outcomes vary considerably (Grossman, Kirst, & Schmidt-Posner, 1986). Even so, while some researchers feel that most reform strategies only set or reinforce traditional goals (Passow, 1984b), recent reform suggestions (Carnegie Forum, 1986) could dramatically force local boards into the fray—or all but eliminate their effectiveness in future improvement efforts.

BOARD DEMOGRAPHICS

The typical school board member is white, male, 41 to 50 years old, and married with one or two children in school. He is a college graduate employed in management or another professional endeavor and earns $40,000 to $50,000 per year. Serving on the board for an average of six years, this Republican tends to express conservative views on education in his moderate-sized district (1,000 to 4,999 students) located in a small or rural town (Cameron, Underwood, & Fortune, 1988). Women, who now make up 39 percent of the school board members, have increased their numbers by about 10 percent since 1978, and their representation has been stable over the last several years (Luckett, Underwood, & Fortune, 1987a). The same cannot be said for minority groups, however. In fact, school board members, just under 95 percent white in 1987, are far from representative of the nation's ethnic diversity (U.S. Bureau of the Census, 1984, pp. 26–34).

These demographics are powerful determinants of how boards behave. As shown by analyses of corporate (Peters & Waterman, 1982) and school cultures (Conway, 1985; Sarason, 1971), the culture—the norms, beliefs, expectations—into which board members are socialized has important implications for what a board values and supports. Male–female differences alone suggest that women would be more open to alternative forms of school district governance, while the current white-male dominance of school boards suggests continuation of hierarchical, power solutions to educational problems (Murphy, 1982). When asked, for example, how they might change the activities of their school boards, increasing attention to curriculum issues was foremost in the minds of the women who responded to the National School Boards Association's annual survey (Luckett, Underwood, & Fortune, 1987b). These women were also less inclined than men to believe that superintendents should be the "absolute" managers of their school systems.

As indicated earlier, school board members do not represent national population distributions. While board membership remains white and male, the school population is becoming blacker and browner—and in many areas poorer. The numbers of children with teenage mothers, handicaps, limited English proficiency, single parents, or no adults at home after school will all increase significantly by the turn of the century (Editors, 1986b). These projections have stark implications for the nature and shape of public schools in the future, and decisions made now will mold the schools for a demonstrably different future (Goodlad, 1983). How such decisions are made *and* implemented will depend, in large measure, on the sensitivity of school boards to our changing, nation-building process (Miller, 1986) and on their ability to initiate or accept efforts to maintain and improve our schools.

THE CALL TO REFORM HAS OVERLOOKED SCHOOL BOARDS

In our nation's long history of reform efforts (Lewis, 1980), the struggle over reform traditionally pits the forces of change against those of the status quo. Such struggles invariably will continue in education. Reports since 1983 on the well-being of education in the United States have focused primarily on graduation requirements, statewide student assessments, teacher competency tests, dollar outlays, minimum pay levels, and student/ teacher ratios (Bridgman, 1985; Editors, 1986a). Whether these reports originate essential reforms or only reiterate well-known needs is debatable (Cuban, 1982; Tyack, Lowe, & Hansot, 1984). Regardless, the major reform reports (cf. Carnegie Forum, 1986; Holmes Group, 1986; National Commission, 1983) and related analyses (cf. Bridgman, 1985; Clark, Lotto, & Astuto, 1984; Edmonds & Frederiksen, 1979; Fullan, 1982; Institute for Educational Leadership, 1986; Passow, 1984a; Purkey & Smith, 1983; Spady & Marx, 1984) establish that few expectations are held for school boards in the reform process.

This oversight has not gone unnoticed. The executive director of the National School Boards Association (NSBA), for one, has pointed out that school boards associations have been systematically overlooked as participants in the reform process (Shannon, 1986); likewise, according to *School Board News*, school boards "have not been passive . . . they have been overlooked" by the reform movement (NSBA, 1986, p. 1). Such protests indicate both the traditional apoliticality of school boards and the perception of many that they are irrelevant to the reform process. Indeed, as Clark, Lotto, and Astuto (1984) note in their review of research on effective schools and school improvement programs, school boards and communities appear to be more effective at preventing change than at promoting it. They quote Fullan, who concludes that "by far the most prevalent case is that school boards and communities do not initiate or have any major role in deciding about innovative programs" (p. 55).

Another review of educational improvement efforts (Crandall, Eiseman, & Louis, 1986) suggests that confused priorities, political cross pressures, stale methods, diverse student populations, and unmotivated and poorly trained staff severely complicate the process of educational improvement. This review identifies several strategies for potentially successful improvement efforts, including "top-down" approaches like external mandates. Once again, however, the role of school boards in impeding or facilitating change is not considered important enough to mention, a point underscored by Kirst, who notes that "in the effective schools literature very little attention is given to the crucial role that school boards and superintendents play in mobilizing school sites and leading a reform effort" (1983, p. 243).

A recent survey of school board members confirms the almost total exclusion of boards of education from state-level policymaking and their glaring omission from most national reports on educational reforms. This same report, however, states the problem succinctly: "Because school boards are charged by states and localities to make policy and govern local public education, their willingness and capacity to lead, in large measure, will determine the long-range success or failure of school improvement efforts" (Institute for Educational Leadership, 1986, p. i). Clearly, boards of education will play a role in the improvement of education. Whether their role will be positive and in the forefront is arguable.

THE CASES

The following two case examples, developed from data collected through participant observation over several years in the mid-1980s, illustrate the governance and implementation issues that will continue to confront the reform movement at the local level. Our analyses both confirm and deny the assertion that school boards have a leading role to play in the improvement process, finding that the nature of this role may depend on several, often situational, factors.

The two boards of education studied differed in that one was a seven-member board in a small suburban/urban community and the other a nine-member board serving a large urban district. These boards were somewhat atypical: the nine-member board had six minority and four female members; the seven-member board had three minority and three female members. Both school systems, however, had predominantly minority student populations and faced similar pressures for educational improvements from the same activist state department of education. These pressures have forced districts in the state—especially minority districts—to make any changes in internal operations to meet mandates on test results, school facilities, and other educationally relevant factors. Thus, both districts had undertaken a number of changes during a five-year period to improve student performance and meet state standards.

The Small District

This small district is one of three school systems with a growing black and Hispanic population in a county of seventy-one districts. Thus pressures on its school board come from the federal and state governments, the board's community, and the surrounding communities to which the district is compared qualitatively (programs, course offerings, college enrollments) or quantitatively (test scores, teacher salaries). Because the state monitors third- and sixth-grade standardized test results and has recently required a high school proficiency test for graduation, districtwide test scores are publicized by the state department of education and appear in local newspapers. The district can now clearly be labeled as a "minority school district," and its scores tend to be lower than those reported for neighboring districts. Neither the community nor the board, however, concedes that the composition of the school population automatically means lower performance. Thus, considerable effort has been expended to maintain high standards and to increase expectations so that the district schools can compare more favorably with their neighbors.

The school board in this district has assumed a very active role in the process of change. Following is a brief but incomplete list of the improvement programs initiated and implemented by this board during the five years prior to 1987:

1. Increased math and science requirements for high school graduation
2. More stringent promotion, retention, and eligibility policies
3. All-day prekindergarten and kindergarten (previously half-day)
4. Better monitoring of districtwide testing with results detailed by school and classroom
5. Formal, public recognition of academic and extracurricular accomplishments
6. Formal teacher recognition programs
7. More thorough administrative accountability measures

With the exception of the all-day kindergarten (proposed by the elementary school principals), the school board in this district—either on its own or in conjunction with its central office administrators—initiated all of these activities.

That the board played such a prominent role was due to a combination of factors that prevailed during the period from 1981 to 1986. First, the board was fairly stable and united. Its seven members were all appointed (or reappointed) by the same mayor, and all except one had served at least four years. For the most part, board members were appointed as representatives of the school community: all but one had or had had children in the school system; three members were themselves educators. Once appointed, the board was allowed to function quite autonomously, without undue political interference or influence. This was significant because of the large private school and nonschool population in the community, members of which had unsuccessfully tried twice in the previous ten years through referenda to change the status of the board to an elected one. Were the board elected or more representative of the larger community, the board's composition, stability, and unity would certainly be very different.

In contrast to the board's stability was the instability of the district's administrators. The lack of administrative leadership was a second factor that accounted for the board's activism. The school district's leadership vacuum lasted for over three years, beginning with a tenured superintendent whose effectiveness had waned considerably. He was followed by a new superintendent who departed after nine months and a succession of three acting superintendents over the next fourteen months. The other two central office positions—assistant superintendent for curriculum and business manager/board secretary—were also unsettled during these same years. The school board, therefore, took initiatives that might otherwise have originated with or have been developed by the district's administrative staff.

The active involvement of black parents, a relatively new phenomenon in the community, further influenced the board's agenda. The leadership of most parent–school organizations had shifted from whites who had primarily focused on maintaining the schools to prevent "white flight." In their place, newly organized black parents increased their participation in school activities, appearing at board meetings and vocally criticizing the district's education of minority children. These parents demanded that a more effective job be done and monitored the district's responses.

All these factors significantly affected both the degree and content of board involvement in districtwide improvements and reforms. The stability of the board, its orientation to and knowledge of educational issues, and its lack of factionalism, combined with a relatively long period of administrative instability, probably accounted for the board's activism. Further, the system's changing demographics, mandates from the state, competition with surrounding districts, and involvement of black parents reinforced the efforts of the board to respond to the spirit of reform in the 1980s.

The Large District

In contrast to the situation in the small district, a lack of stability and unity on the board in the large district impeded effective board decision making. In the mid-1980s, the nine-member board changed from being appointed by the mayor to being elected with three members selected each year. Only two of the original nine members survived the transition, and considerable conflict preceded and followed the change. Among the new members, factions immediately developed.

Noneducational factors had substantial impact on the board's unity. Improving student performance and making the schools more habitable were compelling goals. But, because of its size, the school system is a prominent employer in its beleaguered city and thus a source of power, status, and economic gain.[2] Unemployment is high. Every contract the district awards—for books, food, fuel, even pencils—provides income for someone in the city. School board members, unlike the people who control the large commercial and industrial organizations in the city, are "from the community," and they are elected by that community. They are pressured to provide jobs, award contracts, and underwrite programs for special interests.

Unlike the board, the administration was relatively stable during this period, even though two different administrative teams served three years each between 1981 and 1987. At the time of this study, the second of these was in its third year. Also, with the exception of the previous superintendent, all of the upper-level managers had been fixtures in the system. That policy and program initiatives came predominantly from administrators during this time is due in no small part to the turmoil on the board and the stability of the administrative cadre.

The principal changes in the district's policies and programs during the five years examined included the following:

1. Adoption of a uniform reading series
2. Institution of a stringent Attendance Improvement Plan for staff
3. Formation of a truancy task force
4. Formalization of a school performance monitoring process
5. Implementation over time of new promotion and retention policies
6. Establishment of homework centers and after-school tutorials
7. Formation of school improvement teams in each school
8. Initiation of districtwide staff development programs
9. Implementation of special programs for students retained twice

Although the school board and the community in this large, urban district were quite vocal about the continued low performance of the district's students, most of the initiatives listed above originated with the superintendent or upper-level management staff. The school board primarily voiced anxieties about low student achievement and issued general directives.

Unlike the small district, which competed with its suburban neighbors, the large district compared itself only to other urban districts in the state—most of which face equally dire problems with student performance. No "lighthouse" examples served to challenge these districts. For such urban districts, the primary impetus for school improvement came from the state and the community. State intervention was a constant threat as proposed legislation (now enacted) threatened state department takeover of districts that failed to improve. The message was clear: "If you can't do a better job educating your children, we'll do it for you." This position was the state's interpretation of its constitutional charge to guarantee a "thorough and efficient" education for each child.

Parents, the other prominent source of pressure on the school system, became increasingly aware of test scores as a measure of quality education. Their awareness was heightened by state department publicity and new efforts by the district's testing division. As a result, parents more vocally demanded better education, although their demands were tinged with fears of loss of local control.

Despite their intensity, these state and parental pressures were general rather than specific. That is, the primary message was to urge the system to "do something to make it better." The board echoed these concerns but was unable to agree about the particular strategies. It fell to the administrators—somewhat insulated from the political pressures on the board—to initiate the remedies to raise test scores and avoid a state takeover.

The reforms attempted in this district varied with its two administrations, partly reflecting the changes in the composition of the boards. The earlier board, appointed by the mayor, hired an out-of-state superintendent who, with board support, initiated programs that ultimately had negative repercussions. The teachers, for example, resisted new procedures to improve staff attendance, and the principals rejected attempts to introduce a formal school monitoring process. Calling these attempts "heavy-handed" and top-down management, the opposition organized sufficiently to win a referendum for an elected school board. Subsequently, with the elected board, the balance of power shifted, and the superintendent was replaced by an insider.

This new board and superintendent focused on districtwide staff development and the formation of school improvement teams, which included administrators, teachers, and parents. The administration's slogan was *"Together* we will educate our children." The change in management style—from top-down to participatory—appeared to reflect the change in board membership, partly orchestrated by union organizations, which have played an important and positive role in this district.

Implications

Definitive conclusions about the role of school boards in educational reform certainly cannot be drawn from two cases. Nevertheless, our observations suggest the following hypotheses that could be tested in larger studies. The extent of a board's activity in promoting school reform depends to some degree on its stability, unity, and knowledge base. Boards that are constantly in flux, disunited, continually bombarded by competing demands, unsure of the issues, or indecisive not only will be hampered in reaching workable agreements but also will have difficulty "following through" on their implementation and appraisal functions. Board stability and unity depends, in turn, on autonomy from political influence—particularly if that influence is itself factionalized. Similarly, administrative stability is crucial. Constant change in the top administration, for example, may stimulate stronger board leadership but also can lead a district to depend on part-time laypeople for program change, implementation, and assessment. Unless board members have the necessary time and expertise, reforms may never take hold. Conversely, board instability can lead to continual policy changes, perhaps preventing even the best intentioned, most capable, and most stable administrations from achieving needed improvements.[3]

SOME LARGER ISSUES FOR THE FUTURE

To ignore the role of school boards in educational reform is comparable to saying that city councils have no effect on the delivery of city services. But because school boards play a much more anomalous role on the political stage, they are little understood. Much remains to be done to lessen public ignorance of school board functions, to increase public confidence in the schools, and to improve the capacity of school boards to plan for and manage their schools' futures (Institute for Educational Leadership, 1986).

What has so far been left to chance underscores the fragility of reform in education. For instance, the recent Carnegie report (Carnegie Forum, 1986) calls for increased involvement of teachers in curriculum decisions and increased differentiation among teaching roles. This is a high priority among reformers and requires greater cooperation between and among organizational levels, a notion compatible with the professionalization of teachers and with recent nonhierarchical theories of decision making (Ouchi,

1981). But in militant union districts, staff differentiation schemes (master teachers, merit pay) are anathema since they are perceived as threats to individual and group security. This phenomenon, particularly prevalent in the Northeast, may coincide with other extreme circumstances, as in the large school district described above. Like boards of education, unions at the local level play roles in reform that remain underanalyzed (Graubard, 1984). Nevertheless, their support or nonsupport is significant to whatever reforms are undertaken.

Given that powerful forces—states, reformers, unions, special interests—are seeking in such ways to control the educational agenda in local schools, school boards will be hard pressed to maintain even limited control, let alone participate equally in the reform process. Complicating these conditions is the typical composition of school boards: mostly male, mostly businessmen who tend to espouse hierarchical solutions to problems. Indeed, such tendencies are reinforced by the "cultural psychology" of board membership, the "minimalism" of state standards (reinforced by the economy), and the pervasively unsophisticated accountability systems at all educational levels.

In addition, superintendents, relative to boards, hold a virtual monopoly on information and control the tone of improvement expectations (Clark, Lotto, & Astuto, 1984). Thus, superintendents play a key role in setting the agenda for reform. But, notwithstanding the "ambition" of many school superintendents (DeYoung, 1986) or their innate desires to improve the life chances of children, the ability of superintendents to manage is limited by boards (Beni, Cooper, & Muth, 1984; Minar, 1966), and the tenure of superintendents simply is too often too brief (Cunningham & Hentges, 1982). Because reform takes time, administrative turnover dims the prospects for long-term planning and change. As a result, despite the many external and internal pressures felt by school boards, their governance role remains unquestionably critical. Add to that the financial control that boards of education—and their communities—exercise, and the potential impact of a board on the improvement process rises dramatically.

Reform, change, and innovation have generally been slow, difficult, and often impossible in American education. This initial examination of the role of boards of education in school reform points to a series of structural characteristics, mostly unaddressed by the reform movement, that require focused attention if quality education is to be achieved as the reformers and most others would prefer. As long as policy analysts and policymakers act as though states exercise full control of the reform agenda and local boards remain either unrecognized or unappreciated both as potential change facilitators or impediments, we will fail to produce thoughtful and systematic analyses of present educational realities. We need to know how boards make decisions, how board–superintendent relations affect such decisions, what values board members weigh, what ends they seek (both personally and for their communities), how these values are shaped in the political process, and how they in turn shape our children's educational future.

NOTES

An earlier version of this chapter appeared in *Metropolitan Education*, Fall 1987, pp. 40–56, under the title "School Reform: Whither Boards of Education?" The authors are indebted to Marcia F. Muth for her invaluable assistance in revising that article for this book.

1. In the National School Boards Association's 1987 national survey, state mandates were rated the number two problem nationwide, with board members in the South and Northeast rating them as their number one problem, West and Central members rating them number two, and Pacific members rating them number three (Board Survey, 1987; Luckett, Underwood, & Fortune, 1987c). These results differ sharply from an IEL study which reported that a selected group of school boards ranked state mandates seventeenth in importance (Institute for Educational Leadership, 1986, p. 14). The IEL sample, it seems, felt insulated from state mandates, suggesting that it may not have been representative of school boards nationwide. Results of the 1988 NSBA survey confirm the significance of state mandates to board members nationwide (Board Survey, 1988; Cameron, Underwood, & Fortune, 1988).

2. This district is not alone. Political leaders in both New York and Boston "have charged that their boards of education are more concerned with providing patronage than with leading efforts to improve student performance" (Snider, 1987, p. 1).

3. It may be, at least in large districts, regardless of the intent or preferences of the school board or central administrators, that "street-level bureaucrats"—building-level personnel—will manage their affairs despite the agendas or chaos that reign above them (Crowson & Porter-Gehrie, 1980). Under such conditions and without some internal guidance mechanisms that articulate and clarify districtwide expectations and facilitate ongoing appraisals, school reforms will be minimal at best.

REFERENCES

Beni, V., Cooper, B. S., & Muth, R. (1984, April). *The strong superintendent as "enabler": An ethnographic analysis of the superintendent–board relationship.* Paper presented at the meeting of the American Educational Research Association, New Orleans, LA.

Board survey: Who you are, region by region. (1987). *American School Board Journal, 174*(1), 24–25.

Board survey: Who you are, region by region. (1988). *American School Board Journal, 175*(1), 24–25.

Boyd, W. L., & Kerchner, C. T. (Eds.). (1988). *The politics of excellence and choice in education*. Philadelphia: Falmer Press.

Bridgman, A. (1985, February 13). States launching barrage of initiatives, survey finds. *Education Week*, 1, 31.

Cameron, B., Underwood, K. E., & Fortune, J. C. (1988). Money still is your top problem, but curriculum is making a big comeback. *American School Board Journal*, 175(1), 21, 38.

Campbell, R. F., Cunningham, L. L., Nystrand, R. O., & Usdan, M. D. (1985). *The organization and control of American education* (5th ed.). Columbus, OH: Charles E. Merrill.

Carnegie Forum on Education and the Economy. (1986). *A nation prepared: Teachers for the 21st century*. Hyattsville, MD: Carnegie Forum on Education and the Economy.

Cistone, P. J. (Ed.). (1975). *Understanding school boards*. Lexington, MA: Lexington Books.

Clark, D. L., Lotto, L. S., & Astuto, T. A. (1984). Effective schools and school improvement: A comparative analysis of two lines of inquiry. *Educational Administration Quarterly*, 20(3), 41–68.

Conway, J. A. (1985). A perspective on organizational cultures and organizational belief structures. *Educational Administration Quarterly*, 21(4), 7–25.

Crandall, D. P., Eiseman, J. W., & Louis, K. S. (1986). Strategic planning issues that bear on the success of school improvement efforts. *Educational Administration Quarterly*, 22(3), 21–53.

Crowson, R. L., & Porter-Gehrie, C. (1980). The discretionary behavior of principals in large-city schools. *Educational Administration Quarterly*, 16(1), 45–69.

Cuban, L. (1982, October). Persistent instruction: The high school classroom, 1900–1980. *Phi Delta Kappan*, 113–123.

Cunningham, L. L., & Hentges, J. T. (1982). *The American school superintendency, 1982: A summary report*. Arlington, VA: American Association of School Administrators.

DeYoung, A. J. (1986). Excellence in education: The opportunity for school superintendents to become ambitious? *Education Administration Quarterly*, 22(2), 91–113.

Editors. (1986a). *Education vital signs, vol. II, 1986/1987*. Chicago: National School Boards Association.

Editors. (1986b, May 14). Here they come, ready or not: An Education Week special report on the ways in which America's "population in motion" is changing the outlook for schools and society. *Education Week*, 14–37.

Edmonds, R. R., & Frederiksen, J. R. (1979). *Search for effective schools: The identification and analysis of city schools that are instructionally effective for poor children*. Cambridge, MA: Center for Urban Studies, Harvard University.

Fullan, M. (1982). *The meaning of educational change*. New York: Teachers College Press.

Glazer, N. (1984). Some very modest proposals for the improvement of American education. *Daedalus*, 113(4), 169–176.

Goodlad, J. I. (1983). *A place called school: Prospects for the future*. New York: McGraw-Hill.

Graubard, S. R. (1984). Zeal, cunning, candor, and persistence—to what educational ends? *Daedalus*, 113(4), 75–106.

Grossman, P. L., Kirst, M. W., & Schmidt-Posner, J. (1986). On the trail of the omnibeast: Evaluating omnibus education reforms in the 1980s. *Educational Evaluation and Policy Analysis, 8*(3), 253–266.

Haller, E. J., & Strike, K. A. (1986). *An introduction to educational administration: Social, legal, and ethical perspectives.* New York: Longman.

Haskins, R., & MacRae, D. (Eds.). (1988). *Policies for America's public schools: Teachers, equity, and indicators.* Norwood, NJ: Ablex Publishing.

Holmes Group. (1986). *Tomorrow's teachers: A report of the Holmes group.* East Lansing, MI: The Holmes Group.

Institute for Educational Leadership. (1986). *School boards: Strengthening grass roots leadership.* Washington, DC: Institute for Educational Leadership.

Joyce, B. R., Hersh, R. H., & McKibbin, M. (1983). *The structure of school improvement.* New York: Longman.

Kirst, M. W. (1983). Effective schools: Political environment and educational policy. *Planning and Changing, 14*(4), 234–244.

Knezevich, S. J. (1975). *Administration of public education* (3rd ed.). New York: Harper & Row.

Kyle, R. M. J. (Ed.). (1985). *Reaching for excellence: An effective schools sourcebook.* Washington, DC: U.S. Government Printing Office.

Lewis, S. (1980). *Reform and the citizen: The major policy issues of contemporary America.* North Scituate, MA: Duxbury Press.

Lieberman, A. (Ed.). (1986). *Rethinking school improvement: Research, craft, and concept.* New York: Teachers College Press.

Luckett, R., Underwood, K. E., & Fortune, J. C. (1987a). How men and women board members match up. *American School Board Journal, 174*(1), 26, 41.

Luckett, R., Underwood, K. E., & Fortune, J. C. (1987b). Men and women make discernibly different contributions to their boards. *American School Board Journal, 174*(1), 21–23.

Luckett, R., Underwood, K. E., & Fortune, J. C. (1987c). State mandates are your most serious concern. *American School Board Journal, 174*(1), 27, 41.

Miller, L. S. (1986, May 14). Commentary. Nation-building and education. *Education Week,* 42, 52.

Minar, D. W. (1966). *Educational decision-making in suburban communities.* Cooperative research project no. 2440. Washington, DC: U.S. Office of Education.

Murphy, R. (1982). Power and autonomy in the sociology of education. *Theory and Society, 11,* 179–203.

National Commission on Excellence in Education. (1983). *A nation at risk: The imperative for educational reform.* Washington, DC: U.S. Department of Education.

NSBA: School boards not passive. (1986, November 26). *School Board News,* 1, 3.

Ouchi, W. G. (1981). *Theory Z.* Reading, MA: Addison-Wesley.

Passow, A. H. (1984a). *Reforming schools in the 1980s: A critical review of the national reports.* New York: ERIC Clearinghouse on Urban Education.

Passow, A. H. (1984b). Tackling the reform reports of the 1980s. *Phi Delta Kappan,* 674–683.

Peters, T. J., & Waterman, R. H., Jr. (1982). *In search of excellence: Lessons from America's best run companies.* New York: Harper and Row.

Purkey, S. C., & Smith, M. S. (1983). Effective schools: A review. *Elementary School Journal, 83*(4), 427–452.

Sarason, S. B. (1971). *The culture of the school and the problem of change.* Boston: Allyn and Bacon.

Schlechty, P. C. (1985). District level policy and practices. In R. M. J. Kyle (Ed.). *Reaching for excellence: An effective schools sourcebook* (pp. 117–129). Washington, DC: U.S. Government Printing Office.

Shannon, T. A. (1986, September 17). Phony reasons for excluding school board. *School Board News, 3,* 7.

Snider, W. (1987, January 14). School boards' role is target of criticism in New York, Boston. *Education Week,* 1, 28.

Spady, W. G., & Marx, G. (1984). *Excellence in our schools: Making it happen.* Washington, DC: American Association of School Administrators and Far West Laboratory for Educational Research and Development.

Tyack, D., Lowe, R., & Hansot, E. (1984). *Public schools in hard times: The great depression and recent years.* Cambridge, MA: Harvard University Press.

U.S. Bureau of the Census. (1984). *Statistical abstract of the United States, 1985* (105th ed.). Washington, DC: U.S. Government Printing Office.

Ziegler, L. H. (1975). *School board research: The problems and the prospects.* Bethesda, MD. (ERIC Document Reproduction Service No. ED 132 674).

Ziegler, L. H. (1980). *The politics of educational governance: An overview.* Eugene: University of Oregon. (ERIC Document Reproduction Service No. ED 182 799.)

7

The School Site Level: Involving Parents in Reform

Education Reform: The Neglected Dimension, Parent Involvement
CARL L. MARBURGER

Most of the national reform efforts over the past five years, and there have been many, have ignored the family's role in student achievement and parent involvement in school improvement. Fortunately, over thirty states have initiated and encouraged greater parent involvement (see *Education USA*, Vol. 30, No. 52, p. 374); and governors like Lamar Alexander of Tennessee, Thomas H. Kean of New Jersey, Bill Clinton of Arkansas, Richard Lamm of Colorado, and the former governor of South Carolina Richard W. Riley, among others, have seriously advocated parent involvement as part of the reform efforts in their states (see the *Phi Delta Kappan*, November 1986). Such advocacy, however, is usually couched in voucher or "choice" terms, rather than recognition that the parent/citizen/community involvement in the affairs of the public schools is important, even critical, in its own right.

The evidence is clear. When parents are involved in their youth's schooling, children do better in school and they go to better schools (Hen-

82

derson, 1987). Both families and schools want the best for children: They want to help them learn, grow, and develop into educated, responsible, and caring adults. Because they share the same basic goals, it seems obvious that parents and educators should be working together.

If asked, most parents, teachers, and principals will agree that parents need to be involved in and supportive of education. Yet in many places, parents are not actively involved in the life of the school; instead they are spending most of their time and energies organizing bake sales, if they are involved at all. All too often, families and schools seem to be "worlds apart"—distant and independent, barely communicating with each other, or hostile and at war, giving contradictory messages to each other and to the child who is caught between them.

It is particularly timely to take a fresh look at the relations between families and schools, because of the tremendous changes in family life that have taken place in the last twenty years. The traditional nuclear family where two parents are married to each other and living together, the father the breadwinner and the mother the homemaker, is no longer the dominant model. In fact, the family structures and cultural backgrounds of children in school seem to be becoming ever more diverse and complex.

Educators are understandably uneasy and perplexed about what these changes mean for children, for parents, and for the schools they are expected to run. Current statistics give an idea of their magnitude. In 1955, 60 percent of the households in the United States consisted of a working father, a housewife, and two or more school-age children. In 1980, that family unit was only 11 percent of our homes, and in 1985 it is 7 percent, an astonishing change.

More than 50 percent of women are in the work force, and that percentage will undoubtedly increase. Of our 80 million households, almost 20 million consist of people living alone. The census tells us that 59 percent of the children born in 1983 will live with only one parent before reaching age 18—this now becomes the *normal* childhood experience. Of every 100 children born today:

- Twelve will be born out of wedlock.
- Forty will be born to parents who divorce before the child is 18.
- Five will be born to parents who separate.
- Two will be born to parents of whom one will die before the child reaches 18.
- Forty-one will reach age 18 "normally" (Hodgkinson, 1985).

These trends vastly complicate matters for educators. How can we stimulate more parent involvement if mothers work outside the home? Which parents do we try to reach—the stepparent a child lives with or the father who lives across town, the kindergartner's 34-year-old grandmother or 19-year-old mother? What responsibility do we have to help children cope with the stress of their parents' breaking up? How can we ask over-burdened single parents to help teachers educate their children? How can we be adequately sensitive to cultural, social, and economic differences, and collaborate with parents who cannot speak English or whose cultural background makes our way of thinking almost incomprehensible?

In spite of these and myriad other difficulties that family–school partnerships may entail, working together is critically important for students. As Larry Lezotte says in his forward to *Beyond the Bake Sale:*

1. A child's education is vitally affected by the quality and character of the relationship between home and school.
2. Teachers and administrators at local schools must assume the responsibility for initiating and encouraging parental involvement.
3. Effective practice for enhancing parent involvement in schools have been thoroughly researched, and can be replicated in virtually any school setting.

> No matter how parents choose the schools their children attend, they need to become actively involved in the life of those schools. Despite what we may hear, choice and involvement are not the same thing. (Henderson, 1987)

John Ashcroft, the governor of Missouri, emphasizes the necessity for the involvement of parents when he says: "One of the best guarantees of a child's success in school is his or her parents' involvement in education. Parents are their children's first teacher, and their attitudes about learning and school influence the education of their children from early years through graduation."

He further states: "I believe we can bring more families into the wonder of learning. There are three paths toward that goal. We must *involve parents from the beginning of parenthood.* We must *raise the nation's consciousness* of the importance of parental involvement. And we must reach *out to parents at the local level*" (Education Commission of the States, 1988).

WHAT IS PARENT INVOLVEMENT?

Many educators say they are strongly in favor of parent involvement, yet it is not at all clear what they mean by the term. Most are probably referring to parents' participation in home–school activities—such as bake sales and fairs—to raise funds for the band uniforms or school computer, or they may mean parents helping in the classroom or on school trips. Some may be referring to special programs designed to encourage parents of young children to become more involved with their children in learning activities at home.

Other educators feel less positive about parent involvement, thinking instead about incidents where parents have insisted that certain books be banned from the school library, particular courses not be taught, or a teacher be fired.

Still others are ambivalent about parent involvement, thinking about back-to-school nights or parent–teacher conferences, which on some occasions turn out to be useful and constructive, but on others are boring rituals or even quite hostile encounters.

Parent involvement, therefore, is a broad and loosely defined term. In spite of much official rhetoric in its favor, parent involvement is not always regarded favorably by school personnel.

To clarify the roles parents can play, the activities of parents can be classified in many ways. Williams and Stallworth (1983–1984), Collins, Moles, and Cross (1982), and Epstein (1987) have devised their own classifications. The following is a modification of those and others.

Role 1: Parents as Partners

Parents register their child and ensure that he or she is properly dressed, gets to school on time, and attends each day. They purchase necessary supplies and equipment, and obtain the required vaccinations and medical exams. Parents are expected to read, and often respond to, written communications from the schools about schedules, procedures, special events, and policies. These regular activities and contacts between parents and schools are the core of the family–school relationship.

Role 2: Parents as Collaborators and Problem Solvers

Parents can encourage and reward satisfactory achievement and behavior and show interest in what happens during the school day. Parents can demonstrate how important they believe school is by their reaction to absences, minor illnesses, and truancy; their policies on bedtime and television; and whether they help their child complete homework.

Parents can also stimulate and reinforce learning by providing a variety of enrichment activities: reading to their young child, taking trips to the museums and library, discussing possible careers, and demonstrating their own interest in and curiosity about the world around them.

A major aspect of the parent's role as effective collaborator is its potential to help school personnel resolve problems that may arise with a child's learning or behavior.

Role 3: Parents as Audience

Most elementary and many secondary schools hold open houses during the day or back-to-school nights once a year. In addition, schools invite parents to concerts, plays, exhibitions, and athletic events. These are highly visible steps toward bridging the gap between families and schools.

Role 4: Parents as Supporters

In American public and private schools, there is a strong tradition of parents providing a wide range of volunteer assistance, both to their own children's teachers and to the school as a whole. Parents may serve as room parents in elementary schools, organizing help through telephone trees to obtain needed supplies or assistance with school trips, or to deal with emergencies. Parents can volunteer in school libraries, provide tutoring to children in special need, make attendance calls, or share their special expertise in enrichment programs.

In addition, parent organizations have traditionally played a significant role in sponsoring fund-raising events, such as bazaars, fairs, and auctions, which support the school by paying for special equipment or programs that are not in the school's budget.

Role 5: Parents as Advisors and Co-Decision Makers

In response to increasing dissatisfaction with the remoteness of large, centralized school bureaucracies, school systems in various parts of the country have been experimenting with ways to obtain advice from parents and citizens, or to give them a share in policy decisions.

Perhaps the most common approach is for a principal to name special committees of parent and teacher representatives to work out solutions to a schoolwide problem, such as discipline or safety, or to help introduce a new program or curriculum, such as a sex education unit.

In some school districts, state-mandated school accountability committees or advisory councils function as monitoring or advisory bodies. These groups sometimes play a perfunctory role, approving a bland year-end report; but at other times they can play a crucial role, as in selecting a new principal, creating a new discipline policy, or conducting a school-wide needs assessment. Real power sharing with parents occurs when parents are elected to school governing boards or are equal members on school site councils consisting of representatives of the teachers, parents, and administrators, which make decisions about the expenditure of discretionary school funds.

There are, then, many forms that parent involvement might take. All of them are positive and have an impact on student learning. Henderson (1987: 2) says that the research indicates that there is no one best way to go about it. Instead, what works best is for parents to be involved in a variety of roles over a period of time. The form of parent involvement seems to be less important than that it is reasonably well-planned, comprehensive, and long-lasting.

In spite of research and information available about the importance of parent involvement,

> it is still not unusual to hear experienced educators say that once children are in school, their education is best left to the professionals—that untrained parents might unwittingly interfere with today's sophisticated teaching techniques, or even that turf battles between parents and teachers might disrupt the learning environment. They also argue that the extra time it takes to work with parents would place an intolerable burden on already overworked teachers and principals. (Henderson, 1987: 2)

The work of David Williams, at the Southwest Educational Development Laboratory, is helpful in understanding the discrepancy between the attitude of parents and educators. Williams found that parents are eager to play all roles at school, from tutor to classroom assistant to decision-maker. While they feel that some activities, such as helping their child with homework, should have more priority than others, they also feel that all roles are relatively important. But professional educators tend to consider only the most traditional roles: "school program supporter" or "audience at school functions," to be "important." Educators tend to relegate parents to insubstantial, bake-sale roles, leaving parents feeling frustrated, belittled, and left out.

BUILDING THE PARENT–SCHOOL PARTNERSHIP

There is no blueprint for the school that collaborates effectively with parents. Because schools are so different, there is no single model, no one set of practices or characteristics, to which we can point and say, "That is the definitive Partnership School." But all schools that work well with parents share a fundamental set of principles. Those principles are:

1. *Create a school that's open, helpful, and friendly.*
   - Post a "Parents and Visitors Are Welcome" sign on the front door.
   - Design a special parent lounge.
   - Schedule new family orientations and tours. Set aside weekly drop-in hours for parents to meet with the principal.
   - Have monthly parent–teacher luncheons.
2. *Communicate clearly and frequently with parents (about school policies and programs or about their children's progress).*
   - Send home wall calendars to inform families of school events, holidays, in-service days, and grading schedules.

- Host open houses and back-to-school nights for parents to meet school staff and to ask questions.
- Give teachers opportunities to call the homes of their students to introduce themselves and to encourage parents to visit the schools.

3. *Treat parents as co-workers in the educational process.*
   - Draw up student–parent–teacher Learning Contracts that spell out individualized goals and tasks and are signed annually by parents, teachers, and the child.
   - Request parent–teacher conferences at least once a year for students at all grade levels.
   - Seek assistance from parents in the classroom discipline of students by notifying them of unexcused absences; ask their advice when trying to solve behavior problems in the classroom.

4. *Encourage parents, formally and informally, to comment on school policies and to share in some of the decision making.*
   - Print policy handbooks and distribute them to every family and student.
   - Establish parent advisory committees to deal with specific school concerns.

5. *Get every family involved, not simply those most easily reached. Pay special attention to parents who work outside the home, divorced parents without custody, and families of minority race and language.*
   - Notify employed parents in advance about special daytime events, and offer them times to meet with school teachers outside the regular school hours.
   - Work with the parent organization to make sure parents have arrangements for coping with sudden dismissal (on snow days, for instance).

6. *Make sure that the principal and other school administrators actively express and promote the philosophy of partnership with all families.*
   - Devote one districtwide in-service training day per year to assist teachers in working with parents.
   - Designate a special office or work area near the principal's office for the chairperson of the parent advisory council.

7. *Encourage volunteer participation from parents and other members of the community.*
   - Get volunteers involved in tutoring, internship placement, recreation supervision, field trip coordination, and supplementary education programs.
   - Survey interests and talents of community residents—let them suggest ways in which they would like to work with the school.

If these principles are to work, there needs to be a structure, a systematic way to build that parent–school partnership. One such mechanism is called School-Based (or school site) Management (Marburger, 1985).

School-Based Management (SBM) is a form of school district organization that makes the individual school the unit where many significant decisions about schooling take place. Most districts are now centrally organized. This can create a physical as well as psychological distance between the central office and the local school. It is at that local school that parent/citizen concerns exist and where the teachers and principals can demonstrate that they care. All else—board of education resolutions, administrative and budget decisions, state and federal programs and regulations—has only one purpose: to facilitate what happens at the individual school.

SBM is a decentralized form of organization in which the authority and the decisions now made by the superintendent and school board are shared with those who know and care most about the excellence of the education for students—the teachers, the principal, the parents, the students, and the local school community.

Unlike many educational reforms, SBM is a process, not a prescription. There is no right way to implement SBM because the central theory behind it is the belief that each district and each school within that district is unique. Yet all forms of school-based organization have one thing in common: They reorganize the school district's decision-making structure so that many important decisions that may directly or indirectly affect the education of children are made at the level of the local school.

No one invented School-Based Management. Rather, it seems to have emerged independently as a response to problems that resulted from the centralization of decision making and a shift in society's values away from control and toward autonomy. SBM means both the delegation of some important decision-making authority to the local school and a restructuring of the way decisions are made.

Over the years, our citizens have lost faith in big government and in centralized institutions. Why? Because these institutions are not responsive to individuals. They have also lost confidence in "the professionals"—those doctors, lawyers, and educators who for so long have claimed to know what is best, but who too often do not put their clients' interest first.

SBM is an approach that lets parents, students, teachers, and ordinary citizens make a difference for a change. If School-Based Management is to be more than an idea—if it is a process that is to be tried—there must be a mechanism for its implementation. That mechanism is the school council. The council should follow the democratic model of representative government because (1) the school community is so broad, that it would be impossible to involve everyone directly, and (2) the key concerns in forming SBM councils are the membership categories and size of the council, the selection process, and the council's relationship with the school board and superintendent. The council can be elected or appointed, or can draw representation from existing organizations such as the Parent–Teacher Organization (PTO).

Within carefully drawn but not oppressive limits, the school board and superintendent can delegate a significant portion of their perceived or real prerogatives to that council. Many school districts have such councils. We recommend that councils act within the following guidelines:

• Recognize local school board policies.
• Abide by state and federal law and regulations.
• Stay within budget limits.
• Promote ethical practices.

Each district can determine how it will implement SBM and what authority will be delegated to local school councils. But then each council must be trusted to make decisions that are in the best interests of the children of that school.

CONCLUSION

The public schools of the United States are constantly being exhorted to change. Reforms come and go like hula hoops as new approaches to solving the incredible complexities of schooling and learning are devised.

These past few years have seen another wave of blue-ribbon reports, decrying the conditions of the schools and recommending a multitude of changes, which too often reflect anxiety about the country's economic position in the world or the fact that the United States may not be competitive with some other country.

One significant feature of these recommendations and their resultant statutes or policy mandates is that they are top-down hierarchies. They originate at the state, with orders to school districts to implement policies. Or they begin with the federal government, with orders to the states or local school districts to obey, or to face the consequences.

Regardless of their origin, the result of these actions is a top-down series of commands, often bureaucratically enforced, with a lot of paperwork and reports required. That system is based on fear. If you do not do "it" you will be [fired?—nobody really gets fired], [chastised], [devastated], [chewed out], [audited].

When reforms are initiated from the bottom up, from the school to the district, from the community to the school, from the staff to the principal, we are involved in a process that is based on trust, not fear.

School-Based Management is not a panacea. It is a process that provides the most significant opportunity to create the parent–school partnership. It is a process that can enable concerned superintendents, boards of education, teachers, principals, parents, and students to demonstrate their caring about student learning.

And it is the best mechanism available to involve parents in the affairs of the schools.

NOTE

Portions of this chapter have been adapted from *Beyond the Bake Sale: An Educator's Guide to Working with Parents,* by Anne T. Henderson, Carl L. Marburger and Theodora Ooms. Columbia, MD: National Committee for Citizens in Education, 1986.

REFERENCES

Collins, Carter H., Moles, Oliver, & Cross, Mary. (1982). *The home–school connection: Selected partnership programs in large cities.* Cambridge, MA: Institute for Responsive Education.

Education Commission of the States. (1988, August). *Drawing in the family: Family involvement in the schools.* Denver, CO.

Epstein, Joyce L. (1987, January). What principals should know about parent involvement. *Principal,* 6–9.

Henderson, Anne. (Ed.). (1987). *The evidence continues to grow: Parent involvement improves student achievement.* Columbia, MD: National Committee for Citizens in Education.

Hodgkinson, Harold L. (1985). *All one system: Demographics of education, kindergarten through graduate school.* Washington, DC: Institute for Educational Leadership.

Marburger, Carl L. (1985). *One school at a time: School based management: a process for change.* Columbia, MD: National Committee for Citizens in Education.

8
Teacher Unions: Participation through Bargaining

Collective Bargaining, School Reform, and the Management of School Systems
JOSEPH B. SHEDD

As COLLECTIVE BARGAINING in public education moves into its third decade, scholars are seeking to document, evaluate, and explain its impact on our educational systems. Unlike studies published in the mid-seventies, which focused almost exclusively on the "wage effects" of teacher unionism, more recent studies have focused particular attention on how collective bargaining has affected educational policymaking, the management of school districts, and the work of teachers. Several of the latest studies focus on the relationship between bargaining and efforts to "reform" public school systems.

Most recent studies conclude that collective bargaining has had much more of an impact on educational programs and the management of school districts than earlier observers had expected, but descriptions, interpretations, and explanations of that impact vary dramatically. This article argues that collective bargaining has both affected and been affected by many of the same pressures as those evidenced in the current efforts to "reform" public education. The most distinctive pressure is to include teachers in the formulation of educational policies and programs, with a consequent redefinition of the roles that boards of education, administrators, teachers and their representatives play in the management of school systems.

CONFLICTING EVIDENCE?

The evidence on collective bargaining's effects is confusing, to say the least. Some observers insist that bargaining has introduced rigidity into the management of school systems and has reduced the capacity of school managers to respond to changing public demands (Grimshaw, 1979; Kearney, 1984; Goldschmidt, Bowers, Riley & Stuart, 1984). Others agree that bargaining has changed the way in which schools are managed, but they suggest that those changes may have actually enhanced the flexibility of school systems by providing administrators with new mechanisms for securing their teachers' cooperation and providing teachers with new leverage to insist that they be included in school and district decision making (Kerchner & Mitchell, 1981; Johnson, 1983).

Some observers have suggested that bargaining has resulted in the centralization of authority in district offices and has sharply curtailed the authority of building principals (Goldschmidt et al., 1984); others have concluded that principals continue to play a pivotal role in the management of school systems and retain plenty of influence if they care to exercise it (Johnson, 1983). Some have concluded that collective bargaining has encouraged teachers to think of themselves as "laborers," with a diminished sense of responsibility for the quality of education and the welfare of their students (Leiberman, 1980); others insist that bargaining has enhanced the "professionalism" of teachers, encouraging them to accept *more* responsibility for the quality of educational programs (Kerchner, 1988).

A few scholars have begun to develop a thesis that may help reconcile these seemingly contradictory observations. Kerchner and Mitchell (1986) and Johnson (1987) suggest that collective bargaining in education is itself undergoing a major change, from a system borrowed from and structured along the lines of traditional private sector labor-management relations to one specifically adapted to public education, in which both parties make explicit use of bargaining to address issues of educational policy. If that is what is happening, then it is possible that the seemingly contradictory evidence of bargaining "effects" may be drawn from school systems at different points in such a transition.

The evidence that collective bargaining has produced rigidity, centralization, diminished supervisory authority, and a "laboring" conception of the teacher's role may be drawn from settings where a traditional (industrial) model of collective bargaining continues to predominate. The evidence that bargaining has produced increased flexibility, responsiveness to public concerns, respect for the leadership role of building principals, and teacher involvement in "professional" decision making may reflect labor-management relationships in settings where the parties have made the transition to a newer form of collective decision making. The evidence of conflict and bitterness in education bargaining may be characteristic of relationships in transition between these two approaches, as one party struggles to reconstruct the labor-management relationship along lines that the other refuses to accept.

We agree with the basic outlines of this thesis. It is well-documented in the general research on industrial relations that the parties to collective bargaining relationships tend to adopt substantive and procedural rules that reflect the characteristics of their particular industry (Dunlop, 1958; Kochan, 1980). It is equally well-documented that the most serious conflicts in labor-management relations tend to occur when one or the other party attempts to change the structures and processes of bargaining itself (Weber, 1964; Chamberlain & Kuhn, 1965). There are good reasons to believe that school managers and teacher unions are, in fact, creating a new set of rules to govern their relationship—a set of rules uniquely tailored to their particular environment—and that much of the acrimony attributed to "traditional" collective bargaining is, in fact, a sign of tension between different approaches rather than a characteristic of "traditional" labor relations itself.

But these arguments raise as many questions as they answer. If unions and employers tend to adopt rules that reflect the particular characteristics of their industry, why would the most distinctive feature of this new "generation" of labor relations in public education be teachers' collective participation in school and district education policysetting: a feature that would represent a dramatic *change* in the way school systems have typically been administered? If teacher unions are prepared to insist upon such participation to the point of provoking serious labor-management conflicts, is it accurate to suggest that "professional unions" are more likely to pursue "cooperative" strategies for dealing with their employers than other unions? If teacher unions are particularly concerned with "process" issues—issues of participation, authority, power, and change—is it possible that school bargainers will *never* achieve the level of cooperation that characterized private sector labor-management relationships in, say, the 1950s when the structure of bargaining and division of responsibilities between union and management in the private sector were relatively clear and stable?

EMBRACING—AND OUTGROWING—INDUSTRIAL UNIONISM

Except for restrictions on strikes and the substitution of various third-party impasse procedures, most of the features of collective bargaining in public education were borrowed from the private sector: districtwide bargaining units, the periodic negotiation of comprehensive agreements that last for fixed periods of time, legal restrictions that limit bargaining to so-called "bread-and-butter" issues and that require the parties to negotiate "in good faith," multistep grievance procedures for the resolution of disagreements that may arise during the life of an agreement, and the use of binding arbitration to resolve such disputes if the parties are unable to resolve them on their own.

These features are so familiar today that it is easy to forget that they have not always been the norm. In fact, they were developed for bargaining in the *industrial* sectors of the economy. Craft unionism, which was the "traditional" form of unionism before industrial unions won their organizing victories in the 1930s, was based on principles that were inconsistent with the factory system. Craft unions insisted that workers had to be members of a union *before* they could be hired, that it was the *union's* responsibility to train workers and to certify when they were ready to be employed, and that the *union* would control the work process through its largely unilateral specification of work rules. All three of those principles were incompatible with the labor and product markets, the technologies and the hierarchical management structures on which the mass production factory systems were based.

It is not surprising that the workers and their union leaders in the smokestack industries would have to reinvent the concepts of "collective bargaining" and "union" before their organizing drives could have any hope of success. Although the tactics of industrial unions were militant, and their leaders' rhetoric sometimes radical, the system of collective bargaining that they invented was actually an *accommodation* to the basic features of the factory system (Nadworny, 1955; Piore, 1982). They abandoned the notion that a "real" union must control hiring, training, and the work process, acknowledging (however grudgingly) that control of such processes was the prerogative of management. What they got, in return, were increasingly detailed agreements setting *limits* on the exercise of those prerogatives.

The linchpin in this new arrangement was (and still is) the principle that management "retains" whatever rights it hasn't given up by express contract language or by mutually acknowledged past practice. The industrial union's willingness to respect that basic principle by agreeing to forgo strikes during the life of a contract and to use hierarchical grievance procedures ending in arbitration to resolve disagreements during that period, is the basic "quid" that industrial managers received in return for the negotiated "quos" they ceded at the bargaining table.

It is not difficult to appreciate why teacher unions embraced the basic logic of industrial unionism when they first won bargaining rights in the 1960s. The prevailing logic of education *management* was itself patterned on the industrial model (Callahan, 1962; Cole, 1969; Tyack & Hansot, 1982). The earliest advocates of what came to be called "educational administration" based much of their thinking on the principles of industrial "scientific management" formulated by Frederick Taylor at the turn of the century. Beginning in the late 1950s, with the Sputnik crisis, there were repeated calls to restructure and manage school systems along bureaucratic lines. What, in most school systems, had been a collection of largely autonomous units dominated by building principals was now to be "rationalized" by centralizing the control of educational policies and programs in the hands of district superintendents and central office staff experts.

Although references to school systems as factories or bureaucracies typically carry pejorative implications, the application of industrial/bureaucratic principles to school systems had certain beneficial effects. The level of professionalism of school management staffs was enhanced, employment policies were standardized, and checks were placed on the largely arbitrary, often-capricious authority that principals had exercised in the management of their schools.

But if school systems were to be run like factories, with hierarchical controls and centralized planning and evaluation and policysetting mechanisms, then teacher unions would necessarily have to act like factory unions, resorting to roughly the same sorts of strategies for protecting the interests of their members. Like their industrial sector counterparts, teacher unions often challenged particular management decisions and insisted upon reducing to writing policies that administrators might have preferred to leave to their own discretion. But, at least in the early years, teacher unions played essentially the same reactive role as their industrial union counterparts. They insisted that it was management's job to set policy and manage and the union's job to negotiate and then police protections against abuses of that authority.

The logic of industrial unionism complemented, and in some ways even supported, the management ideology that existed in most school systems when teacher unions first won recognition. Teacher unions did not impose the strategies of "job control" unionism on their employers; those strategies were logical reflections of and responses to the strategies then being pursued by boards of education and central administrators themselves.

But now that "prevailing management ideology" is *itself* the subject of intense scrutiny. With remarkable swiftness, the debate over how to "reform" American public education has shifted from strategies that would have strengthened the bureaucratic controls that boards and central administrators exercise over their subordinates to strategies designed to "empower" those very same subordinates (Carnegie Forum, 1986; Holmes Group, 1986; Conley & Bacharach, 1987). It is this "second wave" of the reform debate that is rising fundamental questions about the appropriateness of industrial unionism to public education.

GROWING INTO WHAT?

The pressures that are forcing a reassessment of collective bargaining in public education are roughly the same as those that have prompted the reform debate itself: new and more complicated public "product" expectations that require changes in the roles of teachers and administrators.

School systems have never really had a single "standardized product" that they offer to a homogeneous group of customers or constituents. Their immediate clients (their students) have a variety of needs and abilities and require a variety of specialized services, tailored to those needs and abilities. Those clients are also a school system's "raw materials" and "first-line workers," whose cooperation is needed if schools are to meet the demands of a host of *other* constituents and audiences, including parents, businesspersons and employers, taxpayers, specialized interest groups, local political officials, and state education officials.

But, despite this diversity, school officials have usually had the luxury of *concentrating* on one kind of expectation at a time. Now, there are increasing calls that public schools pursue "excellence" and "equity" *simultaneously*, promoting basic competence, mastery of new technologies, the development of "thinking skills" and "creative capacities" for all students all at once.

The task of coordinating all these different pressures, of establishing some coherent set of policies, and of forging some common sense of purpose for a district's educational programs is critical to a school system's success (Wynne, 1981; Rosenholtz, 1985). It is no longer a task that can be accomplished, however, by pretending that a district can mass produce a standardized product. Teachers, themselves having to address the needs of individuals and yet orchestrate the activities of small groups and large classes, must have discretion to adapt their day-to-day activities to the changing and often unpredictable situations they confront in their individual classrooms (Lortie, 1975; Conley, 1988).

The task of balancing the need for coordination and the need for adaptability and discretion is emerging as the most challenging aspect of education management. Coordination alone could be achieved by centralization and bureaucratic controls. Adaptability and discretion could be achieved by creating a new program for every need and then leaving individual teachers free to do as they see fit. But enhancing coordination *and* discretion requires a different set of strategies. As in the private sector, where many corporations face analogous market pressures, there is growing evidence that task can *only* be accomplished by including those employees with the most intimate knowledge of work process problems and client needs in the policymaking processes of the organization (Bacharach & Conley, 1986).

It is not difficult to identify parts of the traditional collective bargaining system that may have to be adjusted as a result of these developments, even if the outcomes to those adjustments aren't always clear.

It is clear that the present *scope of bargaining*, which generally (or ostensibly) confines bargaining to teacher compensation issues and to the "impact" of educational policies and programs on teachers' working conditions, will undergo some sort of change. The pressure for change will sometimes come from boards and administrators and sometimes from teachers and their representatives. It will come because policymakers need their teachers' involvement to satisfy external demands, and it will come because the parties are becoming increasingly aware that there is no way of making educational sense out of the private (industrial) sector formula that declares "the nature of the employer's product" to be a management prerogative but "working conditions" to be fully negotiable.

In a service industry, where the work of individual employees is itself the service that the organization provides to its clients, virtually any educational policy or program has a direct and immediate impact on the working conditions of these employees. Indeed, whether school districts *enable teachers to be effective* in their jobs—a question of "policy" or "management prerogative" in most production settings—is one of the most important "working conditions" issues in a service setting. As Johnson (1987), Kerchner (1988), and others have argued, it is quite likely that bargaining over educational policy issues *as* educational issues will represent one of the most distinctive features of future bargaining in public education.

The *forms and forums for bargaining* and the *nature of resulting agreements* will almost certainly undergo changes as well. Boards and administrators will claim that "comprehensive" contract negotiations and fixed-term agreements are inappropriate vehicles for addressing the changing details of complex policies or programs. Teachers and their union representatives will demand guarantees that their "involvement in policymaking" amounts to more than being "consulted" on decisions that have already effectively been made. The result will probably be an increasing reliance on comprehensive negotiations to establish the *structures* and *ground rules* for joint decision making conducted away from the contract bargaining table. Unions and employers in all sectors have used committees to address specialized problems or to develop new programs, but education bargainers are more likely to make permanent use of such mechanisms.

As efforts increase to shift more decision making from central offices to individual schools, bargainers can also be expected to create *new rules governing the application of districtwide agreements to individual schools*. More and more, we can expect to see provisions acknowledging that school principals and their faculties can jointly do what neither has the authority to do unilaterally: make exceptions to some provisions of districtwide agreements. As Johnson (1983) points out, many principals and school faculties already exercise that option without formal authorization; acknowledging and setting rules on when they may do so, without establishing precedents applicable to other schools, would represent an important new development.

The *principle of management's "retained rights"* is almost certain to be modified, but in ways that are difficult to predict. That principle is not only inconsistent with the principle that teachers should be collectively involved in setting basic policies and programs. It is largely inconsistent with the decision-making structures that already exist in most school districts. Although many districts deny teachers the opportunity to participate *collectively* in the setting of district and schoolwide policies, *individual teachers* actually make most of the day-to-day management decisions in school systems: decisions concerning the selection of goals and objectives, the determination of strategies for reaching them, and the marshalling of resources to support those ends (Lortie, 1975; Shedd & Malanowski, 1985; Conley, 1988). The principle that those with administrative titles and supervisory roles "retain" the right to dictate such decisions, to the extent that they have not agreed to limit that right through a negotiated contract, is clearly a fiction. The more attention bargainers focus on educational issues *as* educational issues, the more likely it is that they will *also* address the inapplicability of that principle to the educational setting.

Bargainers will focus more attention on *building closer relationships among teachers.* The growing tendency to define "professionalism" in terms of collective participation in decision making, collegial assistance, and mutual responsibility for the quality of education—rather than in terms of the individual teacher's autonomy—can be expected to keep issues such as team teaching, peer review and coaching, and teacher responsibility for staff development at the forefront of attention (Little, 1987). Such arrangements are foreign to most industrial unions, but they are likely to be received more enthusiastically by teacher unions than observers generally expect. The identification of professionalism with *individual* autonomy has always been one of the obstacles that made it difficult to reconcile the concepts of teachers as professionals and teachers as union members. Defining their professional concerns in terms of *collective participation* and *mutual support* would serve to overcome a source of divisiveness that has sapped the energies and undermined the effectiveness of many local teachers' unions (especially those affiliated with the National Education Association, which had a history of servile professionalism to overcome.)

Some observers confidently predict that these other developments will be reinforced by *changes in the structure of the teaching profession* itself, with the differentiation of teachers' duties and compensation by levels of a "career ladder." Such issues are almost certain to be addressed—repeatedly—in the years ahead, but how they will be resolved is by no means clear. Initial evidence suggests that many of the recent efforts to develop and implement "career ladders" for teachers have been failures for a variety of reasons too complex to address here (see Bacharach, Conley, & Shedd, 1986). One contrast with private sector developments, however, is instructive: Many private sector employers and unions, struggling to achieve greater flexibility and to "involve" employees in decision making, are finding that hierarchical job structures and formal linkages between employees' duties and their levels of compensation are among the greatest obstacles to their efforts (Kochan, 1985). What some educational reformers insist is *a problem*—the formally undifferentiated job structure in education—represents *the ideal* for many private sector managers.

Finally, one of the most widely-held assumptions among those attempting to redirect the future of collective bargaining in public education is that *relationships will become more cooperative* as teachers, administrators, and boards of education turn their attention to policy issues and professional obligations. If the point is simply that there is likely to be more cooperation, more problem solving and less labor-management conflict once the parties quit battling over the basic principle of "negotiated policysetting," and move on to applying that principle, those predictions are likely to be correct. Disputes over basic principles are *always* more acrimonious than disputes over their application, in industrial relations as in any other setting (Bacharach & Lawler, 1981).

But that argument is likely to cut both ways. It is difficult to find empirical support for the widely held conviction that "truly professional" unions will be naturally cooperative and nonconfrontational. Why would parties who jointly set policies and programs for their clients be *less* likely to take "principled" stands than those who have safely assigned the design of the product and the control of work processes to one party or the other? Isn't the opposite more likely?

Teachers, we expect, will always be more sensitive to the need for flexibility and individual discretion, while system managers will continue to be more sensitive to the need for coordination of programs and to the flow of students through the system. The parties will continue, in other words, to have *different* perspectives on what their clients need as well as different interests and priorities in their dealings with each other. Those perspectives, interests, and priorities are not (we trust) mutually exclusive, but they *do* require constant reconciliation. The fact that collective bargaining is well-suited to just such a task is one reason it is likely to assume more prominence in the overall management of school systems in coming years.

But that argument does not justify the assumption that the process of reconciliation will always—or even usually—be harmonious. As in the

1930s, there is reason to believe that a new form of unionism is emerging in the United States: a form of unionism that is likely to be just as vigorous and well-suited to the service and professional employment sectors of the economy as the unionism that was created to fit the characteristics of mass production industries. Indeed, there are reasons to believe that a scrappy new form of unionism is already being delivered naturally by "traditional" collective bargaining itself, while most observers are looking for the stork to deliver a little bundle of love.

REFERENCES

Bacharach, S. B., & Conley, S. C. (1986). Education reform: A managerial agenda. *Phi Delta Kappan, 67*(9), 641–645.

Bacharach, S. B., Conley, S. C., & Shedd, J. B. (1986). Beyond career ladders: Structuring teacher career development systems. *Teachers College Record, 87*(4), 563–574.

Bacharach, S. B., & Lawler, E. J. (1981). *Bargaining: Power, tactics and outcomes.* San Francisco: Jossey-Bass.

Callahan, R. (1962). *Education and the cult of efficiency.* Chicago: University of Chicago Press.

Carnegie Forum on Education and the Economy's Task Force on Teaching as a Profession. (1986). *A nation prepared: Teachers for the 21st century.* New York.

Chamberlain, N. W., & Kuhn, J. W. (1965). *Collective bargaining* (2nd ed.). New York: McGraw-Hill.

Cole, S. (1969). *The unionization of teachers.* New York: Praeger.

Conley, S. C. (1988). Reforming paper pushers and avoiding free agents: The teacher as a constrained decision maker. *Educational Administration Quarterly, 24*(4).

Conley, S. C., & Bacharach, S. B. (1987). The Holmes Group report: Standards, hierarchies, and management. *Teachers College Record, 8*(3), 343–347.

Dunlop, J. T. (1958). *Industrial relations systems.* New York: Holt, Rinehart & Winston.

Goldschmidt, S. M., Bowers, B., Riley, M., & Stuart, L. (1984). *The extent and nature of educational policy bargaining.* Eugene: University of Oregon, Center for Educational Policy and Management.

Grimshaw, W. J. (1979). *Union rule in schools.* Lexington, MA: D. C. Heath.

The Holmes Group. (1986). *Tomorrow's teachers: A report of the Holmes Group.* East Lansing, MI.

Johnson, S. M. (1983). *Teacher unions in schools.* Philadelphia: Temple University Press.

Johnson, S. M. (1987). Can schools be reformed at the bargaining table? *Teachers College Record, 89*(2), 269–280.

Kearney, R. C. (1984). *Labor relations in the public sector.* New York: Marcel Dekker.

Kerchner, C. T. (1988, 20 January). A "new generation" of teacher unionism. *Education Week,* 36.

Kerchner, C. T., & Mitchell, D. (1981). *The dynamics of public sector collective bargaining and its impacts on governance, administration and teaching.* Washington, DC: National Institute of Education.

Kerchner, C. T., & Mitchell, D. (1986). Teaching reform and union reform. *Elementary School Journal, 86*(4), 449–470.

Kochan, T. A. (1980). *Collective bargaining and industrial relations.* Homewood, IL: Irwin.

Kochan T. A. (Ed.). (1985). *Challenges and choices facing American labor.* Cambridge: MIT Press.

Lieberman, M. C. (1980). *Public sector bargaining: A policy reappraisal.* Lexington, MA: D. C. Heath.

Little, J. W. (1987). Teachers as colleagues. In V. Richardson-Koehler (Ed.), *Educator's handbook: A research perspective* (pp. 491–518). New York: Longman.

Lortie, D. C. (1975). *Schoolteacher: A sociological study.* Chicago: University of Chicago Press.

Nadworny, M. J. (1955). *Scientific management and the unions.* Cambridge, MA: Harvard University Press.

Piore, M. J. (1982, March–April). American labor and the industrial crisis. *Challenge,* 5–11.

Rosenholtz, S. J. (1985). Effective schools: Interpreting the evidence. *American Journal of Education, 93*(3), 352–388.

Shedd, J. B., & Malanowski, R. M. (1985). *From the front of the classroom: A study of the work of teachers.* Ithaca, NY: Organizational Analysis and Practice.

Tyack, D., & Hansot, E. (1982). *Managers of virtue: Public school leadership in America, 1820–1980.* New York: Basic Books.

Weber, A. R. (Ed.). (1964). *The structure of collective bargaining.* Chicago: University of Chicago Graduate School of Business.

Wynne, E. A. (1981). Looking at good schools. *Phi Delta Kappan, 63*(5), 377–381.

9
Community Involvement: Parents, Teachers, and Administrators Working Together

Decentralizing and Democratizing the Public Schools—A Viable Approach to Reform?
BETTY MALEN
RODNEY T. OGAWA

O NCE AGAIN, PROPOSALS to decentralize and democratize public schools, to involve teachers and parents in the determination of education policies, are being advanced as potent reform measures. Plans to redefine the professional roles so "teachers participate in key decisions about school policy" (Tucker, 1988:44; Barth, 1988; Lieberman, 1988; Maeroff, 1988), and calls for school improvement councils, site-based management or a host of other building-based measures to make parents "partners" in policymaking (Caldwell, 1987; Guthrie, 1986; Kirst, 1984; National Governors' Association, 1986; Olson, 1987) signal the resurgence of the decentralize–democratize approach to reform. Clearly, initiatives that designate the individual school as the unit of improvement and shared decision-making as the vehicle through which improvements might be stimulated and sustained are prominent features of the "second wave" of education reform (Goodlad, 1984; Wise, 1988).

PURPOSE AND PERSPECTIVE

This chapter analyzes the viability of shared decisionmaking arrangements from the vantage point of site-based governance councils in an urban district. Since proponents claim it is through the alteration of influence relationships that school improvements will be made, the chapter concentrates on the extent to which shared decisionmaking arrangements actually enable teachers and parents to wield significant influence on significant issues at the building level. The chapter draws upon an empirical study of influence relationships on site-based governance councils in Salt Lake City, Utah.[1] The Salt Lake City experience offers a unique but important basis for analyzing the viability of shared decisionmaking arrangements. This district's nationally recognized shared governance policy creates conditions that appear to be particularly conducive to substantial teacher and parent influence on school level policy (Clark, 1979; Davies, 1987). The chapter argues that the Salt Lake case is a "critical test" (Patton, 1980:102) that holds important implications for those who seek to decentralize and democratize schools, for those who seek to create arrangements that enable teachers and parents to exert substantial influence on school policy decisions.

There are a variety of ways to gauge the extent to which particular actors influence policy decisions. The perspective used here rests on several assumptions.[2] First, the decisionmaking influence of actors is contingent on the possession of relevant resources, the skill and will with which those resources are deployed to acquire influence in a particular arena, and the manner in which organizational features and environmental forces operate to magnify the resources of some actors and diminish the resources of others (Mazzoni, 1986). Second, decisionmaking influence is manifest when the actors' involvement at critical stages of the process (formation of agenda, consideration of agenda items, official adoption of an alternative) enables them to preempt, select, modify, block or otherwise affect decision outcomes on subjects that are central to the organization or salient to the individual (Conway, 1984; Malen & Ogawa, 1988). Third, decisionmaking influence is inferred by examining and reconciling participant perceptions of who wields influence in the arena under study with their descriptions of how various resources and strategies combine and interact to produce influence in the arena under study (Gamson, 1968).

Shared decisionmaking arrangements have been the subject of continuous investigation in diverse laboratory, industrial, and organizational contexts (for a synopsis, see Massarik, 1983). They have received, however, rather limited attention in school settings (Conway, 1984; Duke, Showers,

& Imber,1981). Scholars have examined various attempts to decentralize and democratize education policymaking at the district level (see, for example, Boyd & Shea, 1975; Rogers, 1968), but empirical studies of professional-patron influence on policymaking at the site level are rare (see, for example, Mann, 1974; Ornstein, 1983; Wissler & Ortiz, 1986).

The available literature offers little encouragement to proponents of the decentralize–democratize approach to reform because it consistently reveals that teachers and parents rarely exert significant influence on significant issues at the building level. Focused case accounts, broad sentiment surveys and recent reviews of the literature demonstrate that, while participatory decisionmaking arrangements may (or may not) yield some positive benefits such as increased commitment to innovation, improvements in morale, satisfaction and performance, these arrangements do not substantially alter the influence relationships typically and traditionally found in schools (see, for example, Berman, Weiler Associates, 1984; Conway, 1984; Davies, 1978; Guthrie & Reed, 1986; Huguenin, Zerchykov, & Davies, 1979; Shields & McLaughlin, 1986). Essentially, principals retain control over building-level policies; teachers retain control over the instructional component; and parents provide support (Steinberg, 1979).

The available literature does offer some guidance to proponents of the decentralize–democratize approach to reform because it identifies barriers to teacher and parent influence on school-level policymaking and suggests ways in which those barriers might be overcome. The Salt Lake School District's shared governance policy incorporates the suggestions for overcoming barriers to teacher and parent influence. Thus, it is, in many ways, a critical test of the viability of shared decisionmaking arrangements (Patton, 1980:102). If shared decisionmaking arrangements are likely to work anywhere, they ought to work here.

A CRITICAL TEST

Highly Favorable Conditions

The available literature suggests that teachers and parents should be able to wield significant influence on education policy if shared decisionmaking bodies are located at the school site and are granted broad jurisdiction and formal policymaking authority, and if participants, notably principals, teachers, and parents, are given "equal vote" protections and training is provided. All of these conditions are present in the Salt Lake City School District.

The themes developed in this section of the chapter are more extensively illustrated and evidenced in Malen and Ogawa (1988).

Site-Based Councils

In this case, shared decisionmaking bodies are located at the school site, the level reportedly most receptive to teacher and parent involvement in and influence on education policymaking (Davies, 1981:104; Huguenin et al., 1979:99; Boyd & Shea, 1975). The district's shared governance policy requires that each school establish two bodies: a School Improvement Council (SIC), composed of building administrators, teachers, and noncertified staff, and a School Community Council (SCC), composed of parents and SIC members.

Broad Jurisdiction and Formal Authority

The councils are granted broad jurisdiction and formal policymaking authority. Studies indicate that the categorical nature of the councils circumscribes teacher and parent influence by restricting the range of issues that can be discussed. Studies further indicate that teacher and parent influence is constrained because councils "have not been given sufficient formal authority" (Clark, 1979:24; Bastian, Fruchter, Gittell, Greer, & Haskins, 1987). When the jurisdiction and authority of councils is so confined, schools can "create the impression" of substantial influence yet retain control over decision processes and outcomes (Huguenin et al., 1979:54). Presumably the installation of umbrella councils with formal authority to make decisions across a wide range of issues would enhance teacher and parent influence on school policy (Berman, Weiler Associates, 1984; Davies, 1980; Shields & McLaughlin, 1986).

The Salt Lake City councils are set up to function as "individual school policy boards" (Davies, 1987:157; McLeese & Malen, 1987) with "unusual authority" (Clark, 1979:36). Councils can consider virtually any school improvement issue, distribute discretionary funds, review personnel, assess programs, and develop action plans for their respective sites (Morgan, 1980; Thomas, 1980; Wakefield, 1983). The councils can make binding decisions as long as their decisions are consistent with federal and state statutes, general district policies, and accepted standards of ethical practice (Salt Lake City Board of Education, 1978, 1979, 1983–1984).

Parity Protections

Council participants are granted "equal vote" protections. Given the propensity for principal domination of councils' processes (Davies, 1980; Fisher, 1979; Foster, 1984; Mann, 1974) and, in some instances, principal–teacher domination of those processes (Berman, Weiler Associates, 1984; Foster, 1984; Ornstein, 1983), provisions that make principals, teachers, and parents "equal partners" with "equal power" have been identified as the single most important element of a shared governance policy (Clark, 1979:13). The parity clause of Salt Lake City's shared governance policy explicitly grants principals and teachers on the SICs and professionals and parents on the SCCs equal power through equal vote provisions.

Training Provisions

In this case, training has been provided. Both scholarly studies and critical commentaries of attempts to decentralize and democratize schools point to the importance of training as a means to "avoid past failures" (Fruchter, Silvestri, & Green, 1985:202). Many contend that educators and parents must receive training so that each can "define and demand their place in the professional–patron partnership" (Fruchter et al., 1985:202; see also Berman, Weiler Associates, 1984; Hall and Barnwell, 1982; McLaughlin & Shields, 1987; Moles, 1987).

While there is always some discrepancy between formal policy provisions and actual patterns of practice (Bardach, 1982; McLaughlin, 1987), there is also good reason to assume that the shared governance policy would enable teachers and parents to wield significant influence on significant issues. That, however, was not the case.

Unaltered Influence Relationships

Despite the seemingly favorable conditions, teachers and parents did not wield significant influence on significant issues at the building level. Descriptions of the subjects considered and the roles played by teachers and parents in those interactions illustrate that the conventional influence pattern was retained. Principals controlled building policies and procedures; teachers controlled the instructional component; and parents endorsed their efforts.

Subjects Considered

School councils rarely addressed the central subjects of education policy, namely budget, personnel, and program. Budget items might "get mentioned," but there was no evidence that councils discussed budget issues or allocated discretionary funds. Personnel topics surfaced primarily when the district mandated a reduction in work force or a teacher became the object of a complaint. There was no evidence, however, that councils were actively involved in the selection or evaluation of employees. Program issues received what informants termed scant, "superficial" attention. Discussions focused more on supplemental activities such as field trips and extracurricular activities than on required course offerings. They also focused more on program management (e.g., schedules, recess times) than on content. There was virtually no reference to discussions of course objectives, curriculum emphasis, or instructional outcomes in the data.

Moreover, councils rarely addressed subjects salient to teachers and parents. Both teachers and parents characterized topics as "innocuous," "petty" items. Teachers stated that they would like to discuss other topics, such as the academic program, teacher evaluation, teacher morale, and "how to get more democratic input without fear of retaliation." Parents reported that they would like to consider other issues, such as the role of the SCC, minority representation, curriculum, staffing, student discipline, needs assessments, parent training, and student tutoring. But these more salient subjects were not frequently introduced in council meetings.

Councils typically addressed a variety of subjects related to the operation of the school and the implementation of district directives, topics informants termed "routine . . . managerial . . . peripheral." For example, some SICs developed procedures for handling discipline problems and determined how a reduction of work force directives would be carried out. Some SCCs set parent conference times, organized fund-raising projects, made facility safety improvements, sponsored extracurricular activities, and in one instance considered how a reduction in work force directive would be handled.

Roles Assumed

Irrespective of the subjects considered, teachers and parents characterized their role as "listening," "advising," "endorsing the decisions others have already made." Their role was to "rubber stamp," to "take token action." These somewhat general depictions of the role teachers and parents assumed are made credible by the constancy of attributional data and the patterns that emerged from detailed descriptions of council processes at each stage of decisionmaking (Malen & Ogawa, 1985).

Informants maintained that, with rare exception, principals controlled the SICs and professionals controlled the SCCs. In describing SIC processes, virtually all informants reported that the agenda was "set by the principal." Items were "what the principal wishes to bring up." During discussions, teachers "just seem to accept the boss's opinion"; "take [the principal's] lead." When responses were solicited in council meetings, teachers said they "approve what the principal wants." Only two exceptions were noted. If the principal was fairly neutral on a topic, teachers could "get somewhere," and "make a difference." If the principal was eager to defuse an issue or, as principals put it, "take the heat off," teachers were able to "make the call." While informants termed these situations exceptions to principal control, the incidents reveal the extent of principal control in that teachers exerted influence only when the principal permitted them to do so.

In describing SCC processes, virtually all informants reported that agendas were set by the principal, or by the principal and teachers, who, in their informal interactions and separate SIC meetings, agreed on "what needs to be brought to the SCC." During discussions, parents tended to "listen to the principal." If a "sticky" issue surfaced, it was routinely "referred back to the SIC." When formal action was taken, teachers and parents alike contended that the decision conformed to "what the principal wants."

In sum, there was no evidence that teachers and parents were able to exert significant influence on significant issues on site-based governance councils. A review of the subjects considered and an analysis of the roles players assumed illustrates that the decisionmaking relationships typically and traditionally found in schools were not disturbed.

Intervening Factors

A number of factors intervened to offset the ability of teachers and parents to exert substantial influence even under what the existing literature suggests are highly favorable conditions.

Composition of Councils, Predispositions of Participants

Councils were, at least on major demographic dimensions, relatively homogeneous groups. Perhaps because council members had strikingly similar backgrounds, they held strikingly similar views of councils (Conway, 1985). Here, as elsewhere (Davies, 1978; Jennings, 1980), principals, teachers, and parents brought information–service orientations and expectations to the group.

The principals were all white, experienced administrators who, prior to assuming the principalship, had served as teachers or counselors in the district. They saw councils as channels for dispensing information, moderating criticism, and garnering support, not as arenas for redefining roles, sharing power, and making policy.

Teachers were predominantly white, experienced employees, who had spent the majority of their career years at the school or in the district. Few saw membership on school councils as an opportunity to alter school policies or pursue specific interests. Most joined the council to acquire information—that is, to "know what's going on around here," or to fulfill a service obligation—that is, to "take their turn"as a teacher representative on the council.

Parents were, with rare exception, white, middle-class, well-educated women. Most had compiled an extensive record of involvement in schools through employment as social workers, teachers, teacher aides, and teacher substitutes, and through service as "room mothers," Parent Teacher Association representatives, and SCC members at other schools. Council membership did not reflect the economic and ethnic diversity of the school's population. Teachers and parents concurred: "White is visible." "There are minority parents that come to our school all the time, but I guess they have never been brought into the SCC." "There are huge cultural gaps that people don't know how to cross." While a few parent members were concerned about a specific issue or sought to represent an ethnic group or a church viewpoint, most joined the councils because they wanted to "learn about the schools" and "be involved with my child's education."

While participant backgrounds and orientations shape interactions

(Conway, 1985), they do not fully account for them. Individuals who bring listen-and-learn, serve-and-support expectations to groups need not be bound to them. Sometimes the opportunity to participate focuses interests, fuels involvement, and precipitates issue-oriented activities that challenge as well as support existing authority relationships (Salisbury, 1980:95). That potential existed on the SICs and SCCs. Both teachers and parents identified concerns that they wanted to address but chose not to voice. Thus, the predispositions of participants constitute an important factor, but an incomplete explanation of the dynamics.

Positional Power Advantage of Principals and Professionals

While the participants' ability to wield influence is not inextricably linked to their position in the system, position can be important because it affects both the bases of power and the incentives for action. Principals on the SICs and professionals on the SCCs acquired a relative power advantage in large measure because they commanded impressive positional resources and were inclined to use those resources to protect the prerogatives associated with those positions.

Positional power advantage of principals on the SICs. By virtue of their formal position, principals possessed impressive power resources. Principals were perceived as the ones "in charge"; the ones who make assignments, allocate resources, supervise and evaluate employees; the ones who have considerable impact on the working conditions and the career advancements of teachers. Because of their position in the hierarchy, information regarding district directives, building activities and council proceedings went to and through the principals. As a result, this player was perceived as "the one who knows more."

Like principals in other settings (Wiles, 1974) and middle managers in other organizations (Bardach, 1982; Kanter, 1983), principals in this case were inclined to protect what they termed "administrative territory" and "administrative prerogatives." They were in a position to use low-cost strategies—routine activities—essentially to control council processes. For example, principals defined the agenda items, set the meeting times, and presented information on a number of varied topics. Since principals controlled the agenda content, meeting format, and information flow, they held the "supreme instrument of power," the definition of the issues and alternatives to be considered (Schattschneider, 1960:68).

To be sure, teachers also had impressive resources. In this case, they outnumbered principals on the SICs and possessed the option to augment this resource through the creation of ad hoc committees. Teachers had technical expertise, informal information networks, contractual protections, established grievance procedures, the formal assurance of parity in decisionmaking, and the formal right to appeal SIC decisions at the district level. But this impressive inventory of resources was not activated.

Teachers were reluctant to deploy these resources for several reasons. Part of their reluctance was rooted in respect for (or deference to) the principal's authority and expertise. Part of their reluctance reflected an appreciation of the complexity of school operations and the difficulty of the principal's position. The preponderance of their reluctance, however, stemmed from fear of sanction. The fear of sanction was apparent in general comments such as "people feel threatened" or "you can't pit yourself against your boss," and in recurrent concerns about "being labeled" as a "troublemaker." The fear of sanction was pronounced in poignant claims that "If the principal is caused discomfort, the person is made to feel liable. . . . Vindictiveness occurs . . . through innuendo, behind-the-back remarks that ruin your reputation and your chances for advancement." While informants did not provide concrete examples of reprisals, they were apparently constrained by the anticipation (if not the actual application) of them. Consistent with research in other schools and other organizations, the fear of being "known as a troublemaker or malcontent" (Duke, Showers, & Imber, 1981:345; Mann, 1974); the fear of being "cast into disfavor" (Bardach, 1982:123); the fear of "crossing the powerful figure" caused teachers to hold back and allowed principals to "maintain the familiar, rather than experiment with the unfamiliar patterns of decisionmaking" (Kanter, 1982:15).

Positional advantage of professionals on the SCCs. By virtue of their position as school employees, principals and teachers had direct knowledge of school activities and operations, full-time status, technical expertise, and a propensity to assume that most school issues fall "outside the expertise" or outside the jurisdiction of parents. Comments such as "parents need to let those who know do" and "parents shouldn't meddle" reflect adherence to conventional definitions of professional–patron roles and responsibilities. Comments such as parents might "stir up problems that don't really need to be addressed" and "the image of the school" is at stake reveal some of the reasons professionals used their resources to protect those conventional definitions of professional–patron roles and responsibilities.

Like principals and teachers in other settings, the professionals in this study agreed that "parents should not be involved in activities that promote or require power sharing" (Ornstein, 1983:30). Like principals and teacher in other settings, they used low-cost strategies—routine activities— to protect their professional autonomy (Berman, Weiler Associates, 1984; Davies, 1987; Foster, 1984; Gittell, 1968; Mann, 1974). Educators set the agendas. Meetings followed an "information down" and "definite end time" format. "Lots of reports" from the principal, the SIC, or the PTA left "little time for other things." As earlier noted, if a "sticky" issue surfaced, it could be readily contained by referring the matter back to the SIC, the professionals' decision arena. Since educators could set the topics, manage the time, disperse the information, and shift potentially contentious issues to more private arenas, they essentially controlled decision processes and ultimately controlled decision outcomes.

Parents did have some capacity to alter this dynamic. Parents were well educated, experienced council members. They had the formal right to raise a broad range of issues and insist on "equal power" in the resolution of those issues. They had the formal right to expand their representation through ad hoc committees and access to the well-established communication networks of the Mormon Church to do just that. Since ward and school boundaries are often coterminous, parents had the means to canvass and activate a significant number of patrons. There was potential to both persuade and pressure. But this potential was not activated.

Parents were reluctant to use their resources in part because they developed an understanding of and an appreciation for the professional educators. As parents said: "I got to know them . . . I have more respect . . . I am more tolerant." But parents were reticent primarily because they had liabilities that deterred them. First, they were unclear about the parameters of their power on the SCCs. As parents put it, "Nobody really knows what they are supposed to do"; "We're not really sure what we can do." As is the case on other site councils, this ambiguity redounded to the advantage of professionals (Davies, 1981; Jennings, 1980). Second, they were dependent on professionals for both information about school matters and the "invitation" to be involved at all. Parents were selected, for the most part, by the principal and the PTA. The parents' perception was they may not be "asked back" if they were seen as "a troublemaker." Such an arrangement frames participation as a gift to be given to parents, not a right to be exercised by parents and, operates, in Kanter's words, to keep "the giver in control" (1982:12).

The Strength of Engrained Norms

In some situations, norms can nullify policies. In this case, two norms—propriety on issues and civility in interactions—numbed the formal provisions of the shared governance policy. The propriety norm delineates who can legitimately deal with what issues. Although the shared governance policy stipulates that teachers and parents can be involved in many domains, including budget, personnel, and program, informal norms dictated that actors, in a sense, *own* particular domains. As previously noted, budget was seen as the administrator's domain; personnel and program matters were "off limits" for parents.

The civility norm shapes how individuals can interact. Participants were expected to be "pleasant," "harmonious," "agreeable," "civil." This norm operated to cast disagreements as personal affronts, as "pointing the finger." It operated to restrict discussion and suppress conflict. Dissenting views "would be "curbed," "cut off," "squelched." In this case, the norms of propriety on issues and civility in interactions converged to keep contentious issues off the agenda and keep traditional influence relationships intact.

The Nature of District Oversight and Support

School districts can increase the likelihood that policies will alter patterns of practice through steady and strategic blends of oversight and support (Elmore & McLaughlin, 1988). In this case, the district passed a promising policy; developed regulations regarding council meeting times, operating procedures, and membership selection; and sponsored some training for administrators, teachers, and parents. The district did provide oversight and support, but in a modest, intermittent fashion. During the period covered by this study, there was no evidence of district intervention in schools that did not hold regular council meetings, maintain printed agendas and minutes, or balance memberships along ethnic and economic criteria. Council members who had attended district-sponsored training sessions, as well as those who had not, frequently stated that additional training was needed in order for councils to do more than "create the illusion of input." Here, as in other settings, district oversight and support for school councils were present but inadequate (Jennings, 1980:38). Here, as in other settings, modest oversight and intermittent support diminished the ability of policy provisions to penetrate patterns of practice.

Congenial Culture, Stable Environment

The political culture of a community shapes patterns of participation in school decisionmaking (Davies, 1981; Boyd, 1976). Rooted in the tenets and traditions of the Mormon Church, Salt Lake City's political culture can be characterized as congenial. Citizen involvement in public affairs is expected and commended; but to be legitimate, involvement must be motivated by service, based on information, mindful of authority, and managed by consensus (Gottlieb & Wiley, 1984; Hrebenar, Cherry, & Greene, 1987). Even though the broader culture engenders respect for and allegiance to established authority relationships, here as elsewhere, environmental disturbances (e.g., enrollment shifts, fiscal shortages, flagging performance indicators) can trigger intense reactions, precipitating demands that challenge established authority relationships. During the period of this study, the environment was relatively stable. In this case, the congenial culture and stable environment reduced the likelihood that actors inside or outside the system would challenge existing arrangements (Cohen, 1978).

SUMMARY AND IMPLICATIONS

The Salt Lake City experience casts doubt on the viability of the decentralize–democratize approach to reform. Even though evidence from previous attempts to decentralize and democratize schools indicates that teachers and parents rarely wield significant influence on significant issues, there was reason to believe that the Salt Lake experience would be different. The district's shared governance policy addresses major barriers to teacher and parent influence in recommended ways. Thus the Salt Lake City experience represents an attempt to decentralize and democratize schools under highly favorable conditions. It constitutes a critical test in that, if shared decisionmaking arrangements are likely to work anywhere, they should have worked here. Yet, there was virtually no indication that teachers and parents exerted significant influence on significant issues at the building level. For a variety of reasons, the decisionmaking relationships typically and traditionally found in schools remained intact.

As a critical test, the Salt Lake experiment does not rule out the possibility that shared decisionmaking arrangements might work under different circumstances. Rather, it highlights the difficulty of creating arrangements that fundamentally alter decisionmaking relationships in schools and thus holds several important implications for proponents of the decentralize–democratize approach to reform.

First, the Salt Lake City experiment documents the need to refine our understanding of the conditions under which the decentralize–democratize approach to reform might fundamentally alter the decisionmaking relationships of principals, teachers, and parents. This study does not dismiss the importance of establishing structures at the site, granting them school-wide jurisdiction and formal policymaking authority, incorporating parity protections, and providing training programs. It simply demonstrates that, while these conditions may be necessary, they are certainly not sufficient to engender new patterns of decisionmaking. In this case, participants both expected and accepted decisionmaking roles that conformed to familiar definitions of professional–patron relationships.

Second, the Salt Lake City experiment suggests lines of research that might contribute to a clearer understanding of the conditions under which teachers and parents might be able to wield significant influence on significant issues. Several illustrations follow.

1. What is the relationship between the composition of the councils and the patterns of participation? Would changes in council membership make a difference? Councils in this case were homogeneous groups. Members did not, at least on demographic dimensions, mirror the diversity of the community. Members brought information–service expectations and thus imposed few focused demands on the system. Diversifying membership would certainly bring councils closer to the concept of representativeness. Would diversifying council membership significantly alter the decisionmaking dynamic? While some literature on these matters is available, (see, for example, McLaughlin & Shields, 1987), this case reinforces the need to address how membership can be diversified (how those "huge

cultural gaps" might be confronted) and how the composition of decision-making bodies affects the decisionmaking dynamic.

2. What resource configurations are required to balance the positional advantages held by particular players? In this case, principals held positional advantages on the SICs and professionals held positional advantages on the SCCs. Would a more robust redistribution of resources alter the bases of power and incentives for action? In this case, teachers and parents had concerns they wanted to address but chose not to voice. They had resources to mobilize but chose not to deploy them. Would different resource distribution schemes change those decision calculations?

Some argue that if teachers and/or parents were given additional resources, they would be able and eager to wield substantial influence on school policy. Additional resources might include the opportunity to determine the entire school budget, select and dismiss principals and/or teachers, waive district policies, and report proceedings directly to district board members rather than to school administrators (see, for example, Davies, 1987; Garms, Guthrie, & Pierce, 1978; Huguenin et al., 1979). Others contend the power equation can not be balanced unless parents are given consumer *choice* as well as consumer *voice* (Coons & Sugarman, 1978). Unfortunately, there is little empirical data regarding the effect of these various resource configurations on influence relationships in school systems.

3. Given the strength of ingrained norms and the importance of oversight and support, what strategies do reformers need to steadily apply so that changes can be installed and sustained in schools? The literature provides general guidance. For example, scholars suggest that continuous and intensive "norm-based training" would alter the orientations and actions of professionals and patrons (McLaughlin & Shields, 1987). They contend that various combinations of mandates and inducements, oversight and support do enhance the ability of formal policy provisions to permeate patterns of practice (McLaughlin, 1987). But the literature has yet to specify the amounts and kinds of training, the particular blends of oversight and support required to alter the decisionmaking relationships typically and traditionally found in schools.

4. What is the relationship between environmental factors and reform success? Can reformers create favorable opportunity structures, or must they wait for the environment to provide the window of opportunity? In this case, the environment was, on major indicators, a congenial and stable environment. Can schools be decentralized and democratized in this context, or must reformers wait for the environment to generate issues that precipitate or provoke challenges to existing arrangements?

Finally, the Salt Lake City experience reminds reformers that the relationship between structural arrangements and patterned activities is tentative at best. For that reason, the relationship between reform overtures and reform effects can not be taken for granted. The promises and prospects for reform must be guided and gauged by the empirical evidence as well as the ideological appeal. However compelling the call to decentralize and democratize public schools may be, the viability of this approach to reform is in question. The Salt Lake City experience and the evidence of previous experiments suggest that decentralizing and democratizing schools is exceptionally difficult. Empirical investigations that refine our understanding of the conditions under which teachers and parents can wield significant influence on significant issues, empirical investigations that clarify the relationship between various structural revisions and professional–patron influence relationships are needed in order for this second wave of reform to produce results that are fundamentally different from those of previous efforts to decentralize and democratize the public shools.

NOTES

1. The Salt Lake Study was conducted in two phases. The first produced a general profile of all site councils in the district (Malen, Ogawa, Kranz, Mannion, & Steinagel, 1985). The second produced detailed descriptions of site-council processes at eight schools (four elementary, two intermediate and two secondary). Case narratives for each site were developed, then aggregated in a comparative case account (Malen & Ogawa, 1985). Data for the case studies were acquired from in-depth interviews with administrators (10), faculty and staff (48) and parents (43), printed documents and faculty surveys. Data collection and analysis procedures, including steps taken to check for bias and error in the research process, are described elsewhere (Malen & Ogawa, 1988). Unless otherwise designated, quotations are the comments and statements of informants.

2. This perspective is elaborated in Malen and Ogawa (1988).

REFERENCES

Bardach, E. (1982). *The implementation game.* Cambridge, MA: MIT Press.

Barth, R. S. (1988). Principals, teachers, and school leadership. *Phi Delta Kappan, 69*(9), 639–642.

Bastian, A., Fruchter, N., Gittell, M., Greer, C., & Haskins, K. (1987, February 4). Rethinking the agenda for democratic schooling. *Education Week,* 28, 32.

Berman, Weiler Associates. (1984, April). *Improving school improvement: A policy evaluation of the California school improvement program.* Berkeley, CA.

Boyd, W. L. (1976). Community status and conflict in suburban school politics. *Sage Professional Papers in American Politics, 3.* Beverly Hills, CA: Sage.

Boyd, W. L., & Shea, D. W. (1975). Theoretical perspectives on school district decentralization. *Education and Urban Society, 7*, 357–377.

Caldwell, B. J. (1987, March 26–28). *Educational reform through school-site management: An international perspective on the decentralization of budgeting.* Presented at the 1987 conference of the American Education Finance Association, Arlington, VA.

Clark, T. A. (1979). *Improving school site management: A framework for citizen involvement.* Trenton, NJ: School Watch, Inc.

Cohen, D. K. (1978). Reforming school politics. *Harvard Educational Review, 48*(4), 429–447.

Conway, J. M. (1984). The myth, mystery, and mastery of participative decision making in education. *Educational Administration Quarterly, 21*, 11–40.

Conway, M. M. (1985). *Political participation in the United States.* Washington, DC: Congressional Quarterly Press.

Coons, J. E., & Sugarman, S.D. (1978). *Education by choice: The case for family control.* Berkeley: University of California Press.

Davies, D. (1978) *Sharing the power? A report on the status of school councils in the 1970's.* Boston: Institute for Responsive Education.

Davies, D. (1980). School administrators and advisory councils: Partnership or shotgun marriage? *NASSP Bulletin, 64*(432), 62–66.

Davies, D. (1981). Citizen participation in decision making in the schools. In D. Davies (Ed.), *Communities and their schools* (pp. 83–120). New York: McGraw-Hill.

Davies, D. (1987). Parent involvement in the public schools. *Education and Urban Society, 19*(2), 147–163.

Duke, D. L., Showers, B. K., & Imber, M. (1981). Studying shared decision making in schools. In S. B. Bacharach (Ed.), *Organizational behavior in schools and school districts* (pp. 245–276). New York: Praeger.

Elmore, R. F., & McLaughlin, M. W. (1988). *Steady work.* Santa Monica, CA: Rand.

Fisher, A. (1979). Advisory committees: Does anybody want their advice? *Educational Leadership, 37*(3), 254–255.

Foster, K. (1984, March). School partners or handy puppets? *Principal, 27*, 31.

Fruchter, N., Silvestri, K. L., & Green, H. (1985). Public policy in public schools: A training program for parents. *Urban Education, 20*, 199–203.

Gamson, W. A. (1968). *Power and discontent.* Homewood, IL: Dorsey Press.

Garms, W. I., Guthrie, J. W., & Pierce, L. C. (1978). *School finance: The economics and politics of public education.* Englewood Cliffs, NJ: Prentice-Hall.

Gittell, M. (1968). *Participants and participation.* New York: Praeger.

Goodlad, J. I. (1984). *A place called school.* New York: McGraw-Hill.

Gottlieb, R., & Wiley, P. (1984). *America's saints.* New York: G. P. Putnam's Sons.

Guthrie, J. W. (1986). School-based management: The next needed education reform. *Phi Delta Kappan, 68*(4), 305–309.

Guthrie, J. W., & Reed, R. J. (1986). *Educational administration and policy: Effective leadership for American education.* Englewood Cliffs, NJ: Prentice-Hall.

Hall, B., Jr., & Barnwell, E. I. (1982, March). Working with community advisory councils: Key to success in urban schools. *Phi Delta Kappan*, 491–492.

Hrebenar, R. J., Cherry, M., & Greene, K. (1987). Utah: Church and corporate power in the nation's most conservative state. In R. J. Hrebenar & C. S.

Thomas (Eds.), *Interest group politics in the American West* (pp. 113–122). Salt Lake City: University of Utah Press.

Huguenin, K., Zerchykov, R., & Davies, D. (1979). *Narrowing the gap between intent and practice: A report to policymakers on community organizations and school decisionmaking.* Boston: Institute for Responsive Education.

Jennings, R. E. (1980). School advisory councils in America: Frustration and failure. In G. Baron (Ed.), *The politics of school government* (pp. 23–51). New York: Pergamon Press.

Kanter, R. M. (1982). Dilemmas of managing participation. *Organizational Dynamics, 11,* 5–27.

Kanter, R. M. (1983). *Change masters.* New York: Simon & Schuster.

Kirst, M. W. (1984). *Who controls our schools?* New York: W. H. Freeman.

Lieberman, A. (1988). Expanding the leadership team. *Educational Leadership, 45*(5), 4–8.

Maeroff, G. I. (1988). A blueprint for empowering teachers. *Phi Delta Kappan, 69*(7), 472–477.

Malen, B., & Ogawa, R. T. (1985). *The implementation of the Salt Lake City School District's shared governance policy: A study of school-site councils.* Prepared for the Salt Lake City School District.

Malen, B., & Ogawa, R. T. (1988). Professional–patron influence on site-based governance councils: A confounding case study. *Education Evaluation and Policy Analysis.*

Malen, B., Ogawa, R. T., Kranz, J., Mannion, L., & Steinagel, D. (1985). *Salt Lake school district shared governance project interim report.* Prepared for the Salt Lake City School District.

Mann, D. (1974). Political representation and urban school advisory councils. *Teachers College Record, 75*(3), 279–307.

Massarik, F. (1983). *Participative management.* New York: Pergamon Press.

Mazzoni, T. L. (1986). *The choice issue in state school reform: The Minnesota experience.* Prepared for American Educational Research Association Annual Conference.

McLaughlin, M. W. (1987). Learning from experience: Lessons from policy implementation. *Educational Evaluation and Policy Analysis, 9,* 171–178.

McLaughlin, M. W., & Shields, P. M. (1987). Involving low-income parents in the schools: A role for policy? *Phi Delta Kappan, 69*(2), 156–160.

McLeese, P., & Malen, B. (1987). *Site based governance: The Salt Lake City experience 1970–1985.* Prepared for the American Educational Research Association Annual Conference.

Moles, O. C. (1987). Who wants parent involvement? Interest, skills, and opportunities among parents and educators. *Education and Urban Society, 19*(2), 137–145.

Morgan, S. (1980). Shared governance: A concept for public schools. *NAASP Bulletin, 64,* 29.

National Governors' Association. (1986). *Time for results: The governors' 1991 report on education.* Washington, DC.

Olson, L. (1987). Dade ventures self-governance. *Education Week, 7*(13), 1, 18–19.

Ornstein, A. C. (1983). Redefining parent and community involvement. *Journal of Research and Development in Education, 16*(4), 37–45.

Patton, M. Q. (1980). *Qualitative evaluation methods.* Beverly Hills, CA: Sage.

Rogers, D. (1968). *110 Livingston Street*. New York: Random House.

Salisbury, R. H. (1980). *Citizen participation in the public schools*. Lexington, MA: D. C. Heath.

Salt Lake City Board of Education (1978). *Minutes of the Salt Lake City Board of Education* (May 16, 1978). Exhibit 5h.

Salt Lake City Board of Education (1979, July). *Policy manual: A written agreement based on shared governance*. Section 1.8; Articles 8-2-1, 8-2-2.

Salt Lake City Board of Education (1983–84). *Plan for educational excellence*.

Schattschneider, E. E. (1960). *The semi-sovereign people*. New York: Holt, Rinehart & Winston.

Shields, P. M., & McLaughlin, M. W. (1986). Parent involvement in compensatory education programs. *Center for Educational Research at Stanford, 87*(6).

Steinberg, L. S. (1979). The changing role of parent groups in educational decision making. In R. S. Brandt (Ed.). *Partners, parents and schools* (pp. 46–57). Association for Supervision and Curriculum Development.

Thomas, M. D. (1980). Parent participation in education. *NASSP Bulletin, 64*, 1–3.

Tucker, M. S. (1988). Peter Drucker, knowledge, work, and the structure of schools. *Educational Leadership, 45*(5), 42–43.

Wakefield, R. (1983). *Shared governance: Active cooperation for a more effective organization: Training manual* (2nd ed.). Salt Lake City, UT: Salt Lake City School District.

Wiles, D. K. (1974). Community participation demands and local school response in the urban environment. *Education and Urban Society, 6*(4), 451–468.

Wise, A. E. (1988). The two conflicting trends in school reform: Legislated learning revisited. *Phi Delta Kappan, 69*(5), 328–333.

Wissler, D. F., & Ortiz, F. I. (1986). The decentralization process of school systems: A review of the literature. *Education and Urban Society, 21*, 280–294.

UNIT THREE

Defining Good Education: A Political Battleground with Too Many Casualties

*In Unit Two, we saw how there are many interest groups at many
social and governmental levels, all of which are to some extent vying
to define and control the education reform movement. In this unit we
explore the first of those two goals—defining a good education. We
see that defining a good education is a values-based*, intensely political *process.*

*Before we examine the recent results of that political process, it
makes sense to ask whether we are even asking the right question.
Doyle (Chapter 10) makes a very convincing case that* what we
teach our children in school does matter. *He suggests that the
move toward so-called value-neutral or value-free curricula is essentially a fraud. He speaks of the "invisible curricula" determined by
the moral choices that students observe their teachers make.*

*Why did the notion of a value-free education arise? Perhaps it
was because of the need to reconcile the various interest groups' demands for an education that did* not conflict with their basic values. *Perhaps the only way that this genuine cultural diversity could
be successfully accommodated was to remove any reference to values
at all. However, that does not discredit Doyle's argument that* values are an integral part of the process itself.

*Cuban (Chapter 11) puts this in historical perspective, claiming
that for over a hundred years, the pendulum in U.S. public education has swung between various reform movements as the predominant coalition of underlying values has changed. This debate is often
described as the* equity versus excellence argument. *How are*
U.S. public schools to educate large numbers of "children of different
abilities, social classes, religions, and racial and ethnic groups" (Cuban, p. 135)? Should all students be exposed to the same curriculum,
or should curricula be fitted to the different needs of various minorities and socioeconomic classes?*

*The common elementary school and the comprehensive high
school can thus be seen as the structural framework resulting from
many decades of political struggle. The system is set up to offer the
basic core curriculum to all students in the early years, but then to*

offer the prospect of special-needs courses to students of different backgrounds, interests, abilities, and futures. Although there has been a move back to the basics in high school, Cuban claims that few have questioned the compromise itself as a way of reconciling competing values.

Metz (Chapter 12) agrees with this, making explicit the reform movement's assumption that all schools are basically alike. She implies that as long as reform is basically one-size-fits-all, some students will be unaffected (or negatively affected) by reform. For example, the first wave of reform (raising and enforcing tougher standards for all) did not affect the top students, who were already performing above the minimum level, nor did it affect the bottom students, who were probably only encouraged to drop out. Although it was implemented at all comprehensive schools, it was aimed at only a slice of students in the middle.

Another assumption that Metz illuminates is that schools are defined by their homogeneous structure and technology, rather than by their very heterogeneous culture. She uses a powerful theatrical metaphor to show how a kind of cultural tyranny of the majority prevents some students from achieving their potential. Interestingly enough, she mentions the controversy over whether "culturally different groups are better served by stern insistence that they abandon their own culture and accept majority culture or by instruction which attempts to provide a bridge between their home and school cultures." This is a perfect manifestation of the equity-versus-excellence argument.

Her third assumption is that adults determine what happens in schools. Although it is true that adults have the final authority, Metz points out that the degree of cooperation that students give is crucial to the outcome. If the system has been set up in a way that students feel doesn't benefit them, they will opt out, doing only the minimum they need to in order to get through school and out into the "real world." Metz also points out that schools are not in fact separate from their communities, and the social expectations that students bring to school can have a powerful impact on their willingness to work. If Juan expects a life as a picker, why would he bother to study algebra or American literature?

Apple (Chapter 13) picks up this thread with a general discussion of the political and economic context of the current reform movement. He sees the current political alliance between big business and the New Right as resulting in a two-peaked economy, with education being defined according to its economic value. Industrializing the schools is seen as necessary in order for the United States to be economically competitive, even if this means that "those on the bottom will find their schooling even more directly linked to the low-waged, nonunionized, and largely futureless sector of the labor market" (Apple, p. 161).

Monk and Haller (Chapter 14) worry that in their zeal to "industrialize" the schools for greater equity and efficiency (economies of scale), state bureaucrats are unfairly favoring large consolidated school districts over small rural ones. Recent research casts significant doubt on the conventional wisdom that larger school districts are inherently superior to smaller ones. There seem to be significant trade-offs involved in the switch to consolidated school districts. For example, kids seem to socialize better in smaller schools, where they feel less depersonalized and institutionalized. And might not the unique needs of small communities be getting lost in the drive for ever-larger "units of accountability"? In effect, when a system consolidates, it loses some of the flexibility needed to respond equitably to different communities' needs.

In both rural and urban America, this overall bias away from equity and toward excellence is perceived by Medina (Chapter 15) as antagonistic to Hispanic interests. He suggests that the Immigration Reform Act, the English-only movement, and budgetary cutbacks in native-language instruction have combined to create what Hispanics perceive as "an unfavorable national mood toward them." Since efforts to reform practices of segregation and tracking have been ended in favor of across-the-board standards to promote excellence, the Hispanic dropout rate is staying very high.

In summary, defining educational goals is a very political process. Because the reform movement began as an economic crisis was announced (A Nation at Risk) during a conservative resurgence, the alliance of powerful industrial groups and the New Right was able to engineer a large swing of the pendulum away from the value of equity in education toward the value of excellence in education. This has acted to restrict the benefits of reform to specific groups of students who are "ripe" (that is, those who are easiest to affect, rather than those most in need of help). Unfortunately, economically disadvantaged groups and members of minorities have been the ones "favored" for the bottom tier of the two-tier economy that Apple so starkly portrays. In that context, the title of Medina's chapter ("Hispanic Apartheid") is particularly thought-provoking.

10

Does It Matter
What We Teach
Our Children?

Education and Values:
Study, Practice, Example
DENIS P. DOYLE

W HEN I WAS invited to join you for this auspicious occasion,
I was asked to return to my own work to find a quote that would illustrate
the theme of my presentation. Eight years ago this fall I wrote an article
for the *College Board Review* titled "Education and Values: A Consideration."
If anything, it is more apt today:

> Since ancient times, philosophers and scholars have known that values
> and education are indissolubly bound together. Their connection was
> so obvious and important that it was virtually impossible to imagine
> value-free education. Even if education did not transmit values explicitly
> and self-consciously, it did so implicitly and by example. Can anyone
> remember a distinguished teacher or philosopher, ancient or modern,
> who was morally neutral?[1]

As a people we have come to understand that no nation that ignores
values in education can hope to endure. No democracy that neglects values
and education can expect to remain free. The reasons, though they should
be obvious, bear repeating.

The American experiment in self-government is now two centuries old. Indeed, we are not only the oldest democracy in the world; we have an unbroken tradition of self-government marked by a long history of enlarging the franchise. When our experiment began, only white men of property could vote; today all citizens over 18 may do so. They may do so because we are convinced that all adults can responsibly exercise the franchise. They may do so if they are educated.

Philosophically, the reason for including values in education is clear enough: A democracy committed to the twin principles of equality and liberty must have an educated citizenry if it is to function effectively. By *educated* I mean not just people with a knowledge of basic skills, but people who are liberally educated. In this connection it is worth remembering the purpose of a liberal education: It is to suit men and women to lead lives of ordered liberty. It is the embodiment of the Jeffersonian vision of a free and equal people.

Such observations, of course, would hardly surprise the Founders. To them civic virtue was the *sine qua non* of a democratic republic, and it was in some large measure imparted by the formal institutions of society, among them schools. Indeed, without such norms, civilization itself is unimaginable. Born naked, ignorant, and full of appetites, each child must learn the facts and values of the culture anew. It is no surprise that formal schooling plays a major role in that process. Schooling and civic virtue cannot be separated.

In place of the hereditary aristocracy of the Old World, the New World, according to Thomas Jefferson, would witness the emergence of a natural aristocracy of talent. In a great democracy, as all men are equal before God and the law, so too are all men free to develop their talents to the fullest. This elegant and radical idea survives to this day, and for its full development, the people of a democracy must be educated. As Lord Brougham said, "Education makes a people easy to lead, but difficult to drive; easy to govern, but impossible to enslave."[2]

The ancient Greeks, from whom we inherit our intellectual and educational traditions, knew that there was one purpose for education and one only: to fit man to live in the *polis*. And the key to life in the *polis* is values, "civic virtue"; without it the *polis*, the state itself, would flounder. They had the insight to know how one acquires civic virtue. Their threefold lesson is as true today as it was then. It is study, example, and practice.

First, values are acquired by study, knowledge acquired didactically. Teachers teach and students learn. Study requires submission to the discipline of learning. Second, values are acquired by example. Virtuous men and women by example communicate values to the young and to their fellows. Third, and perhaps most important, values are acquired by practice. Virtue is acquired by behaving virtuously.

Long before the excellence movement there were two broad schools of thought in such matters. One is the vision of school as agent of the state, familiar enough to any one who cares to peer beyond the iron curtain. John Stuart Mill, who was spared the excesses of modern totalitarian and authoritarian regimes, thought that no other objective could characterize government schooling. Government education, whether the dominant power be a priesthood, monarchy, or majority of the existing generation, is "a mere contrivance for moulding people to be exactly like one another: and as the mould in which it casts them is that which pleases the predominant power in the government . . . it establishes a despotism over the mind. . . ."[3]

By way of contrast there is the perspective of a supporter of government as the instrument of civic virtue, Simon Bolivar. Addressing the Congress of Angostura, he solemnly observed: "Let us give to our republic a fourth power with authority over the youth, the hearts of men. . . . Let us establish this Areopagus to watch over the education of the children . . . to purify whatever may be corrupt in the republic. . . ."[4]

There is, however, a less extreme way to think about education and civic virtue in a democracy. How should a free people inculcate those values and attitudes essential to public welfare, domestic tranquillity, and the pursuit of happiness? How can order and freedom be reconciled? The task, while not easy, is not impossible. And the American experience of the past century and one-half with public education—or the education of the public—is instructive.

What are the values of civic virtue? First, explicit knowledge, mastered to the point of habit, about the rights and responsibilities of citizenship, and the opportunities and obligations imposed by a constitutional republic. It is knowing, as sociologist Morris Janowitz observed, that the corollary of the right to trial by jury is the obligation to serve on a jury when called. It is knowing that one man's freedom ends where another's begins. It is knowing that rights are earned and must be protected if they are to survive. It is knowing that Supreme Court Justice Oliver Wendell Holmes was right when he observed that "taxes are what we pay for civilized society."[5]

What is it our public schools should do to teach values? What must children acquire to make them virtuous citizens? Let me look first at example, then study, then practice.

The most striking example of citizenship in all of history was offered by Socrates. He accepted the hemlock cup not because he believed himself guilty of corrupting the youth of Athens, but to demonstrate the supremacy of law. His wisdom and his courage are captured by John Ruskin in words that contain the essence of my point: "Education does not mean teaching people what they do not know. . . . It is a painful, continual, and difficult work to be done by kindness, by watching, by warning, by precept, and by praise, but above all—by example."[6]

As a practical matter, this means that our schools must be staffed by moral men and women who care about their calling and their craft. By the pure force of personality they must communicate their sense of commitment to their students. There is no mystery as to who these people are. They are the teachers we each remember, the teachers who made a difference in our own lives. The problem is not identifying them after the fact, but before the fact. They are the teachers who are connected to their disciplinary traditions, who are broadly and deeply educated, and who believe in the life of the mind.

These are not empty homilies. There is an internal dynamic to study and scholarship, and there are canons of the profession that themselves embody the values of a democratic society. They include honesty, fidelity, accuracy, fairness, tolerance for diversity, flexibility, and a willingness to change when new evidence is presented. Indeed, what we expect of our better teachers is precisely the set of traits that we associate with civic virtue.

Another name I use to describe this cluster of attributes and the outcomes they help foster is *the invisible curriculum.* It is the message sent by teachers to students about what is right and what is wrong, what is acceptable and what is not. A school, for example, that sets low standards sends a powerful message: Nothing much matters, get by. That is a dangerous message to give a young person because it programs him for failure. The invisible curriculum undergirds and reinforces the student's visible curriculum.

It has become fashionable in certain circles to think that education is a *process*, a set of skills divorced from their substantive context. That is not true. Education is contextual. It is a substantive experience which requires, among other things, learning about the great documents of citizenship. At a minimum these include an acquaintance with Aristotle's *Politics and Ethics*, Plato's *Republic*, the Magna Carta, *The Prince* by Machiavelli, *An Essay Concerning Human Understanding* by John Locke, the Declaration of Independence, the Tenth *Federalist Paper*, the United States Constitution, John Stuart Mill's *On Liberty*, the Gettysburg Address, Lincoln's Second Inaugural Address, and Martin Luther King's "Letter from Birmingham Jail." Education is an empty concept if it is stripped of the values these documents embody. As King reminds us, "Freedom is never voluntarily given by the oppressor; it must be demanded by the oppressed."[7] This is first and foremost a normative statement, a statement of values.

To be fully educated, the student must master a body of knowledge, fact, myth, history, anecdote, not as an exercise in memory, but as an exercise in understanding and critical thought. History and context are important to education both for themselves and as the instrumentality by which people learn to think and to reason. It is simple but true: People learn to think by thinking and thinking hard. That is the essence of the Socratic dialogue, the most enduring and important teaching technique ever devised.

Think of the centerpiece of the Fifth Amendment as simply a phrase to be recapitulated without an understanding of its underlying meaning:

"nor shall be compelled in any criminal case to be a witness against himself." Without an understanding of its purpose and its historical context, it is truly nonsense. Why should a suspected criminal not have to testify against himself? Protecting all of us from testifying against ourselves emerged from a long and bitter history of the rack and thumb screw—if a man may be compelled to testify against himself, who is to say no to the torturer? Certainly not the victim. Freedom from self-incrimination is no more and no less than freedom from the Inquisitor and the tools of his trade. It is a strange thing in a century so convulsed by violence of every kind that this simple truth is frequently overlooked when people "take the Fifth." It may be the single most important protection a free people enjoy.

In exploring the idea of values and education we must remember that values are a part of our world that is not scientifically derived. They include such human but unscientific attributes as love, loyalty, courage, devotion, piety, and compassion. These attributes give dimension, scope, and meaning to being human. It is precisely with these attributes that great literature concerns itself.

Let me draw upon a particularly telling and appropriate example, Mark Twain's *Huckleberry Finn*, published more than a century ago. It is arguably the greatest American novel, a book of such importance that no American who has not read it can be considered educated. What makes this book important? Its scope and sweep, certainly, but above all, its values. In shape it is a book for the masses. Like the Bible or the *Iliad* it tells a universal story, accessible to all. Just as it contains much with which to agree, it contains much that shocks, provokes, and even offends. As a consequence, reading the book and discussing it in a classroom require sensitivity and discretion. It is not a book to be taken lightly.

It is interesting that the book is attacked today just as it was when first released. The far right believes Huck is venal at best, and hostile to religion at worst. They say his language is abominable, his behavior unacceptable. In sum, he is a poor example. The left is even more outspoken in its hostility to Huck. They level against him the worst of modern epithets: racist.

I will stipulate to this: Twain's purpose was to subvert the state, undermine the morals of the young, and challenge the smugness and complacency of the American *haute bourgeoisie*. To this accusation I plead Twain guilty. And this is precisely the power of the book: to confront the conventional wisdom. Twain railed against the organized religion of the day and its sanctimonious piety and hypocrisy. Indeed, he found organized society, particularly the state, the cause rather than the cure for social ills. Huck and Jim, children of nature, could escape the corrupting forces of contemporary life only by physical escape.

So far as we can tell, Twain really believed that society was a sentence and the only hope was escape. The development of this idea in *Huckleberry Finn* is the best known of Twain's repeated efforts to deal with it. If this interpretation of Twain is correct, as I believe it to be, he is far more dangerous than either the left or right wings know. He is an enemy of the state.

Whether or not he should be read by callow youths, then, becomes a question with meaning. The direction assumed by other great works across the ages is the same. While the first purpose is to entertain, the more important purpose is to instruct. Such literature is almost never the servant of the state nor the advocate of the status quo.

Jean DuBuffet, champion of *l'art brut*, the raw or unschooled art, in a splendid twist on Plato asserted that art was subversive, that the state should attempt to suppress it, and that the artist worked best and most effectively when he was disdained by the prevailing culture. That is, in fact, a rather exaggerated version of my hypothesis here. Suffice it to say that the artist should question, at a minimum, the conventional wisdom and make the *bourgeoisie* uncomfortable.

Without dwelling on Twain, it is useful to consider great literature in general to see if the example is idiosyncratic. Are there common threads? The direction assumed by great literature across the ages is the same. While its first purpose is to entertain, its more important purpose is to instruct. It provides examples of courage, strength, and love. It shows the effects of hubris, greed, and the will to power. It reveals transcendent accomplishment and abject failure. Such literature is almost never the servant of the state or the advocate of the status quo. Great literature challenges assumptions, it breaks with the conventional wisdom.

Not all great books are offensive, or irreverent, or hostile to the state, but they challenge the conventional wisdom, they provoke the reader, they insist upon engagement with the subject. This is even true of science, particularly in its early stages when it is concerned with breakthroughs in basic knowledge. Galileo, Kepler, and Darwin are only the best known examples.

The controversial nature of a work, then, is a product of its power and authenticity, and it is for this reason that the inexperienced reader will frequently find the great book difficult—it is often very tough sledding. It is tough sledding because it raises fundamental questions about right and wrong. For the inquiring mind, it induces an interior Socratic dialogue.

At issue in the teaching of values is an error of judgment that continues to plague our schools. An assumption was made, in all good faith, that our schools could be value-free, neutral, and objective; this would defuse the potentially explosive question of which values to teach and how to teach them. This vision of American education is an old one.

In the nineteenth century, what was described as value-free education was really nonsectarian Protestantism. It was not quite ecumenism, but a robust Unitarianism. Indeed, it is no accident that the early public school reformers were visionary and romantic Unitarians, builders who would use the public schools to uplift and transform each generation. As Horace

Mann, with a striking sense of modernity, said in his *Annual Report to the Board of Education* in 1848: "If all the children in the community from the age of four to that of seventeen could be brought within the reformatory and elevating influence of good schools, the dark host of private vices and public crimes . . . might . . . be banished from the world."[8]

When it came to values education, Mann, as well as his supporters and colleagues, had little problem identifying what schools should do. They knew that most teachers were poorly trained, and they were the inheritors of a classical tradition that brooked little interference. In essence, the curriculum chose itself. So it was in the late nineteenth century that the McGuffey *Reader* enjoyed unparalleled success. It was full of pious homilies and entreaties to civic and religious virtues, the values widely shared by the community that patronized the public schools. In the nineteenth century, the patrons were almost exclusively white Protestants. The emergence of a highly diverse, democratic, and pluralistic modern society means that we can no longer rely on either the classical curriculum or the Protestant consensus of the nineteenth century.

In an attenuated way this disciplinary tradition does exist in the best public and private college preparatory schools. In these institutions, for example, teachers are free to choose Dryden or Donne, Spencer or Marlowe, Shakespeare or Cervantes, Twain or Hawthorne—but the freedom to choose is nearly ephemeral, because the educated person, the student, must eventually read all of them.

What has happened in American education, of course, is the virtual abandonment of the disciplinary tradition. Instead of vertical integration, elementary and secondary schools are organized horizontally. They are not only characterized by self-contained classrooms, they are self-contained organizations with few links to the outside world. Great bands of children are grouped by age, and they are given "problem areas" to study. Communications skills replace English, social studies replaces history and geography; is it any surprise that bachelor living and power volleyball enter the curriculum? Is it any wonder that there are periodic attempts to purge Huck Finn from the classroom? With no intellectual and disciplinary anchor, the school is subject to the fads and vicissitudes of the moment. When the watchwords of the school become "value neutrality," "relevance," and "relativity," anything goes.

Nothing is imposed on anyone, except the notion that there are two sides to every question. The philosophy of the ancient Greeks and the great revealed religions, both based on moral absolutes, no longer provide answers. Not even the existential answer that teachers know more than students can be offered with conviction. It is for these reasons that the disciplinary tradition is essential.

Let me turn briefly to my final point: *practice.* "Happiness," Aristotle tells us, "is activity of the soul in accord with perfect virtue."[9] We achieve this state by practice. Ironically, it is not so much in the exercise of our rights that we learn this, but in meeting our corresponding obligations. It is through submission to a higher principle that we learn to appreciate the importance of our hard-won rights.

At the level of friend and family, *practice* means satisfying the reciprocal demands that loyalty and filial responsibility place upon us. At the level of the community, it means meeting minimum standards of civility and good conduct. More than just obeying the law, it means accommodation to unspoken standards of behavior. At the level of the state, it means honoring the full and explicit demands of citizenship, from honesty in paying taxes, to citizen participation, to the ultimate sacrifice for a higher good in time of mortal danger.

At the level of the school, *practice* means doing what is expected and doing it well. But it could and should mean much more. It could and should mean *service*, both to the school and to the community. Although an old idea in private education, service is just now being taken seriously in the public sector.

The North Carolina School of Science and Mathematics, one of the nation's only public boarding schools, enrolls some of the best and brightest youngsters in North Carolina. There is a special graduation requirement that says no student may graduate without performing three hours a week of school service and four hours a week of community service. Students fron NCSSM spend time in nursing homes, orphanages, day care centers, and hospitals. And they do so week in and week out.

Every high school student in the United States should be expected to perform community service as a condition of graduation. No one is so poor or so elevated as to not profit from it, for that is surely its purpose. The help these young people provide, while important, is the least of what they do. What is really important is that they are learning through practice the habits of service. That is the very foundation of civic virtue and the personal satisfaction it can provide.

What this means, of course, is that we cannot avoid the question of curriculum. What we teach we value, and what we value we teach. The curriculum, both visible and invisible, is value-laden. What is it we need to know as Americans, to have both a shared sense of community and a shared destiny?

At the same time, we need the support, solace, and integrity of the smaller, organic communities of which we are naturally a part. No one can be a member of a "family" of 240 million people. We can be citizens, and owe obligations and expect rights to flow from this larger body politic, but the kinds of association that most of us find deeply satisfying flow from smaller units of organizations.

Any curriculum—particularly a "core" curriculum—must reconcile the demands of a continental democracy and the need to belong to a more intimate community. It must reflect the values of the whole and the part, respecting both while supporting the individual.

The need is acute because in the final analysis "excellence" in any endeavor is a solitary pursuit, requiring self-discipline and commitment. Excellence also assumes many forms—music, art, the quantitative disciplines, languages, and the humanities. And over the life of a student the pursuit of excellence calls for progressively greater specialization and more complete immersion in the peculiarities of a given discipline.

This is not to say that a core curriculum cannot coexist with specialization: It can. It is just more difficult to pull it off successfully. And this raises the most important question of all. If curriculum is central and values are central to the curriculum, who will choose, and of what will the curriculum consist? If it is chosen by the wise and judicious, the penetrating and the discerning, the discriminating and the disciplined—in short, by you and me—the curriculum will be a wonder to behold.

But if it is chosen by the ideologues of the left or right, the Babbitts and buffoons of American intellectual life, it will be a disaster. The fear of the latter is a real one, as anyone who has read Frances FitzGerald's study of U.S. history texts must admit. Anti-intellectualism in the United States is an old, powerful, and even honored tradition, and it is not at all clear that the excellence movement will, even over the long haul, change that.

Lurking beneath the surface of any discussion about the quality of American education is the nagging suspicion that we already have the schools that we both want and deserve. We do have citizen control; we do have a voice in what our schools do and how they do it, however attenuated it may be. Perhaps, after all is said and done, Americans prefer football to the life of the mind. That, after all, is what values are all about.

The life of the school, then, is defined by what is taught, and the life of the student is defined by what is learned.

What has this to do with education and values? A good deal, I think, because we are what we value, and schools cannot escape this simple truth. And at the heart of the excellence movement—if indeed it has a heart— lies the conviction that it makes a difference what children are taught and what they learn.

In conclusion, let me offer the quintessential and timeless expression of values and education that is carved in stone on the B'nai B'rith headquarters in Washington, D.C. The words never cease to move me. "The world stands on three foundations: study, work, and benevolence."

NOTES

This chapter was originally an address prepared for the Angelo State University 1988 University Symposium—"American Values and the Challenges in Education," October 31, 1988, and is reprinted with permission of the author.

1. Denis P. Doyle, "Education and Values: A Consideration," *The College Board Review*, No. 118 (Winter 1980–1981), 17.

2. Lord Brougham, in a speech to the House of Commons, 1828, quoted in Bergen Evans, *Dictionary of Quotations* (New York: Bonanza Books, 1967), 193.

3. Quoted in Charles Leslie Glenn, Jr., *The Myth of the Common School* (Amherst: University of Massachusetts Press, 1988), 12.

4. Quoted in Denis P. Doyle, *Debating National Education Policy: The Question of Standards* (Washington, D.C.: American Enterprise Institute, 1981), 36.

5. Oliver Wendell Holmes, *Campania de Tabacos* v. *Collector*, 275 U.S. 87, 100 (1904).

6. Quoted in Doyle, *Debating National Education Policy*, p. 49.

7. "Letter from Birmingham Jail."

8. Quoted in Glenn, *Myth of the Common School*, p. 168.

9. *The Ethics.*

11

Cycles of History: Equity versus Excellence

Why Do Some Reforms Persist?
LARRY CUBAN

CERTAIN EDUCATIONAL REFORMS have been adopted over and over again to solve particular problems in schools. We can draw three conclusions from this phenomenon. First, since a solution should end a problem, and these reforms have been used again and again, they have failed to remove the problems they were intended to solve. Second, the problems defined as important were either not the problems that needed to be solved and the solutions (reforms) were inappropriate, or the solutions were designed to correct different problems than the ones identified. In short, the problems and solutions are mismatched. Third, perhaps the problems were instead persistent dilemmas involving hard choices between conflicting values. Such choices seldom get resolved but rather get managed; that is, compromises are struck until the dilemmas reappear. I will explore these three statements.

The current passion among states for a traditional education, one in which every student studies a core of academic subjects, is one example of a recurring solution dating back over a century. It is a solution to the problem of how to balance societal values of excellence and equity in tax-supported public schools enrolling children of different abilities, social classes, religions, and racial and ethnic groups.

Requiring academic core subjects does not solve a problem but rather is a compromise to a fundamental dilemma in American schools over conflicting values of excellence and equity in providing an equal education to all children. Solutions are supposed to end problems; however, conflicts over values (dilemmas) produce compromises that are struck and restruck over time.

The situations defined as problems in the arena of public policy are really value conflicts that surface frequently as school issues get dealt with as a series of reforms in structures, rules, staffing, and programs (i.e., solutions), and then disappear from view—for a while. The conflict in values reappears when larger social, political, and economic issues call attention to the school's role in wrestling with these prized but competing values. Hence, there is constancy in reform and repeated efforts to restrike a political consensus over these societal values. When a consensus is reached at the rhetorical level, however, it often breaks down at the level of making policy decisions about programs and allocating resources.

The conflicting values of excellence and equity, proxies for this culture's fundamental values of individual success and group interests, have been dealt with separately, redefined, and combined over the last century and a half to cope with the highly charged emotions and national goals connected to these values. No consensus on which of these values is more or less important or how they can be incorporated easily into public policies involving schools has produced lasting compromises in curricular policymaking. Curricular changes come and go.

Finally, these periodic curricular reforms, inevitably responding to larger socioeconomic and political issues over the last century, have been accommodations to this conflict of highly prized values. A brief description of these compromises would help.

In the mid-nineteenth century, when the idea of tax-supported public schools had become widespread, the prevailing opinion was that all students should be exposed to the same curriculum—the common school. The concept of equality mandated that the conditions of schooling be the same for all. Equity and access to schooling was the ideal, although certain groups of students were excluded in these years. In the post–Civil War decades, however, urban schools, especially high schools, responded to ballooning numbers of students drawn from many social classes and ethnic groups by expanding the numbers of available courses. High schools made erratic and unsystematic efforts to differentiate the content and instruction of classes to match the differences in students. The patchwork quilt of course offerings in grammar and high schools made it correspondingly difficult for colleges and universities to make admissions decisions.

In 1893, the report of the Committee of Ten on Secondary School Studies (sponsored by the National Education Association) recommended for all high schools an academic core of four years of English, three years of history, science, mathematics, and a foreign language. Chaired by Harvard President Charles Eliot, the committee urged that: "Every subject which is taught at all in a secondary school should be taught in the same way and to the same extent to every pupil as long as he pursues it, no matter what the probable destination of the pupil may be, or at what point his education is to cease" (in Krug, 1961, p. 87).

By the time of the First World War, the Committee of Ten's goal to reduce the variety of courses and standardize both the time allotted to a subject and the teaching method had been fulfilled; its recommendations were mainstream practice. What was once good for those going on to college was now defined as good for all. During the same period, however, another generation of reformers—opposed to Eliot and like-minded reformers—sought to resurrect from earlier decades the multiple courses of study tailored to different needs of students, since such variety was more in keeping with their definition of democracy and equal education (Cremin, 1961; Krug, 1964).

In 1918, another national report (also sponsored by the National Education Association), *The Cardinal Principles of Secondary Education*, set forth another generation's manifesto challenging the concept of a single best curriculum for all students. Progressives saw varied curricula designed for different futures as a way for secondary schools to concentrate attention on fulfilling each student's potential while preparing that student for his or her probable niche in society. Elementary schools continued to provide the same curriculum to all students.

Over the next three decades, the gospel of secondary school progressives produced the comprehensive high school with varied curricula for students headed toward diverse futures. Vocational education, college preparatory courses, business classes, and other curricula expanded the familiar academics of earlier years (Krug, 1964; Powell, Farrar, & Cohen, 1985).

By the early 1950s, the earlier solution of varied curricula that had replaced the single academic course of study became the target for even another generation of reformers who saw anti-intellectual flabbiness and a diminished concern for excellence in nonacademic high school courses. Arthur Bestor's *Educational Wastelands: The Retreat from Learning in Our Public Schools* (1953) and Albert Lynd's *Quackery in the Public Schools* (1953), for example, blasted the low academic standards and the quality of teaching in high schools. Seldom were blasts directed at elementary schools, however, where the common core curriculum persisted.

With evidence of the Soviet Union's technological gains orbiting the earth in 1957, further barrages of criticism accelerated concern for the mindlessness of so many high school courses. Generated by fears for national security, federal legislation (the National Education Defense Act, 1958), James Bryce Conant's report on high schools (1959), and new academic programs spilled over schools. More and more high schools raised academic standards by increasing the number of courses in math, science, and foreign languages. Advanced placement courses were established. Subsidized by foundations and federal funds, academics constructed new curricula based upon the nature of the disciplines and how scientists practiced biology, physics, math, and the social sciences. Few of these attacks, however, questioned seriously the previous solution—the comprehensive high school itself—as being inappropriate (Conant, 1959).

But by the mid-1960s and later, political and social movements aimed at freeing the individual from bureaucratic constraints and helping the poor, especially ethnic and racial minorities, swept across schools. If desegregation, compensatory education, and magnet schools became familiar phrases, so did free schools, open classrooms, and flexible scheduling. Many (but not all) of the previous decade's academic reforms evaporated by the early 1970's, as efforts redoubled to differentiate courses and schools to accommodate low-income and minority children with little access to academic curricula. Special programs, alternative schools, and new curricula dotted the urban and suburban school landscape in efforts to recapture students who had been either relegated to the margins of a high school education or pushed out. Concern for access and equal treatment led to further differentiation in curricula (Powell et al., 1985, pp.281–300; Ravitch, 1983, pp.228–266).

By the late 1970s and early 1980s, a renewed call for a core academic curricula in high schools available to all students had again surfaced. *A Nation at Risk* (1983), written by the National Commission on Excellence in Education, urged readers to demand higher academic standards and a common curriculum of their schools. State after state raised its graduation requirements, and more and more students took chemistry, geometry, and foreign languages; fewer students registered for vocational courses. Mortimer Adler's *Paideia Proposal* (1982) renewed discussion of the Great Books curriculum, and calls for a return to traditional curricula have marked the early to mid-1980s' debate on the reform of schooling. In California, a pacesetter among the states in raising graduation requirements of core academic subjects, voters responded warmly to State Superintendent Bill Honig's message for traditional schooling. A graduate of an academically selective San Francisco high school, Honig (1985) said: "A traditional education worked for us; why shouldn't we give at least as good a shot at the common culture to today's children"(p. 55).

For almost a century, this enduring debate over whether all students should take one academic curriculum or varied ones has shuttled back and forth between proponents of different versions of what an "equal education" means in a democracy. The values of equity and excellence, each defined in numerous ways, are entangled in any definition of an equal education. The invention of the comprehensive high school in the first quarter of this century fashioned a workable compromise that both the lay public and professional educators endorsed. But the compromise could not prevent national fears about foreign and domestic policies from penetrating the schools. Each time this debate occurred, administrators and specialists created new courses of study and curriculum guides. New texts appeared.

These changes, however, were again refashioned compromises between competing values of excellence and equity, between the interests of the individual and those of the larger group.

The shifting high school curriculum since the mid-nineteenth century (with many fewer shifts at elementary level) reveals the competing values embedded in the common school curriculum, compared to the differentiated courses of study a generation later, subsequently modified by a partial return to the core academic subjects under the Committee of Ten in the mid-1890s. And so it went through the twentieth century as well. The comprehensive high school, a political and educational compromise, has adapted to the external pressures seeking to restrike the original compromise over a half century ago. These repeated efforts to come to grips with the external demands for the school to serve conflicting values only mirror inherent tensions in the larger culture.

In the 1980s, the debate has been renewed. Calls for excellence have been translated into higher graduation requirements, more homework, a longer school year, and the drive to raise test scores—to make everyone above average. And changes have again occurred. The comprehensive high school again tilts toward the excellence side of the debate, but the institution itself persists as a compromise. Yet the current concern in the big cities for huge percentages of students who leave school early is both a familiar theme over the last century and an early signal for another major effort to adjust the comprehensive high school to the competing values.

Of what policy use is this answer to the initial question that I posed: Why do so many reforms repeatedly appear as solutions to school problems? I have argued that what appear as solutions (e.g., tougher graduation requirements) are really tactical moves to ease political tensions over the role of schools in meeting two competing values. The basic political compromise was worked out in the early decades of this century, that is, the elementary school as the traditional home for a common curriculum and the comprehensive high school as a place offering varied courses of study to deal with the high percentages of students staying on to graduation—rising from one in five to three of every four students nationally. This compromise has successfully managed the hard choices embedded in the dilemma of conflicting values. No solutions here, but important accommodations. Thus knowing the difference between a problem that can be solved and a dilemma presenting difficult choices can help both policymakers and practitioners avoid the excesses of a can-do pragmatism that so frequently leads to ill-defined educational problems and mismatched solutions posing as school reforms.

Of equal importance to policymakers is the clear understanding that the comprehensive high school itself is a durable compromise to this dilemma that has worked. By "worked" I mean that the institution has produced the highest percentages of public school graduates in the world and has managed to accommodate each successive wave of reform energies directed at both equity and excellence. The solution of the comprehensive high school has persisted, I believe, because it contains the ideology, structures, and minimum resources to embrace competing values.

Whether it will continue depends upon a clear understanding of the differences between problems and dilemmas, between solutions and compromises. The present generation of state and federal policymakers active in the reform movement has accepted the historic compromise and wishes to make existing schools lean more to their preferences for what they call excellence. Few, if any, have questioned the very compromise itself. Perhaps the time has come to seriously examine the available alternatives that can compete with the comprehensive high school as a workable way of accommodating tensions between competing values.[1]

NOTE

1. For other interpretations of the origins, development, and consequences of the comprehensive high school and the periodic shifts in public and professional attention to such matters, see James and Tyack (1983) and Cohen and Neufeld (1981).

REFERENCES

Adler, M. (1982). *The Paideia proposal.* New York: Macmillan.

Bestor, A. (1953). *Educational wastelands: The retreat from learning in our schools.* Urbana: University of Illinois Press.

Cohen, D., & Neufeld, B. (1981). The failure of high schools and the progress of education. *Daedalus.*

Conant, J. (1959). *The American high school today.* New York: McGraw-Hill.

Cremin, L. (1961). *The transformation of the school.* New York: Vintage.

Honig, B. (1985). *Last chance for our children.* Reading, MA: Addison-Wesley.

James, T., & Tyack, D. (1983, February). Learning from past efforts to reform the high school. *Phi Delta Kappan,* pp.400–406.

Krug, E. (Ed.). (1961). *Charles W. Eliot and popular education.* New York: Columbia University, Teachers College.

Krug, E. (1964). *The shaping of the American high school.* New York: Harper & Row.

Lynd, A. (1953). *Quackery in the public schools.* Boston: Little, Brown.

National Commission on Excellence in Education. (1983). *A nation at risk: The imperative for educational reform.* Washington, DC: U.S. Department of Education.

Powell, A., Farrar, E., & Cohen, D. (1985). *The shopping mall high school.* Boston: Houghton Mifflin.

Ravitch, D. (1983). *The troubled crusade.* New York: Basic Books.

12

Hidden Assumptions
Preventing Real Reform

Some Missing Elements in the
Educational Reform Movement
MARY HAYWOOD METZ

THIS CHAPTER ANALYZES the educational reform movement as it applies to high schools. It makes explicit what appear to be some unrecognized assumptions that narrow the movement's vision; it considers the sources and consequences of those assumptions and suggests a broader vision. Though the diffuse chorus of voices in the movement makes it difficult to speak of the "reform movement," even when limited to high schools, I will nonetheless address the movement as a whole.

Recently, analysts have been speaking of a first and second wave of reform. The first stresses standardization of curriculum and centralized testing of both students and teachers. It is typified in the report of the National Commission on Excellence (1983), in other discussions of improving and nationalizing school curricula, and in many district and state initiatives to standardize curricula, to institute competency tests, and to increase standardized testing. The second wave, especially in high school reform, stresses upgrading teacher education and restructuring teachers' roles to make them more professional—more collegial, less tied to the classroom, and more inclusive of career stages. It is typified in the report of the Carnegie Forum's Task Force on Teaching as a Profession (1986) and in widespread discussion of "restructuring the high school" that emphasizes staff roles. While both waves of reform share the assumptions analyzed here, there are some relevant differences between them.

In this analysis, I have considered the reform movement in tandem with a study that I have been conducting as part of the work of the National Center on Effective Secondary Schools.[1] This study deals with teachers' working lives at eight "ordinary" high schools in socially diverse settings. My perspective as a sociologist of education with a background of qualitative studies of schools has also informed the argument.

KEY ASSUMPTIONS IN THE REFORM MOVEMENT

Assumption: A School Is a School

The reform movement makes an overarching assumption that schools are much more alike than they are different. They can consequently be reformed with across-the-board policies. The garment of reform comes in one size that will fit all. This assumption is less extreme in the second wave reforms. Here, though restructuring the staffs of high schools is a single change that will improve all schools, that restructuring is suggested in a form that will give increased autonomy to teachers, who can then adjust their behavior to deal with variations in the context and in students.

American educational discourse has long assumed that a school is a school and a student is a student, all fundamentally alike. This attitude reflects our national image of public schools as all essentially the same, a national ritual experience that provides us a common background. It is consonant with our cherished tenet that all American children start out on the same footing, to become differentiated only as they display differential talent and effort.

At the same time, as I will argue in more detail later, everyone knows that schools differ significantly; most are located in communities where housing is homogeneous in class and race, and school boundaries are drawn to encourage homogeneity. Human and material resources are thus highly variable in our "standard" schools. Consequently, across-the-board reforms will have different consequences in different settings. For example, a combination of reasoning and early data suggests that when states increase the number of academic courses required for graduation, affluent communities where students aspire to selective colleges are little affected because their requirements were already that high or higher, while poor areas are likely to experience increased dropout rates because many students do not, or fear they do not, have the skills or the time to accomplish the required work (McDill, Natriello, & Pallas, 1986). It is in the middle-level, average communities that the intended effects will most likely be seen. Schools in these areas will in fact have to raise their requirements, and large numbers of students with the skills but not the desire to take such courses may be pushed into more effort and perhaps into more learning. However, in every context, individual schools may differ from the norm, transforming the impact of the state requirement as they reinterpret it and fit it into the total context of their school—or as enterprising staff shape it to their purposes (Clune, 1987).

Since reformers know that schools really do differ despite the claim that they are formally alike, we can anticipate that recommended reforms will be implicitly targeted toward schools serving one kind of student or another. Reformers pushing increased graduation requirements probably have foremost in their minds average and above-average students heading for skilled and semiskilled work or for colleges with relaxed admissions policies. At the risk of overgeneralizing, it may be fair to say that the first wave of reform is targeted primarily at such average to slightly above-average students, while the second wave is targeted primarily at leading students—though the reports of both waves claim that their recommendations will equally benefit all students.

There are some important dimensions of school life that the reform movement neglects because of its assumption that all schools are alike. By acknowledging these dimensions of school life, a third wave of reform can be based on a more accurate model of the phenomenon it wishes to change. Considering these dimensions would also help a third wave of reform address the schools in the most trouble, those serving predominantly poor and minority children. With one-fourth of our children growing up in poverty and one-third members of minority groups, we cannot afford to consider the education of such children a side issue. Their schooling is the schooling of a substantial portion of the next generation of adults.

Assumption: Structure and Technology Define the Schools

In the last two years, while doing a study that I intended to be policy relevant, I found myself repeatedly presented with a conflict between the confident assumption of the reformers that they could speak easily of the needs of, and reform in, "the American high school" and what I knew about schools from literature in sociology and anthropology, my own previous work, and what we were seeing during our study of eight high schools. I came to see that the reformers' discourse centers on two organizational aspects of schools—their social structure and their technical arrangements. At the same time, our research team was noticing that social structure and technical arrangements were indeed remarkably similar, at least in outline, from school to school.

All of our high schools had similar temporal structures of six to nine class hours, similar "egg crate" physical layouts in which one teacher met with 20 to 30 students for one class hour, five days a week for a year,[2] similar subject offerings with similar scope and curricular sequence, and even the same textbooks, despite radically different academic skills in the student body. Teachers' and administrators' duties and their role descriptions varied little across schools. Rules for students were also similar, though not similarly obeyed or enforced. In short, in the formal elements of social, physical, and temporal structure and in the official curriculum, the schools were alike, just as reformers saw them to be.

The reform movement assumes that these formal characteristics of schools are their most important, defining characteristics. We saw that they form a frame for interaction or provide a script for the play we came to call Real School. All the schools used the same script, but the actors in the different performances at the different schools rendered widely divergent interpretations of both their own characters and the overall meaning of the play. They also freely improvised on their lines and changed their entrances and exits to suit their desires. Nonetheless, all of the school staffs and most of the students found it important to dramatize the legitimacy of the school by following the script for Real School.

The temporal, physical, and social structures and the curricular practices that constitute Real School had varied meaning and, consequently, varied impact on teaching and learning and on the overall experience of both staff and students at the different schools. While social structures might be the same, cultural meanings were different.[3]

Academic learning differed. We often saw the "same" course, such as British literature, American history, or physics, taught at schools in widely differing communities. Students at two schools might, for example, read *Macbeth* and work with it five days a week for two or three weeks in a group of 20 or 30 students with the help of one teacher, but the content of classroom discourse, the questions asked on tests, and students' written work might vary enormously. Similarly, the relationship between the students and the teacher was sometimes radically different in classes that were formally "the same" at different schools, giving the students different messages about how they, as learners and budding citizens, related to the public institution of the school.

The reform movement treats these variations as epiphenomena (insignificant variations around a single theme) or as deviance (the compromise of a valid template for good education). We thought they could be better interpreted as attempts to adjust to significant cultural variation among communities and students (Metz, 1987). But they were incomplete adjustments, and often academically unsuccessful ones, greatly constrained by the structures and expectations associated with Real School.

During the last 20 years, anthropologists of education have built up a sizable literature documenting significant impacts of cultural differences between various groups of ethnic minority students and the mainstream public schools. Some schools have worked successfully with culturally different minorities, some by teaching in their own cultural idiom, and some without making such adjustments (Erickson, 1987). There is also— much more scattered—evidence that there are significant cultural differences among whites according to class, ethnicity, region, and rural-urban differences (e.g., Heath, 1983; Peshkin, 1987; Rubin, 1972).

There is active and legitimate controversy over whether culturally different groups are better served by stern insistence that they abandon their own culture and accept majority culture or by instruction that attempts to provide a bridge between their home and school cultures. However, the reform movement does not join this controversy and scarcely acknowledges that cultural differences with educational implications exist.

In our eight schools, teachers rarely explicitly acknowledged cultural differences—even though they made some pragmatic adjustments for them. Instead, school staffs stayed as close to their own idea of a national curriculum and pattern of relationships as the students would allow. At our middle- and low-income schools, acting out the forms of Real School sometimes became an end in itself, leaving little energy for anything else. The problem was most visible at Charles Drew High School, which had the most economically deprived, lowest-achieving students—black students from a deeply isolated ghetto. An energetic principal seemed torn between efforts, on the one hand, to relax adherence to the rituals of Real School because elements of these rituals alienated or discouraged many students, and efforts, on the other hand, to promote aggressively a demanding academic curriculum that followed and even surpassed the curricular requirements of a Real School. This attempt both to adjust to the students and to maintain a nationally approved pattern resulted in offering courses and using books that resembled those at the high-income schools in our study, while the discourse, the tests, the written work, student attendance, and the general atmosphere at this school were radically different.

The first wave of reform would suggest a firmer enforcement of the rituals of Real School to improve such situations. Its proponents would push for more testing, publishing test scores, stiff academic requirements for graduation, a more detailed centrally prescribed curriculum, and perhaps writing final examinations at the central office. Some of these first-wave prescriptions—for example, the requirement of advanced academic courses for graduation and the publication of test scores—are already in place at this school, but they have had no dramatic impact on its problems. The second wave of reform would suggest a new faculty with more liberal arts training at more cosmopolitan institutions and more time away from students to plan curriculum. These nostrums do not touch the fact that the behavioral and academic rituals of Real School seem to connect poorly with these students.

A third wave of reform should start from the overarching purpose of school to help students develop their full intellectual potential in their own and their parents' terms, while also providing them with academic skills, with an understanding of mainstream culture, and with the ability to participate in it. It would then be possible to cast a critical eye upon Real School, inquiring whether some or all of its patterns are indeed appropriate and constructive for educating particular groups of students. It would be possible to consider and experiment with innovative patterns of curriculum and daily activity that might provide intentional bridges between students' culture and mainstream learning and organizational patterns.

These are thorny issues. Where mainstream culture differs from that of ethnic minorities, rural white communities, or working-class enclaves, one must consider the relative legitimacy of each as a context for the curricular content and relational style of public school education. These considerations lead to fundamental questions concerning what constitutes legitimate school knowledge and what constitutes acceptable school decorum. These issues are too complex to explore in this article, but a third wave of reform should confront them.

Assumption: Adults Determine What Happens in Schools

The reform movement's statements have very little to say about students but much to say about curriculum and staffing. The first and second waves of reform view the appropriate role of teachers in radically different ways, but both assume that reforming teachers' roles and the quality of their performance can reform the schools' performance. This position likewise assumes that students are passive agents who will learn, if only they are taught. Control in the school lies (or should lie) solely with adults.

In practice, teachers must adjust their teaching to a multitude of characteristics of their students. The whole point of teaching—and of schools—is to create changes in the students. We must consider what students are like when they enter the school to determine the appropriate process of change. American students come to high school with a wide variety of academic skills, general knowledge, attitudes, cognitive styles, cultural beliefs, and ambitions. Schools and classroom teachers who take no account of each of these factors are likely to be unsuccessful in creating the changes they plan.

It is always true, as Chester Barnard (1938/1962) pointed out 50 years ago, that authority in formal organizations, of which schools are one example, exists only when subordinates grant their superordinates a legitimate claim upon their obedience, when they "decide to participate" in the organizational system at hand, with its moral claims upon them. (Even though students are legally required to be physically present, they can withhold social participation—and some high school students do.) Even after they decide to participate, subordinates still scrutinize commands from above for consistency with the system of moral claims that support superiors' superordination and for consistency with agreed-upon terms of effort.

Barnard's insight may attract little notice in those schools where students accept parental and community beliefs that the school has a right to expect their obedience to a broad range of commands from school staff. Students' "decision to participate" as subordinates becomes more visibly problematic when they have lost faith in the school and its personnel as an agency that will assist them to prepare for adult life, when they are skeptical of many of the school staff's claims, and when they do not share the values, life experiences, or style of expression that shape teachers' efforts. By now there is a good deal of evidence that such conditions are widespread, not only among minorities (Erickson, 1987; Ogbu, 1987), but among large proportions of majority students, especially those headed for the work force or for less selective colleges after high school (Cusick, 1983; McNeil, 1986; Powell, Farrar, & Cohen, 1985; Sedlak, Wheeler, Pullin, & Cusick, 1986; Sizer, 1984).

At five of our eight schools, the majority of students acted skeptical or otherwise expressed a gulf between the school and themselves. A few students acted this way at the other three schools as well. The three schools that were exceptions were two public and one Catholic school with mostly middle- to upper-middle-class students. Most were headed for college and many for at least somewhat selective colleges.

The teachers we talked with were intuitively aware that their own successes were contingent on students' cooperation and performance. Some were very articulate about that fact. Teachers' efforts and their sense of worth as craftspersons were deeply shaped by the ease or difficulty with which they could win their students' interest in and cooperation with the learning task.

In this situation, it is not sensible for the reform movement to regulate or change training for teachers without helping them increase students' engagement. Even upgrading the skills of teachers will not help, unless such upgrading includes teaching them how to develop methods that take their students' life experience, purposes, and perspectives into account. The first wave of reform responds to students' reluctance to make academic efforts primarily by increasing coercive requirements. Parts of the second wave of reform acknowledge a need to fit schools to community desires and perspectives and to make school tasks more complex and intrinsically interesting, but the second wave still passes lightly over the question of how to bring about these envisioned changes and how to make them attractive to the reportedly 70 percent of students who have lost faith in both the content and the credential of a high school education.

In my previous work, studying desegregated, socially diverse junior high and middle schools (Metz, 1978, 1986), I found that many aspects of children's social and racial backgrounds affect their own behavior and also the perceptions and actions of their teachers. It was also evident in these studies, however, that students' social classes and racial backgrounds were by no means the whole story. At least at the middle school level, curricular approaches, social structures, and cultures developed within the schools could create conditions that went far to counterbalance students' initial readiness or lack of readiness to be cooperative and enthusiastic about school, based on their life situation outside of school (Metz, 1986). Schools are powerfully influenced by the characteristics of their clienteles, but these pressures are not irresistible.

As the reform movement develops, it should address the students' point of view head on. It should analyze the perspectives and prospects of the full range of high school students and consider how to design—or enable and empower school staffs to design—forms of high school education that students in differing life circumstances will find credible, interesting, and helpful for their futures. At the same time, these must still constitute high school educations that the mainstream of society will consider legitimate and socially useful.

Assumption: Schools Are Separate from Their Communities

By paying little attention to differences between schools serving children from different backgrounds, the reform movement assumes that the school's life can be separated from the social context and life trajectories of students outside the schools. But this is a questionable assumption. At the high school level, not only students' backgrounds, but their assessments of their future prospects affect their response to their schools. High school points students toward occupational slots. A few voices (Sedlak et al., 1986) suggest that lack of engagement in school, not only among poor students, but also among middle-income students not headed for selective colleges, is more a function of the lack of relevance or fatefulness of high school performance for their futures than of processes within the schools themselves. Anthropologist John Ogbu (1978) has long argued that minority students who see older relatives, even those with diplomas, chronically unemployed will not make an effort in school as a means to earn a place in the work force.

In our study, teachers were also affected by their anticipation of their students' futures. They often framed answers to questions about their goals in teaching in terms of what they perceived to be their students' destinations. Where those futures were limited and students unconcerned with school, teachers also were at risk of becoming demoralized. At Ulysses S. Grant, a racially mixed low-income school, the secretary to the career counselor summed up staff attitudes when I asked her for the list of destinations for the last year's seniors. She replied, "Our students aren't going anywhere" (but then produced a list of their anticipated destinations).

To ignore the impact of anticipated unemployment or marginally skilled employment upon the attitudes and activities of both students and teachers is to ignore a major reality of school life. If reformers are to help schools where students' backgrounds and futures give them little reason to be interested in school, they must acknowledge the nature and the difficulty of the task such schools face in creating an internal life that attempts to counteract children's social experience on the outside.

Reformers of a third wave who want to improve educational processes within the schools must not only look for ways to insulate the schools from discouraging outside influences, but they must also work to improve the living conditions and future prospects that sap these children's educational commitment. Reformers who argue that schools affect the economy should acknowledge the impact on the schools of economic circumstances in students' homes and communities and of the contracting economic opportunities available to the half of graduates not planning to attend four-year colleges.

SOURCES AND CONSEQUENCES OF THE REFORM MOVEMENT'S ASSUMPTIONS

Why should the reform movement cling to the assumptions I have enumerated? One reason seems to be relatively straightforward. The reform movement is aimed at concrete changes in the formal policy of states, school districts, and teacher training institutions. But managerial intervention will not easily resolve all the complexities I have discussed. Because of its orientation to formal policymaking, the reform movement limits itself to issues that are subject to direct policy manipulation.

While such a stance is understandable, the policy changes it recommends will not succeed if they are based on simple assumptions that ignore processes of perhaps critical importance, even though they are not under the control of educational policymakers. The second wave of reform makes some effort to address this problem by advocating reforms that give teachers in each school considerable flexibility for varied practice. They can then respond to the processes I have discussed in ways that are not legislated.

The reform movement is not only administratively oriented but politically oriented as well. The reports that formed its initial impetus and its manifestos were political rallying cries, designed to enlist popular attention and resources for education. As political statements, they had to take account of political realities. Differences in quality among schools according to social class are well known but still politically explosive in two rather different ways.

The poor, and especially minorities, often suspect that statements that emphasize differences in schools according to their social class or racial composition implicitly condemn their children's intellectual abilities or moral worth. If the reform movement suggests plans to diversify educational strategies in schools serving different clienteles, some citizens might read these plans as proposals for a second-class education for poorer or minority children, something less than Real School. Nor is such a fear illusory. It is not easy to design school programs that are tailored to students' backgrounds while still leading students to knowledge and credentials that give them full access to mainstream culture and economic opportunities. Reformers cautiously stick to the safer ground of proposing reforms across the board, lest they be accused of making invidious distinctions between children on the basis of class or color.

The second political agenda to which these reports respond requires a more complex analysis and is potentially far more subversive of any real educational improvement. Like most public discourse on education, these reports assume that schools are to teach the young the content of the curriculum and some of the social graces required to be a member in good standing of a school community. But education plays another very important role for society in preparing the young to enter into adult roles. It sorts the group of babies born in any year, looking very much alike in their hospital cribs, into groups of 18-year-olds labeled as barely employable, possessing moderate skill, capable of much further development, or showing extreme promise. The public schools rank the students who emerge from their doors after 13 years in ways that are decisive for those young people's work, their economic fortunes, and their status among other members of society.

Imagine what would happen if some year the reports' apparent goals were suddenly actually accomplished. All the graduates of all of the high schools in the country were successfully educated, so that all of them scored in the 99th percentile on standardized tests and made perfect scores on the Scholastic Aptitude Test,[4] not to mention having perfect A grades throughout their schooling.

Chaos would ensue. Colleges would not have room for everyone but would have little basis for accepting some and rejecting others. Employers looking for secretaries, retail salespersons, waiters, bus drivers, and factory workers would have jobs unfilled as every student considered such work beneath his or her accomplishments.

As long as education is used to rank young people and sort them into occupational futures that differ substantially in their attractiveness and intrinsic as well as monetary rewards, good education, or students' success at education, must remain a scarce commodity. Those who do succeed have less competition to deal with if large numbers of others do not.

In the United States, we say we do not believe in passing privilege from parent to child. We expect individuals to earn the favored slots in society through talent and hard work. The schools have been given the task of judging that talent and diligence. Consequently, it is important to our national sense of a justly ordered social system that all children have an equal opportunity through education. If we are to say that success in education is a fair and just criterion by which to award each child a slot in an adult occupational hierarchy based upon individual merit, then the poorest child must have access to as good an education as the richest.

How, then, to guarantee an equal education? By guaranteeing the *same* education. The reform movement speaks of high schools as all alike because it is important to our political sense of fairness that they *be* all alike. The similar social structures and the near standardization of curricula across high schools give a skeletal reality to that claim. The reform reports reflect a strong public consensus on the importance of offering a standard high school experience to all American children.

Nonetheless, there is unspoken public knowledge of an opposing principle in operation. In practice, the public perceives schools as actually very *un*equal. Middle-class parents will make considerable sacrifices to enroll their children in schools perceived to be superior. Communities of parents with the economic and political means to do so will construct superior schools for their own children and see to it that others are denied access to them.

This process is such an open secret that, in communities large enough to have several schools, realtors advertise houses according to their school attendance area when those houses are located close to schools with a reputation for high quality—usually because they draw a large number of children from well-educated or affluent families. Houses in such neighborhoods can cost thousands of dollars more than equivalent structures in neighborhoods with less reputable schools.

Separate suburban school districts allow residents far more control in creating superior schools. Ordinances requiring certain sizes for lots or specifying single occupancy housing can keep out lower-income families. Fair Housing groups across the country document the continued practice of racial steering by real estate agents to keep many suburban communities all or mostly white. These districts can also take advantage of their higher tax base to add the amenities of higher salaries for teachers, small class sizes, and richer stores of materials to their "standard" schools.

As a political entity, Americans live with this contradiction between officially equal education based on standardized curriculum and activities, on the one hand and, on the other, tremendous variety in the quality and content of public education because it is linked to local funding and to housing that is segregated by social class as well as race. We rarely see, let alone openly acknowledge, the contradiction between these two principles. Political scientist Murray Edelman (1977) argues that simultaneous acceptance of such contradictory perspectives is a common feature of our political life.

Society's blindness to this contradiction serves the interests of the well-educated middle class. Children in schools with better prepared peers and better prepared teachers have a considerable advantage when competing with other students from America's standard and equal public schools. But middle-class leaders feel no inconsistency in claiming that the young are rewarded according to merit even though they take care to place their own children in schools that foster merit much more actively than those to which other children find themselves consigned. Our blindness to these contradictory perceptions of American schools allows large segments of society to perceive as fair a "race" for societal rewards in which competitors are given unequal resources depending on their parents' status.

The reform movement's implicit endorsement of the official view of public schools as all alike and its near silence about the tremendous variations in American schools endorses and reinforces the continuance of this contradiction in American education.

CONCLUSION

I believe the reform movement is correct in perceiving serious problems in a large proportion of public schools. My critique of its solutions stems from a perspective based on prolonged contact with individual schools and from a grounding in sociological and anthropological literature. It is easier to see the problems that a third wave of reform might address after living in the schools awhile—and participating in schools of varied communities. It is important to acknowledge the genuine dilemmas and the real distress that lie behind the resigned, indifferent, or angry facades of both students and teachers in schools for the poor and, increasingly, in schools for the broad middle band of society.

Since the "old" reforms of the 1960s and 1970s, policy analysts have learned some hard lessons. They have seen that their policies are sometimes not implemented at all, despite fervent promises, and frequently not implemented as planned. Even more important, analysts have seen that when policies are implemented, they often do not have the desired effects, but they do have other unanticipated and often unwanted effects. Milbrey McLaughlin (1987, p. 172) summarizes this experience by arguing that "policymakers can't mandate what matters." However, to say this is not to say that "what policymakers mandate doesn't matter." It does matter, though it may not have the intended or desired effects.

Both waves of the reform movement have laudable goals. But policymakers will do education a disservice if they attempt reforms that take no account of cultural differences between communities, students' perspectives, and conditions of students' lives outside as well as inside the school. Reformers will aggravate the problems of many students and teachers if they impose on all of them patterns that are designed for the needs of only some of them, in the name of the American myth of standardized and therefore equal schools.

NOTES

Author's Note: The research on which this article is based was supported by the National Center on Effective Secondary Schools at the Wisconsin Center on Education Research, which is supported by a grant from the Office of Educational Research and Improvement Grant G-00869007. Any opinions, findings, and conclusions expressed in this article are those of the author and do not necessarily reflect the views of the Office of Educational Research and Improvement or of the United States Department of Education.

    1. Our study was a double one; one group, which I led, concentrated on the work of teachers in the eight schools, and the other group, led by Professor Richard Rossmiller, concentrated on the work of administrators. Other research staff working with us were Nancy Lesko, Annette Hemmings, Alexander K. Tyree, Jr., and Jeffrey Jacobson.

    2. One of the schools we studied, a large Catholic school, had a different temporal structure and grouped students into large and small instructional groups. This pattern of "flexible scheduling" was developed during the seventies, but the school had informally developed many of the structural features that the second wave of reform suggests. It had flexible instructional strategies, collegial consultation among teachers, mentoring by and involvement of department chairs in evaluation, and teachers' participation in policymaking.

    3. I have argued the central role of school culture, as it is created within individual schools, in two extended studies of desegregated schools (Metz, 1978, 1986). In the eight high schools, different cultures imported from the communities often shaped the schools' internal cultures.

    4. I am assuming sudden change to make a point. There would be no time to rewrite or renorm tests to create a new broad distribution of scores. Whether a broad distribution would reemerge, given radical improvements in instruction and students' motivation, is an empirical question to which we have no answer.

REFERENCES

Barnard, C. I. (1962). *The functions of the executive.* Cambridge, MA: Harvard University Press. (Original work published 1938.)

Carnegie Forum on Education and the Economy's Task Force on Teaching as a Profession. (1986). *A nation prepared: Teachers for the 21st century.* New York.

Clune, W. (1987). *Findings on student standards from the state wave and implications for further research.* Unpublished manuscript, Center for Policy Research in Education, University of Wisconsin, Madison.

Cusick, P. (1983). *The equalitarian ideal and the American high school*. New York: Longman.

Edelman, M. (1977). *Political language: Words that succeed and policies that fail*. New York: Academic Press.

Erickson, F. (1987). Transformation and school success: The policies and culture of educational achievement. *Anthropology and Education Quarterly, 18*, 335–356.

Heath, S. B. (1983). *Ways with words: Language, life and work in communities and classrooms*. New York: Cambridge University Press.

McDill, E. L., Natriello, G., & Pallas, A. M. (1986). A population at risk: Potential consequences of tougher school standards for student dropouts. *American Journal of Education, 94*, 135–181.

McLaughlin, M. W. (1987). Learning from experience: Lessons from policy implementation. *Educational Evaluation and Policy Analysis, 9*, 171–178.

McNeil, L. M. (1986). *Contradictions of control: School structure and school knowledge*. New York: Routledge & Kegan Paul.

Metz, M. H. (1978). *Classrooms and corridors: The crisis of authority in desegregated secondary schools*. Berkeley: University of California Press.

Metz, M. H. (1986). *Different by design: The context and character of three magnet schools*. New York: Routledge & Kegan Paul.

Metz, M. H. (1987, November). *The impact of cultural variation on high school teaching*. Paper presented at the annual meeting of the American Anthropological Association, Chicago.

National Commission on Excellence in Education. (1983). *A nation at risk: The imperative for educational reform*. Washington, DC: U.S. Government Printing Office.

Ogbu, J. U. (1987). *Minority education and caste: The American system in cross-cultural perspective*. New York: Academic Press.

Peshkin, A. (1978). *Growing up American: Schooling and the survival of community*. Chicago: University of Chicago Press.

Powell, A. G., Farrar, E., & Cohen, D. K. (1985). *The shopping mall high school: Winners and losers in the educational marketplace*. Boston: Houghton Mifflin.

Rubin, L. B. (1972). *Busing and backlash: White against white in an urban school district*. Berkeley: University of California Press.

Sedlak, M. W., Wheeler, C. W., Pullin, D. C., & Cusick, P. A. (1986). *Selling students short: Classroom bargains and academic reform in the American high school*. New York: Teachers College Press.

Sizer, T. R. (1984). *Horace's compromise: The dilemma of the American high school*. Boston: Houghton Mifflin.

13
Creating Inequality: The Political/Economic Context

What Reform Talk Does: Creating New Inequalities in Education
MICHAEL W. APPLE

IN ONE OF HIS most insightful arguments, the late philosopher Ludwig Wittgenstein (1953) reminded us that it is wise to look for the meaning of language in its use. That is, words receive meaning from their use in particular historical periods and settings. Thus we should not ask what words mean in general; rather, we should examine how they are being used in a variety of ways by different groups. This principle is of special importance if we are to understand the meaning of the current movement to "reform" our educational system. In fact, with all of the discussion of reforming education in the popular media, in professional and scholarly journals, and in government agencies at all levels, we may be in danger of forgetting Wittgenstein's principle.

In the current context, what does reform talk do? I recognize that there may be serious problems with the curriculum and teaching that now go on in many of our schools; I have criticized them and suggested alternatives in a series of volumes (Apple, 1979, 1985, 1986). I want to claim here that the way we talk about reforming education actually diverts our attention from many of the root causes of the problems we are experiencing. To see this, we shall need to focus both on the relationship between schooling and the larger society and on the structure of inequalities in that society. For the crisis we are facing in American society goes far beyond the school and will not be solved by blaming educators.

Part of the outline of this crisis is visible in the following analysis of the current state of American political and economic life:

> The powers of the American state are now deployed in a massive business offensive. Its basic elements are painfully clear. Drastic cutbacks in social spending. Rampant environmental destruction. Regressive revisions of the tax system. [Looming trade wars.] Loosened constraints on corporate power. Ubiquitous assaults on organized labor. Sharply increased weapons spending. Escalating threats of intervention abroad. (Cohen and Rogers, 1983, p. 15)

Of course, the fact that many people see a crisis does not mean that they see it in the same way, a point made very clear in Cohen and Rogers's preceding statement about government response. For progressive groups in the United States, the crisis is seen in the increase in poverty, the defunding of the educational and social programs that took many years to win and that are still crucially necessary, the attempts by rightist groups to impose their beliefs on others, the widespread deskilling of jobs, the lowering of wages and benefits for many others, and the loss of whole sectors of jobs, as industries engage in what economists call "capital flight" (moving their plants to other nations) thereby destroying whole communities in the process (Apple, 1986; Carnoy, Shearer, & Rumberger, 1984).

In contrast, powerful conservative groups see the crisis largely from above, simply as an economic and ideological one. Profits and production are not high enough. Workers aren't as disciplined as they should be. We aren't "competitive" enough. People have begun to expect "something for nothing." All institutions, especially schools, must be brought more closely into line with policies that will "reindustrialize" and "rearm" America so that we will be more economically competitive. The impact of this conservative definition of the crisis has had a truly major impact on official policy toward education (Apple, 1986).

Nowhere is this effect clearer than in what is perhaps the most influential government-sponsored document on the relationship between schooling and the economy, *A Nation at Risk*. In language that leaves no false hope that education is performing anywhere near what is necessary, the reports's authors state in their now-famous quote:

> Our nation is at risk. Our once unchallenged preeminence in commerce, industry, science, and technological innovations is being taken over by competitors throughout the world. . . . [The] educational foundations of our society are presently being eroded by a rising tide of mediocrity

that threatens our very future as a nation and a people. What was unimaginable a generation ago has begun to occur—others are matching and surpassing our educational attainments. (National Commission on Excellence in Education, 1983, pp. 12–16)

The report continues:

If an unfriendly power had attempted to impose on America the mediocre educational performance that exists today, we might have viewed it as an act of war. As it stands, we have allowed this to happen to ourselves. . . . We have, in effect, been committing an act of unthinking, unilateral educational disarmament. (National Commission on Excellence in Education, 1983, pp. 12–16)

In these words, we see the crisis as reconstructed around particular themes: international competition, capital accumulation, a reassertion of "toughness" and standards. The crisis is *not* one of the immense inequalities that are so visible in American society. Instead, it is redefined by dominant groups to fit their own interests. We must focus upon the more general question of how dominant interests work in the larger social context in which the role of education is now being dramatically changed if we are to understand how many of the educational "reforms" now being proposed may embody social values that many educators might not find to their liking.

In an article of this size, I can only note tendencies that either are reaching an advanced state or still loom on the horizon. The reader can find more detail and supporting evidence in the references.

INDUSTRIALIZING THE SCHOOL

We will miss what is happening in education unless we focus on the larger context in which educational change is occurring.[1] We have seen a breakdown of the largely liberal consensus that has guided a good deal of educational policy since World War II. Powerful groups within government and the economy have been able to redefine, often regressively, the terms of debate in education, social welfare, and other areas of "the common good" (Raskin, 1986). What education is *for* has been transformed. It is no longer seen as part of a social alliance that combines many minority groups, women, teachers, administrators, government officials, and progressively inclined legislators who act together to propose social democratic policies for schools, such as expanding educational opportunities or developing special programs in bilingual and multicultural education and for the handicapped. A new alliance has been formed, one that has increasing power in educational and social policy. This power bloc combines industry with the New Right. It is less interested in redressing the imbalances in life changes of women, people of color, or labor than in aiming at providing the educational conditions believed necessary for both increasing profit and capital accumulation and returning us to a romanticized past of the "ideal" home, family, and school (Apple, 1986, 1987; Giroux, 1984; Hunter, 1987; Omi and Winant, 1986).

The power of this alliance can be seen in a number of educational policies and proposals: (a) calls for voucher plans and tax credits to make schools like the idealized free-market economy (Apple, 1985); (b) the movement in state legislatures throughout the country to "raise standards" and mandate both teacher and student "competencies" and basic curricular goals and knowledge, usually by employing management and evaluation techniques originally developed not by educators but by business and industry (see Kliebard, 1986; Apple, 1979); (c) the increasingly effective attacks on the school curriculum for its anti-family and anti-free enterprise bias, its "secular humanism," and its lack of patriotism (Arons, 1983); and very important for my discussion here, (d) the growing pressure to make the perceived needs of business and industry into the primary goals of the school (Apple, 1985, 1986).

In essence, the new alliance in favor of the conservative restoration (Shor, 1986) has integrated education into a wider set of ideological commitments. The objectives in education are the same as those that guide its economic and social welfare goals. These include the expansion of the "free market," the drastic reduction of government responsibility for social needs, the reinforcement of the intensely competitive structure of mobility, the lowering of people's expectations for economic security, and the popularization of what is clearly a form of Social Darwinist thinking (Bastian, Fruchter, Gittell, Greer, and Haskins, 1986, p. 14). The effects of this realignment on how we think about education are becoming clearer every day.

As I have argued at length elsewhere, the political right in the United States has been very successful in mobilizing support *against* the educational system, often exporting the crisis in the economy to the schools. Thus one of its major victories has been to shift the blame for unemployment, underemployment, and the supposed breakdown of "traditional" values and standards in the family, education, and the paid workplace *from* the economic, cultural, and social policies of business and industry *to* the school and other public agencies (Apple, 1985, 1986).[2] The commitments that are embodied in the quotes from *A Nation at Risk* and that stand behind its policies bear eloquent witness to these tendencies.

This process is heightened by the federal and state governments that bombard the public with a particular *selection* of statistical data about the well-being, or lack of it, of our society. I say selection here because the United States government sets up "great manufactories of 'facts' and 'figures' " that are distributed to the public. These are usually economic and serve to construct a view of reality as fundamentally revolving around the economics of profit and loss, of accumulation and profit (Horne, 1986, pp. 189–190).

In the process, the value of education is reduced to economic utility (Apple, 1986, 1987). Other goals such as critical understanding, political literacy, personal development, mastery and skill, self-esteem, and shared respect are beside the point or "too expensive" (Bastian et al., 1986, p. 157). The issues of care and connectedness—issues that, as feminists have so crucially reminded us, count critically in building a society based on the common good—are disenfranchised as well (Gilligan, 1982). Instead, schools are to perform one primary function for society: supply the "human capital" to underwrite "the promise of individual success in competitive labor markets and national success in competitive global markets" (Bastian et al., 1986, p. 21).[3]

Simultaneously, as education's purpose is being drastically reduced to its role in reaching the economic goals established by the new alliance, its inner world has continuously adopted accompanying procedures of standardization and rationalization. Increasingly, teaching methods, texts, tests, and outcomes are being taken out of the hands of the people who must put them into practice. Instead, they are being legislated by state departments of education, state legislatures, or other centralized authorities, a process that is being supported or stimulated by reports such as *A Nation at Risk*.

The effects have been widespread. The tendency for the curriculum to be rationalized and industrialized at a central level focuses largely on competencies measured by standardized tests and encourages the use of more and more predesigned commercial materials and texts written specifically for those states that have the tightest centralized control and thus the largest guaranteed markets (Apple, 1985, 1986). The most obvious result is the *deskilling* of teachers. When individuals cease to plan and control a large portion of their work, the skills essential to doing these tasks well and self-reflectively atrophy and are forgotten. The skills that teachers have built up over decades of hard work—setting relevant curriculum goals, establishing content, designing lessons and instructional strategies, individualizing instruction based on an intimate knowledge of students' desires and needs, and so on—are lost. In many ways, given the centralization of authority and control and given the reduction of the primary mission of the school into, mainly, its economic utility, they are simply no longer needed (Apple and Teitelbaum, 1986).

In the larger economy, this process of separating conception from execution and deskilling has been called the degradation of labor. Importing these procedures into the school under the banner of improving educational quality, as many of the conservative national reports advocate, can have exactly the same effects as when they are employed in industry: a loss of commitment and respect, bitter battles over working conditions, a lowering of quality, and a loss of skill and imagination (Edwards, 1979.).[4] In the economic workplace, this process has also ultimately reduced the power of employees to have any significant say in the goals and procedures of the institutions in which they work. All these characteristics run directly counter to what we are beginning to know about what will lead to effective education in schools (Bastian et al., 1986).

It is not just at the level of the social goals or the curricula and teaching that the "industrialization" of the school has proceeded, however. The Right has attempted to alter our very perception of schooling itself, turning it away from the idea of a common ground in which democracy is hammered out (an intensely *political* idea involving interactive notions of citizenship in a polity). Instead, the common ground of the school no longer is based on a set of democratic political commitments; rather it is replaced by the idea of a competitive marketplace. The citizen as a political being with reciprocal rights and duties is lost; instead is the self as *consumer*. Schooling becomes a "retail product" (Bastian et al., 1986, p. 16; see also Giroux, 1984). Freedom in a democracy is no longer defined as participating in building the common good but as living in an unfettered commercial market; in such a view, the educational system now must be integrated into the mechanisms of such a market (Apple, 1989).

I have discussed the inherent weaknesses of these proposals—such as voucher plans and the like—elsewhere (Apple, 1985). The important point is to see the ideological reconstruction that is going on—to understand that in the process of making the school into a product to be bought and sold, we are radically altering our definitions of what it means to participate in our institutions. Participation has been reduced to the commercialization of all important public social interaction (Hall, 1986, pp. 35–36). The unattached individual, one whose only rights and duties are determined by the marketplace, becomes ascendant. The ideological imprint of our economy is hard to miss here.

Convincing the public at large to see education as a product to be evaluated for its economic utility and as a commodity to be bought and sold like anything else in the "free market" has required a good deal of hard ideological work on the part of the Right. It has meant that the citizenry must be convinced that what is public is bad and what is private is good.

Hugh Stetton evokes the tenor of these claims when he says:

> The commonest trick is this: of people's individual spending, mention *only the prices they pay*. When they buy a private car and a public road to drive it on, present the car as a benefit and the road as a tax or a cost. Tell how the private sector is the productive sector which gives us food, clothing, houses, cars, holidays and all good things, while the public sector gives us nothing but red tape and tax demands. (Horne, 1986, pp. 172–173)

Perhaps the ideological comparison can be made clear when we realize that in, say, the United States and Britain, there is a tendency to treat welfare and other forms of public education, health, or legal assistance as somehow not really deserved or as "abnormal." Yet, in countries such as Sweden, in social studies courses, students are taught about the range of public benefits to which each citizen is *entitled* as part of his or her very citizenship (Horne, 1986, p. 175).

While the convictions of a majority of the American people may not have been totally swayed by such conservative ideological tendencies, it is clear that the processes of redefinition are part of the larger strategies involved in the conservative restoration. As recent polls have shown, however, there has been clear movement within the larger society toward accepting some of the positions embodied by the Right (see Bunzel, 1985; Apple, 1987).

WILL CHANGES IN SCHOOLS CHANGE THE ECONOMY?

Even with this brief analysis of the encroachment of economic interests, ideologies, and procedures into the educational system, a major question remains. Will the results in the economy be what the Right assumes, if it is indeed successful in totally reorienting schooling? There is reason to doubt it.

Bastian et al. (1986) have called it a myth that "national economic growth and individual mobility are contingent on establishing more rigorous standards of educational competition" and on industrializing the school (p. 8). In these authors' review of the history and current status of the relationship between education and the economy, they propose considerably more democratic changes in schooling and showing the other side of this argument. Rather than linking declining school performance with declining economic performance, and rather than claiming that stressing high standards (defined by whom?) and discipline will somehow "restore economic productivity, competitive advantage, and job creation," the very opposite may be true. We instead may be creating discrimination and a new cultural elitism, one that will be justified by rhetorical artifice but not by results (Bastian et al., 1986, pp. 50, 60). The further result will be the reproduction of a double-peaked economy in which those on the bottom will find their schooling even more directly linked to the low-waged, nonunionized, and largely futureless sector of the labor market (Apple, 1986).

Bastian et al. (1986) summarize these arguments in the following way:

> Economic realities do not justify the claim that a more competitive school regime will raise productivity and widely enhance job opportunities. The growing polarization of the workforce into a small professional strata and a large pool of low wage, de-skilled service and production workers indicates that our increasingly bureaucratized and

industrialized education will mean more for a few and less for many, in terms of economic reward. The logic of today's marketplace is to lower expectations and limit chances for the majority of children, and competitive elitist schooling reinforces this logic. (p. 163)

Such a logic might, of course, lead to a "rearmed" America. However in the guise of the public good, a public largely consisting of the powerful will be the major beneficiaries (Apple, 1987).

CONCLUSION

In this brief article, I have tried to show how education has become increasingly dominated by economic interests that can result, not in enhanced equality, but in its opposite. I have pointed to the changing relations of power that have stimulated, and been stimulated by, such "reform" documents as *A Nation at Risk* and to the ideological shifts that have resulted. I have also noted that such shifts in what education is for are not the only significant changes that are occurring. We are witnessing important alterations in the control of curriculum and teaching at the level of policy and practice. This development has been accompanied by an attempt to not only enhance the influence of economic needs on schools, but to make education itself an economic product like all others.

In making these arguments, I have highlighted the negative side of what is happening. I am not defending the status quo nor claiming that schools don't need improvements—of course they do. Instead, I have tried to point out that we so often are asked to ride bandwagons without paying sufficient attention to what other baggage might be taking the trip with us. While bandwagons are certainly not new to education, the current wave of reform could result in antidemocratic tendencies, in worsening working conditions in schools, in even fewer resources ultimately being given to education, and to policies that will lead the public to blame education even more for things over which it has little control. Such outcomes would be tragic for millions of children and for the teachers and administrators who now work so hard every day in uncertain conditions to provide an education worthy of its name.

NOTES

1. What follows is based on a larger discussion in Apple (1988).
2. As many social analysts have argued, our kind of economy must subvert traditional values and communities and substitute an ethic of commodity pur-

chasing and monetary status if it is to survive. Placing the blame on our educational system is a form of category error. See Heilbroner (1985).

3. Of course, the educational system of the United States as well as other countries has always had close links to the economy (Apple, 1979). However, this relationship has always been a source of conflict, with many groups attempting to democratize both its goals and procedures. See Reese (1986) and Hogan (1985).

4. As I have demonstrated elsewhere, the critical fact that teaching, especially at the elementary level, has been socially defined as largely *women's work* makes the issues surrounding the probable deskilling of teachers even more important. See Apple (1986).

REFERENCES

Apple, M.W. (1979). *Ideology and curriculum.* Boston: Routledge & Kegan Paul.

Apple, M. W. (1985) *Education and power* (revised ARK ed.). New York: Routledge & Kegan Paul.

Apple, M. W. (1986). *Teachers and texts: A political economy of class and gender relations in education.* New York: Routledge & Kegan Paul.

Apple, M. W. (1987). Producing inequality: Ideology and economy in the national reports on education. *Educational Studies, 18,* 195–220.

Apple, M. W. (1988). Economics and inequality in schools. *Theory Into Practice, 27,* 282–287.

Apple, M. W. (1989). The redefinition of equality in the conservative restoration. In W. Secada (Ed.), *The meaning of equity.* Philadelphia: Falmer.

Apple, M. W., & Teitelbaum, K. (1986). Are teachers losing control of their skills and curriculum? *Journal of Curriculum Studies, 18,* 177–184.

Arons, S. (1983). *Compelling belief.* New York: McGraw-Hill.

Bastian, A., Fruchter, N., Gittell, M., Greer, C., & Haskins, K. (1986). *Choosing equality: The case for democratic schooling.* Philadelphia: Temple University Press.

Bunzel, J. (Ed.). (1985). *Challenge to American schools.* New York: Oxford University Press.

Carnoy, M., Shearer, D., & Rumberger, R. (1984). *A new social contract.* New York: Harper & Row.

Cohen, J., & Rogers, J. (1983). *On democracy.* New York: Penguin.

Edwards, R. (1979). *Contested terrain.* New York: Basic Books.

Gilligan, C. (1982). *In a different voice.* Cambridge: Harvard University Press.

Giroux, H. (1984). Public philosophy and the crisis in education. *Harvard Educational Review, 54,* 186–194.

Hall, S. (1986). Popular culture and the state. In T. Bennet, C. Mercer, & J. Woolacott (Eds.), *Popular culture and social relations* (pp. 22–49). London: Open University Press.

Heilbroner, R. L. (1985). *The nature and logic of capitalism.* New York: Norton.

Hogan, D. (1985). *Class and reform.* Philadelphia: Temple University Press.

Horne, D. (1986). *The public culture.* Dover, NH: Pluto.

Hunter, A. (1987). *The politics of resentment and the construction of middle America.* Unpublished paper, University of Wisconsin, Department of History, Madison.

Kliebard, H. (1986). *The struggle for the American curriculum.* New York: Routledge & Kegan Paul.

National Commission on Excellence in Education. (1983, April 27). A nation at risk: An imperative for educational reform. *Education Week,* pp. 12–16.

Omi, M., & Winant, H. (1986). *Racial formation in the United States.* New York: Routledge & Kegan Paul.

Piven, F., & Cloward, R. (1982). *The new class war.* New York: Pantheon.

Raskin, M. (1986). *The common good.* New York: Routledge & Kegan Paul.

Reese, W. (1986). *Power and the promise of school reform.* New York: Routledge & Kegan Paul.

Shor, I. (1986). *Culture wars.* New York: Routledge & Kegan Paul.

Wittgenstein, L. (1953). *Philosophical investigations.* New York: Macmillan.

14
The Question of Size:
To Consolidate or Not?

Keeping an Eye on the Reformers:
State Education Bureaucrats and
the Future of Small, Rural Schools
DAVID H. MONK
EMIL J. HALLER

R̶EGARDLESS OF WHETHER the impetus for educational reform stems from the pen of a scribbling academic, an opportunistic politician, or a faceless bureaucrat, a reform movement proceeds in steps, involves many actors playing a wide variety of roles, and can evolve to such a degree that it is difficult to discern the original intent from the ultimate impact. The point is not to stress the self-evident fact that reforms can be transmuted in various ways as they proceed from perceptions of need to concrete programs for improvement. Rather, the point is to note that these modifications can also be made to serve the interests of the persons doing the modifying. More broadly still, the point is that the impetus for reform can be captured and put to uses not intended by those who came earlier in the reform process. Indeed, drives to reform can be turned to purposes patently contrary to the ideas that gave rise to them. It is well, then, to keep an eye on reformers, lest a reform popular and sensible at its early states be transmuted into practices far removed from original intentions.

A good case in point is the impact that the current reform movement, an effort now codified into law in many states, is having on small rural schools. There is reason to believe that this reform movement is being used by state education officials to engineer another round of school district consolidations in rural regions. Such a development would be painfully ironic, since it runs counter to virtually all recent research on school size and to the expressed objectives of some of the reformers themselves.

THE REFORM MOVEMENT AND SCHOOL SIZE

While the modern reform movement has numerous themes and is difficult to capture in a single statement, many of its central concerns focus on the nature and level of schooling outcomes. Making schools offer a better mix of courses (e.g., requiring more science and mathematics) at higher levels of achievement (e.g., testing for minimum competency) at less cost to taxpayers (e.g., paying teachers according to their actual contributions) are all consistent with the thrust of the reform movement. This is the "hard" side of school reform. *A Nation at Risk* (National Commission on Excellence in Education, 1983) is paradigmatic.

In addition to the "stiffen academic requirements and make schools more accountable" theme, there is a second, "softer" dimension to the reform movement. Here the focus is on the social and moral side of student's schooling (e.g., reducing dropout rates), on greater cooperation among teachers and administrators (e.g., developing a climate of trust and shared responsibilities), and on a stronger role for parents and building administrators in school affairs (e.g., decentralizing decision making). Lightfoot's *The Good High School* (1983) is illustrative.

The hard and soft themes in the reform movement have different implications for the future of small rural schools. As we shall show in the following section, in some quarters there is a widespread and deeply entrenched belief that large size is a prerequisite for a cost-effective, diverse, and specialized curriculum. Moreover, there is a parallel belief that greater standardization and accountability follow from dividing a state into a small number of similarly organized, relatively large units. According to this belief, the fewer districts the better for the sake of exercising state oversight. Thus, expanding educational offerings and making educators more accountable to the state—the hard dimension of the reform movement—is very much consistent with a "larger is better" point of view.

In sharp contrast, researchers have concluded that large schools have adverse effects on certain aspects of the education and social development of youth. Beginning with the seminal work of Barker and Gump (1964), it has become clear that students in smaller schools participate more actively in the extracurriculum, have better self-concepts, and exhibit lower levels of alienation. (See Hamilton, 1983, for a thorough review of this research.) Moreover, there is some evidence that smaller schools are more closely tied to their communities (Carlsen & Dunn, 1981; Kay et al., 1981; Peshkin, 1978) and operate with less hierarchical, more collegial decision-making structures than do their larger counterparts (Dunn, 1977).

Thus, the two central themes of the modern school reform movement have contradictory implications for the future viability of small rural schools. In light of this, it is not surprising that modern reformers have had little to say explicitly about size or small rural schools per se. In the few instances where size is mentioned (Boyer, 1983; Goodlad, 1984; Lightfoot, 1983; Powell, Farrar, & Cohen, 1985), big schools are either viewed as a clear-cut source of undesirable outcomes (as in Goodlad, 1984) or as the source of a dilemma wherein officials must balance the opportunities for an expanded curriculum against the drawbacks for student social development or increased parental involvement (as in Boyer, 1983).

Further, the leaders of the reform movement have not explicitly rejected the long-standing belief that a more diversified curriculum can be more cost-effectively offered in large school systems. Instead, they seem more concerned about the nature of the specialization that is offered. For example, Powell and his colleagues decry the lack of coherence in high school courses; they do not question the virtue of offering a diversified curriculum (Powell, Farrar, & Cohen, 1985). Moreover, several reformers suggest ways of achieving the advantages of small size within the context of large districts and schools. Even Goodlad (1984), who is most explicit in his denunciation of large schools, notes that creating five or six small schools within a single large one means that each can benefit from sharing common facilities, such as libraries and gymnasiums. He concludes: "It is not impossible to have a good large school; it simply is more difficult" (p. 309). Boyer (1983) makes similar points. Such suggestions imply that whatever the virtues of small schools, they need not be lost in the process of creating large ones.

We conclude that the modern reform movement sends two inconsistent messages regarding school size. By not repudiating the idea that larger size facilitates an enriched academic curriculum, and by explicitly endorsing an expansion of academic opportunities through increasing graduation requirements, the hard side of the movement tacitly supports the further consolidation of small rural school districts. However, by simultaneously stressing the importance of the social outcomes of schooling; the necessity of a cooperative, caring climate; and the need for vastly increased parent involvement, its soft side helps to undercut the case for consolidation.

Which of these two themes will prevail in rural areas depends on more than their relative strength. Current reforms must be viewed in light of the legacy of past reforms, particularly those that have been directed uniquely at small rural schools. We consider this history next.

THE LEGACY OF RURAL SCHOOL REFORM

The history of rural education in this country provides remarkably compelling evidence against the view that educational institutions are highly resistant to change. The successive waves of school consolidations that washed over rural regions in the last half-century have been among the most successful educational reforms ever undertaken—if one defines *success* as the realization of the reformers' goal. They have transformed rural education, replacing tiny schools serving a few students and a single village with large, complex organizations serving hundreds or even thousands of pupils from several distinct communities.

The magnitude of this transformation is easy to document. For example, the number of school districts in the United States declined from 128,000 in 1930 to slightly over 14,000 today. In the same period, the number of one-room elementary schools went from nearly 150,000 to fewer than 1,500 (Sher & Tompkins, 1977). But to appreciate the real magnitude of this transformation, one must remember that this wholesale abolition of local school boards meant, in fact, the abolition of thousands of local governments. Further, these governments were not obscure entities performing some trivial social task; they were governmental bodies that daily touched the lives of citizens in a critically sensitive area, the welfare of their children.

The rationale offered for this massive reform rested on the idea that larger schools and school districts were more equitable and more efficient. They were more equitable because small schools denied rural students equality of educational opportunity by not providing the variety of programs offered by larger institutions. Similarly, larger schools were more efficient because they could offer any given program at a lower per-pupil expense, or they could offer a wider variety of programs at no greater expense.

Both the equity and efficiency arguments are highly problematic. For almost two decades, accumulating research suggests that making large rural schools from small rural schools does not dependably result in either greater equity or efficiency (see, for example, Monk & Haller, 1986; Sher & Tompkins, 1977; Walberg & Fowler, 1987). At the same time, and as we noted previously, other research suggests that small schools have important social and educational advantages.

This massive reform of U.S. education was carried out over the sometimes fierce resistance of parents and residents of small communities. Indeed, the consolidation of small rural schools in this country belies the notion that strong community support is essential for substantial educational change to occur. District consolidations were often achieved in fractious, tempestuous conflicts that pitted a small number of professional educators and their allies against large segments of local communities (see, for example, Monk & Haller, 1986; Peshkin, 1982; Tyack, 1974; Weaver,

1977). The frequency with which the educators won these battles (as the statistics on the declining numbers of districts attest) is remarkable.

The last big wave of rural school consolidations took place during the 1960s. In that decade the number of school districts in the United States was halved, and the one-teacher elementary schools virtually disappeared (National Center for Education Statistics, 1982). By the 1970s, district consolidations had slowed to a trickle. In New York, for example, mergers occurred on the average of 20 per year between 1963 and 1967. A decade later they were averaging one per year (Monk & Haller, 1986).

It is important to note that this decline did not result simply because there were no small districts left. Today in New York there are 723 K–12 school districts. Two hundred and forty-five (33 percent) serve fewer than 1,000 pupils, 120 (17 percent) fewer than 500, and 41 (6 percent) fewer than 200. Rather, many districts *chose* to remain small. That is, in sometimes bitter, protracted struggles (Woodward, 1986) they successfully resisted the efforts of educators and state officials to merge them with their neighbors.

Educators who now hold positions of authority in local educational authorities (LEAs) and in state educational bureaucracies began their administrative careers during these "school wars." They received their administrative training during the 1950s and 1960s, when educational research, administration texts and such influential books as Conant's *The American High School* (1959) were uniformly praising large size. Their training, their successes in the 1960s, and their subsequent failures have indelibly marked their views of rural schools. These experiences will influence their strategies for implementing current reforms in this country's hinterlands.

Evidence for this prediction comes from our study of the effects of school district consolidation in New York (Monk & Haller, 1986), which included interviews with school administration, superintendents of intermediate-level school districts (who are state education department officials), and officeholders in the state education department, among numerous others. Ignorant of two decades of research, the large majority of these officials continue to attribute high levels of inequality and inefficiency to small districts and to claim these result from their small size (Davis, 1986:60). As just one example, in 1981, after evidence contraindicating consolidation had been accumulating for years, one state official wrote concerning New York's earlier efforts to merge districts:

> I am sure that there are many who felt the school districts were being pushed too fast and too far [into consolidation]. But in truth, it was too slow and not far enough; and the great majority of school districts in New York State are still too small to adequately function in our present society. Their size, or rather their lack of it, inhibits the school's flexibility to solve the difficult problems they currently face. . . . Continuing such a school system is a luxury we cannot afford and is difficult to justify. (Ramer, 1981, quoted in Davis, 1986:47)

Further, their experience with school consolidations has left New York officials with the firm conviction that rural residents resist mergers because they do not understand the benefits that will accrue to their children. Their resulting perception is that consolidation must be *sold* to a skeptical and ignorant public. In New York this selling takes various forms. State education department officials visit small districts and speak to citizens and board members about the advantages of consolidation, but not its disadvantages. The state has published various pamphlets on the virtues of consolidation and distributed these to LEAs. It will underwrite the cost of a study of consolidation's possibilities. And it is willing to send experts to a community to help organize a campaign to promote a merger.

The selling of consolidations in New York also takes less straightforward guises. For example, a district consolidation must be preceded by a study to evaluate its merits. These studies are carried out by hired consultants, nearly always current or retired state officials. We have found no studies that recommended against consolidation. In fact, few even suggested that there were any disadvantages to a merger. Certainly, the authors of these studies never mentioned to community residents or to the school boards that hired them that there was an extensive body of research that was highly equivocal about any improvements district consolidation might have on equality or efficiency.

What was notable about these various activities was not so much that state officials engage in various selling tactics to convince rural people to consolidate their schools nor that this selling often took on a decidedly disingenuous cast. Rather, what best illustrates how deeply ingrained is this commitment to consolidation is the fact that many did not see these activities as "selling" at all. In fact, some took considerable umbrage at this suggestion, viewing their one-sided presentations as "educating" relatively ignorant people about the desirability of abandoning their local school district.

Another notable aspect of officials' views was their understanding of residents' motives for resisting school consolidation. Besides ignorance, we were frequently told that people oppose consolidations for capricious reasons. For example, old athletic rivalries, jealousies between communities, unwillingness to locate a new school in another town, and of course the "If it was good enough for me, it's good enough for my kids" rationale were all cited as the "real" reasons that people resist a reform that is in their own interest.

Finally, resistance was sometimes attributed to illegitimate motives. Consider these comments about school board members:

> [There] are two types of men and women who serve on school boards without pay. One type is the altruistic person who serves without any selfish motive and whose main objective is to improve the program of the school. The other type is that person who has power and likes

power and doesn't always put the needs of pupils first. He or she can be tempted to keep the status quo [i.e., to resist a consolidation] for a variety of reasons even including protection of friends or relatives who work for the school district. (Davis, 1986:86)

At times this attribution of capricious and illegitimate motives promotes a profoundly antidemocratic attitude among these officials. Some clearly believed that, since rural people refuse to do what is patently right for their own children, they need to be forced to do what officials know to be right. Consider these comments:

All small districts . . . should be eliminated, if need be by the [state] Commissioner's office. They are and have been expensive, inefficient and indefensible in this day.

[L]egislation is the only answer. Albany, in conjunction with the District Superintendents, should decide which schools are too small to operate efficiently. Legislation should be enacted that would greatly reduce aid for the inefficient. Then only those who could afford it would want to or should be able to remain small. (Davis, 1986:63–64)

The first person believes that all "expensive and inefficient" districts should be dissolved by an appointed official, regardless of residents' wishes. The latter person has an even more remarkable view. He believes that wealthy districts should be permitted to remain small. Poor ones should be starved into submission.

The continuing push to consolidate small rural schools does not depend simply on the attitudes of aging state bureaucrats. The probability of school consolidations is substantially enhanced because powerful legal and structural mechanisms supporting reorganization are in place. These are the relics of the push to abolish small rural districts several decades ago. For example, New York provides very large financial incentives for districts to merge. It can also withhold aid for building construction from districts identified in a state document as too small. Further, when two or more districts decide to hold a referendum on a proposed merger, as the law requires, the same law mandates that the ballots of residents in all concerned districts be mingled and then counted. Thus, a large majority of the residents of a relatively small community can oppose a consolidation, yet find their district merged with a larger neighbor. Finally, it is very important to note that in New York's State Education Department there is a Bureau of School District Organization. One of this bureau's major functions is to monitor school consolidations and to administer the procedures that govern them. But monitoring and administering, obviously, require that consolidations occur. Thus, a state agency and its associated officials have a vested interest in insuring that district mergers regularly take place.

We conclude that in New York State a reform movement of historical

proportions, district consolidation, has become thoroughly institutionalized. Supporting belief systems, legal authority, and social structures are
all deeply rooted in the state's educational landscape. The modern reform
movement, then, is laid on top of this legacy of earlier reform and, we
believe, will be shaped by it.

But our data derive from only one state. We do not know the extent
to which New York's experience differs from that of others. Undoubtedly
it does in many respects. Nevertheless, and as we shall show, there is
reason to believe that the consolidation movement has been institutionalized in other states as well—and with the same consequences for current
reform efforts.

THE FUTURE OF SMALL RURAL SCHOOLS

We can now draw conclusions about the modern reform movement's likely
impact on small rural school districts. There are two points to make. On
the one hand, there is an unmistakable congruence between the long-
standing effort to consolidate small rural schools and the hard dimension
of the current school improvement effort, with its emphasis on enhanced
academic offerings and accountability. Officials in state education departments across the land can be expected to resonate to these calls for improved, cost-efficient programs. It is an old and reassuring refrain to the
ears of those in positions of power.

On the other hand, there is no comparable congruence between the
consolidation movement and the "soft" side of the modern reform effort,
with its emphasis on the social development of youth, keeping schools
close to their communities, increased parent involvement, and decentralized decision making. These are new to the landscape of state education
officials, and there is no tradition into which they comfortably fit. Indeed,
these ideas are in many respects antithetical to some of their more cherished
beliefs.

Moreover, there is the matter of cost. As states proceed to increase
graduation requirements, the poorest and the smallest districts with the
most minimal programs will face the greatest strain. This strain may persuade residents in these districts to believe assertions that consolidation
will reduce school costs, especially when those assertions are made by
"experts" who fail to cite contradictory evidence. Further, residents' willingness to accept reorganization as a solution to their fiscal problems will
be accentuated by the large fiscal incentives offered for district mergers.
(In New York these typically amount to several million dollars of additional
state aid awarded over a period of fifteen years.) Thus, the modern reform
movement is likely to prompt additional school district reorganization ef-

forts, despite its virtual silence on the question of size and its concern for social development of youth, parent involvement, and decentralized decision making.

Much of what we have said is speculative and based on research in one state. Nevertheless, it is worth noting that recently at least eight states (Georgia, Illinois, Iowa, Massachusetts, New York, North Carolina, Utah, and Vermont) have evidenced renewed efforts to consolidate their small school districts. Our analysis suggests that this renewed interest has come about, at least in part, because the seeds of hard reform have fallen on fertile ground in state education bureaucracies.

This suggestion is supported by additional evidence. As our analysis would predict, these renewed efforts spring from state-level sources. For example, in Illinois an executive branch initiative prompted a state department study recommending further consolidation (Illinois State Board of Education, 1985). North Carolina's efforts followed a similar course (North Carolina Department of Public Instruction, 1986). In New York and at the state education department's behest, the legislature has made available "efficiency study grants" of up to $20,000 to two or more districts willing to study cooperatively the possibilities of consolidating or otherwise sharing programs. (It is worth noting that even the title of this program implies that enlarging school districts promotes efficiency.) Our own study of reorganization in New York was prompted by small districts' concerns over what the Regents Action Plan (New York's "hard" side of reform) would mean for their future. In Vermont, the governor appointed a Special Commission on Public School Governance, which called for further consolidation of Vermont schools, in October 1987.

Moreover, state-level officials continue to ignore the large body of research that questions the wisdom of creating larger school districts. In 1986 in North Carolina, officials of the state education department prepared a document urging a sweeping, mandated reorganization of the state's schools, creating one district per county. These officials concluded that "recent research" showed that North Carolina's school districts should serve at least 5,000 students each and that the optimal number was 10,000. As Sher (1986) points out in a scathing critique, the authors of this report relied on no research conducted after 1971; and, like their New York counterparts, they failed even to mention studies (one conducted by a member of their own department) that questioned the value of large size. Sher also found, as we did, that when these officials conducted studies of the feasibility of specific consolidations, they *always* found in favor of the proposed merger.

Thus, the sudden reawakening of interest in consolidation among state education officials is no accident. It stems from the compatibility of hard reforms with old and deeply embedded ideas about the virtues of large schools. In addition, the mechanisms for consolidation are in place in many states, and consolidation is a familiar tool for "improving" small rural schools. To paraphrase an old adage, "When your favorite tool is a hammer, every problem is a nail."

Perhaps most fundamentally, the renewed interest in consolidation may be another example of the common political phenomenon we noted in the beginning of this chapter. We have seen numerous examples of the power of local, state, and federal agencies to "capture" a public policy, especially a policy aimed at reforming the agency itself or the enterprise it is supposed to oversee. In this process, public policy can be transformed to serve the agencies' own ends, sometimes in ways contrary to the intentions of the reformers who proposed an idea and the legislative body that codified that idea into law (Harrigan, 1976; Stone, Whelan, & Murin, 1986). Indeed, we have seen examples of this phenomenon in education (Rodgers, 1969; Zeigler, Tucker, & Wilson, 1976).

It will be unfortunate if the current reform effort is captured by state bureaucrats and used for a largely discredited purpose, the further consolidation of small rural schools. Few current reformers have given much thought to the implications of their recommendations for the issue of school size. Those who have thought about size do not view large schools as a desirable goal. We suspect that this is also true of those who are mute on the matter. Further, while the effect of school size on many educational outcomes is problematic, it is least so in regard to reform's soft objectives. That is, large, complex, and bureaucratized schools are inimical to the social and moral goals sought by reformers. It would be a bitter irony, then, were a successful reform movement to spawn in the nation's small rural schools some of the very pathologies that the reformers were seeking to cure.

REFERENCES

Barker, G., & Gump, P. V. (1964). *Big school, small school.* Stanford, CA: Stanford University Press.

Boyer, E. L. (1983). *High school.* New York: Harper & Row.

Carlsen, W. S., & Dunn, F. (1981). Small rural schools: A portrait. *High School Journal, 64,* 299–309.

Conant, J. B. (1959). *The American high school today.* New York: McGraw-Hill.

Davis, C. E. (1986). *If we can haul the milk we can haul the kids: A personalized history of school district reorganization in New York State.* Ithaca, NY: Department of Education, Cornell University. (ERIC Document No. 016356.)

Dunn, F. (1977). Choosing smallness: An examination of the small school experience in rural America. In J. P. Sher (Ed.), *Education in rural America* (pp. 81–124). Boulder, CO: Westview Press.

Goodlad, J. I. (1984). *A place called school.* New York: McGraw-Hill.

Hamilton, S. F. (1983). The social side of schooling: Ecological studies of classrooms and schools. *Elementary School Journal, 83,* 313–334.

Harrigan, J. T. (1976). *Political change in the metropolis.* Boston: Little, Brown.

Illinois State Board of Education (1985). *Student achievement in Illinois: An analysis of student progress.* Springfield, IL.

Kay, S., et al. (1981). *Public school organization and community development in rural areas.* Frankfort: Kentucky State University. (ERIC Document Reproduction Service No. ED 201 433.)

Lightfoot, S. L. (1983). *The good high school.* New York: Basic Books.

Monk, D. H., & Haller, E. J. (1986). *Organizational alternatives for small rural schools.* Ithaca, NY: Department of Education, Cornell University. (ERIC Document Reproduction Service No. ED 281 694.)

National Center for Education Statistics. (1982). *Digest of educational statistics, 1982.* Washington, DC: U.S. Government Printing Office.

National Commission on Excellence in Education. (1983). *A nation at risk.* Washington, DC: U.S. Government Printing Office.

North Carolina Department of Public Instruction. (1986). *Report of the state superintendent on schools and school districts in North Carolina.* Raleigh, NC.

Peshkin, A. (1978). *Growing up American: Schooling and the survival of community.* Chicago: University of Chicago Press.

Peshkin, A. (1982). *The imperfect union: School consolidation and community conflict.* Chicago: University of Chicago Press.

Powell, A. G., Farrar, E., & Cohen, D. K. (1985). *The shopping mall high school.* Boston: Houghton Mifflin.

Rodgers, D. (1969). *110 Livingston St.* New York: Vantage Press.

Sher, J. P. (1986). *Heavy meddle.* Raleigh: North Carolina School Boards Association.

Sher, J. P., & Tompkins, R. B. (1977). Economy, efficiency, and equality: The myths of rural school and district consolidation. In J. P. Sher (Ed.), *Education in rural America* (pp. 43–80). Boulder, CO: Westview Press.

Stone, C. N., Whelan, R. K., & Murin, W. J. (1986). *Urban policy and politics in a bureaucratic age* (2nd ed.). Englewood Cliffs, NJ: Prentice-Hall.

Tyack, D. B. (1974). *The one best system.* Cambridge, MA: Harvard University Press.

Walberg, H. J., & Fowler, W. T. (1987). Expenditure and size efficiencies of public school districts. *Educational Researcher, 16,* 5–13.

Weaver, T. (1977). Class conflict in rural education: A case study of Preston County, West Virginia. In J. P. Sher (Ed.), *Education in rural America* (pp. 162–204). Boulder, CO: Westview Press.

Woodward, K. L. (1986). *Reorganization and rancor: The aftermath of a troubled reorganization.* Unpublished doctoral dissertation, Cornell University, Ithaca, New York.

Zeigler. L., Tucker, H. J., & Wilson, L. A. (1976). How school control was wrested from the people. *Phi Delta Kappan, 57,* 534–539.

15
Effects on a Minority: Hispanic Apartheid

Hispanic Apartheid in American Public Education
MARCELLO MEDINA, JR.

NATIONAL REFORM REPORTS transformed 1983 into a watershed year, unparalleled in the history of American public education (Pipho, 1986). The subsequent education reform movement progressed faster than any public policy reform in modern history (Odden, 1986). Fueled by the need to restore the nation's lagging economic competitiveness, policy-makers in every state took up the reins of leadership, while the federal government chose to remain on the sidelines, cheerleading the states' initiatives (Jennings, 1987). However, to view this unprecedented and dynamic policy environment from a Hispanic perspective, three other contemporaneous policy agendas must be considered. For Hispanics, these issues describe the climate and tone of an increasingly ethnocentric policy environment.

In 1986, after 15 years of heated national debate, Congress passed the

Immigration Reform and Control Act, primarily to prevent illegal immigration by Mexican and other Hispanic aliens. Mexican American groups criticized earlier unsuccessful versions as the most blatantly anti-Hispanic bills ever considered. These groups' primary concern was that the inclusion of employer sanctions would lead to increased discrimination and harassment against Hispanic citizens in the work-place. Despite these concerns, the immigration reform legislation became law, with the employer sanction provision in place (Fuchs, 1987).

The second policy effort affecting Hispanics has been the English-only movement, coordinated by the advocacy group U.S. English. Founded in 1983 by S. I. Hayakawa, this group's ultimate goal is to promote a constitutional amendment establishing an official language. In the fall of 1986, Californians overwhelmingly voted English the official state language. A total of 9 states have now passed such measures, and 31 more are considering them. U.S. English views bilingualism as a threat to English and has warned that Hispanics are promoting national disunity by insisting on retaining their native language and cultures. Hispanic leaders have denounced the English-only movement as divisive, exclusionary, and racist (Crawford, 1987b). Larmouth (1987) investigated whether linguistic heterogeneity erodes national unity, as claimed by U.S. English, and concluded that the Hispanic community's support of Spanish is a function of continued immigration and would not undermine national unity. In fact, Hispanics have demonstrated a high degree of assimilation and linguistic anglicization to enhance their economic opportunities.

A third policy issue salient to Hispanic interests has been the highly publicized efforts by the nation's top education officer, Secretary William J. Bennett, to alter the Bilingual Education Act (BEA) requirement that virtually all federal monies supporting limited English proficient (LEP) children's instruction must go to native language programs (Crawford, 1987a). Bennett has already slashed the BEA budget by 47 percent in constant dollars between 1980 and 1986 (Jennings, 1987). The U.S. General Accounting Office (1987) received a congressional request to assess the validity of the Department of Education's position to eliminate the requirement of native language teaching from the BEA. Based on the judgments of a panel of 10 experts, the report found that a sizable majority differed from the views of the department. A total of 8 experts found sufficient research support for native language instruction, while 7 did not for English-only methods to promote English acquisition by LEP children. Department of Education officials characterized the report as seriously flawed.

Hispanics perceive an unfavorable national mood toward them, produced by heated public debates surrounding the above three issues of immigration reform, official language amendments, and native language instruction. In this atmosphere, some Hispanics and policymakers have observed an ominous side to school reform policy.

Oakes (1986c) criticized the reform reports for imposing a single standard of excellence, an undeniably white and middle-class standard. She further asserted that current reforms have not addressed such equity issues as desegregation, tracking, inadequate school facilities and counseling, nor the effects of racism and poverty on the educational treatment of minority students. In a critical review of four major reform reports, Stedman and Smith (1983) concluded that careful treatment of school outcomes data suggests that reform should have been focused on poor and minority urban school children. Still others (Boyer, 1984; Kirst, 1986; Miller, 1986) have expressed concern that school reform has occurred without regard for the rapidly changing ethnic and racial composition of our schools. Orfield (1986) stated that the reform agenda has overlooked one of the most critical and urgent developments of this century—the widespread educational problems facing Hispanics. Arias (1986), concerned with increased school segregation of Hispanic children and their declining academic attainment, supported Orfield's contention of neglect by the school reform movement. Meanwhile, others (Jones, 1986; McDill, Natriello, & Pallas, 1987; Valdivieso, 1986) have reported that current reforms focusing on increased academic rigor may have aggravated already high Hispanic dropout rates. According to Jennings (1987), the special needs of Hispanic students were not the object of state school reform legislation between 1980 and 1986. Only one state has enacted a major new program aimed at the needs of poor children, a classification that disproportionately includes Hispanics. Thus there is a frequently reported conclusion that reform agendas have ignored Hispanic interests.

From a Hispanic perspective, an even more ominous aspect of the educational excellence movement is its bias in the enduring polarity of educational equity and excellence. Howe (1987) has described the tension between equity and excellence as educators grappled with how best to serve an increasingly diverse student population. The economic motives driving current reform efforts, with little time to waste on equity, have encouraged policymakers to largely ignore the dilemma of educating ever larger numbers of minority children. Equity issues and the pursuit of social justice have been critical dimensions in earlier reforms (Lightfoot, 1987). Willie (1987) said that educational eminence was a function of high standards and diversity—not one without the other, but each complementing the other.

By itself, excellence has resulted in abuse, as schools discard individuals who do not measure up. The current reform agenda is not only indifferent but actually antagonistic to Hispanic interests. Earlier reform agendas in the 1960s attempted to ameliorate conditions for castelike Hispanics (Ogbu, 1978). Unfortunately, they were largely unsuccessful, perhaps due to faulty premises. The new reform agendas essentially abandon egalitarian efforts for an undifferentiated focus on excellence. Seeking to promote a unidimensional vision of excellence and thus ignoring meaningful social and cultural differences among minority groups, these new reforms, however well intended, can injure Hispanic educational and social interests. Unsurprisingly, some Hispanics interpret those harms as the actual goals of policymakers, intent on promoting only majority interests.

This article addresses four issues that apparently have not been of concern to current school reformers. The first issue relates to the rapidly growing demographic prominence of the Hispanic in the United States and the importance of this fact to schools and to the future economic well-being of this country. Two other ignored issues, Hispanic school segregation and school tracking practices, enhance structural inequality and are morally and ethically abhorrent to a democratic republic. These two prominent factors contribute to the fourth ignored issue, high dropout among Hispanic caste group members.

HISPANIC DEMOGRAPHICS

Arias (1986) has called the population growth rates of Hispanics one of the most compelling social developments of the last 25 years. According to the U.S. Census Bureau (1987), the Hispanic population has increased by 30 percent since 1980, a rate five times greater than non-Hispanics. Valdivieso (1986) has contended that high birth rates and continued immigration make Hispanics the youngest, fastest-growing population. Census figures for 1987 indicate median ages for Mexican Americans, Puerto Ricans, and non-Hispanics to be 23.5, 24.3, and 32.6, respectively. Hispanics, with 87 percent living in metropolitan areas, are the most urban population (Orum, 1985), yet they are very heterogeneous both culturally and linguistically (Arias, 1986). However, Hispanics tend to be more homogeneous when economic and educational factors are considered. The 1987 poverty rate of Hispanics is almost three times that of non-Hispanics, and their 1987 unemployment rate is 67 percent greater (U.S. Census Bureau, 1987). Hispanic youth, in their increasing numbers (Orum, 1985), are achieving at the lowest quartiles of the academic ladder for reading, mathematics, and science (Arias, 1986).

The United States already has the seventh largest Hispanic population in the world (Fradd, 1987), and by the year 2000, it will have the fifth largest (Boyer, 1984). By 2080, the majority of Americans will be from minority populations, and Hispanics will comprise the largest minority cohort (Fradd, 1987). Between 2005 and 2015, Hispanics will surpass black Americans as the largest minority group (McNett, 1983). These trends reveal a rapidly changing nation. Today, unconcerned by this titanic iceberg looming on the horizon of economic self-destruction, state and national policymakers formulate school reforms with their short-term vision focused on the next election.

HISPANIC SCHOOL SEGREGATION

On May 17, 1954, the U.S. Supreme Court issued its landmark decision *(Brown v. Board of Education,* 1954, p. 495) that found, in part, that "separate educational facilities are inherently unequal." More than 30 years later, Clark (1984) has observed that de facto segregation still exists and, indeed, is proliferating. He noted that resegregation is occurring in American public education to a point where urban schools may be more segregated now than at the time of *Brown.* Clark decried this condition as institutional injustice, reinforcing racial prejudice and violating this nation's democratic principles.

Hispanic children are now the most segregated group in our schools. In 1984, 70.6 percent of Hispanic students attended "predominantly minority" public schools (those where minorities made up more than half the student body). Equally disturbing, 31 percent attended "intensely segregated" schools where more than 90 percent of the student body were minorities. These percentages have risen consistently since these data first became nationally available in 1968 (Fiske, 1987).

Orfield (1983) and Orfield, Monfort, and George (1987) have also noted this disturbing trend toward increasing Hispanic isolation and have postulated two probable and related causes—demographics and discrimination. Table 15.1 presents a rank order of states with the largest Hispanic enrollments as well as a ranking of states by highest levels of segregation. Three measures of segregation levels are used. Two of these measures, defined above, are "predominantly" and "intensely" segregated. The third, most reliable, measure is the percentage of white students in schools typically attended by Hispanic students (Orfield et al., 1987).

Through 1984, as revealed in Table 15.1, consistent state growth in Hispanic enrollment occurred as well as high and increasing levels of segregation for each of the three measures.

Legal and policy decisions of the 1960s and early 1970s led to much lower black segregation than in 1968, while Hispanic segregation increased (Orfield et al., 1987). Regrettably, Hispanic students of the mid-1980s had much less interaction with English-speaking whites during their schooling than did those attending school 16 years earlier. This emergent Hispanic urban underclass may have been more comprehensively isolated than were black children of the South prior to their desegregation over three decades ago. The paucity of Hispanic school desegregation orders has clearly encouraged isolationistic trends that are uniform across state and metropolitan settings. As no policy initiatives or reforms are under consideration to reverse them, it is quite apparent that they will continue.

Orfield (1983) and Orfield et al.(1987) have maintained that America is a metropolitan society. This nation's economy has been organized at that level. Therefore, economically speaking, it is important to remember that Hispanics have been the fastest-growing metropolitan population. The same

Table 15.1   **States with Largest Hispanic Enrollment and Highest Levels of Segregation of Hispanic Students According to Three Measures, 1984**

Rank	Hispanic Percentage of Total Enrollment	Percentage of Hispanic Students in Predominately Minority Schools	Percentage of Hispanic Students in 90–100% Minority School	Percentage of White Students in School of Typical Hispanic Student[a]
1	New Mexico (43.4)	New York (85.1)	New York (59.1)	New York (18.9)
2	California (29.2)	Illinois (79.2)	Illinois (41.2)	Texas (27.6)
3	Texas (27.9)	Texas (77.9)	Texas (40.0)	Illinois (28.0)
4	Arizona (21.5)	New Jersey (75.1)	New Jersey (37.1)	New Jersey (29.5)
5	Colorado (15.7)	New Mexico (74.0)	Connecticut (29.4)	California (32.7)
6	New York (13.6)	California (73.9)	Pennsylvania (29.4)	New Mexico (33.0)
7	New Jersey (8.8)	Florida (68.4)	California (26.8)	Florida (35.2)
8	Florida (8.1)	Connecticut (66.5)	Florida (25.6)	Connecticut (35.9)
9	Illinois (8.0)	Pennsylvania (62.9)	Mississippi (25.2)	Pennsylvania (38.0)
10	Connecticut (6.8)	Arizona (59.3)	Arizona (18.0)	Arizona (40.9)

Source: Orfield, G., Montfort, F., & George, R. (1987). *School segregation in the 1980s: Trends in metropolitan areas.* Washington, DC: Joint Center for Political Studies.

[a]Lowest percentage represents greatest segregation; thus states in this column are ranked in order of increasing percentage. That is, New York has the smallest percentage of white students in the school of a typical Hispanic student.

metropolitan areas where Hispanic segregation has dramatically increased are linked to the nation's economic future. These cities include Los Angeles, San Francisco–Oakland, San Diego, Houston, San Antonio, Chicago, Miami, and New York; and the only cities where Hispanic integration has increased, through school desegregation orders, are Denver, Las Vegas, Austin, Sacramento, and San Jose.

The relationship between the nation's economic competitiveness and quality education has been recurrently emphasized during the school reform movement (Jennings, 1987; Kirst, 1986). Therefore, a study by Espinosa and Ochoa (1986) that investigated the impact of Hispanic school segregation on academic achievement should be of interest to reformers. Their report sampled all 5,059 public elementary and high schools in California, investigating Hispanic reading and mathematics achievement levels for grades 3, 6, and 12. In addition, they examined the relationship between Hispanic segregation in schools and their achievement outcomes. They found that by the third grade, 80 percent of Hispanic children were already below average for reading and mathematics achievement. Their low patterns of academic growth began in grades 1 through 3 and continued through grade 12. They also found a statistically significant negative relationship between Hispanic school segregation and school achievement. As Hispanic school segregation increased, Hispanic achievement in reading and mathematics decreased for grades 3, 6, and 12. Rightfully, Orum (1985) has observed that Hispanic children have the dubious distinction of being, not only the most undereducated, but the most highly segregated as well.

If these prevalent patterns of segregation are ever to be rectified, Hispanics must draw on the lessons learned from earlier Hispanic and black school desegregation efforts (Orfield et al., 1987). However, two recent developments have blunted the thrust of such efforts. The excellence over equity movement and an unsympathetic Reagan administration have reduced federal pressure and financial support for desegregation (Hawley, 1983). Braddock, Crain, and McPartland (1984) have reported on long-term benefits of school desegregation by studying minority adults who graduated from desegregated schools. They found that minority students educated in desegregated schools, when compared to their segregated counterparts, were more likely to attend white universities, make better grades, have higher university graduation rates, work in more integrated settings, and perceive less racism and have better attitudes toward whites. They concluded that desegregation revitalizes the socialization function of schools. American society cannot avoid the pain of desegregation simply by improving segregated schools and then expect to produce assimilated, economically successful, and socially well-adjusted minorities as adults.

HISPANICS AND TRACKING

The increasing segregation of most Hispanics has been further exacerbated by the pervasive practices of tracking in middle and secondary schools, dividing students by achievement levels into separate curricula (i.e., academic, general, and vocational), and further grouping them by ability in academic subjects (particularly English, mathematics, and science). This practice is firmly embedded in the school culture. It has been a major structural element of schooling, untouched by reform, and is responsible for a large measure of day-to-day schooling inequity and mediocrity (Oakes, 1985).

Research over 60 years has produced virtually no clear-cut evidence of beneficial effects from tracking on academic achievement (Oakes, 1985; Sorensen & Hallinan, 1986; Winn & Wilson, 1983). Yet, this dominant school practice has persisted, impervious to reform (Oakes, 1986a).

At the secondary school level, Hispanics have been disproportionately represented in low-ability academic subjects (Oakes, 1986a). These low-ability classes were distinctly different and damaging to Hispanic student performance. Hispanics in low-ability English classes rarely read great or even good literature. Their learning involved only simple memory tasks or comprehension, while high-ability English classes demanded critical thinking, problem solving, and synthesizing knowledge. Hispanics in low-ability mathematics classes focused on basic computational skills and arithmetic facts, while high ability mathematics classes taught sophisticated concepts about number systems, probability, and statistics (Oakes, 1986a).

Generally, Hispanics in low-ability classes experienced a greater emphasis on student conformity, study habits, and punctuality, while high-ability classes encouraged critical thinking, self-direction, and creativity. Teachers in low-ability classes spent less time on learning, assigned less homework, and exhibited fewer behaviors thought to be beneficial to learning than did their counterparts in high-ability classes (Oakes, 1985).

For Hispanics, the dilemma of the secondary schools' sorting system has been their disproportionate assignment to nonacademic tracks. Often, the placements have been associated with lower academic performance based on achievement scores and grades (Oakes, 1985, 1986a, 1986b). Valdivieso (1986) reported that in 1982, at-risk Hispanic seniors were taking the fewest academic courses of all student groups, and 75 percent were in nonacademic tracks. He also found that 92 percent of Hispanic dropouts had been enrolled in nonacademic tracks. In addition to poor school performance, student assignment to nonacademic tracks has fostered lower self-esteem, negative school attitudes (Winn & Wilson, 1983), decreased effort and motivation (Sorensen & Hallinan, 1986), and greater misconduct and delinquent behavior (Oakes, 1985).

Secondary school reforms that raised academic standards may foster more achievement-based tracking (Jones, 1986) and increase the distinction between the college-bound and the two lower tracks, general and vocational (Pipho, 1986). However, there is little evidence that reformers have addressed the issue of tracking and its debilitating effect on Hispanic students' educational opportunities (Oakes, 1986c). Oakes (1985) has shown that heterogenous grouping substantially counteracted all the negative attributes associated with tracking. Others (Goodlad, 1984; Romberg, 1983; Slavin, 1983) have suggested alternatives for restructuring classroom instruction and teacher practices to untrack schools. Yet differentiated schooling has continued to result in an unequal distribution of learning opportunities that clearly favors the already privileged (Oakes, 1986c).

HISPANICS AND DROPOUT RATES

Mann (1987) has observed that the number of students dropping out of high school has become nearly scandalous in education. Yet some (Jones, 1986; McDill et al., 1987; Valdivieso, 1986) suggest that school reforms aimed at standardizing curriculum and raising academic standards may have accelerated already high dropout rates. Hispanic youngsters have dropped out at a higher rate than all other students, even when socioeconomic status has been held constant (Steinberg, Blinde, & Chan, 1984).

Of the Mexican American and Puerto Rican students who enter high school, 45 percent never finish (National Commission on Secondary Schooling for Hispanics, 1984a, 1984b).

A national and metropolitan review of varying Hispanic dropout rates illustrates the magnitude of this problem. In 1974, the Hispanic dropout rate was reported to be 30 percent, but by 1979 it had risen to 40 percent, substantially higher than the 25 percent national average (Steinberg et al., 1984). The Department of Education (1987) currently places the Hispanic (Mexican American and Puerto Rican) dropout rate at 45 percent, while the rate for non-Hispanic whites is 17 percent. Valdivieso (1986) used the "High School and Beyond" data base and calculated that 40 percent of the 1982 Hispanic cohort had dropped out. Nationally, more Hispanics drop out than blacks or whites (Steinberg et al., 1984).

In metropolitan areas critically important to the economic future of the nation, Hispanics generally have the highest dropout rates for all groups. For example, Valdivieso (1986) reported the following metropolitan Hispanic dropout rates: Chicago, 70 percent; Los Angeles, 50 percent; Miami, 32 percent; New York, 80 percent; and San Antonio, 23 percent. Hammack (1987), using data obtained directly from large, urban school districts, reported the following Hispanic dropout rates: Boston, 20 percent; Chicago, 46.9 percent; Los Angeles, 43 percent; and Miami, 29.3 percent. Interestingly, Astin (1981) reported a nonmetropolitan Hispanic dropout rate of 44.8 percent compared to 15.5 percent for nonmetropolitan whites. These devastating data do not seem to attract the attention of or stimulate action by school reformers.

Hispanic dropouts have several factors in common. Some commentators (Ekstrom, Goertz, Pollack, & Rock, 1987; Valdivieso, 1986) have concluded that low grades are the most important variable in Hispanics' decision to drop out. Overage Hispanics also run a high risk of dropping out, as do those exhibiting high absenteeism and repeated suspensions (Orum, 1985). Valdivieso (1986) reported that Hispanic students had the highest labor participation rates, worked more hours per week, and held more full-time jobs than all other groups. He noted that attraction to work, poor grades, and being overage resulted in Hispanic dropout.

Other researchers have produced similar data. Hiramo-Nakanishi (1986) reported that 43 percent of all Hispanic dropouts left school before reaching grade 10, and 55.6 percent of LEP Hispanics left that soon. She also found that poor Hispanics left before reaching high school at two to five times the rate of more advantaged Hispanics. Still others (Steinberg et al., 1984) found that language-minority Hispanics had the highest dropout rates of all language-minority students, as much as 1.5 to 2.0 times greater. Barro and Kolstad (1986) found that Hispanic dropout rates were greatest from general and vocational tracks. Valdivieso (1986) observed that only 8 percent of Hispanic dropouts emerged from academic tracks. Curiously, several scholars (Curiel, Rosenthal, & Richek, 1986) reported that

Hispanic secondary students exposed to an elementary bilingual education program experienced significantly less grade retention, lower dropout rates, and were younger due to appropriate age-grade placements than Hispanic counterparts in an English-only traditional curriculum. All these studies identify a complex of interactive, powerful factors that contribute to the numbing Hispanic dropout figures.

Mann (1987) has asserted that our national policy toward school reform has been "teach the best and to hell with the rest"(p.13). McDill et al. (1987) contend that reform reports have neglected dropouts and that this oversight may have aggravated the problem. They have noted three consequences for at-risk students emerging from the current reforms. First, restricted core-curriculum requirements may have limited these students' opportunities to succeed by exposing them to repeated academic failure. Additionally, lengthening the school day and assigning more homework may have created economic and academic conflict for those students who need to work to stay in school. Finally, raising academic standards may have resulted in perceptions by at-risk students that these standards were unobtainable. If this occurred, these students may have disengaged from school, becoming more apathetic and finally dropping out.

Valdivieso (1986) has agreed with these contentions. He has asserted that more academic rigor for at-risk Hispanic students, who made up 25 percent of the entire Hispanic cohort and 43 percent of those who graduated in 1982, would push them out of school. At-risk Hispanic students would have to show the most academic growth and substantial changes in school attitudes and work habits to succeed. A reform agenda addressing the dropout might include enhanced counseling, integration of work with school (Valdivieso, 1986), smaller schools, enhanced governance, reward structures, and normative emphasis on academics (McDill et al., 1987).

The ultimate cost of dropping out is economic (McDill et al., 1987). For Hispanics, dropping out results in a $441,000 loss in lifetime earnings over those of a typical high school graduate, and $1,082,000 in lost earnings compared to a college graduate. For the nation, $68 billion is lost in yearly tax revenue from dropouts in each national high school class of dropouts. In 1985, Los Angeles spent $488 million in local government cost for dropouts (Department of Education, 1987). All dropouts, over their lifetimes, will earn $237 billion less than graduates from high school (Mann, 1987). In this future of diminishing resources, can we withstand the incredible cost of Hispanic dropouts?

CONCLUSIONS

In turning from equity issues, the school reform movement has left intact an inferior, dual-state educational system that will perpetuate Hispanic economic and social apartheid. Driven by a myopic vision of trickle-down excellence (Oakes, 1986c), state policymakers have formulated and implemented myriad school reforms, thematically unified by increased academic rigor for students and by higher standards for teachers (Pipho, 1986). Motivated primarily by national interests in maintaining worldwide economic competitiveness, the reform agenda included increased graduation requirements, lengthened school days, more homework, and teacher compensation systems based on merit and career ladders. These excellence agendas have virtually stopped policy initiatives aimed at continuing this nation's brief struggle for equity in our schools. An apparent casualty was a national vision of an integrated society, where schools functioned to educate Hispanic students successfully and that sought to be just and tolerant toward their cultural and linguistic differences. The excellence reforms have fostered schools that socialize Hispanic students in highly segregated school settings, educational arrangements that were found to be "inherently unequal" by the U.S. Supreme Court more than 30 years ago.

It is the role of the federal government to explicitly question the effects of educational reform movements that fail to address or even exacerbate the "dilemmas of difference" (Minow, 1985) posed by heterogeneous subpopulations of this country. If these reform agenda ignore these differences, then regardless of their perceived societal value, they must be considered exclusionary as well as intellectually and morally bankrupt within our constitutional framework. Moreover, although states are implicitly responsible for their own educational systems and their reform, the national interest, embodied by the 14th Amendment, requires that these questions be confronted and answered. State educational reformers must accept the affirmative duty to educate all children effectively. When states apparently place a higher reform priority on increasing student homework than on abolishing pervasive, segregated schooling of Hispanics, the excellence movement has both trivialized and eroded the foundation of our democratic republic.

NOTE

Author's Note: Preparation of this chapter was supported in part by the Mexican American Studies and Research Center, University of Arizona. I appreciate the help of those colleagues who offered useful comments on earlier drafts: Walter Doyle, Celestino Fernandez, Paul Heckman, Judy Mitchell, Luis Moll, and Michael Sacken. Request reprints from Marcello Medina, Jr., Division of Education Foundations and Administration, College of Education, University of Arizona, Tucson, Arizona.

REFERENCES

Arias, M. B.(1986). The context of education for Hispanic students: An overview. *American Journal of Education, 95*(1), 26–57.

Astin, A. W. (1981). *Minorities in higher education.* San Francisco, CA: Jossey-Bass.

Barro, S. M., & Kolstad, A. (1986). *Who drops out of high school? Findings from high school and beyond.* Washington, DC: SMB Economic Research.

Boyer, E. L. (1984). Reflections on the great debate of '83. *Phi Delta Kappan, 65*(8), 525–530.

Braddock, J. H., Crain, R. L., & McPartland, J. M. (1984). A long-term view of school desegregation: Some recent studies of graduates as adults. *Phi Delta Kappan, 66*(4), 259–264.

Brown v. *Board of Education,* 347 U.S. 483 (Supreme Court of the United States, 1954).

Clark, K. B. (1984). Educational trends and U.S. commitments since the *Brown* decision. *Educational Leadership, 41*(4), 83–85.

Crawford, J. (1987a, April 1). Bilingual education: Language, learning and politics. *Education Week: A Special Report,* pp. 19–20.

Crawford, J. (1987b, April 1). California vote gives boost to "English-only" movement. *Education Week: A Special Report,* p. 26.

Curiel, H., Rosenthal, J. A., & Richek, H. G. (1986). Impact of bilingual education on secondary school grades, attendance, retentions and dropout. *Hispanic Journal of Behavioral Sciences, 8*(4), 357–367.

Department of Education. (1987). *What works: Schools that work—Educating disadvantaged children.* Washington, DC: U.S. Government Printing Office.

Ekstrom, R. B., Goertz, M.E., Pollack, J. M., & Rock, D. A.(1987). Who drops out of high school and why? Findings from a national study. In G. Natriello (Ed.), *School dropouts: Patterns and policies* (pp. 52–69). New York: Columbia University, Teachers College Press.

Espinosa, R., & Ochoa, A. (1986). Concentration of California Hispanic students in schools with low achievement: A research note. *American Journal of Education, 95*(1), 77–95.

Fiske, E. B. (1987, July 26). Segregation growing for Hispanic students. *New York Times,* Sec. 1, p. 24.

Fradd, S. H. (1987). The changing focus of bilingual education. In S. H. Fradd & W. J. Tikunoff (Eds.), *Bilingual education and bilingual special education: A guide for administrators* (pp. 1–44). Boston: Little, Brown.

Fuchs, L. H. (1987, August). *The immigration reform and control act of 1986: A case study in legislative leadership and pluralistic politics. A triumph for the civic culture.* Paper presented at the American Political Science Association, Chicago, IL.

Goodlad, J. I. (1984). *A place called school: Prospects for the future.* New York: McGraw-Hill.

Hammack, F. M. (1987). Large school systems' dropout reports: An analysis of definitions, procedures, and findings. In G. Natriello (Ed.), *School dropouts: Patterns and policies* (pp. 20–37). New York: Columbia University, Teachers College Press.

Hawley, W. D. (1983). Achieving quality integrated education—with or without federal help. *Phi Delta Kappan, 64*(5), 334–338.

Hiramo-Nakanishi, M. (1986). The extent and relevance of pre-high school attrition and delayed education for Hispanics. *Hispanic Journal of Behavioral Sciences, 8*(1), 61–76.

Howe, H. (1987). Remarks on equity and excellence in education. *Harvard Educational Review, 57*(1), 199–202.

Jennings, J. F. (1987). The sputnik of the eighties. *Phi Delta Kappan, 69*(2), 104–109.

Jones, B. F. (1986). Quality and equality through cognitive instruction. *Educational Leadership, 43*(7), 4–11.

Kirst, M. W. (1986). Sustaining the momentum of state education reform: The link between assessment and financial support. *Phi Delta Kappan, 67*(5), 341–345.

Larmouth, D. W. (1987). Does linguistic heterogeneity erode national unity? In W.A. Van Horne & T. Tonnesen (Eds.), *Ethnicity and language: Volume 6. Ethnicity and public policy series* (pp. 37–57). Milwaukee, WI: University of Wisconsin System, Institute on Race and Ethnicity.

Lightfoot, S. L. (1987). On excellence and goodness. *Harvard Educational Review, 57*(1), 202–205.

Mann, D. (1987). Can we help dropouts? Thinking about the undoable. In G. Natriello (Ed.), *School Dropouts: Patterns and policies* (pp. 3–19). New York: Columbia University, Teachers College Press.

McDill, E. L., Natriello, G., & Pallas, A. M. (1987). A population at risk: Potential consequences of tougher school standards for school dropouts. In G. Natriello (Ed.), *School dropouts: Patterns and practices* (pp. 106–147). New York: Columbia University, Teachers College Press.

McNett, I. (1983). *Demographic imperatives: Implications for educational policy.* Washington, DC: American Council on Education.

Miller, L. S. (1986). The school-reform debate. *Journal of Economic Education, 17*(3), 204–209.

Minow, M. (1985). Learning to live the dilemma of difference: Bilingual and special education. *Law and Contemporary Problems, 48*(2), 157–211.

National Commission on Secondary Schooling for Hispanics.(1984a). *Make something happen: Hispanics and urban high school reform* (Vol.1). New York: Hispanic Policy Development Project.

National Commission on Secondary Schooling for Hispanics. (1984b). *Make something happen: Hispanics and urban high school reform* (Vol. 2). New York: Hispanic Policy Development Project.

Oakes, J. (1985). *Keeping track: How schools structure inequality.* New Haven, CT: Yale University Press.

Oakes, J. (1986a). Keeping track, part 1: The policy and practice of curriculum inequality. *Phi Delta Kappan, 68*(1), 12–18.

Oakes, J. (1986b). Keeping track, part 2: Curriculum inequality and school reform. *Phi Delta Kappan, 68*(2), 148–154.

Oakes, J. (1986c). Tracking, inequality and the rhetoric of reform: Why schools don't change. *Journal of Education, 168*(1), 60–80.

Odden, A. (1986). Sources of funding for educational reform. *Phi Delta Kappan, 67*(5), 335–340.

Ogbu, J. U. (1978). *Minority education and caste: The American system in cross-cultural perspective.* New York: Academic Press.

Orfield, G. (1983). *Public school desegregation in the United States, 1968–1980.* Washington, DC: Joint Center for Political Studies.

Orfield, G. (1986). Hispanic education: Challenges, research and policies. *American Journal of Education, 95*(1), 1–25.

Orfield, G., Monfort, F., & George, R. (1987). *School segregation in the 1980s: Trends in metropolitan areas.* Washington, DC: Joint Center for Political Studies.

Orum, L. S. (1985). *The education of Hispanics: Selected statistics.* Washington, DC: National Council of La Raza. (ERIC Document Reproduction Service No. ED 262 121.)

Pipho, C. (1986). Kappan special report: States move reform closer to reality. *Phi Delta Kappan, 68*(4),K1–8.

Romberg, T. A. (1983). A common curriculum for mathematics. In G. D. Fenstermacher & J. I. Goodlad (Eds.), *Individual differences and the common curriculum* (pp. 121–159; 82nd Yearbook of the National Society of Education). Chicago: University of Chicago Press.

Slavin, R. L. (1983). *Cooperative learning.* New York: Longman.

Sorensen, A. B., & Hallinan, M. T. (1986). Effects of ability grouping on growth in academic achievement. *American Educational Research Journal, 23*(4), 519–542.

Stedman, L. C., & Smith, M. S. (1983). Recent reform proposals for American education. *Contemporary Education Review, 2*(2), 85–104.

Steinberg, L., Blinde, P. L., & Chan, K. S. (1984). Dropping out among language minority youth. *Review of Educational Research, 54*(1), 113–132.

U.S. Census Bureau. (1987). Current population reports. Population characteristics (Series P-20, No. 416). Washington, DC: U.S. Government Printing Office.

U.S. General Accounting Office. (1987). *Bilingual education: A new look at research evidence* (GAO/PEMD-87-12BR). Washington, DC.

Valdivieso, R. (1986). *Must they wait another generation? Hispanics and secondary school reform.* New York: Columbia University, Teachers College. ERIC Clearinghouse on Urban Education. (ERIC Document Reproduction Service No. ED 273 705).

Willie, C. V. (1987). When excellence and equity complement each other. *Harvard Education Review, 57*(1), 205–207.

Winn, W., & Wilson A. P. (1983). The affect and effect of ability grouping. *Contemporary Education, 54*(2), 119–125.

UNIT FOUR

Redefining Good Education: Preparing Students for Tomorrow

191

In the previous unit, we concluded that defining the goals of a good educational system is an intensely political process. Historically, that process has swung between two extremes, equity *(making sure that everybody, regardless of background, has the same chance at making it in society), and* excellence *(giving everybody the same "best" possible education). In recent years, the New Right and big business interests have allied to shift away from equity and toward excellence as a goal in education. The assumption was that the U.S. work force had become lazy and that we should begin to discipline the students of today to be the workers of tomorrow.*

In a sense, Unit Three described *how the current reform movement arose out of the politics of interest group pluralism. In this unit, several reformers will take the basic theme of preparing today's students for tomorrow, and* prescribe *some changes in the reform movement.*

Robert Reich (Chapter 16) looks at education from a business perspective, asking what types of traits workers will need to succeed in the next economy. Interestingly, he claims that there are two routes to success. Either firms will have to compete in the world economy on the basis of lower cost *(implying Third World wages), or else they will have to compete on the basis of* higher quality *that is customized to meet the buyer's needs. Reich claims that this second method is the only way to retain our nation's high standard of living in the long run, and thus we need a very different kind of educational system than the one we have now, which was set up to prepare workers to do simple, repetitive tasks on long assembly lines. Instead, we now need workers who can be creative, innovative, and flexible.*

The need for people with higher order cognitive skills turns out to be a recurring theme in this unit. Hawley (Chapter 17) laments the fact that today's schools are not set up for today's demographic realities (one-parent families, for example), and that in the attempt to cram enough "knowledge" into kids so that they can pass the standardized tests, inadequate attention is paid to the development of problem-solving and decision-making skills. This latter approach (aimed at developing problem-solving and decision-making skills) has been called intentional learning, *and the key to it appears to be student involvement.*

Unfortunately, unless our society radically changes its priorities to give much more support to socially and economically disadvantaged families (both inside and outside of school), it will be difficult to close the gap between the haves and the have-nots, as our public education system has historically helped to do between the generations. This is because the development of higher order skills ap-

pears to be strongly linked to the levels of cognitive demand placed on the child during social experiences outside of school (Hawley).

Given that U.S. society is unlikely to change its economic and social inequality, what can we do with the structure of education to motivate student involvement (intentional learning, as noted previously)? Bishop (Chapter 18) addresses this question by suggesting that there is a serious problem with docility and apathy in our schools today. He points out that our society does not substantially reward academic accomplishment in the job market. Because of this, students have little incentive to do anything more than pass. In addition, the system is set up as a zero-sum game, where obtaining a good class ranking means you are hurting your best friends' rankings, thus creating a powerful social disincentive to work too hard.

Until we remove these structural impediments *to intentional learning, Bishop claims, the apathy problem will remain. He suggests that employers have a special responsibility to give academically successful students their due in increased pay and responsibility, and that schools should award diplomas based on competencies achieved rather than on time served.*

This emphasis on developing thinking *students to be effective participants in the economy is a good response to the first wave reformers and the back-to-basics people who would impose ever-tighter regulations and standardize the learning process. As Futrell (Chapter 19) points out in her thoughtful essay, however, education should serve as more than an economic weapon in the international trading arena. She suggests that we overemphasize the* economic value *of an education while underemphasizing its* intrinsic value *in elevating character. Can an economic value be put on such virtues as civic responsibility, morality, and aesthetic sense, or on an appreciation of music and the arts?*

Finally, Futrell, reminding us of the global village metaphor, suggests that an education defined to serve the cause of economic nationalism may be entirely inappropriate. The values of the future are likely to be transnational. *"That goal is an education . . . that prepares them not only for a life of work but for a life of worth. . . ."*

16

Preparing Students for Tomorrow's *Economic* World

Education and the Next Economy
ROBERT B. REICH

INTRODUCTION

What kind of education will Americans need in the emerging economy? The conventional view is that Americans will need *more* and *better* education, but there is surprisingly little agreement about what *more* and *better* actually mean. The answer should not depend on occupational projections—that is, on estimates about which jobs are likely to be plentiful should the economy continue in the direction it is now moving—for that direction is toward a continuing decline in the living standard of most Americans. We first need to define where we want our economy to go, and then ask what kind of education will help to propel us in that direction.

The purpose of this chapter is to explore where the economy is heading, where it should be heading, and what education can and should contribute. Its modest goal is to provide a framework for continuing discussion about these vital matters. By focusing on the relationship between education and the next economy, I do not mean to suggest that education's only, or most important, purpose is economic. To the contrary: A truly educated person is motivated by, and can find satisfaction in, a wide array of things that are not traded in markets or that cost very little. A just and democratic society depends on a citizenry educated in civic responsibility rather than in economic aggrandizement.[1]

THE CURRENT MESS

The stock market crashed on October 19, 1987, but the deterioration of the American economy had begun long before. America has been busy consuming more than it has produced. In 1986, for example, the nation generated some $800 billion more in goods and services than it had in the recession year of 1982, but it spent about $900 billion more.

We have been able to ignore this profligacy only because foreigners have kept lending us money, buying our corporations, and purchasing our real estate. By the time of the crash, we were $350 billion in debt, almost one-half of the commercial real estate of downtown Los Angeles (among many other cities) was in foreign hands, and foreign creditors were growing sufficiently nervous about our ability to repay our debts that the dollar was heading downward.

A nation living beyond its means faces precisely the same choice as a person living in the same manner; either it may grow poorer, or it may improve its means by becoming more productive. America has been exercising the first option. The steadily declining dollar has rendered more expensive everything we purchase from abroad; in most families, two wage-earners are necessary to make ends meet, whereas years ago one would do; average family size is shrinking; young people are having difficulty affording houses nearly as nice as the homes they grew up in; for the first time since the 1930s the percentage of Americans who own their own homes is declining; over one-fifth of our children are now born into poverty. The average American family is no better off today than it was fifteen years ago, even though America is now living off borrowed funds. Were the borrowing to stop, our standard of living would fall precipitously.

As the present work force matures, moreover, the first option (to grow poorer) becomes ever more likely. The number of American young people is declining while retirees are increasing. By the year 2030, when the proportion of our population 65 years of age and older will nearly have doubled from what it is now, the number of workers supporting each retiree will have dropped from 3.3 to a bit over 2. Unless each remaining worker becomes far more productive than now (or unless retirees continue to work long after retirement age, or unless we allow into America large numbers of new immigrants), our average citizen will have to get by on a much smaller income.

The second option (becoming more productive) has been pursued less vigorously. Our indebtedness to the rest of the world would not be alarming were the proceeds invested in our future productivity, but such has not been the case. Net investment in plant and equipment, as a percentage of gross national product, has been no higher in the 1980s than in the perilous 1970s, supply-side predictions to the contrary notwithstanding. Meanwhile, public investments have lagged. Government spending on commercial research and development has declined 95 percent from its level two decades ago; even when added to private-sector research and development, the total is still less than 2 percent of GNP, lower than comparable research and development expenditures in all other advanced industrial nations. Spending to upgrade and expand the nation's infrastructure—the roads, bridges, ports, tunnels, and communications facilities through which our commerce travels—has dropped from 2.3 percent of GNP two decades ago to 0.4 percent today. Federal support for education, job-training, and preschool care has declined as well.

Thus, while manufacturing productivity has risen slightly as a result of advances in automation and efforts at cutting costs, overall productivity gains, weighed down by slow or negative gains in the increasingly important service sector, have dropped to only 1 percent a year, from over 3 percent a decade before. In the last two years, even a declining dollar has barely helped American producers regain market share from foreigners who continue to supply world markets with relatively cheap, high-quality goods. At this rate the dollar will have to drop significantly lower if the trade balance is to be restored.

Most of the panaceas now being offered by politicians and business leaders are alternative means of growing poorer—for example, allowing the dollar to continue to fall, cutting wages, reducing environmental and safety regulations, slashing welfare expenditures, protecting American goods from foreign competition, and even bringing on a recession. These strategies impose the burden of becoming poorer on different groups of citizens over slightly different periods of time, but their overall effects are much the same. There is no secret to becoming poorer. To repeat: The *only* becoming-richer strategy is to become more productive—adding ever-greater value to the world economy.

WORK IN THE OLD ECONOMY

Productivity, however, is no longer simply a matter of making more of what we already make at less cost per unit. To add greater value to the world economy, we have to provide higher quality goods, and tailor our products and services to the particular needs of consumers. This is a new challenge, entailing a very different organization of work.

In the early postwar years, most young people could look forward to jobs requiring only that they be able to learn some relatively simple tasks that could be repeated, over and over. That's because the American economy was organized around economies of scale. The goal was high-volume, standardized production in which large numbers of identical items could be produced over long runs, allowing fixed costs to be spread as widely as possible. Whether it was wheat, steel, or even insurance, the same overarching rule prevailed: Every step along the production process was to be simple and predictable, so that it could be synchronized with every other step. Productivity was a function of high volume and low cost.

There was little room or need for innovation. Once in a while someone came up with a major invention—e.g., continuous casters for making steel, automobile stamping machines, plastics—but these big breakthroughs were relatively few and far between. Indeed, innovation often was seen as a problem rather than as a solution. Innovation meant changes in products and production processes, and such changes cost money. If the changes happened too often, it was difficult to achieve the economies of scale necessary to pay for them and still make a profit.

Sometimes competitors quietly agreed not to innovate very much for fear of rocking the profitable boat. These were the days when most industries were dominated by a few large companies—the Big Three automakers, a handful of steel producers, three or four major food processors—who roughly coordinated prices and investments in order to achieve the kind of stability and predictability necessary for vast economies of scale. The tailfins on our cars grew longer, but underneath the hoods the autos remained about the same year after year, and it didn't matter very much which brand you bought.[2]

Under high-volume, standardized production, a few people at the top made all the decisions. They designed the system and planned all the standard operating procedures by which it would run. Most people followed orders. Indeed, for the production system to be stable and predictable, the majority had to follow orders exactly. Rigid work rules and job classifications posed no challenge to this hierarchical system, because every job was rigid to begin with—like cogs in a wheel.

A primary goal of public education within this stable system was to prepare most young people for such "cog" jobs. They had to be trained to comprehend and accept instructions, and then to implement them conscientiously. Discipline and reliability were core virtues.

A much smaller number of young people had to be prepared to act as decision makers at the top. They needed to be trained to gather information, translate the information into abstract symbols, manipulate the symbols to find answers, turn the answers into operating instructions, and then communicate the instructions downward. Here, abstract logic, clarity, and firmness were the core virtues.

Our schools were reasonably effective at preparing Americans for these two kinds of jobs. Most children graduated from high school or vocational school ready to accept cog jobs. A few were set on an advanced track through high school and into colleges that prepared them either for careers as professional managers or for the related professions of law, banking, engineering, and consulting. Productivity soared.[3]

ENTER THE GLOBAL ECONOMY

High-volume, standardized production can no longer provide the productivity gains we need to maintain our standard of living. There has been a sea change in the world economy. Beginning in the 1960s and continuing to the present day, the cost of sending things or information around the globe has fallen dramatically. This is a result, principally, of rapid advances in the technologies of transporting and communicating—of innovations such as container ships, satellites, and computers that allowed the production process to be fragmented and parceled out around the globe to wherever pieces of it could be undertaken most cheaply and efficiently. Until recently most goods were produced close to where they were to be consumed; the main exceptions were certain minerals, agricultural goods, and economically unimportant exotica. This pattern has been breaking down at an increasing pace. Consumers of cars, refrigerators, televisions and television programs, insurance policies, and even money, often live in different nations or on different continents from the producers. The producers, in turn, often depend on far-distant sources for components, designs, and information. It is now often cheaper to ship raw steel across an ocean than across the United States. Slight differences in interest rates may induce a New York corporation to raise money in Tokyo or in Bonn instead of on Wall Street.

Two decades ago international trade hardly figured in the American market; today, more than 70 percent of the goods we produce are actively competing with foreign-made goods. Whoever can do it best and cheapest, anywhere in the world, now sells to whoever is willing to pay the best price, anywhere in the world. The elegant curves of supply and demand that so charm economists are meeting up in the oddest of places.

In a world where routine production is footloose and billions of potential workers are ready to underbid American labor, we can no longer expect to be competitive by simply producing more of the same thing we produced before, at lower cost. As the production of commodities shifts to other nations, America's competitive advantage correspondingly must shift toward work whose value is based more on quality, flexibility, precision, and specialization than on its low cost. For example, only a small fraction of the American work force is still employed on the farm. But the food industry nevertheless accounts for close to one-quarter of the jobs in the United States. That's because most of what Americans and consumers in other advanced nations now spend for food goes to the people who process, package, market, and retail it, and to the agricultural epidemiologists, geneticists, international bankers, commodity traders, chemists, and process engineers who supply the technology and money for producing it, rather than to those who actually grow and harvest it. Similarly, most of what is spent on appliances, clothing, cars, computers, air travel, or a host of other things is for designing, engineering, fabricating, and advertising, rather than for standardized, routine work. In fact, much of the growth in what has been termed services within the American economy is attributable to just such businesses.

Nor can we hope to be competitive by relying, as before, on major inventions that occur from time to time. These days, breakthrough inventions get away. Americans continue to lead the world in big breakthroughs and cutting-edge scientific discoveries. But the big ideas that start in this country now quickly travel abroad, where they get produced at high speed, at low cost, and with great efficiency. All too often, Americans get bogged down somewhere between invention and production. We fail to incorporate new ideas into our products and processes nearly as fast as we should. Several product histories make the point. Americans invented the solid-state transistor in 1947. Then in 1953, Western Electric licensed the technology to Sony for $25,000—and the rest is history. A few years later, RCA licensed several Japanese companies to make color televisions—and that was the beginning of the end of color television production in the United States. Routine assembly of color televisions eventually shifted to Taiwan and Mexico. Americans came up with video recorders, basic oxygen furnaces, microwave ovens, and computerized machine tools. But these big ideas and many others found their way into routine, standardized production in other nations.[4]

Keeping a technology requires elaborating upon it continuously, developing variations and small improvements in it that better meet particular needs. Where innovation is continuous, and products are ever more tailored to customers' needs, the distinction between goods and services further blurs. Thus when robots and computerized machine tools are linked through software that allows them to perform unique tasks, customer service becomes a part of production. When a new alloy is molded to be a specified weight and tolerance, service accounts for a significant part of the value added.

Reports that American workers can no longer compete in manufacturing and must shift to services are thus only half right. More precisely, they can keep high wages only by producing goods with a large component of specialized services, or to state the same thing differently, by providing services integral to the production and use of specific goods. There is no longer any meaningful distinction between the two categories, goods and services.

The point is this: In the new global economy, nearly everyone has access to big breakthroughs and to the machines and money to turn them into standardized products at about the same time, and on roughly the same terms. The only factor of production that is relatively immobile internationally, and on which the future standard of living of the nation uniquely depends, is *us*—our competence, our insights, our capacity to work productively together.

The older industrial economies like America thus have two options: (1) they can try to match the wages for which workers elsewhere are willing to labor, or (2) they can compete on the basis of how quickly and how well they can transform ideas into incrementally better goods and services. Both paths can boost profits and improve competitiveness in the short run, but only the second can maintain and improve the standard of living of most Americans over time.

THE ORGANIZATION OF WORK: TWO PATHS TO THE NEXT ECONOMY

The first path—toward stable mass production—relies on cutting labor costs, and leaping into wholly new product lines as old ones are played out. For managers this path has meant undertaking (or threatening) massive layoffs, moving (or threatening to move) to lower-wage states and countries, parceling out work to lower-cost suppliers, automating to cut total employment, and diversifying into radically different goods and services. For workers this path has meant defending existing jobs and pay scales, grudgingly conceding lower wages and benefits, shifting burdens by accepting lower-pay scales for newly hired workers, seeking protection from foreign competition, and occasionally striking.

The second path involves increasing labor's *value*. For managers this path means continuously retraining employees for more complex tasks, automating in ways that cut routine tasks and enhance worker flexibility and creativity, diffusing responsibility for innovation, taking seriously labor's concern for job security and giving workers a stake in improved productivity via profit-linked bonuses and stock plans. For workers this second path means accepting flexible job classifications and work rules, agreeing to wage rates linked to profits and productivity improvements, and generally taking greater responsibility for the soundness and efficiency of the enterprise. The second path also involves a close and more permanent relationship with other parties that have a stake in the firm—suppliers, dealers, creditors, even the towns and cities in which the firm resides. On this second path, all those associated with the firm become partners in its future, sharing downside risks and upside benefits. Each member of the enterprise participates in its evolution. All have a commitment to its continued success.

The second path requires a fundamentally different organization of work from that which has come before, as well as a different work force within that new organization. The old hierarchical arrangement in which a relatively few well-trained individuals planned and maintained the production system from the top, and almost everyone else undertook cog jobs below, is not up to the challenge. The technologies upon which we must continuously improve, and the tastes to which we must continuously respond, are changing so rapidly that no set of decision makers at the top can hope to keep up. Much of the relevant information lies below—among production workers, production engineers, sales people and others in direct contact with suppliers, production processes, and customers. There is not enough time for all the relevant information to be passed upward to the top decision makers and then down again in the form of new operating instructions. With valuable information and expertise dispersed throughout the organization, top managers cannot hope to solve problems and provide answers; their jobs must be to create environments in which people can identify and solve problems for themselves.

Thus the division between workers and managers will blur. Because production is a continuous process of reinvention, efforts will focus on many thousands of small ideas rather than on just a few big ones. Small-scale innovations will occur everywhere in the organization—and must occur quickly and continuously, in response to changing opportunities. One idea should lead to another. Producing the latest generation of automobiles involves making electronic circuits that govern fuel consumption and monitor engine performance; developments in these devices might lead to improved sensing equipment and software for monitoring heartbeats and moisture in the air. Producing cars also involves making flexible robots for assembling parts and linking them by computer; steady improvements in these technologies, in turn, may lead to expert production systems that can be applied anywhere. What is considered to be an "automobile manufacturer" thus is transmuted into a broad collection of skills evolving toward all sorts of applications that flow from the same strand of technological development.

Ideally, individual skills are integrated into a group; this collective capacity to innovate becomes something greater than the sum of its parts. Over time, as group members work through various problems and approaches, they learn about each others' abilities. They learn how they can help one another perform better, what each can contribute to a particular project, and how they can best take advantage of one another's experience. Each participant is on the lookout for small adjustments that will speed and smooth the evolution of the whole. The net result of many such small-scale adaptations, effected throughout the organization, is to propel the enterprise forward.

Workers also learn how they can better meet customers' needs: Sales people no longer simply "sell" goods and services. They help customers clarify and redefine what they need, and devise new solutions based upon what the firm might potentially provide. Thus sales people must have a complete understanding of the enterprise's capacity to design and deliver specialized products; and designers and engineers must be equally familiar with sales and marketing. In short, the firm's ability to adapt to new opportunities and capitalize on them depends on the capacities of all of its employees to share information and involve themselves in a systemwide search for ways to improve, adjust, adapt, and upgrade.

As workers add value through judgment and knowledge, computers become tools that expand their discretion rather than further simplify their jobs. Computer-generated information can give workers rich feedback about their own efforts, how they affect others in the production process, and how the entire process can be improved. One of the key lessons to emerge from the General Motors–Toyota joint venture in California is that the Japanese automaker does not rely on automation and technology to replace workers in the plant. In fact, human workers still occupy the most critical jobs—those where judgment and evaluation are essential. Instead, Toyota uses technology to allow workers to focus on those important tasks where choices have to be made. Under this approach, technology gives workers the chance to use their imagination and their insight on behalf of the company.

THE NEW EDUCATIONAL CHALLENGE

The second path to the next economy—increasing the value of labor rather than cutting its costs—relies, above all, on a work force capable of rapid learning. The most important skills will be transferred informally among workers as they gain experience on the job, rather than gleaned through formal education and training. But the ability to learn on the job will depend on learning skills and attitudes developed long before.

The old system of education mirrored the old organization of production: Most people spent eight to twelve years of their childhood training for cog jobs, while a few were propelled toward top policy and planning positions. The new system must prepare far more people to take responsibility for their continuing education, and to collaborate with one another so that their combined skills and insights add up to something more than the sum of their individual contributions.

Today's education is different from what it was two or three decades ago, of course. We surely spend more on education—about $300 billion in 1988 alone, which is almost 7 percent of our total annual output of goods and services, or about the same amount of money we spend on national defense.[5] Between the early 1950s and the mid-1980s, per pupil expenditures in American public schools tripled, as measured in constant dollars (although they have hardly increased at all since then).[6]

And we are getting a lot more education than before: Over 57 million of us are formally enrolled in schools and colleges, with millions more in job training and less formal educational activities. Three-quarters of our adults have completed high school; over 86 percent of younger adults in their twenties have done so—twice the percentage of 1940. Six out of ten of our high school graduates begin some form of more advanced education, and one-quarter of our younger adults have completed four years of college—up from 12 percent as recently as 1960.[7]

The quality of public education also has changed, particularly over the last several years. In 1983, the National Commission on Excellence in Education reported that American schools were failing to educate (23 million adults and 13 percent of our 17-year-olds were functionally illiterate); they compared badly with those of our trade competitors (our children came in last in 7 out of 19 academic tests, first or second in none); and they failed to teach our children the basics of American history and culture.[8] In response to this report and to others that followed, broad reforms have been initiated: All but five states have raised the minimum requirement for graduation from high school. Most states have also bolstered math and science curricula. Two dozen states, mainly in the South, have inaugurated comprehensive educational reforms including tightened standards, more academic discipline, and higher teacher salaries.[9] Forty states now have programs in technological education; New York even requires all junior high school students to take a year of introductory technology.[10] Efforts have been made to reduce truancy and dropout rates, introduce computer literacy and foreign languages in the early years, establish after-school programs, require more basic academic courses for a high school diploma, extend the school year, and enhance job-readiness programs.

There have been modest gains. Although, as we shall see, standardized examinations are questionable criteria of success, they offer useful comparisons. In South Carolina, which in 1984 enacted one of the most comprehensive reforms, average Scholastic Aptitude Test (SAT) scores have risen by 36 points. In Florida, where the high school day has been lengthened, SAT scores have increased modestly over the same period. In New York, which also imposed more stringent academic requirements, scores on the Pupil Evaluation Performance test for third graders rose from 77 to 79 percent. In California, the number of students taking three or more years of mathematics has increased by 15 percent and of science by 20 percent.[11]

But the task has just begun. The gains so far have been small. Education is so central to our place in the new world economy that we will have to do a better job—particularly in two respects: helping all our children to become minimally numerate and literate, and preparing them for jobs involving responsibility and collaboration. The challenge is not simply or even most importantly to provide our children with more education, but to provide them with a different kind of education founded upon new premises about the world they will meet in the future.

BASIC NUMERACY AND LITERACY

Although a higher proportion of our young people are better prepared for productive lives than ever before, the worst-prepared third of our young people—disproportionately lower income—are almost totally unprepared. They cannot do simple calculations, understand written directions, or read road signs, charts and maps.[12] And they often lack certain basic information about history, literature, geography, and the natural sciences.[13]

These deficiencies are already affecting American business. When the New York Telephone Company undertook a large-scale recruiting effort in 1987, for example, it found that over 80 percent of its New York City applicants failed entry-level examinations in basic reading and reasoning skills. Some 1,700 of Polaroid's employees—about one-third of the firm's hourly work force—are enrolled in a company program teaching them elementary reading and writing. All told, one of three American corporations now provides some form of basic skills training for its employees. The American Society for Training and Development Study predicts that American industry will have to spend as much as $25 billion yearly on remedial education.

Perhaps we are too impatient—maybe the reforms need more time to take hold. Or perhaps they are inadequate to the task of dealing with all the problems that accompany poverty and broken homes. Twenty-two percent of our children are now born into poverty, up from 15 percent in 1970, and it is projected that 60 percent of today's 3-year-olds will live in a single-parent home before they turn 18.

Or it may be that formal schooling comes too late in the lives of our neediest children, by which time learning habits and attitudes are already firmly established. While there is overwhelming evidence that preschool programs designed to develop the intellectual and social skills of poor children have large payoffs later on, less than one-half of 1 percent of our national spending on education goes to children under the age of six.[14] Or perhaps the reforms have backfired upon the neediest: Stricter promotion and graduation requirements may have prompted more of them to drop out. In many of our largest cities, nearly half fail to graduate. Forty percent of Florida's students drop out, as do almost half of Louisiana's. Overall, between 15 and 25 percent of our young people never finish high school.[15]

Whatever the cause, raising the lowest achievers to minimal levels of productive competence is a large part of the challenge of American education in the next economy. Not only do we need a larger population of productive people to help pay off our international debt, but we also need them to support a growing population of retirees.

RESPONSIBILITY

Achieving basic numeracy and literacy is only part of the challenge. If our economy is to transform itself—if we are to take the second path, toward higher-value production—we can no longer train the majority of our young people for cog jobs requiring primarily discipline and reliability. They must be prepared to take advantage of whatever opportunities present themselves for improvements in product and process. To recognize such opportunities, they must be educated to think critically and to continually learn on the basis of new data and experience.

In some respects, the training of young people in the old economy resembled the system of high-volume, standardized production in which they were to take part when their training was complete: Responsibility was exercised by a very few, at the top. The majority of students were pushed, as if on an assembly line, through a preestablished sequence of steps. Each step involved particular routines and practices. Teachers—the production workers—had little discretion over what they had to do to each batch that passed through; students passively received whatever was doled out. Inspectors tried to weed out the defects, sometimes returning them to an earlier step for reworking. Most got to the end of the assembly line, more or less ready to take their places along real assembly lines somewhere in the economy.

The premises of education in the next economy must be quite different. Just as productivity can no longer be a matter of making more of what we already make at less cost per unit, productivity in education cannot be solely a function of the numbers of children who pass standardized examinations at a lower cost per unit.

Because our future economy will depend to an ever greater extent on thinking rather than repeating learned information, future reforms must motivate teachers and students alike to love learning, and not prescribe to them exactly what should be learned and how and when the information should be doled out. Responsibility must be pushed downward, to students and teachers. They must be allowed and encouraged to take more initiative in deciding what is learned, and when and how it is learned. Education modeled around long lists of facts that "every adult should know" and standardized tests will produce robots adept at Trivial Pursuit but unable to think for themselves or to innovate for the future.

First, instead of giving students information along a preestablished sequence of steps, and then asking them to "play back" the information on tests, the emphasis in teaching should be on educating young people to formulate problems and questions for themselves. Thus, rather than teach students to assume that problems and solutions are generated by others (as they were under high-volume, standardized production), students should be taught to understand that problems and questions are created, that students can have an active role in creating them, and that such critical and creative approaches can guide them through their careers.[16]

Second, instead of teaching through repetition and drill, the emphasis should be on allowing students to experiment for themselves with solving the problems they help define. Thus, rather than conveying particular pieces of information or imposing established routines—a type of teaching and learning relevant to high-volume, standardized production—teachers must help students gain the experience of working through problems, and thus discovering underlying principles that help define and solve related problems.

The difference between absorbing information and gaining understanding depends on how much responsibility students are taught to accept for their own continuing learning. It is like the difference between learning how to get from one location to another in a city by having someone drive you or by driving yourself with a guide sitting beside. In the first instance you may eventually learn the way, but you probably will learn sooner by being in the driver's seat. Indeed, if your guide also allows you to experiment a bit, warning you only when you're going down blind alleys or heading in the wrong direction, you may gain even more understanding of the terrain, and thus learn how to find other places as well.[17]

An understanding of underlying principles and patterns allows discovery of other information, and gives that new information added context and meaning. The new information, in turn, permits deeper insight into the principles and patterns. As Michael Polanyi has written, "[w]e cannot comprehend the whole without seeing its parts, but we cannot see the parts without comprehending the whole."[18]

The habits and techniques of experimentation—of iterative discovery of parts and wholes—will be critical in the next economy, where technologies, tastes, and markets are likely to be in constant flux. Informal, on-the-job education will be a central aspect of work. Formal education and training will no longer be limited to young people, but will be available on a continuing basis to workers throughout their working lives—an accepted and expected aspect of one's career. A work force capable of taking responsibility for its own continuous learning will prove a more precious national asset than countless new factories and equipment.

COLLABORATION

Specialized skills also will be needed, of course. More of our young people will have to be able to communicate in foreign languages (for every American who now speaks Japanese, there are at least ten Japanese who speak English), and gain a working knowledge of foreign nations and cultures. More of them will need advanced education in mathematics, science, and engineering. (Despite a growing need, fewer bachelor's degrees were awarded in science and engineering in 1987 than on average during the 1970s.) There will be a greater need for people who can cross disciplines—from, say, physics to computer programming, from biology to Chinese language and culture.

But our culture has never had much difficulty educating the most talented and fortunate fifth of our young people to do complex intellectual tasks. Analytically sophisticated students already graduate from our universities, trained for narrow specialties in which they manipulate symbols and concepts in wonderous ways. We may want to change the mix somewhat—more engineers and foreign experts, fewer lawyers and financiers—but there is no fundamental problem mustering talented people and getting them educated. The greater challenge is to transform the individual talents and specialized skills of the top 20 percent into collective capacities broadly shared across American enterprise.

In the old economy, a relatively few people at the top could analyze and plan the production process by themselves, and then issue operating instructions to everyone else. So long as professional managers and their professional aides—bankers, lawyers, accountants, and engineers—got it "right" on paper, it was assumed that the rest would follow automatically. But paper professionals are far less relevant to the future. As we have seen, the weakest link in the American economy is between ideas and implementation, between paper and product. Thus if our business enterprises are to be as flexible and innovative at all levels as they need to be, our youngsters must be prepared to work with and through large numbers of people. While there will always be a need for a certain number of solo practitioners, the more usual requirement will be that combinations of individual skills are greater than their sums. Most of the important work will be done by groups, rather than by individual experts.

Learning to collaborate suggests a different kind of education than one designed to prepare a relatively few talented young people to become professional experts. Instead of emphasizing the quiet and solitary performance of specialized tasks, a greater emphasis should be placed on interactive communications linked to group problem-definitions and solutions.[19] Students should learn to articulate, clarify, and then restate for one another how they determine questions and find answers. Rather than be trained to communicate specialized instructions and requests—skills relevant to high-volume standardized production—students should learn how to share their understandings, and build upon each others' insights.[20]

Communication skills are only one aspect of collaboration. Young people also must be taught how to work constructively together. Instead of emphasizing individual achievement and competition, the emphasis in the classroom should be on group performance. Students need to learn how to seek and accept criticism from their peers, to solicit help, and to give credit to others, where appropriate. They must also learn to negotiate—to articulate their own needs, to discern what others need and see things for others' perspectives, and to discover mutually beneficial outcomes.

The "tracking" system, by which students are grouped in the classroom according to the speed of their learning, is another vestige of high-volume, standardized production—the deluxe models moving along a different conveyor belt from the economy cars. This may be an efficient way to cram information into young minds with differing capacities to absorb it; but tracking or grouping can also reduce young peoples' capacities to learn from and collaborate with one another. Rather than separate fast learners from slow learners in the classroom, all children (with only the most obvious exceptions) should remain together, so that class unity and cooperation are the norm. Faster learners would thus learn how to help the slower ones, while the slower ones would be pushed harder to make their best effort.[21]

In sum, it is not enough to produce a cadre of young people with specialized skills. If our enterprises are to be the scenes of collective entrepreneurship—as they must be—experts must have the ability to broadly share their skills and transform them into organizational achievement; and others must be prepared to learn from them.

THE DANGER OF FRAGMENTATION

Numeracy, literacy, responsibility, and collaboration: this is a tall order for public education. But it is a necessary one if we are to succeed in the world economy in coming years. It will require that we do in our schools what we must do in our business enterprises: push responsibility downward toward teachers and students; invite continuous, incremental innovation at all levels; foster collaboration among parents, teachers, principals, community groups, and the private sector; and encourage flexibility.[22]

Meeting the challenge also requires that we invest substantially in one another. We will have to pay more to educate our children—especially to attract and retrain talented teachers to do the educating. Between 1987 and 1993, American schools must recruit some 1.3 million new teachers—over half of the current force. According to present trends, the labor market will not meet this need. The choice will be either to lower recruitment standards or to raise teachers' salaries. The former choice will be far more costly to the nation than the latter. (It is worth noting in this regard that starting pay for Japanese school teachers exceeds that for any other public servants in Japan, and is higher than or equal to that of engineers.) Teachers and educational administrators, in turn, will have to accept even more accountability.

We also will have to bear more of the cost of educating our fellow citizens before and after their formal schooling. If our children are to be adequately prepared for school, Head Start and other preschool programs for ages 3 and 4, and day care for toddlers, must become the norm. If our older workers are to be adequately prepared for jobs that are continuously changing, they must have easy access to retraining and continuing education.[23]

Do we have the will to make the needed investments and undertake the necessary changes? Much depends on the extent to which we consider ourselves one people whose fates are linked.

I have before emphasized our choice of path toward the next economy—either cutting labor costs or increasing labor value. The first path will result in a lower standard of living for most Americans; the second requires that we all sacrifice in the short term in order to reap long-term gains. It should be noted, however, that the fates of our most talented and fortunate citizens are not necessarily linked to the educational attainments of the rest. The new world economy makes it possible for the top fifth of our population to sell their expertise directly in the global market, and thus maintain their standard of living and that of their children, even as that of other Americans declines. Improvements in the technologies of communications and transportation are facilitating the development of global corporations, partnerships, and consulting businesses that transcend the organization of production within any single nation. The most talented and fortunate fifth—sitting astride these global businesses—are thus losing any unique connection to the American economy.

There are signs that a two-tier society is already developing. Increasingly, our largest cities are inhabited by paper professionals at the top— lawyers, financiers, consultants, managers—and by unskilled service workers at the bottom—sales clerks, fast-food employees, custodians, hospital orderlies, cab drivers. Nationally, the gap appears to be widening. For 80 percent of American families, the last decade was a time of declining real income. But the wealthiest fifth of our population experienced no decline. In fact, the richest tenth enjoyed an increase of about 16 percent; the top twentieth, an increase of 23 percent; and the real income of America's richest 1 percent rose 50 percent.[24] Since 1980 the median income of a married couple, each of whom has had five or more years of education beyond high school, has risen to $61,130; the median income of a couple with only high school degrees has risen more slowly, to $36,888. Since 1980 the bottom fifth of the income distribution has lost, on average, one dollar out of every six in earnings, while the top fifth has increased its share of total national income by 8 percent.[25]

Without the active support of the most talented and fortunate fifth of our population, however, it will be difficult to muster the political will necessary to change the present direction. But unless we change, the gap between the top fifth and the rest of us will widen further; and most

Americans will continue to grow poorer. Therein lies one of the sharpest dilemmas of our time.

NOTES

This chapter is reprinted by permission of the author from "Education and the Next Economy," National Education Association—Professional and Organizational Development/Research Division. Copyright © 1988 National Education Association of the United States.

1. "[H]owever deserving of attention may be the *economical* view of the subject which I have endeavored to present, yet it is one that dwindles into insignificance when compared to those loftier and more sacred attributes of the cause." Horace Mann, *Fifth Annual Report of the Board of Education* (Boston: Board of Education, 1842).

2. For a more detailed description of this stable production system, see my *The Next American Frontier* (New York: Penguin Books, 1983).

3. Almost one-fifth of the growth in net national product per worker between 1948 and 1973 was a result of increased education of the work force. See Edward Denison, "The Interruption of Productivity Growth in the United States," *The Economic Journal* 93 (1983).

4. See my "Enterpreneurship Reconsidered: The Team as Hero," *Harvard Business Review* 65, No. 3 (May–June 1987).

5. In 1987, about $184 billion was spent for public and private elementary and secondary schools, about $124 billion for colleges and universities. For these and related data, see Center for Educational Statistics, U.S. Department of Education, *Digest of Education Statistics, 1986–1987* (Washington DC: U.S. Government Printing Office); U.S. Bureau of the Census, *Educational Attainment in the United States*, Current Population Reports, Series P-25 (Washington DC: The Bureau, various years).

6. Between 1980 and 1986, states and local school districts increased their educational expenditures by about $4.2 billion, in constant dollars, while the federal government's contribution declined by approximately the same amount. *Digest of Education Statistics 1986–1987*. See also, National Education Association, *Estimates of School Statistics, 1985–1986* (Washington, DC: The Association, 1987).

7. See U.S. Bureau of the Census, *Educational Attainment in the United States*, Current Population Reports (Washington, DC: The Bureau, 1986, 1987).

8. National Commission on Excellence in Education, *A Nation at Risk* (Washington, DC: U.S. Government Printing Office, 1983).

9. As recently as 1980, 10 of 15 states belonging to the Southern Regional Education Board required no more than one year of high school science. Now every state requires at least two years, and several require three.

10. "Reading, 'Riting, and 'Rithmetic, and Now Technological Education," *Business Week* (October 19, 1987), 114.

11. As reported in the *New York Times*, August 8, 1987, A14.

12. See, for example, Irwin S. Kirsch and Ann Jungeblut, *Literacy: Profiles of America's Young Adults* (Princeton, NJ: Educational Testing Service, 1986).

13. See, for example, Chester Finn, Jr., and Diane Ravitch, *What Do Our 17-Year-Olds Know?* (New York: Harper & Row, 1987); Committee for Economic Development, *Children in Need: Investment Strategies for the Educationally Disadvantaged* (New York: Committee for Economic Development, 1987).

14. The Committee for Economic Development, op. cit., recommends that more emphasis be placed on preventing teenage pregnancy, providing better nutrition and medical care to poor pregnant women, giving them advice on parenting, providing better postnatal care for high-risk mothers, and making quality child care and preschool programs more available. On the economic effects of preschool education, see, for example, J. R. Berreuta-Clement et al., *Changed Lives: The Effects of the Perry Pre-School Program on Youths Through Age Nineteen* (Ypsilanti, Mich.: High/Scope Press, 1984).

15. Only one in four finishes high school on schedule; there are no clear data on how many who do not finish on schedule finish later on.

16. A description of this method of teaching question-raising can be found in Marcia Heiman, "Learning to Learn: A Behavioral Approach to Improving Thinking." Paper presented at the Harvard Conference on Thinking, Cambridge, MA, 1984.

17. There is a rich literature on "experiential" learning. See, for example, D. A. Kolb, "On Management and the Learning Process," in *Organizational Psychology: A Book of Readings,* 2nd ed., edited by D. Kolb et al. (Englewood Cliffs, NJ: Prentice-Hall, 1974); Arthur Whimbey and Jack Lockhead, *Problem Solving and Comprehension* (Philadelphia: Franklin Institute Press, 1982); Lillian C. McDermott, "Helping Minority Students Succeed in Science," *Journal of College Science Teaching* (January, March, and May 1980).

18. Michael Polanyi, *The Study of Man* (Chicago: University of Chicago Press, 1958), 29.

19. The emphasis in Japanese schools upon teamwork in the classroom is thought to explain Japan's low rates of absenteeism on the job, and its firm's quick responsiveness to new opportunities. See Benjamin Duke, *The Japanese School: Lessons for Industrial America* (New York: Praeger, 1986).

20. See generally, Ernest L. Boyer, "Reflecting on the Great Debate of '83," *Phi Delta Kappan* (March 1984); Boyer, *High School* (New York: Harper & Row, 1983).

21. Japanese children are not grouped or "tracked"; the assumption in the Japanese classroom is that it is better for all the children to have the class as a whole progress together. See Mary White, *The Japanese Educational Challenge: A Commitment to Children* (New York: Free Press, 1987).

22. See generally, Judith Little, "Norms of Collegiality and Experimentation: Workplace Conditions and School Success," *American Educational Research Journal* 19, no. 3 (Fall 1982).

23. The sacrifices we will be called on to make in the years ahead are not only pecuniary, of course. We will have to spend more time with our children and perhaps with other children as well. It will be necessary for us to work closely with our childrens' teachers and principals. We will need to join with other parents to ensure both that the schools are meeting our expectations and that our childrens' lives outside of school are adequately stimulating and emotionally and physically secure.

24. Calculated from data supplied by the Congressional Budget Office, November 1987. See also Frank Levy, *Dollars and Dreams: The Changing American Income*

Distribution (New York: Basic Books, 1988). In 1969, a man three-quarters of the way up the income ladder earned $28,659 (in 1984 dollars); a fellow worker at the 25th percentile earned $8,981. The ratio between them was about 3 to 1. But in 1984, the ratio between them became 4 to 1.

25. Calculated from data from the U.S. Department of Labor, Bureau of Labor Statistics.

17

Preparing Students from Today's Families for Tomorrow's *Cognitive* Challenges

Missing Pieces of the Educational Reform Agenda: Or, Why the First and Second Waves May Miss the Boat
WILLIS D. HAWLEY

AMERICA RECURRENTLY ATTEMPTS to reform its schools. The most recent reform movement gained its momentum from a number of reports and studies about American education that began to gain public attention in 1983 with the publication of the National Commission on Excellence in Education's *A Nation at Risk*. To the surprise of many, the movement is not only still alive but has progressed, at least in some states and communities, beyond its essentially regulatory beginnings to concerns that address fundamental and enduring weaknesses in our schools. Indeed, should those who seek to ride the "second wave" of educational reform be successful, our schools will be better than they have ever been.

While improvements in our schools are being made, our needs and expectations are accelerating. Thus, the changes that are being achieved will probably seem inadequate. Because this could lead to the idea that "we've done what we can reasonably do," or to more cynical conclusions about the futility of investing in public education, the chance to do what needs doing will be lost for the foreseeable future unless we expand the agenda.

There are two general reasons why the current reform agenda is incomplete. First, the proposals that compose the second wave reforms are encumbered both by an undertow of first wave proposals and assumptions and by stated justifications for significant proposals that are unlikely to gain popular support. Second, even if this undertow could be overcome, and political support for the advocated changes developed, the second wave proposals now on the policy agenda fail to address two major problems: (a) the separation of schools and families and (b) the need to develop, beyond the goals policy makers have heretofore owned, the cognitive *capabilities* of our young people.

To argue that the first and second waves will come up short raises the question: short of what? The success of the case I am trying to build depends on the ultimate purposes of education reform to which one subscribes. I believe that two of the most important goals of educational reform should be:

1. significantly improving the performance of low-achieving students so as to narrow the current gap in academic learning between them and high-achieving youngsters and eliminating the inequalities of opportunity and condition that result from that deficit; and
2. developing among almost all children greater interest in and cognitive capacity for learning, "higher-order thinking," and problem solving.

Tall orders, these. It would be possible to compile considerable data to demonstrate that we are a long way from achieving these goals, but I assume that both this reality and the desirability of these goals need no validation.

THE FIRST WAVE OF EDUCATIONAL REFORM

While the first wave has not yet broken on the shores of all states—much less all school systems—and may not reach some schools at all, it does seem possible to identify its major concerns, themes, achievements, and limitations.

The Fundamental Assumption of the First Wave

For several years preceding the 1980s, public and policymakers were bombarded with information about declining test scores, the low achievement levels of American students compared to the students of other nations, conflict resulting from desegregation, the debate over prayer in the schools, and other social controversies. The public mind was not so much shaped as it was mirrored by the hyperbole of the 1983 report of the National Commission on Excellence in Education, *A Nation at Risk*, whose title became the rationale of the first wave reforms. It seemed easy to argue that at least part of our problem resulted from the nation's preoccupation with equal opportunity rather than high standards. Accordingly, Wave 1 policies and initiatives paid little attention to students who were physically, mentally, or environmentally handicapped, and federal spending for programs serving such children declined (National Coalition, 1985).

While many who could influence educational policy were concluding that our schools' effectiveness was at a new low, there was, in fact, little evidence that this was so (Hawley, 1985). Indeed, while test scores most relevant to measuring student achievement had declined somewhat in the 1960s and early 1970s, most measures of student learning were on the way up by the mid-1970s (Congressional Budget Office, 1987). In spite of this fact, even most of those who knew better decided to ride the wave to obtain more resources for schools.

Thus the first wave of reform was energized by a conviction that we had fallen from a higher state of grace to a desperate situation that threatened not only individual school children but the nation's economic and military security. As one of the more widely cited passages of *A Nation at Risk* put it:

> If an unfriendly foreign power had attempted to impose on America the mediocre educational performance that exists today, we might well have viewed it as an act of war. As it stands, we have allowed this to happen to ourselves. We have even squandered the gains in student achievement made in the wake of the Sputnik challenge. We have in effect, been committing an act of unthinking, unilateral educational disarmament. (National Commission, 1983, p. 3)

The logical response to such a conclusion was to quickly and forcefully repair the sinking vessel, chart a simpler course, and insist that the sailors—the nation's teachers—shape up or ship out. Thus, while the flood of reform proposals that burst upon the schools in the mid-1980s had many currents, most reflected the view that change would come only by a combination of regulations and incentives that would tell educators what to do and insist that they work smarter and harder. (For a specification of first wave proposals, see Passow, 1987.)

CONSEQUENCES OF WAVE 1

Empirically grounded reports on the impact of Wave 1 reforms are limited; it seems fair to say that it is too early to tell what the results will be over time. Public spending for schools has apparently increased more rapidly than one would have predicted from trend lines and increases in the cost of living (Stern, 1988, Chart 1.12), with much of the new money going to improve teachers' salaries. There is reason to believe that the number and academic ability of whites who want to be teachers has increased (Hawley, Goldman, & Austin, 1988).

At this point, the impact of reforms on student achievement cannot be clearly discerned. More students do appear to be taking more math and science courses in high school, and curricula have been aligned with standard tests in many places. Some observers believe that increased emphasis on academic courses and greater use of retention practices have increased the high school drop-out rate, but there is little evidence that this is so, at least in the aggregate (Stern, 1988, Chart 1.8).

Almost everyone who has written about the reforms agrees that, taken together, these measures have reduced discretionary decision making for school boards, school administrators, and teachers. In particular, a number of the critics of the reform movement point to the "mechanization" and "routinization" of teaching as the most unhappy consequence of the Wave 1 reform efforts (e.g., Wise, 1988, and McNeil, 1986).

Simplification, prescription, and performance measurement were the policy mechanisms that were most common to Wave 1 reforms. Those who believed that schools' problems could be traced to low standards for students and teachers and a lack of focus on academic achievement felt these strategies were sensible. But others, who diagnosed the problems differently, charged that the reforms, on the whole, limited the prospects for quality education by oversimplifying the solutions and restricting rather than facilitating basic changes.

The Wave 1 reforms not only centralized authority for educational policymaking, thus increasing rules and regulations, they reinforced the climate of distrust that had initially motivated the reforms. Moreover, many policymakers riding the first wave apparently assumed that the problem was to right the ship and get it *back* on course rather than working to streamline the prow, add more sail, or reorganize the command structure. Thus the first wave did not add new capacity to our educational system or try to take on fundamental problems that diminished and constrained the intellectual capacity of children.

THE SECOND WAVE

Some believed in the necessity of the first wave reforms but recognized that the reforms were both limited and limiting. This recognition, combined with a concern for a likely shortage of qualified teachers, a worsening trade deficit, and the pent-up energies of would-be reformers who had been waiting for a wave they felt better about riding than the first, gave rise to a second set of priorities for educational improvement. This does not mean that the energy of the first wave is spent. Indeed, it is precisely because the two waves overlap, and sometimes move in different directions, that the potential benefits of the reform movement are so problematic.

The origins of the second wave of reform proposals can be traced to a series of studies that captured considerable attention, at least among those most concerned about improving the nation's schools. *Time for Results*, prepared by the National Governors' Association in 1986, represented both the political ascendance of educational issues and efforts to broaden the reform agenda. The two reports of the Committee for Economic Development, *Investing in Our Children* (1985) and *Children in Need* (1987), represented a growing awareness of the link between economic prosperity and education and, more importantly, an effort to restore the problems of children with special needs to the nation's list of priorities for public spending. The report of the 1986 Carnegie Forum on Education and the Economy drew attention to the importance of effective teaching to effective schools and added the professionalization of teaching and the related restructuring of schools to the reform agenda.

The second wave of reform gained additional momentum from other studies and reports, all of which suggested a need to go beyond the essentially regulatory steps that characterized the major thrust of earlier proposals. But, perhaps because Wave 2 proposals have tried to focus our attention on the need to reach shores we have not yet reached, the calls for change it encompasses have been less angry and more diffuse. Thus the roar of the second wave is less distinct than that of the first and its pull less clearly felt by policymakers and the public at large.

THE SECOND WAVE AGENDA

The second wave appears to have two main emphases that differ from Wave 1 proposals for school improvement. The first of these—the concern for addressing the needs of "children at risk" because of poverty, poor physical or mental health, or family instability—calls for recommitment to a spate of social programs and, in particular, for preventive policies that address the needs of prospective parents and preschool children. Let me refer to this set of policies as "investment in children strategies."

The other set of second wave reform efforts, which I will call the "investment in teaching strategies," has two complementary but not necessarily dependent emphases. The first centers on attracting and retaining effective teachers, with particular concern for increasing the proportion of academically talented persons in the teaching corps. The policies derived from this goal link readily with first wave reforms: reform of teacher education, higher overall salaries, higher standards for entry to teaching, and differentiated staffing, with higher pay for teachers who manifest exceptional performance and/or are willing to take special responsibility. It is the second focus of the investment in teaching strategies that makes this set of policies second wave: improved working conditions and greater professional discretion for teachers combined with (a) the restructuring of schools to provide teachers opportunities to define and administer school policy and (b) school site management—the devolution of greater authority over curriculum, instructional strategies, and resource allocation to the school level.

Other proposals might be thought of as second wave reforms—including the reform of undergraduate college education and the need to make better use of technology to enhance learning—but they do not appear to be high on the political agenda.

LIKELY OUTCOMES OF THE SECOND WAVE

If it is difficult to assess the impact of the first wave, predicting the consequences of the second is even more speculative. But making such predictions can serve two purposes: first, identifying obstacles to these reforms may contribute to efforts to overcome them; and, second, such speculation can reveal that the policies being proposed are importantly incomplete.

In assessing the potential outcomes of second wave reforms, we should characterize their political consensus and technical certainty. Political consensus—how desirable a given policy is among those with the resources and interest to shape the decision to enact and implement that policy—is the product of several factors. Two that seem most important are the extent to which (a) it is perceived that a given problem has both direct and indirect consequences for large numbers of people and (b) how the potential solutions to the problem fit prevailing values about the appropriate role of government in a given policy arena.

By "technical certainty," I mean the confidence one can have about the extent to which the policy can bring about the desired outcome. Certainty depends, among other things, on the strength of the demonstrated cause-effect relationships and the capacity of the individuals and institutions involved to maximize the predicted outcome.

The probability that the chance a given policy will be enacted and effectively implemented is affected, of course, by the amount of money it will require. As the amount required grows, so does the degree of political consensus and technical certainty required. Moreover, as the amount of money required to implement a policy increases, the more the test of technical certainty will take the form of implicit or explicit estimates of return on investment. Technical and political concerns are, of course, interrelated.

WAVE 2 PROPOSALS FOR INVESTING IN CHILDREN

I have already suggested that such political consensus that will result in new or reinvigorated programs for children at risk appears to be developing. This consensus transcends conventional divisions between liberals and conservatives, though specific mechanisms to implement programs may yet prove divisive. Advocacy groups like the Children's Defense Fund (1984) are finding support for children at risk among governors, corporate executives, chief state school officers, teachers' organizations, constituent members of the Education Commission of the States, and conservative members of Congress. These support groups are aware of the severity of the problems many children face, realize that society will depend increasingly on those who have traditionally been least well-educated and most prone to social pathologies, and are convinced that the growing evidence of technical certainty of some child investment policies is high (Committee for Economic Development, 1987; Baumeister, Dokecki, & Kupstas, 1987).

Space does not permit a detailed analysis of policy options for addressing all of the problems of children at risk, but three general propositions seem reasonable. First, if we expect to succeed with the set of child investment strategies, we must see them *as* a set. Preventative policies aimed at reducing the incidence of low birth weight and infant malnutrition and poor health respond to easily understood problems with high and relatively certain benefit/cost ratios. However, it is wishful thinking to suppose that we can "intervene" early in children's lives and, in effect, inoculate them against the forces that will later impede their cognitive and social development. The pathologies associated with poverty, family instability, and community disorder continue to influence children as they grow to young adulthood. Because the technical certainty of extant programs for older children is much lower than for those programs aimed at younger children and because some older children with special needs engage in antisocial behavior, political consensus to support a comprehensive child investment strategy is difficult to obtain.

A second generalization about child investment programs is that they are the responsibility of multiple public agencies and that no institution other than the child's family is in a position to ensure adequate attention to the needs of children at risk. Obviously, when families are unstable or lack the resources to make demands on the various institutions on which their children must depend, children's needs go unmet. Many children have special needs *because* of their situation. This problem is confounded when private services are available because the exit of wealthier families from public service providers reduces the effectiveness of parents' demands for improved public services (Hirschman, 1970).

A third generalization about investment in children programs is that their success—with the possible exception of those aimed at nutrition and illness prevention—depends on the persons delivering the service. Formula treatments for children with multiple problems are seldom effective; rather, the therapy needed must be determined through diagnoses that take into account the changing circumstances and needs of the child being served. Ideally, the service provider must be intelligent, flexible, and committed and must serve only a small number of children. But because service providers cannot be with children continuously, the most successful programs for children with special needs are those in which parents are trained (and reinforced continuously) to provide the service needed. This, in turn, means that children from stable and well-educated families would profit most from investment in children's programs, though the children who most need such programs often do not have stable and well-educated families.

WAVE 2 PROPOSALS FOR INVESTING IN TEACHING

Policies related to the qualities of teachers. Policies aimed at securing certain qualities in our teachers—such as screening devices, salary increases, and so on—are logically related to the outcomes desired, although there is little hard evidence to link specific teacher qualities and student performance (Evertson, Hawley, & Zlotnik, 1985). Of course, the high cost of implementing teacher salary policies limits how much will be done in most places. While most recognize the desirability of attracting and retaining teachers of higher quality (however defined), they are unclear as to the technical certainty of the strategies to achieve this goal. Not surprisingly, policies have proliferated that screen out people without the qualities we want. The policies are certain (in the sense that screening is effective), and they don't cost much. Because of the high cost of across-the-board salary increases, we have witnessed policymakers' pursuit of ways to stratify teachers by performance and responsibility so as to focus the largest salary increases on a limited number of teachers. This strategy, however, seldom has been accompanied by changes in the organizational structure of schools that actually differentiate teacher functions. This is one reason why so-called ladder plans appear to be unstable wherever they have been introduced. Some proponents of significantly increasing the salaries of teachers argue that much of the money needed to finance such a policy could be obtained from the reallocation of funds now allocated to other educational expenditures (Carnegie Foundation, 1986). But such reallocation proposals weaken the political consensus needed to obtain support for increasing teacher salaries.

Most agree on the desirability of increasing teacher salaries (Gallup, 1987; Louis Harris, 1986), but they are uncertain about its efficacy. There is evidence that increasing teacher salaries will increase the supply of teacher candidates (Kershaw & McKean, 1962), but what a given teacher salary increase will buy in enhanced teacher quality is unknown. Indeed, there is some popular suspicion, reinforced by the emphasis teachers and parents place on the importance of "Mrs. Jones"'s love for children in explaining why she is a good teacher, that paying teachers very well would attract the wrong kind of people to the profession. Moreover, it is easy to believe that our teachers should be literate and of above-average intelligence, but it is not clear how literate or how much above average in intelligence teachers must be to facilitate student learning (Evertson et al., 1985). While I know of no direct studies on the questions, it seems likely that most people do not *expect* the average teacher to be as bright as the average engineer, doctor, lawyer, or successful businessman and thus will not think it necessary to pay teachers accordingly.

Another reason for the technical uncertainty of teacher salary increases is that Americans may believe that their children's future success is shaped less by their education than by upbringing, luck, contacts, peer and community influences, and innate ability. For example, Stevenson, Lee, and Stigler (1986) found that American mothers were much more likely than Japanese or Chinese mothers to attribute their child's success in school to innate ability than to effort.

Policies relating to the restructuring of schools. The political and technical limits of regulatory policies and salary increases, coupled with evidence showing that the opportunity to help others learn, is a powerful incentive for people to enter and stay in the profession (Hawley & Rosenholtz, 1984, chap. 3), have given rise to proposals to change the structure of schools and the roles of teachers in ways that would allow talented teachers to maximize their effectiveness and attract and retain talented people in teaching.

However, these proposals, which I will label "restructuring," face considerable difficulties. On the one hand, restructuring proposals are often ambiguous, and the language and symbols they invoke do not promise to foster sufficient political consensus to achieve widespread change. On the other hand, the technical certainty of these proposals is considerably less obvious to those who have not joined the bandwagon than to their advocates. The lack of consensus, of course, contributes to technical uncertainty. Let me elaborate on each of these points.

Like change in general, restructuring in the abstract is a popular idea. But current discussions suggest that those affected by restructuring like the idea only if it does not portend a loss of authority, status, or discretion for them. Proven models of restructured schools do not dot the landscape. Such schools exist, of course, but they are treated in the literature as aberrations that thrive because of unusual circumstances or because of exceptional leadership either among teachers or principals (the latter usually get the credit).

The most common theme in the calls for restructuring is teacher "empowerment." Aside from the vagueness of term, there are at least five reasons why the idea is unlikely to generate much political consensus:

- The first wave of reform rested heavily on the idea that many teachers are incompetent or not hard-working.
- Research and commentary on effective schools frequently emphasizes the importance of strong leadership from the school principal.
- Many school administrators have seen themselves in adversarial relations with teachers, a position complicated by their increased responsibilities for teacher evaluation.
- Many parents appear to feel that teachers already have too much power. For example, more than 50 percent of parents nationwide believe that parents should have more say in curriculum and 5 percent believe they should have less; more than 40 percent of parents believe they should have more say over instructional materials and the types of books available in the school library and only 10 percent believe they should have less (Gallup, 1987, p. 21).
- Even a good many teachers seem to be doubtful about the desirability of significantly changing the relative authority they have vis-à-vis school administrators (Bacharach, Bauer, & Shedd, 1986).

If teacher empowerment is the most common theme of restructuring, the most common rationale for restructuring seems to be to make teaching "a true profession." But here again the symbol may not be a rallying cry that appeals to many who have not historically advocated more status for teachers. Two decades ago, for example, the professionalization of public sector jobs was seen as a problem because it allegedly distanced public servants from those they were to serve. The product of this concern was proposals for educational vouchers, community school boards, parent advisory councils, and more accountability. And, while professionals such as doctors and lawyers are often envied and paid well, sizable numbers of us speak of the impersonality of physicians and the self-interest of lawyers, traits we do not seek in teachers. Moreover, it is not common to think of a heavily unionized work force—and most teachers are union members—as professionals.

Proposals for school site management seem to be making little progress largely because they directly confront the centralizing and standardizing effects of the first wave reforms. Moreover, international comparisons, which drove our collective awareness of the need for change, led the pundits, including many political leaders, to conclude that central direction, a uniform curriculum, and the like, held the answer to our problems. In 1987, the Gallup Poll showed that a whopping 84 percent of the American citizens favored having the *federal government require* local districts to meet minimum educational standards (Gallup, 1987, p. 23).

Some critics of the first wave marveled at how quickly Americans (or at least their elected representatives) seemed to abandon presumably cherished traditions of local control over education. But the power of the first wave to swamp localism suggests that the commitment was not deeply rooted and that our thinking about educational authority had not adapted to changes in the diversity and mobility of our populations. Moreover, the successful efforts to ensure civil rights and civil liberties in our schools had not been rationalized with the value of local control (Ravitch, 1986), and the very foundations of local control—local school boards—had been substantially weakened (Institute for Educational Leadership, 1986).

In short, the justifications given for restructuring often seem to focus on improving the status, autonomy, and income of teachers, and on decentralizing educational decision making generally. It seems likely that many school board members, school administrators, parents, first wave reformers, and other citizens may have trouble understanding why this will improve student learning. Which brings us to the question of technical certainty of restructuring.

The problem in knowing about the technical certainty of restructuring is that the case for its effects must be largely inferential. It is not that we have not tried restructuring. Many school systems experimented with "differentiated staffing," and "alternative schools" once flourished with the support of federal funds. But research analyzing the effects of these experiments on students is scarce, and the uncertain efficacy of these efforts is suggested by their high mortality rate.

Will restructuring lead to improved student performance? It is possible to conclude from extant research that the conditions identified with restructuring are associated with high student achievement (Hawley & Rosenholtz, 1984). But apparently there are no careful before and after studies of student achievement in restructured schools. It is possible, therefore, that schools with high-achieving students can be structured differently and attract teachers with different qualities. In other words, the directions of the causal arrows are unclear.

If restructuring will lead to improved student achievement, and, on balance, it seems that it will, it will be for one or more of four reasons: (a) the mix of teacher qualities will be different, (b) teachers will be more motivated to do what they know how to do, (c) teachers will be able to do better the things they know how to do, or (d) the opportunities for peer and administrative support will allow teachers to improve their competence.

Those who assert that restructuring will lead to higher teacher salaries argue that restructured schools will attract teachers with qualities society will want to reward more generously. The available evidence does not clearly show this. A competing hypothesis is that if restructuring does attract teachers with desirable qualities, the perceived need to increase salaries will be reduced, since there is some evidence that the conditions associated with restructuring are also associated with teacher job satisfaction and retention (Hawley & Rosenholtz, 1984, chaps. 2–3). While there is no research on the effects of these conditions on teachers with different qualities, it does seem reasonable to assume that schools where such conditions are present can selectively attract and retain people. But restructuring could lead to higher teacher morale without significantly changing teacher effectiveness; a host of studies of changes in working conditions in private industry demonstrate that job satisfaction can increase without increases in productivity (Katz & Kahn, 1978).

In any case, the reasons restructuring could lead to student achievement are conditioned by the individual and collective competence levels of the teachers involved. Since competence is usually defined, both in current practice and research, as knowledge and behaviors that are correlated with student performance on standardized tests, we cannot assume that restructuring will lead to outcomes other than those conventionally assessed by such tests. How will restructuring figure significantly in teacher knowledge and teaching competence? Recent calls for restructuring do not typically incorporate resources and conditions that would allow teachers to learn more than their collective experiences in a given school could teach them.

If restructuring does lead to better teaching, the impact of that teaching will be affected by outside factors that influence student learning (outside the school). Thus far, restructuring proposals have not tried to change the relationships between schools and families. Indeed, some versions of restructuring would reduce the claims parents might make on schools just as the professionalization of law and medicine rendered clients and patients more dependent on lawyers and physicians.

Finally, the technical certainty of restructuring is undermined by some of the first wave proposals, especially those that prescribe student outcomes and teacher behaviors very explicitly. In those schools where Wave 1 reforms have been implemented, restructuring efforts are not likely to replace these newly established policies and procedures. Thus restructuring proposals will have to accommodate to constraints imposed by the first wave, and the Wave 2 reformers have not yet tackled this very difficult task.

THE MISSING PIECES: FAMILIES AND
COGNITIVE DEVELOPMENT

I have argued that first wave reforms are both limited and limiting. While they may seem to raise the tide level, they lack the power to take our schools beyond mediocrity. Second wave reforms grapple with two more fundamental problems: enhancing mental capacity and remediating sources of learning difficulties among the disadvantaged and handicapped, on the one hand, and enhancing the quality of teaching on the other. Both of these second wave policies are essential, but neither goes far enough to solve the problems they seek to address if our goals are to significantly reduce the inequalities in student achievement and to enhance the intellectual capacity of the nation.

I have argued that neither of the two general strategies of the second wave come to grips with the role of families in educating our children. Further, I have argued that the proposed investment in teaching strategies probably cannot develop political consensus throughout the nation and takes for granted that changes in teacher quality and teaching conditions will markedly change the way learning is defined and facilitated in schools. These political and technical uncertainties are exacerbated by the almost total omission from teaching strategies of a role for parents, so that the family—the social institution upon which the schools are most dependent politically and technically—is not only without a new reason for engaging in efforts to improve schools but could also be estranged further.

Thus I conclude that the reform movement needs to be broadened and deepened in two major ways. First, families and schools need to be reconciled. Second, we must redefine the role of the teacher and change the way we conceptualize and facilitate learning.

RECONCILING THE FAMILY AND THE SCHOOL

For at least the last 50 years, those educators and social reformers who have seen schools as the mechanism through which individuals are prepared for social change have worried about the powerful influence the family has in preserving the status quo. This problem is confounded by the local and popular control of schools to a degree unmatched in any other industrialized nation. These worries have resulted, at best, in mixed signals to parents about their welcome in the schools (Berger, 1985).

Investment-in-children strategies have reflected a more pragmatic view of families. But, while most investment in children strategies recognize the family as part of the problem of increasing the cognitive capacity of babies and young children, the solutions proposed often take the current pathologies of "families" as givens and limit efforts to strengthen the family's role in education to preschool and, perhaps, primary grades.

So, what can be done to reconcile the family and the school? I think there are two types of strategies that deserve consideration; programs and practices to involve parents in the education of their children and efforts to strengthen families. Obviously the first is easier and certainly less controversial than the second.

Involving parents in their children's education. Virtually all researchers who study student achievement agree that it is significantly related to the extent to which parents are actively involved in and otherwise provide support for their children's learning (Constable & Walberg, 1987). Programs aimed at enhancing student learning, which provide parents with the resources and responsibility to assist their children, have a remarkable success rate (Hawley & Rosenholtz, 1984, Chap. 6). And, if there is one thing we should learn from studies of Japanese education, it is that parental involvement in children's education, more than any other factor, helps explain the high achievement of Japanese children (White, 1987; OERI, 1987).

So, if it is clear that parental involvement helps children learn, why isn't this a major part of the education reform agenda? There are many possible answers to this question, but two stand out: (a) many educators believe that many parents are not willing to devote much energy to their children's education, and (b) the demographics of dual-career couples and single-parent households and divorce, which complicate parental involvement in their children's education, are seen as inevitable and beyond remediation.

Despite the despair about parental involvement that seems to discourage related reforms, there are things that can be done.

- Teacher initiatives can eliminate differences in parent involvement between middle-class and lower-class parents and between one-parent and two-parent families (Epstein, 1986).
- Parents can learn how to help their children in preschool settings, in community organizations, and in churches, synagogues, and mosques.
- Electronic technology, such as computer-based telephone systems, can provide daily information to parents about student assignments.
- Homework assignments can provide opportunities for students to learn from parents and provide parents chances to be of help.
- Schools could be located in or near workplaces—such an experiment is now underway in Miami—to provide parents opportunities to be in schools, meet regularly with teachers, and talk with their children on the way to and from school and work.

No doubt there are other proposals that could involve parents more in their children's education. No one should expect things to change over-

night, even with imaginative programs. The process that currently es-
tranges families from schools has been underway for decades (Berger,
1985), and the social forces rewarding parents for activities other than those
related to their children's education and contributing to family instability
are powerful. But it is hard to imagine that schools can be as effective
without significant parent involvement as they can be when the interests
and priorities of families and schools are congruent.

    Strengthening families. This is not the place to assess the strength of
American families. It does seem safe to say that the rate of divorce is too
high, that the proportion of children born to unwed teenagers is appalling,
and that too many marriages are characterized by verbal and physical abuse
(Bergman, 1986). It also seems safe to say that, other things being equal,
children whose parents divorce, who are born to unwed teenagers, and
who witness or are the victims of abuse will not do as well in school as
children who do not have such experiences.

    If the health of families is important to children's learning, why isn't
the health of families an important part of the school curriculum? One
answer is that the moralistic character of family health has caused schools
to stay away from the topic. Another answer is the feeling that we should
be teaching academic subjects, not social behavior, in schools. Ironically,
the increasing state control of curriculum may resolve some of the concerns
that family-related curricula will become ways of teaching particular religious doctrines or offending the sensibilities of those who believe there
should be no public posture about the value of strong families. There is
nothing inherently nonacademic about the study of families. Their role in
history, the impact of social change on families, ways of dealing with
intrafamily stress, and the role of parenting in child development are all
matters of serious scholarly inquiry. In any case, if schools are to transmit
a nation's culture and build its capacity, neglecting curricula that might
strengthen families probably predicts the future. Deciding what such curricula should look like could, in itself, be a first step toward reconciling
families and schools.

ENHANCING COGNITIVE DEVELOPMENT

Let me recall two points made earlier. First, if school reform is to significantly alter the quality of life for individuals and help the nation solve its
economic and social problems, it must go beyond improved performances
on standardized tests and develop a capacity to learn, to be intellectually
resilient, and to make better decisions in seeking to solve complex problems. Second, to assume that Wave 2 reforms in themselves will change
how and what students learn because teachers are smarter or freer to

pursue their own insights is a leap of faith that contradicts the central argument for the reforms—that teaching is a complicated enterprise requiring special knowledge and competence that justifies calling it a profession.

Investment-in-children strategies do address cognitive development by seeking to prevent health-related limitations on intelligence and by seeking to enrich the environments and learning opportunities of younger children.

Paradoxically, strategies for investing in teaching do not typically try to change the ways children learn. No doubt much of the problem is that the design of ways to foster cognitive development, like strategies for restructuring, have been speculative, and even the term itself lacked much precision. These difficulties persist, and are reflected both in sloppy conversation about what we are after and suggestions of unproven and unlikely solutions (like stand-alone courses on thinking, curricula based on right brain-left brain research, and teaching strategies based on convictions that learning styles are the causes rather than the products of learning).

In the last few years, however, research has emerged that could lead to preconceptions of the role of teachers and students in the teaching-learning process (Resnick, 1987; Gardner, 1985). Carl Bereiter and Marlene Scardamelia (1987) have recently reviewed research on cognitive development and concluded that the linguistic and verbal reasoning abilities, literary standards and sophistication, and the moral values and precepts traditionally associated with elites are within the reach of most students. Other researchers have shown that new understandings of learning could dramatically enhance the capabilities of children to learn about science (Sherwood, Kinzer, Bransford, & Franks, 1987). But not if teachers structure learning opportunities as most teachers do. Bereiter and Scardamelia developed a composite model of teaching, the essential elements of which call for teachers to help students, on their own initiative, to activate prior knowledge, relate old knowledge to new in systematic and reflective ways, organize disparate pieces of information, and reach conclusions and assess those conclusions before settling on them. Bereiter and Scardamelia call this intentional learning. Students who engage in intentional learning not only are able to do the things outlined above, they are self-conscious about what they have learned in the process of learning and, even, why they learned what they did.

In fostering intentional learning, interests and motives are not treated as factors that influence what is learned; they are part of what is to be learned. Bereiter and Scardamelia (1987) suggest how Teacher C, their model teacher, would do this:

> Teacher C asks students themselves to recognize what is new and what is old information. Instead of asking questions of the students, Teacher C models the process of asking questions of the text or of oneself, and

coaches the students in carrying out the modeled process. In writing, Teacher C makes use of external prompts, modeling, and peer cooperation to enable students to carry on their own Socratic dialogues, by means by which their knowledge is not only activated but reconsidered and evaluated in relation to what they are trying to write. Whereas Teacher B [our conventional model of an effective teacher] tries to minimize students' difficulties in comprehending and composing, Teacher C will sometimes assign reading or writing tasks that present special difficulties in order to provide occasions for teaching problem solving strategies. When difficulties arise they are treated as interesting phenomena for investigation, with the result that the students themselves become students of cognitive processes in reading and writing. (pp. 10–11)

Bereiter and Scardamelia argue that conventional modes of teaching focus on adaptive learning, the development of the competency to deal with the world as students experience it. This means that the students' immediate environments create the levels of cognitive demand they engage. Thus, as study after study shows, the students' social experiences (family, peers, community), rather than what is being taught in school or a particular educational program, accounts for the bulk of variations in student performance. It follows that the goal of significantly reducing the gap between the high- and low-achieving youngsters, which I posited at the outset of this section, can best be achieved, perhaps only be achieved, if we change the way students learn. This, of course, will happen only if we change the way students are taught.

How can we foster "intentional learning"? A precondition is the restructuring of schools so that teachers have the opportunity and are motivated to create appropriate learning situations. As noted earlier, many of the first wave reforms assume that what children learn is more important than and independent from how they learn, so that good teaching is described in mechanistic terms and measured by student test performance that tell us little about student capacity for intentional learning.

It should be noted that the influence of first wave reforms lies not in the changes they brought about in teaching but in the fact that they reinforced and fine-tuned dominant practices that in turn were supported by the way schools are organized. Evidence for this conclusion can be found in the remarkable similarity of teaching styles and structure in American schools over time and across schools (Cuban, 1988; Goodlad, 1983).

There are three general ways to help teachers acquire greater competence and knowledge: preservice education, formal in-service training, and enriching opportunities for "incidental learning" in the context of teaching.

Proposals for reforming teacher education abound in both waves of reform, but they are without content (see, for example, proposals by the Holmes Group, 1986, and the Carnegie Forum, 1986). That is, they focus on requirements for prospective teachers and the process of teacher education largely in terms of the number of courses taken and the mix of classroom and field or clinical experience. They give little attention to what is to be learned by teachers about teaching, learning, and schools.

In-service education and other formal opportunities for professional development generally receive low marks from teachers (Bacharach et al., 1986) and little attention from reformers. Presumably, teachers are to learn new ways to facilitate student learning on their own. Many restructuring proposals do create opportunities for learning from peers and from personal experiences. But this is not usually the focus of such proposals; thus the conditions that would best produce incidental learning receive little attention.

The idea that teachers will change the way they teach because we free them from bureaucratic constraints and provide them with opportunities to shape school policies and practices has a mystical quality to it. If we really want teachers to teach more effectively, we will have to teach them how. This means retraining teacher educators, creating induction processes (like so-called professional development centers), developing ways within school systems to enhance teacher learning, and using restructuring to empower teachers intellectually as well as politically and emotionally.

How technically certain is teaching that fosters intentional learning? There is considerable evidence that variations have worked in experimental situations, and the theoretical bases for this approach are supported by research. But like other promising educational innovations, we will not know whether they will work on a large scale until we try them on a large scale. That, in turn, will require considerably more research and development work and well-supported pilots.

Since we do not seem able to implement less ambitious improvements in teaching and learning, why set such high goals and invest in a somewhat utopian scenario? As I noted in the opening, the proposed investments in children and teaching that make up the second wave of the reform movement hold the promise of major changes in educational quality. But these improvements will not keep pace with our need and will fall short of our aspirations. While restructuring is needed to promote intentional learning, it is not sufficient. Most teachers do not intuitively teach with the sophistication outlined above. Achieving intentional learning capabilities for all children can move us within reach of the two goals outlined earlier. No other reform really does.

There is another, less altruistic reason for pursuing new approaches to teaching based on cognitive research. We have a better chance of achieving this high goal than do most other nations. For example, the Japanese government is seeking school reforms, hoping to achieve the outcomes that intentional learning produces—students who are self-directed and active learners who can solve complex problems in creative ways (OERI, 1987, chap. 6). But Japanese schools and Japanese cultural values will have to change considerably more than ours will to achieve these results. On the other hand, there is no conceivable way that the first and second wave reforms now on the agenda will either (a) raise the level of mass education to Japanese levels when the measures are the acquisition of knowledge and basic skills or (b) socialize our young people to the values of perseverance and commitments to family and community that Japanese schools achieve. In short, our comparative educational advantage lies in upping the ante with respect to cognitive development.

CONCLUSION

I have tried to suggest the limitations of many of the proposals and the assumptions that compose the mainstream of both waves of the educational reform movement. I have argued that two important additional initiatives are essential if we wish to achieve greater equality of educational outcomes, significantly enhance capabilities to learn, and actively use such capabilities to solve problems. These complementary initiatives are to strengthen the role of parents in the education of their own children and to develop among teachers a capacity for new approaches to teaching that result in intentional learning.

Let me conclude by drawing attention to two ugly facts that represent the unposted undertow of the reform movement efforts and that significantly reduce both the political and technical certainty of almost all our reform efforts, especially those that seek to address fundamental and historic weakness in our schools. The first of these is the massive differences in social condition that set American students, as a whole, apart from the students of other industrialized societies. These differences can be ameliorated by quality education, but not much. The second fact that undermines efforts at educational improvement is the differences between our best and our worst schools. These differences are linked to differences in the resource base upon which schools can draw and, of course, to the problems that come from children living in poverty.

These realities have received remarkably little attention in the current debates over school reform (for an exception, see National Coalition of Advocates for Children, 1985). It is as though mentioning them would be an excuse not to undertake reform, or it would destroy the fragile consensus that keeps the reform efforts moving forward. But, unless we address these issues, the outcome of the reform movement is predictable: Differences in school quality and social condition will increase, even if our worse schools improve somewhat and the effects of social disadvantages on children are somewhat ameliorated.

Addressing this undertow is beyond the reach of educational policy alone, of course. But the two pieces of the reform movement that I have argued are missing do speak directly to differences in the educational experience of children that are related to the inequalities we have trouble acknowledging.

REFERENCES

Bacharach, S. B., Bauer, S. C., & Shedd, J. B. (1986). The learning workplace: The conditions and resources of teaching. *Organizational Analysis and Practice*. Ithaca, NY.

Baumeister, A., Dokecki, P., & Kupstas, F. (1987). *Preventing the "new morbidity": A guide for state planning efforts to prevent mental retardation and related disabilities associated with socioeconomic conditions.* A report prepared for the President's Committee on Mental Retardation in Conjunction with the Prevention Subcommittee.

Bereiter, C., & Scardamelia, M. (1987). An attainable version of high literacy: Approaches to teaching higher-order skills in reading and writing. *Curriculum Inquiry, 17*(1), 9–30.

Berger, B. (1985). *Challenge to American schools: The case for standards and values.* Oxford: Oxford University Press.

Bergman, B. (1986). *The economic emergence of women.* New York: Basic Books.

Carnegie Forum on Education and the Economy's Task Force on Teaching as a Profession. (1986). *A nation prepared: Teachers for the 21st century.* New York.

Children's Defense Fund. (1984). *American children in poverty.* Washington, DC.

Committee for Economic Development. (1987). *Children in need: Investment strategies for the educationally disadvantaged.* Washington, DC.

Committee for Economic Development. (1985). *Investing in our children: Business and the public schools.* Washington, DC: Research and Policy Committee.

Congressional Budget Office. (1987). *Educational achievement: Explanations and implications of recent trends.* Washington, DC.

Constable, R., & Walberg, H. J. (1987). The new thrust toward partnership of parents and schools. *Journal of Family and Culture, 3*(12), 15–34.

Cuban, L. (1988). The fundamental puzzle of school reform. *Phi Delta Kappan, 69,* 341–344.

Epstein, J. (1986). Parents' reactions to teacher practices of parental involvement. *Elementary School Journal, 86,* 277–294.

Evertson, C., Hawley, W., & Zlotnik, M. (1985). Making a difference in educational quality through teacher education. *Journal of Teacher Education, 36,* 2–12.

Gallup, G. (1986). The 18th annual Gallup poll of the public's attitudes toward the public schools. *Phi Delta Kappan, 68,* 45–59.

Gallup, G. (1987). The 19th annual Gallup poll of the public's attitudes toward the public schools. *Phi Delta Kappan, 69,* 17–30.

Gardner, H. (1985). *The mind's new science: A history of the cognitive revolution.* New York: Basic Books.

Goodlad, J. (1983). *A place called school.* New York: McGraw-Hill.

Louis Harris & Associates. (1986). *The American teacher 1986: Restructuring the teaching profession.* New York: Metropolitan Life.

Hawley, W. (1985). False premises, false promises: The mythical character of public discourse about education. *Phi Delta Kappan, 11,* 183–187.

Hawley, W., Goldman, E., & Austin, A. (1988). *Changing the education of teachers.* Atlanta: Southern Regional Education Board.

Hawley, W., & Rosenholtz, S. (1984). Good Schools: A synthesis of research on how schools influence student achievement [Special issue]. *Peabody Journal of Education. 4*, 1–178.

Hirschman, A. O. (1970). *Exit, voice and loyalty.* Cambridge, MA: Harvard University Press.

Hobbs, N., Dokecki, P., Hoover-Dempsey, K., Moroney, R., Shayne, M., & Weeks, K. (1984). *Strengthening families.* San Francisco: Jossey-Bass.

The Holmes Group. (1986). *Tomorrow's teachers: A report of the Holmes Group.* East Lansing, MI: Michigan State University.

Institute for Educational Leadership. (1986). *School boards: Strengthening grass-roots leadership.* Washington, DC.

Katz, D., & Kahn, R. (1978). *The social psychology of organizations* (2nd ed.). New York: Wiley.

Kershaw, J., & McKean, R. (1962). *Teacher shortages and salary schedules.* New York: McGraw-Hill.

McNeil, L. (1986). *Contradictions of control: Social structure and school knowledge.* New York: Methuen/Routledge & Kegan Paul.

National Coalition of Advocates for Children. (1985). *Barriers to excellence: Our children at risk.* Boston.

National Commission on Excellence in Education. (1983). *A nation at risk.* Washington, DC: U.S. Government Printing Office.

The National Governors' Association. (1986). *Time for results: The governors' 1991 report on education.* Washington, DC.

Office of Educational Research and Improvement, U.S. Department of Education (1987). *Japanese education today.* Washington, DC: U.S. Government Printing Office.

Passow, H. (1987). *Present and future directions in school reform.* Paper presented at a conference on Restructuring Schooling for Quality Education: A New Reform Agenda at Trinity University, San Antonio.

Resnick, L. B. (1987). *Education and learning to think.* Washington, DC: National Academy Press.

Ravitch, D. (1986). *The troubled crusade.* New York: Basic Books.

Sherwood, R., Kinzer, C., Bransford, J., and Franks, J. (1987). Some benefits of creating macro-contexts for science instruction: Initial findings. *Journal of Research in Science Teaching, 24*, 417–435.

Stern, J. (1988). *The condition of education.* Washington, DC: U.S. Government Printing Office.

Stevenson, H. W., Lee, S., & Stigler, J. W. (1986). Mathematics achievement of Chinese, Japanese and American children. *Science, 231*, 693–699.

White, M. (1987). *The Japanese educational challenge: A commitment to children.* New York: Free Press.

Wise, A. E. (1988). The two conflicting trends in school reform: Legislated learning revisited. *Phi Delta Kappan, 69*, 328–332.

18
A System Wherein Students Become Active *Learners*

Docility and Apathy:
Their Cause and Cure
JOHN BISHOP

ALL TOO OFTEN docile, compliant, and without initiative" (p. 54). This is how Theodore Sizer (1984) characterized American high school students at the end of his massive two-year study of high schools. John Goodlad (1983) described "a general picture of considerable passivity among students" (p. 113). The high school teachers surveyed by Goodlad ranked "lack of interest by students" and "lack of interest by parents" as the two most important problems in education.

Studies of time use and time on task in high school show that students actively engage in a learning activity for only about half the time they are scheduled to be in school. Absence rates of 15 percent or more are common. Even when students are in class, the teacher and/or students are on task only part of the time. A study of high schools in Chicago found that public schools with high-achieving students averaged about 75 percent of class time for actual instruction; for schools with low-achieving students, the average was 51 percent of class time (Frederick, 1977). Other studies have found that for reading and math instruction the average engagement rate is about 75 percent (Fischer et al., 1978; Goodlad, 1983; Klein, Tyle & Wright, 1979); for vocational classes it is about 56 percent (Halasz & Behm, 1983). Overall, Frederick, Walberg, and Rasher (1979) estimated 46.5 percent of the potential learning time was lost due to absence, lateness, and inattention.

In 1980, high school students spent an average of 3.5 hours per week on homework. When homework is added to engaged time at school, the total time devoted to study, instruction, and practice is only 18 to 22 hours per week—between 15 and 20 percent of the student's waking hours during the school year. By way of comparison, the typical senior spent 10 hours per week in a part-time job and about 24 hours per week watching television (A. C. Nielsen unpublished data, 1987). Thus, television occupies as much time as learning. Students in other nations spend much less time watching TV: 60 percent less in Switzerland and 44 percent less in Canada (Organization of Economic Cooperation and Development, 1986, Table 18.1).

The lack of student interest makes it difficult for teachers to be demanding. As Theodore Sizer has observed: "A lot of the honors students aren't questers. They dodge the hard problems, the hard courses, to keep their averages up" (p. 53). Teachers find it difficult to escape being infected by the lassitude. The students can be cruel if they are not entertained or if they perceive the work load to be too heavy. Ms. Shiffe's class, as described by Sizer, was strikingly similar to one of the classes I visited in my research:

> Even while the names of living things poured out of Shiffe's lecture, no one was taking notes. . . . They did not want to know them and were not going to learn them. Apparently no outside threat—flunking, for example—affected the students. Shiffe could not flunk them all, and if their performance was uniformly shoddy, she would have to pass them all. Her desperation was as obvious as the students' cruelty toward her. (p. 157–158)

How does a teacher avoid this treatment? Sizer's description of Mr. Brody's class provides one example.

> He signaled to the students what the minima, the few questions for a test, were; all tenth- and eleventh-graders could master these with absurdly little difficulty. The youngsters picked up the signal and kept their part of the bargain by being friendly and orderly. They did not push Brody, and he did not push them. . . . Brody's room was quiet, and his students liked him. No wonder he had the esteem of the prin-

cipal who valued orderliness and good rapport between students and staff. Brody and his class had agreement, all right, agreement that reduced the efforts of both students and teacher to an irreducible and pathetic minimum. (p. 156)

Some teachers are able to overcome the obstacles and induce students to undertake tough learning tasks. But for most the students' lassitude is demoralizing. Everyone in the system recognizes that there is a problem, but each group fixes blame on someone else. As one student put it:

As it stands now, there is an unending, ever increasing cyclic problem. Teacher and administrator disinterest, apathy, and their lack of dedication results in students becoming even more unmotivated and docile, which in turn allows teachers to be less interested and dedicated. If students don't care, why should teachers? If teachers don't care, why should the students? (Krista, 1987)

Yes, it is a classic chicken-versus-egg problem. We assign teachers the responsibility for setting high standards, but we do not give them any of the tools that might be effective for inducing student observance of the academic goals of the classroom. They finally must rely on the force of their own personalities. All too often teachers compromise academic demands because the majority of the class sees no need to accept them as reasonable and legitimate. One must wonder whether, even if salaries were much higher, it would be possible to attract and retain large numbers of teachers who can succeed in teaching difficult material in the face of the obstacles just described.

Student apathy and student motivation are not the entire problem. Parental apathy and parental motivation should also concern us. A comparative study of education in Taiwan, Japan, and the United States shows that *even though American children were learning the least in school, American parents were the most satisfied with the performance of their local schools* (Stevenson, Lee, & Stigler, 1986). Why do Japanese and Taiwanese parents hold their children and schools to a higher standard than U.S. parents?

The U.S. lag in mathematics was revealed by the First International Mathematics Study in 1967. Test scores turned down in 1968. Why did it take until 1981 for a major educational reform movement to get underway? Thus the problem of apathy and motivation is as much a societal problem as it is a parental, a teacher, or a student problem.

REASONS FOR APATHY

The fundamental cause of the apathy and motivation problem is the way we recognize and reinforce student effort and achievement. During the

1960s and 1970s we adopted practices and developed institutions that hid from ourselves our failure to teach, protected adolescents from the consequences of failing to learn, and prevented many of those who did learn from reaping the fruits of their labor. The problem is that although there are benefits to *staying in* school, *most students realize few benefits from working hard in school.* The lack of incentives for effort is a consequence of three phenomena:

- The labor market fails to reward effort and achievement in high school.
- The peer group actively discourages academic effort.
- Admission to selective colleges is not based on an absolute or external standard of achievement in high school subjects. It is based instead on aptitude tests that do not assess the high school curriculum and on such measures of student performance as class rank and grade point averages, which are defined relative to classmates' performances, not relative to an external standard.

Absence of Economic Reward for Effort in High School

The educational decisions of students are significantly influenced by the costs (in money, time and psychological effort) and benefits (praise, prestige, employment, wage rates, and job satisfaction) that result. Any number of empirical studies confirm this (Freeman, 1971, 1976a, 1976b; Bishop, 1977). When asked why they work hard in school and/or why they care about grades, college-bound students typically respond "to get into college" or "to get into a good college." For students who plan to look for a job immediately after high school, however, the situation is different. They typically spend less time on their studies than do those who plan to attend college, in large part because most of them see very little connection between performance in high school and their future success in the labor market. Their teachers, of course, tell them that they are wrong, that they will be able to get a better job if they study hard. But when the students observe the success of prior graduates, they can see that success does not depend on how much they learned in high school. Fewer than a quarter of tenth-graders believe that geometry, trigonometry, biology, chemistry, and physics are needed to qualify for their first-choice occupation (Longitudinal Study of American Youth, 1988). Statistical studies of the youth labor market confirm their skepticism about the economic benefits of taking tough courses and studying hard:

- For high school students, high school grades and performance on academic achievement/aptitude tests have essentially no impact on labor market success. They have

—no effect on the chances of finding work when one is seeking it during high school

—no effect on the wage rate of the jobs obtained while in high school (Hotchkiss, Bishop, & Gardner, 1982)

• For those who do not go to college full time, high school grades and test scores had

—no effect on the wage rate of the jobs obtained immediately after high school in Kang and Bishop's (1984) analysis of High School and Beyond seniors and only a 1 to 4.7 percent increase in wages per standard deviation (SD) improvement in test scores and grade point average in Meyer's (1982) analysis of class of 1972 data

—a moderate effect on wage rates and earnings after four or five years [Gardner (1982) found an effect of 4.8 percent per SD of achievement and Meyer (1982) found an effect of 4.3 to 6.0 percent per SD of achievement]

—a small effect on the probability of being employed immediately after high school

• In almost all entry-level jobs, wage rates reflect the level of the job, not the worker's productivity. Thus, the employer, not the worker, benefits from a worker's greater productivity. Academic achievement and higher productivity make promotion more likely, but it takes time for the imperfect sorting process to assign a particularly able worker a job that fully uses that greater ability—and pays accordingly.

The long delay before labor market rewards are received is important because most teenagers are present-oriented, so benefits promised for ten years in the future may have little influence on their decisions.

Benefits to Society of Academic Achievement
Although the economic benefits of higher achievement to the employee are quite modest and do not appear until long after graduation, the benefits to the employer (and therefore to national production) are immediately apparent in higher productivity. Over the last 80 years, industrial psychologists have conducted hundreds of studies, involving many hundreds of thousands of workers, on the relationship between productivity in particular jobs and various predictors of that productivity. They have found that scores on tests measuring competence in reading, mathematics, science, and problem solving are strongly related to productivity on the job (Ghiselli, 1973).

Figure 18.1 compares the percentage effect of mathematical and verbal achievement (specifically, a difference of three grade-level equivalents in test scores or 0.7 grade point average (GPA) points on a 4-point scale) on the productivity of a clerical worker, on wages of male clerical workers (from Taubman & Wales, 1975), and on the wages of young women who

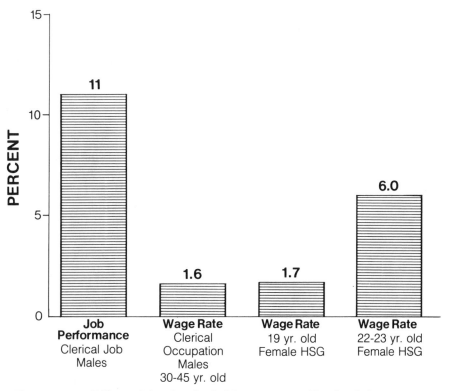

Figure 18.1 Effect of Academic Achievement on Productivity

Note: The source of the estimate of the effect of academic achievement on productivity is as follows. Studies that measure output for different workers in the same job at the same firm, using physical output as a criterion, have found that the standard deviation of output varies with job complexity and averages about .164 in routine clerical jobs and .278 in clerical jobs with decision-making responsibilities (Hunter, Schmidt, & Judiesch, 1988). Because there are fixed costs to employing an individual (facilities, equipment, light, heat, and overhead functions such as hiring and payrolling), the coefficient of variation of marginal products of individuals will be considerably greater (Klein, Spady, & Weiss, 1983). On the assumption that the coefficient of variation of marginal productivity for clerical jobs is 30 percent [1.5*(.33*.278 + .67*.164)], a .5 validity for general mental ability implies that an academic achievement differential between two individuals of one standard deviation (in a distribution of high school graduates) is associated with a productivity differential in the job of about 11 percent (.5*.74*30%). The ratio of the high school graduate test score standard deviation to the population standard deviation is assumed to be .74.

have not gone to college (from Kang & Bishop, 1984, and Meyer, 1982). Productivity clearly increases much more than wage rates. *Apparently it is a youth's employer, not the youth, who benefits the most when a non-college-bound student works hard in school and improves his or her academic achievements.* The youth is more likely to find a job, but not one with an appreciably higher wage.

Why Wage Rates Do Not Vary According to
Productivity on the Job

Employers are competing for better workers. Since research demonstrates that academic achievement is a good predictor of productivity, why doesn't this competition result in much higher wages for graduates with high GPAs and achievement test scores? The cause appears to be the lack of objective information available to employers on the applicant's academic accomplishments and skills.

Tests are available for measuring competency in reading, writing, mathematics, science, and problem solving; but court decisions (e.g., *Griggs* vs. *Duke Power Company*, 1971), and pressure from the Equal Employment Opportunity Commission (EEOC) resulted in a drastic reduction in their use after 1971. A 1987 survey of a stratified random sample of small and medium-sized employers who were members of the National Federation of Independent Business (NFIB) found that aptitude test scores had been obtained in only 2.9 percent of the hiring decisions studied (Bishop & Griffin, forthcoming).

Other potential sources of information on effort and achievement in high school are transcripts and referrals from teachers who know the applicant. Both these means are underused. In the NFIB survey, transcripts had been obtained prior to the selection decision for only 14.2 percent of the hiring events in which a high school graduate was hired. If a student or graduate has given written permission for a transcript to be sent to an employer, the Buckley amendment obligates the school to respond. Many high schools are not, however, responding to such requests. Nationwide Insurance, one of Columbus, Ohio's, most respected employers, sent over 1,200 such signed requests to high schools in 1982 and received only 93 responses. Employers reported that colleges were much more responsive to transcript requests than were high schools. High schools have apparently designed their systems for responding to requests for transcripts around the needs of college-bound students, not around the needs of those students who seek a job immediately after graduating.

There is an additional barrier to the use of high school transcripts in selecting new employees—when high schools do respond, it takes a very long time. For Nationwide Insurance, the response almost invariably took more than two weeks. Given this time lag, if employers required transcripts prior to making hiring selections, a job offer could not be made until a month or so after an application had been received. Most jobs are filled much more rapidly than that. The 1982 NCRVE employer survey of employers found that 83.5 percent of all jobs were filled in less than a month, and 65 percent were filled in less than two weeks.

The only information about school experiences requested by most employers is years of schooling, diplomas and certificates obtained, and area of specialization. Probably because of unreliable reporting and the threat of EEOC litigation, only 15 percent of the NFIB employers asked the applicants with 12 years of schooling to report their grade point average. Despite their limited use in selecting employees, employers apparently believe that GPAs are good predictors of future productivity. A policy capturing experiment with a nationwide sample of 750 employers found that employer ratings of completed job applications were more affected by high school grade point average than by any other single worker characteristic (Hollenbeck & Smith, 1984).

Hiring on the basis of recommendations by high school teachers is also uncommon. In the NFIB survey, when someone with 12 years of schooling was hired, the new hire had been referred or recommended by vocational teachers only 5.2 percent of the time and referred by someone else in the high school only 2.7 percent of the time.

Consequently, hiring selections and starting wage rates often do not reflect the competencies and abilities students have developed in school. Instead, hiring decisions are based on observable characteristics (such as years of schooling and field of study) that serve as signals for the competencies the employer cannot observe directly. *As a result, the worker's starting wage primarily reflects the average productivity of all workers with the same set of educational credentials rather than that individual's productivity or academic achievement.* A study of how individual wage rates varied with job performance found that when people hired for the same or very similar jobs are compared, workers who are 20 percent more productive than the average received wage offers that were only 1.6 percent higher than average (Bishop, 1987). After a year at the firm, the more productive workers were more likely to be promoted, but the impact of reported productivity on a worker's relative wage was still quite low. A 20 percent productivity differential generated a 4 percent wage differential at nonunion firms with about 20 employees and no wage differential at unionized establishments with more than 100 employees and at nonunion establishments with more than 400 employees.

Employers have a number of good reasons for not varying the wage rates of their employees in proportion to their perceived job performance. All feasible measures of individual productivity are unreliable and unstable. Workers are reluctant to accept jobs in which the judgment of one supervisor can result in a large wage decline in the second year on the job (Hashimoto & Yu, 1980; Stiglitz, 1974). Most productivity differentials are specific to the firm, and this reduces the risk that not paying a particularly productive worker a comparably higher salary will result in his going elsewhere (Bishop, 1987). Pay that is highly contingent on performance can also weaken cooperation and generate incentives to sabotage others (Lazear, 1986). Finally, in unionized settings, the union's opposition to merit pay will often be decisive.

This evidence implies that the benefits of developing one's verbal, mathematical, and scientific capabilities are considerably greater to society than to the individual. Despite their higher productivity, *young workers who have achieved in high school and who have done well on academic achievement tests do not receive higher wage rates immediately after high school.* The student who works hard must wait many years to start really benefiting, and even then the magnitude of the wage and earnings effect—a 1 to 2 percent increase in earnings per grade level equivalent on achievement tests—is considerably smaller than the actual change in productivity that results.

The Zero-Sum Nature of Academic Competition in High School

The second root cause of the lack of real motivation to learn is peer pressure against studying hard. Students report that "in most of the regular classes . . . [i]f you raise your hand more than twice in a class, you are called a 'teacher's pet.' " It's O.K. to be smart, you cannot help that. It is definitely not O.K. to study hard to get a good grade. This is illustrated by the following story, related by one of my students:

> Erroneously I was lumped into the brains genus by others at school just because of the classes I was in. This really irked me; not only was I not an athlete but I was also thought of as one of those "brain geeks." Being a brain really did have a stigma attached to it. Sometimes during a free period I would sit and listen to all the brains talk about how much they hated school work and how they never studied and I had to bite my lip to keep from laughing out loud. I *knew* they were lying, and they knew they were lying too. I think that a lot of brains hung around together only because their fear of social isolation was greater than their petty rivalries. I think that my two friends who were brains liked me because I was almost on their level but I was not competitive. (Tim, 1986)

The primary reason for peer pressure against studying is that pursuing academic success forces students into a zero-sum competition with their classmates. Their achievement is not being measured against an absolute, external standard. In contrast to scout merit badges, for example, where recognition is given for achieving a fixed standard of competence, the schools' measures of achievement assess performance relative to fellow students through grades and class rank. When students try hard to excel, they set themselves apart, cause rivalries and may make things *worse* for friends. *When we set up a zero-sum competition among close friends, we should not be surprised when they decide not to compete.* All work groups have ways of sanctioning "rate busters." High school students call them "brain geeks," "grade grubbers" and "brown nosers."

Young people are not lazy. In their jobs after school and at football practice they work very hard. In these environments they are part of a team, where individual efforts are visible and appreciated by teammates.

Competition and rivalry are not absent, but they are offset by shared goals, shared successes, and external measures of achievement (i.e., satisfied customers or winning the game). On the sports field, there is no greater sin than giving up, even when the score is hopelessly one-sided. On the job, tasks not done by one worker will generally have to be completed by another. In too many high schools, when it comes to academics, there is no greater sin than trying hard.

The second reason for peer norms against studying is that most students perceive the chance of receiving recognition for an academic achievement to be so slim they have given up trying. At most high school awards ceremonies, the recognition and awards go to only a few—those at the very top of the class. By ninth grade most students are already so far behind the leaders that they know they have no realistic chance of being perceived as academically successful. Their reaction is often to denigrate the students who take learning seriously and to honor other forms of achievement—athletics, dating, holding your liquor, and being "cool"—that offer them better chances of success.

The lack of external standards for judging academic achievement and the resulting zero-sum nature of academic competition in the school also influences parents, the school board, and local school administrators. Parents can see that setting higher academic standards or hiring better teachers will not improve their child's grade point average or class rank. Raising standards at the high school will have only minor effects on how one's child does on an SAT that is purposely designed to be curriculum-free, so why worry about standards? In any case, doing well on the SAT matters only for the small minority who aspire to attend a selective college. Most students are planning to attend a public college, many of which admit all high school graduates from the state who have completed the requisite courses. Scholarships are awarded on the basis of financial need, not academic merit.

The parents of children who are not planning to go to college have an even weaker incentive to demand high standards at the local high school. They believe that what counts in the labor market is getting the diploma, not learning algebra. They can see that learning more will be of only modest benefit to their child's future, and that higher standards might jeopardize what is really important—the diploma.

Only when educational outcomes are aggregated at the state or national level do the real costs of mediocre schools become apparent. The whole community loses because the work force is less efficient, and it becomes difficult to attract new industry to an area. As competitiveness deteriorates, the whole nation's standard of living declines. This is precisely the reason that employers, governors, and state legislatures have been the energizing force behind school reform. State governments, however, are far removed from the classroom, and the instruments available to them for imposing reform are limited. If students, parents, and school board officials perceive the rewards for learning to be minimal, then state efforts to improve the quality of education will not succeed.

INCENTIVES TO LEARN IN OTHER NATIONS

The tendency to underreward effort and learning in school appears to be a peculiarly American phenomenon. In Japan and many European countries, the educational system administers achievement test batteries (e.g., the O Levels in the United Kingdom, or the Baccalaureate in France) that are closely tied to the curriculum. Performance on these exams is the primary determinant of the university and the field of study to which a student is admitted. The credentials that are awarded to secondary school completers signal not only that the individual has passed a particular set of exams, but also the level of the pass. Top companies in Japan and Europe often hire lifetime employees directly out of secondary schools; and performance on these exams, together with teacher recommendations and schools grades, has a significant impact on who is chosen to work at the more prestigious firms (Leestma et al., 1987; Reubens, 1969). Germany has no common national or provincial exams, so grades in school are a crucial determinant of the employer with whom a German youth apprentices and the university and specialty college–bound students are able to enter.

In Japan the best jobs are available only to those who are recommended by their high school. The most prestigious firms have long-term arrangements with particular high schools, to which they delegate the responsibility of selecting new employees for the firm. It is universally understood that when more than one student is interested in a particular job, the student with the highest grades and best exam results is to be referred. The number of graduates that a high school is able to place in this way depends on its reputation and the company's past experience with graduates from the school. Schools with poorly prepared students find it difficult to place them in good jobs. A school that does not live up to this implicit understanding loses the opportunity to make referrals in the future, The following incident demonstrates what happens when meritocratic principles are set aside by the school.

> A couple of years ago, after the school decided to recommend a student for a job, another student told us that he wished to apply for the same firm, and he [and his parents] said he had strong personal connections with an executive in the firm. Although we were not comfortable about doing this, we allowed the second student to apply [and we] withdrew the other [better qualified] student. Later, the firm complained that the student lacked the requisite ability and they have stopped offering a job to us since then. We visited and explained what happened, but,

after all, we lost the relation with the firm. (Furikawa, 1986, article written by a teacher in charge of job placement in a high school, quoted in Rosenbaum & Kariya, 1987, p. 10)

Japanese parents know that their son or daughter's future economic and social rank in society critically depends on which high school is attended and on how much is learned in school. Entry into the better high schools depends primarily on the child's performance in junior high school, not on where the parents can afford to live, as in the United States. Because the reputation of the high school is so important, the competitive pressure reaches down into junior high school. Forty-five percent of junior high school students attend *juku*, private schools that provide tutoring in the subjects that will be tested on the exam given to determine the high school to which one is admitted. Because of the importance of the national exams in the allocation of students to high school, colleges, and jobs, learning achievement tends to be measured in relation to everyone else in the state or nation, not just relative to one's classmates in the school. These are the reasons that Japanese parents demand so much of their children and of their schools. It is why Japanese fifth-graders spend 32.6 hours a week involved in academic activities, while American youngsters devote only 19.6 hours to their studies (Stevenson, Lee, & Stigler, 1986).

Japanese adolescents work extremely hard in high school, but once they have entered college they stop working. For most students, a country club atmosphere prevails. The reason for the change in behavior is that employers apparently care only about which university the youth attends, not about the individual's academic achievement at the university. *Studying very hard is not a national character trait; it is a response to the way Japanese society rewards academic achievement.*

American students, in contrast, take it easy in high school but generally work quite hard in college. This change is caused in large part by the fact that when higher level jobs requiring a bachelor's or associate's degree are being filled, employers pay much more attention to grades and teacher recommendations than they do when they hire high school graduates. The NFIB survey found that when college graduates were hired, 26.5 percent of the employers had reviewed the college transcript before making the selection, 10.9 percent had obtained a recommendation from a major professor, and 6.5 percent had obtained a recommendation from a professor outside of the graduate's major or from the college's placement office.

If learning were defined by an absolute standard and not by one's ranking in the school, and if the rewards for learning were as attractive as they are in Japan, everyone—students, teachers, parents, and school boards—would behave very differently. Parents would demand that their school be the best and would be willing to tax themselves heavily to achieve that result. The status and salary of secondary school teachers would rise, the requirements for entry into the profession would increase, and standards of teacher performance would improve. If parents were not satisfied with their child's academic progress, they would send him or her to a tutor, just as Japanese parents do. Adolescents would no longer be such reluctant learners.

HOW TO IMPROVE THE QUALITY OF EDUCATION

The rapid gains in academic achievement overseas and declining achievement here spell trouble for the U.S. economy (Koretz, 1986; Bishop, 1989). The problem is so serious and so long-standing that nothing short of radical reform will help. Most of the reforms now underway are desirable, but by themselves they are insufficient.

Proposed reforms of secondary education include stricter graduation requirements; more homework; increases in the amount and difficulty of course material; greater emphasis on the basics (English, math, science, social science, computer science); and improvements in the quality of teaching through higher salaries, career ladders, and competence tests for teachers. Though important, these reforms are limited in that they emphasize changes in the content and quality of what is offered by the school and require the student to work harder, without giving sufficient attention to how to *motivate* students to work harder. Learning is not a passive act; it requires the time and active involvement of the learner. In a classroom with 1 teacher and 18 students, there are 18 learning hours spent to every 1 hour of teaching time. Student time is, therefore, very important, and how intensely that time is used affects learning significantly. Clearly, then, attention needs to be given to how much time and energy students devote to learning.

The key to motivation is recognizing and rewarding learning. Individual learning goals should be established that challenge the student to the maximum extent possible. Achievement of these goals would be assessed by the school and recognized at an awards ceremony. The student would receive a competency profile describing these achievements that would aid in securing employment. If employers know who has learned what, they will provide the rewards.

The second way schools can generate stronger incentives for learning is to restructure schoolwide and classroom recognition of student achievement so that everyone has a chance to be recognized for his or her contribution: Greater effort by everybody makes everybody better off, and there are significant rewards for learning and real consequences for failing to learn. As Theodore Sizer has advocated, "The better the performance, the greater [should be] the latitude given the student" (1984, p. 67). Bloom's theory of mastery learning says that there are no differences in *what* people can learn, only differences in the *rate* at which people learn. Given enough time, almost everyone can achieve mastery. Students who fail to learn on the first try should commit extra time to learning task, with extra classes scheduled after school and during the summer. *Learning* would be defined as gaining in competence and knowledge, not as meeting an absolute standard of performance. The gifted and the handicapped would be stretched, as would everyone else. The reward for effort and for learning would be free time. Schools would be open all day and all year, and enrichment programs designed to attract all students would be offered during the additional time. Everyone would be encouraged to participate, but only the unsuccessful learners would be obligated to participate.

Some might respond to these proposals by stating a preference for intrinsic over extrinsic motivation of learning. This, however, is a false dichotomy. Nowhere else in our society do we expect people to devote thousands of hours to a difficult task while receiving *only* intrinsic rewards. Public recognition of achievement and the symbolic and material rewards received by achievers are important generators of intrinsic motivation. They are, in fact, one of the central ways a culture symbolically transmits and promotes its values.

It goes without saying that these reforms involve a radical restructuring of our schools. No-fault adolescence and the zero-sum nature of academic competition would pass from the scene. The incentives faced by everyone in the system would change and this would probably lead to a major increase in public investment in education. The proposed reforms are not simple to implement and they need not be implemented all at once. The following discussion of these recommendations is organized into five sections, dealing with these topics:

1. Improving measures of academic achievement
2. Getting the peer group to encourage learning
3. Creating new learning opportunities in school
4. Generating additional recognition and reward for learning
5. Helping students obtain good jobs

Improving Measures of Academic Achievement

Institute Statewide Examinations

States should adopt statewide tests of competency and knowledge that are specific to the curriculum being taught, like New York State's Regents Examinations. If a state does not have such exams, a school district (or the members of each department of a school) could establish its own exams. Such examinations would offer several benefits. They would:

- Better inform students and parents about how well the student is doing, and thus help parents work with teachers to improve their children's performance.
- Make the relationship between teachers and students more cooperative, with the teacher and students working jointly to prepare the students for the exam.
- Strengthen students' incentives to learn because they would now be able to signal to their parents and employers their competence in specific curriculum areas.
- Create a data base that school boards and parents could use to evaluate the quality of education being provided by their local school.
- Enable employers to use scores on these examinations to help improve their selection of new employees. If the uncertainties involved in hiring are reduced, expanding employment will become more profitable, total employment will increase, and recent high school graduates will be better able to compete with more experienced workers.

Reform the SAT and ACT Tests

Although national tests are necessary, the Scholastic Aptitude Test (SAT) is not the kind of test that is helpful. The SAT suffers from two very serious limitations: the limited range of the achievements that are evaluated and its multiple-choice format. The test was designed to be curriculum-free. To the extent that it evaluates students' understanding of material taught in schools, the material it covers is vocabulary and elementary and junior high school mathematics. Most subjects studied in high school—science, history, civics, technology, computers, trigonometry, and statistics—are completely absent from the test. As a result, it fails to generate incentives to take the more demanding courses or to study hard. The multiple-choice format is also a severe limitation. National and provincial exams in Europe are predominantly essay examinations. The absence of essays on the SAT and the American College Testing Program's ACT test contributes to the poor writing skills of U.S. students. The test advertises itself as an ability test but is, in fact, an achievement test measuring a very limited range of achievements.

Jencks and Crouse (1982) have made many of the same criticisms of the SAT and have recommended that it evaluate a much broader range of achievements. I support their position. A portion of the test should involve writing an essay. Knowledge and understanding of literature, history, technology and science, and higher order thinking skills should all be assessed.

Colleges should require that students take at least two subject-specific exams. The advanced placement exams are examples of the kind of examinations we need. These exams should not be limited to the multiple-choice format. Foreign language exams, for example, should test conversational skills as well as reading and writing. Students taking science courses should be expected to conduct experiments and demonstrate the use of laboratory equipment.

Certifying Competencies

Schools should provide graduates with certificates or diplomas that certify students' knowledge and competencies, not just their attendance. Competency should be defined by an absolute standard, just as Scout merit badges are. Different types and levels of competency need to be certified. Minimum competency tests for receiving a high school diploma do not satisfy the need for better signals of achievement in high school. Because some students arrive in high school so far behind, and the consequences of not getting a diploma are so severe, we have not been willing to set the minimum competency standard very high. But once they satisfy the minimum, many students stop putting effort into their academic courses. What is needed is a more informative credential that signals the full range of student achievements (e.g., statewide achievement exam scores, competency check lists).

Competency Profiles

Another way to motivate students is to give them feedback on their accomplishments through the mechanism of a criterion-referenced competency profile. Competency profiles are a checklist of competencies needed in a specific occupation that the student either has or can develop through study and practice. The ratings of competence that appear on a competency profile are relative to an absolute standard, not relative to their classmates. By evaluating students against an absolute standard, the competency profile avoids a negative feedback of one student's effort into another student's grade. Unlike the present zero-sum game, it does not discourage students from sharing their knowledge and teaching each other.

A second advantage of the competency profile approach to evaluation is that students can see their progress as new skills are learned and checked off. The skills not yet checked off are the learning goals for the future. Seeing such a checklist get filled up is inherently reinforcing.

With a competency profile system, goals can be tailored to the student's interests and capabilities, and progress toward these goals can be monitored and rewarded. Students who have difficulty in their required academic subjects could nevertheless take pride in the developing occupational competence now recognized just as prominently as course grades in academic subjects. Upon graduation, the competency profile would be encased in plastic and given to the student to serve as a credential certifying occupational competencies.

Getting the Peer Group to Encourage Learning

Cooperative Learning

One effective way of inducing peers to value learning and support effort in school is to reward the group for the individual learning of its members. This is the approach taken in cooperative learning. Research results (Slavin, 1985) suggest that the two key ingredients for successful cooperative learning are as follows:

- A cooperative incentive structure—awards based on group performance—seems to be essential for students working in groups to learn better.
- A system of individual accountability is needed in which everyone's maximum effort must be essential to the group's success and the effort and performance of each group member must be clearly visible to his or her group mates.

For example, students might be grouped into evenly matched teams of four or five members that are heterogeneous in ability. After the teacher presents new material, the team works together on worksheets to prepare each other for periodic quizzes. The team's score is an average of the scores of team members, and high team scores are recognized in a class newsletter or through group certificates of achievement.

What seems to happen in cooperative learning is that the team develops an identity of its own, and group norms arise that are different from the norms that hold sway in the student's other classes. The group's identity arises from the extensive personal interaction among group members in the context of working toward a shared goal. Because the group is small and the interaction intense, the effort and success of each team member is known to other teammates. Such knowledge allows the group to reward each team member for his or her contribution to the team goal, and this is what seems to happen.

Creating New Opportunities for Learning in School

Turn Schools into All-Day Learning Centers
Schools should remain open after the end of the regular school day. A full range of remedial and enrichment programs, extracurricular activities, and interscholastic sports should be offered. The library should remain open during this period, and the auditorium could be used for showing educational films and videotapes. Extra help would be available for students having difficulty with the core curriculum. Volunteers to provide tutoring and to offer special-interest courses could be recruited from the community. Private teachers of music, art, and other subjects could also use school facilities during these hours. The benefit of this reform is that (1) the regular school day would be freed up for more intensive study of the core curriculum, (2) slower students would be given the extra instruction they need, and (3) the phenomenon of the latchkey child would be significantly reduced or eliminated.

Keep the Schools Open During the Summer

Longitudinal studies of learning have found that the pace of learning slows considerably during the summer and that disadvantaged students, especially, lose ground during the summer months (Heyns, 1987). Experimental evaluations of STEP, a program for disadvantaged youth that combines a part-time summer job with about 90 hours of remediation, has found that adding the remediation to the summer job results in gains in academic achievement of 0.5 grade-level equivalents (Corporation for Public–Private Ventures, 1988). It would appear that summer programs targeted on educationally and economically disadvantaged children are likely to have high payoffs.

A variety of remedial, enrichment, and special-interest short courses should be offered during the summer. Although many of the teachers would be regular school staff, an education degree and state certification would not be required. Private teachers of music, art, athletics, and academic subjects could also offer their own courses at the school. Where appropriate, academic credit would be given for the summer school courses. The school district would provide transportation.

Generating Additional Recognition and Rewards for Learning

A Massive Dose of Mastery Learning

Students who are not learning at the desired rate should be expected to commit additional time to the task after school and during the summer. At the beginning of the school year, school personnel would meet with each student and his or her parents to set goals. Students who are not performing at grade level in core subjects and who do not make normal progress during the school year should be kept after school for tutoring and remedial instruction and required to attend summer school. Assessments of progress should be made at appropriate points during the school year to inform students of their progress and to enable those who are participating in remedial programs after school to demonstrate that they are now progressing satisfactorily. Course grades and teacher evaluations would be a central part of the assessment process, but there should be an external yardstick as well. This might be a competency checklist, a mastery test keyed to the textbook, or an examination specified by the state, by the school, or collectively by the teachers, in that grade level or department. The assessment tools would be established at the beginning of the school year. The external yardstick helps ensure that students perceive the standard to be absolute rather than relative to others in the class, and helps create a communality of interest between teacher and student. Teachers need to be perceived as helping the student achieve the student's goals, not as judges meting out punishment. Final decisions regarding who would be required to attend summer school could be made by committees of teachers, possibly with some administrative representation. Because students will want to avoid being required to get remedial instruction after school and during the summer, this will be a powerful incentive for them to devote themselves to their studies.

Honoring Academic Achievement

Schools should strengthen their awards and honors system for both academic and nonacademic accomplishments. The medals, trophies, and school letters awarded in interscholastic athletics are a powerful motivator of achievement on the playing field. Academic pursuits need a similar system of reinforcement. Public school systems in Tulsa and a number of other cities have started awarding school letters for academic achievements. Awards and honors systems should be designed so that almost every student can receive at least one award or honor before graduation if he or she makes the effort. Outstanding academic performance (e.g., high grades or high test scores) would not have to be the only way of defining excellence. Awards could be given for significant improvements in academic performance since the previous year or since the beginning of the school year, for public service in or out of school, for leadership and participation in extracurricular activities, for participation in student government, for perfect attendance records, and for student of the week (criteria could vary weekly). The standard for making an award should be criterion-referenced: If greater numbers achieve the standard of excellence, more awards should be given.

A prominent place in the school should be reserved for bulletin boards where pictures of the most recent winners and reasons for their receiving recognition could be posted. Another form of recognition could be displays of student work: art, science, social studies, vocational education projects, and so forth. Periodically, the parents of the most recent award winners and sponsoring teachers should be invited to an evening assembly, where the principal would award the students the certificate or plaque recognizing their accomplishments. Although the primary purpose of this system would be to improve the school's educational climate, a secondary effect would be the creation of a tool to help the student obtain a good job. The potential of these awards as an aid to improving employability should be made clear to students and parents.

Allow Employers to Use Scores on Achievement Tests in Selecting New Hires

There is now a great deal of evidence that scores on tests measuring competence in mathematical reasoning, language arts, science, and technical knowledge are good predictors of job performance in a great variety of jobs and do not discriminate against minorities or women (Hunter & Hunter, 1984; Bishop, 1988). Despite this, Equal Employment Opportunity

Commission (EEOC) regulations and case law have in the past required that a very expensive validation study be conducted before a firm can use any test to help select employees. The result has been to diminish greatly the use of tests for employee selection and to reduce the rewards for learning. There is a strong public interest in strengthening the incentives to learn; government regulations should not prevent the use of tests and should encourage the use of broad-spectrum achievement tests covering the high school curriculum, rather than so-called aptitude tests. Adverse impacts on minority groups can be avoided by race-norming the test (as the General Aptitude Test Battery [GATB] currently does) and through affirmative action. Because other instruments are available for achieving societal goals for integration on the job, decisions about employment testing should be based on the effects of these tests on incentives to learn and efficient sorting of workers across jobs.

Helping Students Obtain Good Jobs

Schools can help their graduates avoid unemployment and get better jobs by improving the quality and facilitating the flow of employment-related information to students and their potential employers. Improving the information available to all parties in the job search/hiring system will have the following consequences:

- A greater share of school graduates will find employment.
- The jobs they obtain will pay better and offer more training and job security.
- The better jobs will be distributed more in accordance with the objective merit of the candidate.
- Students will commit a greater amount of time and effort to their studies as they perceive the greater payoffs for doing so.

Policies that facilitate information flow make the connection between effort in school and later labor market success more visible. Such policies include the following.

Offering Courses in Job Search Skills
Schools have an important role to play in preparing youth to navigate in the labor market. Career guidance and career counseling have been viewed as important school functions for many decades. Realizing that a career choice cannot be implemented unless a job can be obtained in the chosen field, many schools are now teaching youths how to search for work (Wegmann, 1979). Students need practice in writing a résumé, in interviewing, and in using the more effective informal methods of searching for a job.

Acting as a Source of Informal Contacts

School personnel can be a reference and a source of job contacts for their students. Some students may feel that they do not have and cannot develop good employment contacts. School personnel can help them by building and maintaining trusting relationships with local employers and then helping to match employer and student needs. Students from disadvantaged backgrounds have a special need for this kind of help because their relatives and neighbors typically lack the employment contacts of middle-class families.

Many schools provide job placement and referral services for their students and graduates. Three and a half million people found their current job through a referral by a teacher, school, or college (Rosenfeld, 1975). This function of schools is much more important than is generally thought.

Whenever possible, there should be a one-to-one relationship between a specific teacher or administrator and an employer. A study by McKinney, Franchak, Halasz-Salster, Morrison, and McElwain (1982) found that *when schools formalize this relationship by creating a placement office, the number of jobs found for vocational students tended to decrease.* The best example of an informal contact system is the one that exists for many vocational students. Vocational teachers often know local employers in related fields; they also know students well enough to recommend them. This kind of informal system could be expanded to include all students not planning to attend college.

Guiding Students in Assessing Jobs and Employers

Students need help in assessing jobs, and schools can give them the information necessary to make these assessments. Career guidance tends to focus on the individual's choice of occupation, but attention also needs to be given to selecting an employer and matching employer and employee needs. Young people who find good, high-paying jobs with promotion opportunities will end up changing jobs less often. Students need to learn how to assess such dimensions of a firm as training opportunities, promotion opportunities, job security provisions, maternity leave rules, vacation policies, policies regarding tardiness, friendliness of co-workers, effectiveness of supervision, medical insurance, educational leave, and tuition reimbursement.

Releasing Student Records

The school can help students provide employers with information by developing an equitable and efficient policy for releasing student records. While developing this policy, school officials should keep in mind their dual responsibilities of protecting the student's right to privacy and helping students find good, suitable jobs. The student and his or her parents should receive certified copies of the transcript and other records that might be released.

Schools can develop a form that would explain to parents and students their rights, as well as the pros and cons of disclosing information. The Buckley Amendment requires that the form specify the purpose of disclosure, which records are to be released, and who is to receive the records. The law allows the student to specify a "class of parties." The class specified could be "all potential employers contacted by the student," which would cut down on the necessary paperwork. Once the student has filed a request, the school is required by law to comply. Schools can best serve students by handling all inquiries expeditiously and without charge.

Developing a Job Search Portfolio

Schools should consider providing students with a job search portfolio or competency profile that records all their accomplishments in one place. Students attempting to market themselves to employers will have greater success if all their school achievements are summarized in one compact, standardized document. Compactness and standardization make it easier for employers to use information in their hiring decisions, and this facilitates information flow.

The coverage and format of the document are probably best worked out cooperatively by a committee that includes school administrators, employers, and other interested parties. Developing and using such a document might be a part of a campaign to enlist commitments from major local employers to hire the school's graduates. Developing the information system cooperatively is a good way to ensure that the finished form will be beneficial to schools, employers, and students.

Students have many talents and skills that can be highlighted in such a document. The job search portfolio should emphasize accomplishments and performance indicators that are most useful in identifying a good match between a job and a youth. Students and parents receive copies of it, and students should be encouraged to bring copies with them when they apply for jobs. Employers should be encouraged to ask to see the portfolio and keep a copy when a job application is filed.

SUMMARY

Institutional arrangements of schools and the labor market have profound effects on the incentives faced by students, teachers, parents, and school administrators. When educational credentials are awarded for time served rather than for learning achievements, the incentive to devote time and energy to learning is significantly weakened. The passivity and inattention of students, the low morale of teachers, the defeat of so many school levies, and low U.S. rankings on international measures of achievement are all logical outcomes of institutional arrangements that weaken student incentives to study and parental incentives to fund a high-quality education. Only with an effective system of rewards within schools and in the labor market can we hope to overcome this pervasive apathy and achieve excellence.

NOTES

The research that has culminated in this chapter was sponsored by the Center for Advanced Human Resource Studies, the National Center for Research in Vocational Education, and the Commission on Testing and Public Policy.

Author's Note: I would like to thank Peter Mueser and Richard Murnane for helpful comments on an earlier version of the chapter. The opinions and conclusions expressed herein are solely those of the author and should not be construed as representing the opinions or policies of any agency of the United States government. This chapter has not undergone formal review or approval of the faculty of the New York State School of Industrial and Labor Relations. It is intended to make results of Center research available to others interested in human resource management in preliminary form to encourage discussion and suggestions.

REFERENCES

Bishop, John. (1977, Summer). The effect of public policies on the demand for higher education. *Journal of Human Resources.*

Bishop, John. (1987, October). The recognition and reward of employee performance. *Journal of Labor Economics.*

Bishop, John. (1988) *The productivity consequences of what is learned in high school.* Center for Advanced Human Resources Working Paper #88-18, Cornell University, Ithaca, New York.

Bishop, John. (1989). Is the test score decline responsible for the productivity growth decline? *American Economic Review.*

Bishop, John, & Griffin, Kelly. (Forthcoming). *Recruitment, training and skills of small business employees.* Washington, DC: National Federation of Independent Business Foundation.

Corporation for Public–Private Ventures. (1988). *Summer Training and Education Program (STEP): Report on the 1987 experience.* Philadelphia.

Fischer, C. W., et al. (1987). *Teaching behaviors, academic learning time and student achievement: Final report of phase III-B.* Technical Report V-I. San Francisco: Far West Laboratories.

Frederick, W. C. (1977, January). The use of classroom time in high schools above or below the median reading score. *Urban Education, 11*(4):459–464.

Frederick, W., Walberg, H., & Rasher, S. (1979, November–December). Time, teacher comments, and achievement in urban high schools. *Journal of Educational Research, 73*(2):63–65.

Freeman, Richard B. (1971). *The market for college-trained manpower: A study in the economics of career choice.* Cambridge, MA: Harvard University Press.

Freeman, Richard. (1976a, January). A cobweb model of the supply and starting salary of new engineers. *Industrial and Labor Relations Review, 29*:236–248.

Freeman, Richard. (1976b). *The overeducated American.* New York: Academic Press.

Gardner, John A. (1982). *Influence of high school curriculum on determinants of labor market experience.* Columbus: National Center for Research in Vocational Education, Ohio State University.

Ghiselli, Edwin E. (1973). The validity of aptitude tests in personnel selection. *Personnel Psychology,* 1973: 26, 461–477.

Goodlad, J. (1983). *A place called school.* New York: McGraw-Hill.

Griggs vs. *Duke Power Company,* 3 FEP 175 (1971).

Halasz, Ida M., & Behm, Karen S. "Time on Task Selected Vocational Education Classes." Columbus: National Center for Research in Vocational Education, Ohio State University, January 1983.

Hashimoto, M., & Yu, B. (1980). Specific capital, employment and wage rigidity. *Bell Journal of Economics, 11*(2):536–549.

Heyns, Barbara. (1987). Schooling and cognitive development: Is there a season for learning? *Child Development, 58*(5):1151–1160.

Hollenbeck, K., & Smith B. (1984). *The influence of applicants' education and skills on employability assessments by employers.* Columbus: National Center for Research in Vocational Education, Ohio State University.

Hotchkiss, Lawrence, Bishop, John H., & Gardner, John. (1982). *Effects of individual and school characteristics on part-time work of high school seniors.* Columbus: National Center for Research in Vocational Education, Ohio State University.

Hunter, J. E., & Hunter, R. F. (1984). The validity and utility of alternative predictors of job performance. *Psychological Bulletin, 96* (1):72–98.

Hunter, John E., Schmidt, Frank L., & Judiesch, Michael K. (1988, June). *Individual differences in output as a function of job complexity.* Department of Industrial Relations and Human Resources, University of Iowa.

Jencks, Christopher, & Crouse, James. (1982). Aptitude vs. achievement: Should we replace the SAT? *The Public Interest,* pp. 21–35.

Kang, S., & Bishop, J. (1984). "The impact of curriculum on the non-college bound youth's labor market outcomes." In *High School Preparation for Employment* (pp. 95–135). Columbus: National Center for Research in Vocational Education, Ohio State University.

Klein, M. F., Tyle, K. A., & Wright, J. E. (1979, December). A study of schooling curriculum. *Phi Delta Kappan, 61*(4):244–248.

Klein, Roger, Spady, Richard, & Weiss, Andrew. (1983). *Factors affecting the output and quit propensities of production workers.* New York: Bell Laboratories and Columbia University.

Koretz, Daniel. (1986). *Trends in educational achievement.* Washington, DC: Congressional Budget Office.

Krista. (1987). *Paper for ILR 360.* Ithaca, NY: Cornell University.

Lazear, Edward P. (1986, April). *Pay equality and industrial politics.* Stanford, CA: Hoover Institution, Stanford University.

Leestma, Robert, et al. (1987). *Japanese education today.* Report of the U.S. Study of Education in Japan, prepared by a special task force of the Office of Educational Research and Improvement Japan Study Team.

Longitudinal Survey of American Youth. (1988). Data file user's manual. Dekalb, IL: Public Opinion Laboratory.

McKinney, Floyd, Franchak, Stephen, Halasz-Salster, Ida, Morrison, Irene, & McElwain, Douglas. (1982). *Factors relating to the job placement of former secondary vocational educational students.* Columbus: National Center for Research in Vocational Education, Ohio State University.

Meyer, R. (1982). Job training in the schools. In R. Taylor, H. Rosen, & F. Pratzner (Eds.), *Job training for youth.* Columbus: National Center for Research in Vocational Education, Ohio State University.

Nielsen, A. C., Company. (1987). Unpublished raw data.

Organization for Economic Cooperation and Development. (1986). Living conditions in OECD countries: A compendium of social indicators. *Social Policy Studies,* No. 3. Paris.

Reubens, Beatrice. (1969). *From learning to earning: A transnational comparison of transition services.* Washington, DC: R&D Monograph 63, U.S. Department of Labor.

Rosenbaum, James, & Kariya, Tobe. (1987, August). *Market and institutional mechanisms for the high school to work transition in Japan and the U.S.* Paper presented at the American Sociological Association Meeting, Chicago.

Rosenfeld, Carl. (1975). Job seeking methods used by American workers. *Monthly Labor Review, 98*(8):39–42.

Sizer, Theodore R. (1984). *Horace's compromise: The dilemma of the American high school.* First report from a study of high schools, cosponsored by the National Association of Secondary School Principals and the Commission on Educational Issues of the National Association of Independent Schools. Boston: Houghton Mifflin.

Slavin, Robert E. (1985). When does cooperative learning increase student achievement? *Psychological Bulletin.*

Stevenson, Harold W., Lee, Shin-Ying, & Stigler, James W. (1986, February). Mathematics achievement of Chinese, Japanese and American children. *Science, 231,* 693–699.

Stiglitz, Joseph E. (1974, April). Risk sharing and incentives in sharecropping. *Review of Economic Studies, 61*(2):219–256.

Taubman, P., & Wales, T. (1975). Education as an investment and a screening device. In F. T. Juster (Ed.), *Education, income, and human behavior* (pp. 95–119). New York: McGraw-Hill.

Tim. (1986). *Paper for ILR 360.* Ithaca, NY: Cornell University.

Wegmann, R. G. (1979). Job-search assistance: A review. *Journal of Employment Counseling, 16:*197–228.

19
Preparing Students for Tomorrow's *Political* World

Redefining National Security: New Directions for Education Reform
MARY HATWOOD FUTRELL

". . . AN ACT OF WAR"

To revisit the seminal work in the education reform movement of the 1980s—the 1983 report *A Nation at Risk*—is to experience a revelation. In retrospect, this opening salvo of the modern reform movement proves consistently prophetic, occasionally profound.

A Nation at Risk prefigures, in uncanny fashion, the host of issues that in time came to dominate our national dialogue on education reform. It presents, in tight and eloquent prose, a syllabus for a course on the future of American education, hinting at problems only dimly perceived in 1983 but soon deeply pursued and passionately debated.

A Nation At Risk touches all the bases: illiteracy, the decline in basic skills and graduation standards, the specter of a society deeply divided between a scientific elite and a lay citizenry bewildered by the rush of technological advances, the challenge of ethnic pluralism and the threat to the ideal of equity, the dropout syndrome and the teacher shortage, diluted curricula, banal textbooks, student discipline, teacher preparation, federal leadership, parental responsibility, and a portrait in miniature of a teaching profession under siege, undervalued, and underpaid.

A Nation at Risk is a remarkable document.

And yet, despite its scope, a single paragraph dominates the whole. All else becomes a footnote. And what prevails is an analogy, bluntly militaristic,that defines education—decisively—as an *instrumental* value rather than an *intrinsic* value:

> If an unfriendly foreign power had attempted to impose on America the mediocre educational performance that exists today, we might well have viewed it as an act of war. . . . We have, in effect, been committing an act of unthinking, unilateral, educational disarmament.[1]

It is only a bit hyperbolic to contend that these two sentences set the initial tone for the entire reform debate and dictated the direction of all but a few early reform initiatives. For these sentences defined the mission of education. The mission was decidedly utilitarian: Education was a weapon. This tenet was seldom challenged. It swiftly became the axiomatic foundation of education reform.

The mission of education was to serve the national interest. The destiny of American democracy, it was argued, demanded what revitalized education alone could deliver: technological prowess in the service of military security, economic rejuvenation in the service of reclaimed dominance within the international marketplace, the smooth social and political integration of new waves of immigrants in the service of national harmony.

Education was in the service now.

Not surprisingly, politicians volunteered for action. And, not surprisingly, what would later be termed the first wave of reform emanated not from the schoolhouse, but from the statehouse. Dictates from on high proliferated. An army of governors and state legislators swept into action. And their rallying cry—their battle cry—was "more": more tests for teachers, more credits for graduation, more hours in the school day, more days in the school year, more regimentation, more routinization.

Between 1983 and 1985, legislatures enacted more than 700 statutes stipulating what should be taught—and when, how, and by whom it should be taught.

The reaction to this statutory mania was not swift, but it was inevitable. And when the reaction arrived, it ushered in the second wave of reform.

THE CHANGING OF THE GUARD

The second wave arose from the recognition that if education was to be an instrument for social and economic revitalization, the instrument ought to be wielded by educators, not legislators. Appearing before the annual meeting of the American Educational Research Association in April 1986, I presented the National Education Association's (NEA's) thesis that the time had come to reform the reform movement:

Every attempt at reform that dilutes the authority of the classroom teacher dilutes the quality of instruction in our nation's classrooms.

Teachers cannot hope to prepare students for a world of perpetual flux if they themselves are condemned to static, externally imposed conceptions of effective pedagogy.

Teachers cannot hope to prepare students for the information age if they themselves are condemned to organizational structures derived from the industrial age.

Teachers cannot hope to ready students for responsibility within a participatory democracy if they themselves are condemned to an autocratic bureaucracy.[2]

That was, in brief, the rhetoric of the second wave—and its substance. By 1986, a growing body of research supported the contention that a rising tide of regulation, by wrenching decision-making authority away from teachers and principals, had produced a web of inefficiency. And in 1986, no fewer than five prestigious national reports condemned that inefficiency. The sources of those reports were the Holmes Group, the Carnegie Commission, the National Governors' Association, the Education Commission of the States, and the Association for Supervision and Curriculum Development.

Second-wave reform soon rested on a solid, research-based consensus. Scholars Theodore Sizer and Samuel Bacharach, each with a single statement, added exclamation points to the sentence that exiled first-wave reform. Said Sizer: "The decentralization of substantial authority to the persons closest to the students is essential."[3] Said Bacharach: "Unless faculty are granted appropriate decision-making authority, education reform will remain a poorly disguised political sham—promising everything, delivering nothing."[4]

During this second wave, professional recognition and professional autonomy for teachers became less distant, more realistic goals. The notion of top-down reform had been vanquished. Reform from the bottom up would now hold sway. Teacher empowerment would become at last more than an aspiration. NEA empowerment programs—the Mastery in Learning Project, Operation Rescue, and TABS (the Team Approach to Better Schools)—were launched in 1985 and 1986. All gave substance to the principle that effective reform must be designed and defined by teachers at the local level, working in concert with the local community.

The second-wave thrust was toward reform efforts that would bring together teachers, principals, superintendents, school board members, parents, and business and community leaders in a culture of cooperation. The local school site would be the focus of reform, and reform initiatives would be tailored to local needs.

But exiles return. More precisely, what remained from first-wave reform was the emphasis on education as an instrumental rather than an intrinsic value. Most reforms, even the most creatively crafted, continued to be justified purely on the grounds of national interest. Economic imperatives took the place of legislative mandates. This emphasis, this economic utilitarianism, generated the third wave of reform. Its parentage could be traced, not to the second, but to the first wave of reform. The "top," this time more economic than political, was again driving the reform agenda.

It was at this point that educators recognized the need to forge a broader agenda—an agenda that defined education as *both* an instrumental *and* an intrinsic value.

THE ECONOMIC BATTLEGROUND

In the United States today, the prevailing assumption remains that all will be right with our nation if only education is so reformed that it is guided exclusively by the twin goals of catching the Japanese economically and matching the Soviets militarily. These goals, however, cannot in themselves prepare today's students for the world they will inherit tomorrow. For that world—the "global village"—will demand zealous compassion as much as competitive zeal. Just as surely, it will demand emotional resiliency, mental agility, moral stamina, and the creative savvy to improvise successfully in the face of unrelenting change and unforeseen challenges. These virtues represent the *intrinsic* values of education that, until now, the reform debate has too frequently neglected.

How do we explain this flaw? And how do we prevent this flaw from becoming fatal? We might start by examining the vocabulary that now dominates discussions of education. We are told with increasing regularity that knowledge is a *commodity*, education an *industry*, learning an *asset*, research an *enterprise*. Talk of intellectual *capital* is commonplace. A stubborn consensus holds that the business of education is business.

There is, of course, no denying that the business community and the education community must work together more closely and more cooperatively. Indeed, the corporate community may be public education's most valuable ally. But when the language of commerce so thoroughly saturates discourse on education, something is amiss. Is a mercantile mentality compatible with the traditional mission of public education? Can an education that is *both* an *instrumental value* in the service of national interests *and* a *noninstrumental, nonutilitarian value* that elevates character and educates "the whole child" be forged on the anvil of economic imperatives?

Not likely.

Harvard University economist Robert Reich, author of the landmark treatise *Education and the Next Economy*, which addresses precisely the issue of how to make education a more powerful *economic instrument*, nonetheless takes care to issue a stern caveat:

By focusing on education and the next economy, I do not mean to suggest that education's only, or most important, purpose is economic. To the contrary: A truly educated person is motivated by, and can find satisfaction in, a wide array of things that are not traded in markets or that cost very little. A just and democratic society depends on a citizenry educated in civic responsibility rather than in economic aggrandizement.[5]

Reich goes on to fortify his position by quoting with approval the eloquent statement Horace Mann issued to the Boston Board of Education in 1842. Defending the cause of public education, Mann ended his address by saying:

[H]owever deserving of attention may be the *economical* view of the subject which I have endeavored to present, yet it is one that dwindles into insignificance when compared to those loftier and more sacred attributes of the cause.[6]

None of this is to deny that education is the engine that drives our economy. *But it does not follow that our economy ought to be the engine that drives education.* The simple fact—the incontrovertible fact—is that we will do a disservice to students if we offer them no more than a curriculum designed to advance economic goals or serve utilitarian objectives.

During the past two decades, we have seen the dangers of education designed to serve narrow, provincial priorities—priorities defined by the crisis of the hour. We have also seen the results of this subservience: graduates who are skilled but uneducated, short on creativity, incapable of synthesizing new information. Graduates who draw a blank when asked what images come to mind when they hear the words Soweto and Gdansk, Managua and Phnom Penh, Hiroshima and Auschwitz. Graduates who (the greatest irony of all) are condemned to routinized, dead-end jobs that deprive them of pride and drive them toward debt.

These students are ill prepared for both the world we know and the world we know is approaching. In this, there is no surprise. The obsolete curriculum they were offered—this subservient curriculum—advances *neither* the ethical *nor* the economic agendas our nation embraces.

Education—even if defined only as an instrument to advance national goals—conquers ignorance. A more balanced education—education free from subservience and forged with at least one eye to its intrinsic value— has the potential to conquer intellectual myopia. The education that emerges from this broader agenda will not bow to parochial interests.

Those parochial interests will, of course, persist—and rightly so. Parents may seek an education that offers their children a route to fortune or fame. Corporate executives may seek an education that prepares their future employees to increase corporate earnings. Governments may seek an education that prepares students for active and responsible citizenship. These respective agendas are beyond reproach, and educators must both respect these agendas and remain responsive to them. At the same time, we can never allow a single goal to define our mission.

Educators must accept the premise that the mission of education is of necessity defined by a coherent vision of the kind of world we wish our children to inherit. More important still, it is defined by a vision of the values that will prepare students to cope, indeed to flourish, in that new world.

What now seems clear, as the intellectually demanding and precariously balanced world of the the twenty-first century comes into view, is that the mission of education must not be to train people to *serve* the purposes of others, but to develop their capacity to *question* the purposes of others. We must equip students with stupidity detectors. We must bolster their will to seek wisdom. We must enable them to think complexly and creatively, to act responsibly, and—when necessary—to act selflessly. We must convince them that the gross national product is not a measure of our worth as a people.

The fourth wave of reform will demand a return to schools that are organized to facilitate bottom-up reform. The goals of education—defined as both an instrumental and an intrinsic value—must become less parochial, more expansive, more animated by good will, less determined by economic forces.

PEACE

The curricula that will emerge from fourth-wave reform will, because forged at the local level, exhibit no uniformity. But they will, if reform does indeed become less wed to instrumentalist goals, share a common feature. Specifically, our curricula—designed to prepare students for a radically pluralistic, "shrunken" world—will be less deeply rooted in the classics of Western civilization. The classics will not be forsaken nor traditional curricula jettisoned. But those curricula will be expanded, supplemented, stretched.

We can, of course, learn much—and much of value—from the giants of the classical tradition. Pythagoras, to cite only one example, has more than a few lessons for fourth-wave reformers. For Pythagoras might be characterized as a radical interdisciplinarian. It was he who insisted that the most intimate of all disciplines are mathematics . . . and music.

The strict back-to-basics advocates might want to give this puzzle some thought. For these advocates, in the interest of producing a citizenry (more precisely, a work force) that can read and count, all too often define the arts—and music in particular—as inadequately instrumental, as educational frills. This characterization is unacceptable to anyone who believes that education must serve personal human needs at least as much as it serves national economic goals.

Music is among the keys that offers us access to the souls of civilizations past and civilizations still in the making. It is the language of the emotions. Not raw emotion, but emotion rendered articulate, emotion corralled by intellect. Anyone who understands the difference between cacophony and a symphony has begun to understand the meaning of civilization—the meaning of the quest to wrench order from chaos.

Is there utility in that understanding? Very likely. Is there intrinsic value? Most assuredly. Similar statements could be made about sculpture and painting, literature and dance, foreign languages and geography. These disciplines are—to borrow the fashionable cliché—windows of opportunity. Those windows must remain open, for through them flows the air that awakens and sustains the understanding that fosters self-understanding.

But a balanced curriculum demands still more. Fourth-wave education must have both instrumental and intrinsic value, must help the United States meet both economic and moral imperatives. To that end, that education must neglect neither artistic nor scientific content.

Today, more than ever before, a well-trained cadre of scientists is essential if our global village is to be free from pestilence, free from hunger, free from fear. Acquired immune deficiency syndrome, to invoke the obvious example, has taught us that viruses do not respect national boundaries and do not discriminate on the basis of race, gender, or ethnicity. Nor should science. Any scientific discovery that can improve the lot of the human family belongs to that family. This fact is decisive. It points to the need for an education that serves our *national* interest even as it awakens us to the *common* interests we share with all nations and all peoples. Our highest aspirations cannot be achieved and our most sublime intentions cannot find expression without an education in which instrumental and intrinsic values intersect.

Perhaps no ideal conveys this lesson more powerfully than the ideal of peace, the kind of peace President Kennedy described—"peace that enables men and nations to grow and to hope and to build a better life *for their children*—not merely peace for Americans, but peace for all men and women . . . not merely peace in our time, but peace for all time" [emphasis added].[7] With the introduction of this issue, the dichotomy that has informed this chapter can no longer be sustained. Peace is an instrumental value, and peace is an intrinsic value. The issue of peace brings into focus the most compelling argument for an education defined by an intersection of values, values that are economic, political, social, ethical, national—and *transnational*.

The goal of fourth-wave reform is no longer obscure. That goal is an education that prepares tomorrow's adults to meet economic imperatives as well as ethical imperatives, that prepares them not only for a life of work but for a life of worth, that steels their resolve to exhibit fidelity not only to the most sacred principles that unite the American family, but to principles that can bring harmony to the human family.

The fourth wave of education reform has the potential to so transform the educational landscape that in years hence, the question "Is education an instrumental value or an intrinsic value?" will be unintelligible. This either/or question will be unintelligible because the answer—the one right answer—will be "Yes."

If that happens—*when* that happens—we will have fulfilled the promise of American education. We will have met the mandates of *A Nation at Risk* without yielding to the one-dimensional, instrumentalist ideology of *A Nation at Risk*. That's the best of both worlds. That's the promise—and the challenge—of fourth-wave education reform.

NOTES

1. U.S. Department of Education, National Commission on Excellence in Education, *A Nation at Risk: The Imperative for Educational Reform* (Washington, DC: U.S. Department of Education, 1983), p. 5.

2. Mary Hatwood Futrell, "Restructuring Teaching: A Call for Research," address to the annual meeting of the American Educational Research Association, San Francisco, April 17, 1986.

3. Theodore R. Sizer, remarks to the National Education Association Board of Directors, March 1986. Cf. Arthur E. Wise, *Legislated Learning: The Bureaucratization of the American Classroom* (Berkeley: University of California Press, 1979), pp. 98–103, 206–212.

4. Samuel Bacharach, "Management: The Hidden Agenda of Education Reform," speech delivered at the Leadership Conference, Northeast Education Association, Hartford, CT, January 1986.

5. Robert B. Reich, *Education and the Next Economy* (Washington, D.C.: National Education Association, 1988), p. 7.

6. Horace Mann, *Fifth Annual Report of the Board of Education* (Boston: Board of Education, 1842). Quoted in Reich, *Education and the Next Economy*, p. 27.

7. John Fitzgerald Kennedy, "The Strategy of Peace," American University, June 10, 1963.

One Structural Remedy: Public Choice

In the previous two units, we have struggled to define some basic goals of a good education. The recurring struggle between the forces and interest groups representing the underlying values of equity and excellence was the theme of Unit Three, and Unit Four focused on the goals of education in terms of output—namely, making education more worthwhile for the students. *This unit moves beyond the goal-setting stage in an attempt to discuss one* structural *remedy for our educational system.*

One way to discuss the system is by studying the impact of societal values *on the administration of schools. In Chapter 20, Kerchner suggests that the primary social values of the nineteenth century were those of* morality *and* industriousness, *and that as a result school administrators believed themselves to be (and behaved as such)* evangelical ministers. *With the need for more operating efficiency,* achievement *became the new value, and as a result administrators acted like* social engineers. *When the need for more* equity *became dominant, administrators had to become* street-level politicians *in an attempt to balance out the interest group pressures. At this point, Kerchner sees* public choice *as the dominant value (remember the success of economist Milton Friedman's television series "Free to Choose"?).*

What is choice? *Briefly, it involves restructuring the system so that parents and students can decide which school to attend, and schools can decide which students to admit (see Chapter 20 by Kerchner). There are several different ways of operationalizing this (vouchers, tuition tax credits, magnet schools, etc.), and this section is not here for the purpose of arguing which would be the best. Kerchner talks instead about the implications of the choice metaphor for school administrators. He suggests that they would become less like street-level politicians and more like* public entrepreneurs. *If schools had to compete with each other for "clients" (students), then those school administrators who could make their staffs feel like an* ownership team *would be the most successful. Kerchner also uses the concept of* loosely coupled systems *to describe some of the benefits that could acrue to schools that gave their members more of an "ownership stake" in them.*

Is this realistic, given the enormous inertia of our public school system? In Chapter 21, Cooper puts education reform in the context of the conservative revolution of recent years, and shows us how the New Right, led by Prime Minister Margaret Thatcher in Great Britain, is undertaking to disassemble completely the British equivalent of a school district, called a local education authority (LEA). Schools within a district have a right to "declare independence" from their LEA and submit their own budget directly to the government.

Although things have not come that far yet on this side of the Atlantic, Cooper does emphasize that the idea has philosophical roots in the question of whether government has any proper role at all in education, and, if it does, whether or not it has any business owning schools. One of their strategies is to talk about education as being a business, *and to talk about the virtues of making the "market" a* competitive *one, which is a popular idea in our free enterprise system. Indeed, this gets to the heart of what the public choice argument is all about. Nevertheless, even the Reagan administration has had to realize how difficult it is to change the nature of schools. Cooper says that "the Reagan administration appears to be most successful in changing schools when it works 'within the public school system' through school effectiveness efforts, more school autonomy, and, most notably, magnet schools."*

Working within the public school system *is what Chapter 22 by Urbanski talks about. He argues that the metaphor of* public choice *is already being implemented with substantial success in the Rochester, New York, public schools. Although he strongly defends the special role that* public *education should play in this country, Urbanski cries out for major reform, not just tinkering. Reading his chapter, I was struck by the parallel with Mikhail Gorbachev's efforts to deregulate economic markets in the Soviet Union. Perhaps our public school districts could use a little* perestroika?

After first dismissing the vouchers and tuition tax credits ideas as being undemocratic (public funding for private choices without public accountability!), Urbanski claims that the public schools are *salvageable, and that the public* will *pay for it, if they believe they will get better results. He cites a recent Harris poll demonstrating this.*

For choice to be real, there must be differentiation. This takes us back to Metz's arguments (Chapter 12) about the assumption of homogeneity, despite widely varying conditions, in high schools across the country. Urbanski argues persuasively that the system fails to take into account the societal changes that have occurred. Because students come from many different family backgrounds and have many different learning styles, they need to be able to choose the most appropriate school structure, curriculum, and style. Instead of being only a safety valve for problem situations, Urbanski argues that choice should be a routine and normal process of fitting options to a student's situation.

Urbanski's enthusiasm comes from a belief that the Rochester example is working now. It is working because schools that compete for students and that have a theme build a sense of cohesiveness and shared purpose, which is an effective ethos. This sense of teamwork promotes greater teacher responsibility, which results in collegiality, shared governance, and many of the goals of the teacher empowerment movement. In this way, Urbanski sees teachers and the administration working together to implement realistic reform.

20
Educational Administration: Choice as a Reflection of Today's *Social* Values

Bureaucratic Entrepreneurship: The Implications of Choice for School Administration
CHARLES T. KERCHNER

CHANGING HISTORICAL PERIODS AND CORE VALUES

Historical periods in school administration carry labels that, with reasonable accuracy, capture the social role and underlying value prescriptions for those occupying leadership positions. In succession, school administrators have been called on to be moral exemplars in the tradition of Protestant evangelicals, social engineers molding the youth of today for the society of tomorrow, and street-level politicians balancing and brokering the demands of potent interest groups. In each of these periods, the problems schools were assigned to solve were presumed to be different, and so, too, were understandings about how school organizations worked and how they were linked to universities. In the last decade, we have seen a renewed emphasis on choice as a central social value. Choice influences school policy decisions as disparate as individualized instruction, magnet schools, and tuition tax credits. If choice became the dominant metaphor of education, it would fundamentally alter the nature of school adminis-tration, ushering in a new generation of administrators who are substan-tially different from their occupational parents.

Historical Periods and Values

Capturing the essence of school leadership with a metaphor is the center-piece of David Tyack and Elizabeth Hansot's (1982) insightful *Managers of Virtue*. For most of the nineteenth century, the role of schools was to further the republican version of the second great religious awakening, joining Christian principles and government. The educator became, in John Dew-ey's words, "the prophet of the true God and the sharer in the true kingdom of God" (in Tyack & Hansot, 1982, p.3). Beginning with the Progressive Era, circa 1910, the educators followed the wave of rationality generated by Frederick Taylor's (1911) scientific management movement, and lead-ership became explicitly tied to authentic expertise in curriculum and school organization. As political reforms divorced school boards from partisan politics, the phrase "neutral professional competence" began to describe the ethos of school administrators as well as that of city managers and other civil servants (Iannaccone & Lutz, 1970).

Beginning in the mid-1950s, the rise of explicit interest groups in education shattered the progressive political consensus. A central vision of education disappeared to be replaced by an era in which politics itself defined the role of educators. If teachers became street-level bureaucrats, to use Michael Lipsky's (1980) phrase, then surely administrators had be-come street-level politicians, their jobs functionally defined by the neces-sary brokering of services and balancing of potent interests. Politics became recognized as an explicit part of school administration and political met-aphor as part of administrative language (Morgan, 1986).

The Metaphors of Leadership

Each core value shapes administrative practice, thus creating a new met-aphor of leadership, a unique problem to be solved, and a distinct attach-ment to the organizational thought of the time. As Table 20.1 illustrates, if school administrators in the nineteenth century were Protestant evan-gelicals, those during the Progressive Era were social engineers, and those during the period of discontent were street-level politicians, then school administrators in a choice era will become bureaucratic entrepreneurs.

Table 20.1   Implications of Four Periods of Educational Leadership

	Evangelical Period	*Progressive Period*	*Period of Discontent*	*Period of Choice*
Metaphorical role for administrators	Evangelical ministers	Social engineers	Street-level politicians	Bureaucratic entrepreneurs
Primary problem to solve	Getting organized	Efficient operation	Coalition and organizational maintenance	Engagement of clients and employees
Core values	Morality, industriousness	Achievement	Equity	Liberty or choice
Organizational concepts				
Social system	Closed	Closed	Open	Loose
Authority	Autocracy	Bureaucracy	Polity	Ownership
Rationality	Revealed truth	Categorical	Calculative	Adaptive
Techniques	Charisma	Accounting, field studies	Systems analysis, management science	Network management, empowerment, acculturation
University/field relationship	Developing	Sponsorship of administrative careers	Elite universities study education, most universities train and certify	Partnership? (not yet developed)

Although they were the forebears of school administration, educational leaders in the nineteenth century were depicted more as advocates of a social movement than as chief executive officers. They formed an "aristocracy of character" that both set the tone and gathered converts for public education (Tyack & Hansot, 1982, p. 7). Their success was extraordinary. In 1850, public schools at all levels accounted for only about half of the funds expended on education; but, by the turn of the century, they had become nearly a monopoly. Leaders did not so much manage as preach a civil religion: "The common school, like the Fourth of July oration, inaugural address, or revival sermon, provided symbols and rituals that strengthened patriotism and pan-Protestant piety" (p. 94).

The social engineers were the proper bureaucrats leading rational, hierarchical institutions. Such an array of public services was possible because schools were depicted as closed systems, worlds unto themselves. Schools used the dominant rationality of the time: correct categorization. Administration existed to create a rational set of categories that could then be put in place throughout a school system, bringing uniformity and standardization that would assure quality. Accreditation standards, teacher certification, and integrated curriculum grew during this era.

Street-level politicians are savvy survivors. They often appear colorless because they have learned the fine art of knowing when to duck, but they have highly developed skills in understanding fundamental interests and satisfying unstable coalitions. Such skills are required to exist in a pluralist and sometimes anti-institutional political environment that simultaneously demands increased public services (such as special education) and a much less institutional environment (such as individualized instruction). The perception of schools as organizations also changed when viewed with open systems theory, which recognizes external demands and supports and a tidal wash of influence between organization and environment. The rationality of administration is one of calculation: thinking problems through before decisions are made. Decision trees, systems analysis, and coalition analysis have become part of the stock in trade of school administration.

Each of these historical periods fashions a different relationship with the university. During the evangelical period, the university relationship was still being developed. However, during the social engineering era, in an explicit effort to professionalize, school administration sought and obtained legitimacy within the university; professors and deans formed the apex of a highly integrated educational elite. University professors became the sponsors and brokers, guiding administrators and also establishing the standards for good schools.

During the street-level political period, the relationship between the universities and the schools bifurcated according to university status. Faculties in elite, research-oriented universities began to *study* education rather than *do* education; and in a curious way, the social distance between the university and the schools became a hallmark of high status among education graduate programs. In the words of one assessment, the message in the graduate schools of education is "Do not prepare teachers or schools personnel or educational administrators. No credit will come to us for dealing with schools that are messy or difficult" (Judge, 1982, p.41).

Meanwhile, the less selective schools expanded their administrative training programs, many of them offering doctorates and other advanced credentials for the first time. They did not, however, inherit the level of sponsorship formerly enjoyed by the elite schools. School district internal promotion practices, along with requirements for open job posting and antidiscrimination practices, blunted the ability of deans or professors to place students in particular jobs. Also, there were relatively few jobs to be filled as the children of the baby boom passed out of adolescence and into yuppiedom.

"BUREAUCRATIC ENTREPRENEUR": THE CHOICE METAPHOR OF LEADERSHIP

Reduced to the basics, choice involves bilateral selection: Students choose schools, and schools choose students. Choice can be structured in many different ways ranging from vouchers to magnet schools, and the debate still rages over which structures best honor the different values of equity, excellence, and efficiency (see Kerchner & Boyd, 1988, for a review). However, rather than join the debate over how choice would be provided, this section speculates on the implications of choice as a defining value for school administrators.

If choice were the dominant value, school administrators would become bureaucratic, or public, entrepreneurs, each offering a mix of services and styles of learning designed to attract the students for whom the schools could be most successful. Such an organizational role stands in sharp contrast to that found in the street-level politics era, where administrators were required to accommodate any potent, politically relevant interest. Schools operated under a choice system would require an administrator to attract and hold a clientele but not to serve all comers.

In this environment, schools would be, in some ways, a less protected institution, and like other services that fail to attract a following (family counseling or dentistry, for example), they could face bankruptcy and reorganization. Clients would have an interesting bargaining relationship with schools, one simultaneously more and less powerful than under street-level bureaucracy. Clients could threaten to withdraw children from school more easily than is now the case. But schools could also feel free to release or even expel students and parents whose ideas about education were in great conflict with their own. Schools would, simultaneously, gain more institutional integrity and self-definition and feel pressures toward bland noncontroversiality. Schools that had successfully defined their market would become relatively unresponsive to clients who demanded other options, just as many traditional colleges change only glacially over the years. Other schools that had not been successful in defining a market would find themselves chasing whim, fad, and trend, just as tuition-dependent colleges now do.

Attracting clients and accommodating interest groups are fundamentally different social processes. Whereas interest group accommodation requires that each potent, potentially disruptive group be listened to and answered, client satisfaction requires an individual rather than a group response. Knowing and understanding the client, and creating the cognitive "fit" between client expectation and perception of the school, becomes a central problem.

Organizational Concepts During the Choice Era

In each social period, managerial concepts have been played out within prevailing organizational thought. Thus it is interesting that, in many respects, the current wave of organizational thought about social systems, authority, and rationality has been developed through research into schools and colleges and subsequently applied to corporations and other organizations.

Loose Systems

The idea of loose coupling, or organizations whose parts are not tightly coordinated, grew from observations of how schools and colleges operate. Loose coupling intentionally conveys the image that "coupled events are responsive, but that each event also preserves its own identity and some evidence of its physical or logical separateness" (Weick, 1976, p. 3). This description captures the identity of organizations, such as schools, whose activities are characterized by a relative lack of coordination, planned unresponsiveness, situations when any one of several means will produce the same results, poor observational abilities, and occasions when, no matter what you do, things always come out the same (p. 5). Schools appear tightly coupled in terms of certification (the classification of teachers, students, and topics to be taught) and very loosely coupled in terms of inspection (evaluation, authority, and the technology of curriculum) (Meyer & Rowan, 1978).

Under the rules of bureaucracy, loose coupling equals bad management. But current interpretation finds a virtue in the would-be vice of looseness. Consider the problem of deviant behavior, for instance. Part of the folklore of the firms heralded as excellent in the new management literature is their tolerance of heresy within the organization and even a belief that heresy is necessary to innovation and market response. The phrase *skunk works* was created in these organizations to describe a tolerated but extralegal subunit whose inhabitants were busy doing useful things by breaking the organization's own standard operating rules.

Looseness also suggests that too much coordination may be a bad thing. Organizational looseness makes it possible for parts of an organization to function successfully, even when other parts are having trouble. The east coast power grid, whose 1979 failure plunged New York City and environs into darkness, has become the symbol of systems too tight to successfully adapt to an emergency.

Finally, loosely coupled organizations require that we revise our opinions about economies of scale. Large, integrated companies and large schools are no longer seen as models of efficient operation. On the contrary, they are seen as having hurdled into a sea of high transaction and coordination costs while smaller, leaner organizations retained the ability to know and understand their markets. Peters and Waterman (1982), in the best-selling management book of the decade, injected the loose coupling idea into the mainstream of management thought.

Authority through Ownership

Choice as a value legitimates the authority of ownership. As social engineers and street-level politicians, educators acted on behalf of the commonweal and the interest group, both of whom were thought to be surrogates for education's clients (Blau & Scott, 1962). In a choice environment, clients would be expected to pursue their own best interests, and school administrators could flexibly use their resources like proprietors in the private sector as long as they satisfied their clients. Unlike the typical public school principal, an owner can proclaim an attachment to a product or service based on nothing more than personal desire or taste. In a delightful demonstration of this prerogative, a recent article on small brewers quoted Fritz Maytag, president of Anchor Brewing in San Francisco, singing the praises of his barley wine: "It'll never have wide popularity, but I own the place, and I can do what I like. A brewery should have a hallmark—a drink of absolute distinction" (Moon, 1987, p. 84).

Ownership, however, does not necessarily imply a personal economic stake. A human capital investment of self in an idea or vision of a school is altogether as precious a stake as is an investment of physical capital. The central problem for administrators in a choice environment is to gain commitment, matching one's investment of self with the investments of clients and teachers. In this context, ownership becomes broadly spread: corporate rather than a proprietorship.

Successfully creating ownership requires that ownership itself become a motivating factor. Students have to want to work hard and to get into schools that require them to work hard. Teachers have to value their investment in the curriculum. The work itself—teaching, studying, managing—has to carry an incentive value. Extrinsic rewards are a necessary condition in this kind of work but not a sufficient one.

Adaptive Rationality

Ideas about rationality have changed with those about authority. Having the right answers, or being able to figure them out, was the taproot grounding administrative authority in the social engineering and street-level politician periods. However, both educational practice and organizational theory have come to question the existence of unique right answers, and a new genre of administrative texts have started to appear emphasizing leadership in a "nonrational" world (Patterson, Purkey, & Parker, 1986; McPherson, Crowson, & Pitner, 1986). Nonrational in this sense does not mean irrational, and the more apt description is that education appears to be adaptively rational rather than calculatively rational. Educational organizations gain knowledge of themselves heuristically, through trial and error. "What works" in one location or circumstance is not necessarily successful in another. This tendency, already recognized in the literature, would certainly be emphasized in a choice environment where matching client and organizational preferences would be paramount to maintaining an orthodox pedagogy.

Managerial Techniques

In a setting characterized by loosely coupled systems, symbolic ownership, and adaptive rationality, school administration would rely on a different set of techniques than those typically emphasized during earlier eras.

Loosely coupled systems require network analysis and management. Because client-responsive organizations are seldom as compartmentalized as existing public bureaucracies, managers will need to analyze the set of interdependencies required for client response. Then, they will have to devote time to create groups of teachers and others with the capability of responding without the high structural overhead and long lag times associated with public bureaucracies. Part of this process involves the management of coupling: choosing those few elements in the organization that will be watched in great detail. These become the touchstones of an organization, almost its trademark, as is IBM's penchant for service (Peters & Waterman, 1982, p. 159). Part of the process is understanding the system maintenance costs of interpersonal and intraorganizational communications implied by networks.

Ownership implies empowerment, that which Kanter (1983, p. 142) calls, "the freedom to act, which arouses the desire to act." The ability to act is created by distributing the "basic commodities" of the organization: its information (data, technical knowledge, political intelligence, expertise); its resources (funds, materials, space, time); and its support (endorsement, backing, approval, legitimacy)(p. 159). Without creating an ability to respond to clients, it is impossible to create the lean, hands-on, close-to-the-client characteristics so prized by writers on entrepreneurial organizations.

Adaptive rationality implies the establishment and management of organizational cultures, whose strong beliefs substitute for bureaucratic rules as an organizational control mechanism (Smircich, 1983). However, cultural norms, unlike bureaucratic rules, have the property of situational adaptivity; they allow teachers, principals, and students to "know" what to do even in the absence of a directive. Cultures are transmitted in story, slogan, and legend, an organizational mythology that often obscures the process of culture creation. Managers create cultures through clear visions, well stated, and by recognizing that mundane events such as visiting classrooms or conducting weekly school meetings are part of an ongoing process of reality construction.

Schools and Universities

The shape of a new relationship between schools and universities is not yet clear. If choice is constructed along strongly professional lines, as is the case in medicine, the role of the university in legitimating educators' professionalism and in advancing the field of practice is likely to strengthen. No occupation has gained professional status without connection to a university. The growing connection between schools and universities some 70 years ago strongly influenced the development of "neutral professional competence" among school administrators. However, the relationship is not likely to be as one-sided as it once was. Traditionally, we believed that the university's role was largely educative and that education preceded practice. Much professional education is still based on this notion. But in fluid, entrepreneurial organizations, learning continues over a lifetime of practice, and knowledge often flows from the field of practice to the university. The potential for authentic partnership arrangements is a strong one. Although the model of such partnership does not yet fully exist, some interesting trials are John Goodlad's national network and Theodore Sizer's coalition of schools.

Is Choice a Likely Metaphor?

The emergence of choice as the defining metaphor for school administration is by no means preordained, but it is likely. Choice or liberty is a powerful social value that attracts populists and libertarians as well as traditional conservatives. It is also a public policy option that represents a compromise between other, competing educational values: excellence, equity, and efficiency.

Americans have diverse social values, not easily captured in the two-dimensional liberal-conservative political scale. During the last decade, political theorists have begun to speak of a society in which identifiable groups join with traditional liberals and conservatives but identify with only part of their values. Libertarians share with conservatives an aversion to government intervention. Populists share with traditional liberals a desire for responsible government. Electoral victories require attracting voters from at least three groups and shaping policies that have strong cross appeal.

In education, choice is a particularly potent appeal. The ability to get the kind of education one wants for one's self or one's children serves both as a reward for those with a pedagogical interest and as a means of defusing fights between interests over who should have the ability to impose universal requirements on the system. It is no wonder that a vast array of choices have emerged within public school systems (Lewis, 1987). Schools now offer so many options that they endanger their own ability to form a strong internal identity (Chubb & Moe, 1988). Because offering choice is now part of the established policy arsenal, both clients and policy analysts come upon problems with an expectation of finding options rather than single solutions (Elmore, 1988).

In this respect, the excellence revolution creates a situation of serious and growing political tension. The era of external review and reform initiated in the early 1980s has been, if anything, a frantic effort to reestablish a central political consensus about the purposes of education. The current round of educational reform is ample evidence that those who would alter education have grown intolerant of the belief that some sort of educational truth will emerge from the clash of existing interests.

However, a single definition of excellence is probably impossible. A national core curriculum is highly unlikely, particularly one associated with a common set of values, as Doyle (1988) advocates. We are more likely to see the diversity of preference and active educational interests continue simultaneously. These interests grew for very clear historical reasons, namely, the inability or unwillingness of the existing educational establishment to attend to the various needs of handicapped children, inner-city youth, teacher welfare, and other core needs around which advocacy groups have developed.

The idea that a new conception of education administration built on "excellence" would simply override existing interests fails to understand the relationship of each metaphorical era to the previous ones. The administrator of today is the heir of the past, "receiving a handsome legacy from a distant relative" (Tyack & Hansot, 1982, p.4), and those of the future will labor under history's unseen hand. The metaphor of choice is not so much a repudiation of the past symbol as it is a value that somehow envelops it.

The contradiction between specific interests and general support of excellence will become more apparent when the excellence movement fails to deliver on its promises, as it surely will. The cost of the existing educational reform movement is probably well in excess of the capacity of the states to finance it. In economic terms, we will have created an excess of demand over supply.

The contradiction between social wants and social conditions is, of course, nothing new. What is new, however, is the tendency to resolve these problems through quasi market structures and deregulation. The impulse to provide services and meet client needs that, at one time, would automatically have triggered an appeal to charity or the establishment of a government program is now just as likely to trigger a search for a mechanism that allows people to choose the kind of service they want.

Indeed, the period of educational interests and system responsiveness has increased the expectation that options would be provided. Even the pedagogy built around individual instruction for all children (particularly individual instructional plans for special education students) increases the impetus toward choice.

Choice is an attractive political symbol because it can be made to function as a compromise between the other values. In addition it is attractive to those who value choice for its own sake (Drucker, 1985). Whereas high standards are entirely consistent with the administrative dominance of the progressive era, choice is not. The interest groups—from teacher unions to special education parents—have succeeded in penetrating education to such an extent that individual treatments for children are now considered the norm. Schools are expected to accommodate individual differences in student treatments, and to respect student/parent choice of treatments within the public school setting. As the inconsistency between demands for choice within schools and demands for curricular integrity become apparent, a system of choice between schools is likely to become more widespread. If it does, we will have established new demands upon school leadership and, ultimately, a new metaphor of administration.

REFERENCES

Blau, P. M., & Scott, W. R. (1962). *Formal organizations.* San Francisco: Chandler.

Chubb, J. E., & Moe, T. M. (1988). No school is an island: Politics, markets and education. In W. L. Boyd & C. T. Kerchner (Eds.), *The politics of choice and excellence in education: The politics of education association yearbook* (pp. 131–142). London: Falmer.

Doyle, D. P. (1988). The excellence movement, academic standards, a core curriculum and choice: How do they connect? In W. L. Boyd & C. T. Kerchner (Eds.), *The politics of choice and excellence in education: The politics of education association yearbook* (pp. 13–36). London: Falmer.

Drucker, P. (1985). *Innovation and entrepreneurship.* New York: Haper & Row.

Elmore, R. F. (1988). Choice in public education. In W. L. Boyd & C. T. Kerchner (Eds.), *The politics of choice and excellence in education: The politics of education association yearbook* (pp. 79–98). London: Falmer.

Iannaccone, L., & Lutz, F. W. (1970). *Politics, power and policy: The governing of local school districts.* Columbus, OH: Merrill.

Judge, H. (1982). *American graduate schools of education: A view from abroad.* New York: Ford Foundation.

Kanter, R. M. (1983). *The change masters: Innovation and entrepreneurship in the American corporation.* New York: Simon & Schuster.

Kerchner, C. T., & Boyd, W. L. (1988). What doesn't work: An analysis of market and bureaucratic failure in schooling. In W. L. Boyd & C. T. Kerchner (Eds.), *The politics of choice and excellence in education: The politics of education association yearbook* (pp. 99–116). London: Falmer.

Lewis, A. (1987). Public schools offer vast choices. *The School Administrator, 44*(8), 8–11.

Lipsky, M. (1980). *Street-level bureaucracy: Dilemmas of the individual in public services.* New York: Russell Sage.

McPherson, R. B., Crowson, R. L., & Pitner, N. J. (1986). *Managing uncertainty: Administrative theory and practice in education.* Columbus, OH: Merrill.

Meyer, J. W., & Rowan, B. (1978). The structure of educational organization. In M. Meyer (Ed.), *Environments and organizations.* San Francisco: Jossey-Bass.

Moon, W. L. H. (1987). A glass of handmade. *The Atlantic, 260*(5),75–87.

Morgan, G. (1986). *Images of organization.* Beverly Hills, CA: Sage.

Patterson, J. L., Purkey, S. C., & Parker, J. V. (1986). *Productive school systems for a nonrational world.* Alexandria, VA: Association for Supervision and Curriculum Development.

Peters, T. J., & Waterman, R. H. (1982). *In search of excellence.* New York: Harper & Row.

Smircich, L. (1983). Concepts of culture and organizational analysis. *Administrative Science Quarterly, 28*(3), 339–358.

Taylor, F. W. (1911). *Principles of scientific management.* New York: Harper Brothers.

Tyack, D., & Hansot, E. (1982). *Managers of virtue: Public school leadership in America: 1820–1980.* New York: Basic Books.

Weick, K. E. (1976). Educational organizations as loosely coupled systems. *Administrative Science Quarterly, 21*(1), 1–19.

21

An International Comparison: *Political* Forces for Choice

School Reform in the 1980s: The New Right's Legacy
BRUCE S. COOPER

SCHOOL REFORM IN this decade is filled with irony. Ronald Reagan, who came into office as the most anti-education president in recent memory, has done more, perhaps, to fasten national attention on school improvement than any before him. The U.S. Department of Education, slated to die in the early Reagan years and be "reborn" as the lowly Foundation for Educational Assistance, has blossomed into a primary outlet for neoconservative ideas and programs. While trying to diminish the "federal role" in education, the Reagan administration has, in fact, made school reform a major national issue (see Boyd, 1987; Doyle & Hartle, 1983).

To be sure, the New Right has advanced its message. The language of "choice," "competition," and even the "marketplace," is being adopted by bipartisan, often liberal, groups that a decade ago would not have been caught dead saying things like: "Markets have proven to be very efficient instruments to allocate resources and motivate people in many sectors of American life. They can also make it possible for all public school students to gain access to equal school resources." That was not from the American

Enterprise Institute nor from a tract by Milton Friedman. It was written by the Carnegie Task Force on Teaching, including the heads of the nation's two teachers' unions, Albert Shanker of AFT and Mary Hatwood Futrell of NEA (Carnegie Forum, 1986).

The issue of conservative revision of education is interesting from an international perspective as well, since Britain under Margaret Thatcher is also committed to breaking the monopoly of public school services and introducing more choice, competition, and measurable results. However, it appears for various reasons that Thatcher's Britain has moved ahead of the United States in "privatizing" education (Sexton, 1987; Cooper, 1988a; Hillgate, 1987). Parliament is now considering a law to disassemble local education authorities (school districts) and to allow individual public schools to "go independent" (governed by their own boards while receiving full funding from the *national* government).

While much of the Reagan reform effort, according to critics, has been "rhetoric and symbolic politics" (Boyd, 1987)—valuable in redefining the nature of education—Thatcher's government moved toward a range of major structural reforms, including aid to private and parochial school, school-site management, national curriculum and testing, school choice, and breaking the monopoly and control of school districts. Thus Reagan, while working within the existing public school structure, has made relatively minor changes in American schools; Thatcher, in contrast, has altered the very structure of British schools, leading to a kind of education revolution.

Are the critics right? To what extent have the New Right goals of extending choice, competition, and school improvement been accomplished (Clark & Astuto, 1987)? Beside the "war of words"—the symbols and rhetoric that have surrounded the Reagan years—what real-life changes have occurred, particularly along the ideological lines from whence Reaganism grew?

It is essential to examine the ideological roots of Reagan's New Right program to understand this fundamental redirection in school policy. Ideology is not a dirty word. It lets scholars unearth the deeper philosophical positions that have long supported major change. In the past, analysts have either attempted to depoliticize educational change, entirely transforming it into a kind of technical, rational process, or to assume rather bland, pluralist, and basically nonideological views (Butts, 1978). However, in Britain, with its long Socialist and Conservative party histories, ideology is recognized as a valuable platform from which to base reforms. It cannot be ignored.

The New Right ideology of the Reagan administration can be understood by asking three fundamental questions, all of which stem from discussions by intellectuals as far back as John Stuart Mill: What is the legitimate role of the state in education, if any? Second, why can the government simply not fund schools without also owning and controlling them? And third, how can the public sector introduce greater freedom of choice and competition into government schools if it must fund, own, and control them?

GOVERNMENT'S ROLE IN EDUCATION

What is the fundamental interest of the government, particularly at the federal level, in education—if any? (Or, should government be involved in education at all?)

The New Right holds the role of government in education in undisguised disdain. In part, this apprehension stems from the long-held belief that government monopolies—like any protected "industry"—are inherently inefficient, ineffective, and slow to respond to change in society and consumer demands. Free marketeers such as Milton Friedman and F.A. Hayek have turned a jaundiced eye on public school hegemonies, instead favoring private education or devices like "vouchers" to reintroduce freedom, competition, and choice into educational provision systems (Seldon, 1986). Friedman (1975, p. 272), for example, explains his preference for alternate suppliers of education as follows:

> As Adam Smith wrote 200 years ago, "Those parts of education, it is observed, for the teaching of which there are no public institutions, are generally the best taught." That is true today: music or dance, secretarial skills, automobile driving, airplane piloting, technical skills—all are taught best when they are taught privately. Try talking French with someone who studied it in public schools, then with a Berlitz graduate.

Friedman compares the food industry to the education industry, wondering what our dinners would look like if government owned all the grocery stores and required us to use them. The modern supermarket, he asserts, would be replaced by government farms and commissaries, long queues, shortages, and boring menus. "How can the market be used to organize schooling more effectively?" he demands. "The most radical answer is to put schooling precisely on a par with food: Eliminate compulsory schooling, government operation of schools and government financing of schools except for financial assistance to the indigent. The market would then have full rein" (p. 272).

Conservative economists thus advocate that government stop being the prime provider of education. As Hayek (1960, p. 381) explains, "Indeed, we may soon find that the solution has to lie in government ceasing to be chief dispenser of education and becoming the impartial protector of the individual against all uses of such newly found powers."

Secondly, the New Right, fearing the power of government in controlling the minds of students through the creation of a state-imposed orthodoxy, often cites *On Liberty* by John Stuart Mill (1946), which explains the dangers of state education:

> A general State education is a mere contrivance for molding people to be exactly like one another and the mold in which it casts them is that which pleases the predominant powers in the government, whether this be a monarch, a priesthood, an aristocracy, or the majority of the existing generation. In proportion as it is effective and successful, it establishes a *despotism over the mind,* leading by natural tendency to one over the body. (p. 130; italics added)

In more recent times, Bertrand Russell (1955, p. 57) warned that government-controlled education might produce "a herd of ignorant fanatics, ready at the word of command to engage in war and persecution as may be required of them." Some far right conservatives would argue that ignorance is better than centralized state control over education. Russell further averred that "the world would be a better place if State education had never been inaugurated" (p. 58). And conservative economist Hayek (1960, p. 132) believes that the power of education is so great that "it may be better that some children go without formal education than that they should be killed in fighting over who is to control that education."

Quite clearly, Reagan came into office intending to extend private initiative and reduce the federal government's role, expenditure, and control in education (Doyle & Hartle, 1983). In part, he took this view because of the Democratic party's key role in establishing the U.S. Department of Education, as symbolized by the National Education Association's fervent support for President Jimmy Carter. But the feeling was deeply ideological as well, based on a dislike of government monopolies and a gut-level fear of government control over the education of children.

Given these beliefs, why then, has the U.S. Department of Education continued to control large budgets and, furthermore, grabbed the national spotlight? Or, as the Republican National Committee chair, Frank Fahrenkopf, exclaimed, how is it that Education Secretary Terrel Bell now "holds the most important job next to the President of the United States?" (Fund & Wooster, 1983, p. 16).

Some would argue that efforts to abolish the department were defeated by a combination of bureaucratic inertia, Bell's political skill, and the White House's realization that education reform was a beautiful platform from which to preach New Right ideology. Ironically, then, a major plank in the New Right platform—the destruction of the department—has not been realized, and major programs such as student loans and Title I have survived relatively untouched despite earlier threats.

However, other related conservative goals have been reached: (a) shifting of greater options to states and localities by the use of block grants, replacing the plethora of 33 federal "entitlement" and "categorical" programs; (b) cutting personnel at the department by almost a third; (c) "contracting out" student loan collection to private companies; (d) means tests for student loans; and (e) cutting back regional departmental offices and personnel.

Since the Reagan years began, we have seen the New Right platform appearing in state after state. A total of 43 states have increased graduation requirements since 1981, and "choice" and "competition" have become favorite words, even for bipartisan groups such as the National Governors' Association (Snider, 1987, pp. C1–C5) and the Carnegie Task Force on Teaching as a Profession (Carnegie Forum, 1986).

In its *Time for Results,* the National Governors' (1986) group sounded almost Friedmanesque: "If we first implement choice, true choice among schools, we unlock the values of competition in the education marketplace" (p. 6). The Task Force of the Carnegie Forum on Education and the Economy (1986), which included a number of school establishment figures, concluded, in early New Right lingo with an interesting liberal twist, that "in the public sector, as in business and industry, there are essentially two possible approaches to the improvement of performance and productivity: administrative—or management—methods, and the 'unseen hand' of market mechanisms. . . . These approaches are not contradictory" (p. 20).

In a sense, President Reagan and his second secretary of education, William J. Bennett, may have few new national programs to show. But they appear to have won the hearts and minds of the nation. National symbols may be more important than national programs over the long haul. And, in fact, the federal role has never been more obvious. Bennett, his assistant secretary, Chester E. Finn, Jr. and others exert great influence—fighting a crusade for more choice and competition and using the "bully pulpit" (Jung & Kirst, 1986, p. 81) of their office to evangelize for more conservative efforts to improve schools (see also Finn, 1987). While the school establishment may not always like Bennett and Finn, school leaders cannot ignore them and likely appreciate efforts to move educational concerns off the back page of newspapers and into the headlines.

This irony is not only American. Thatcher's Tory government has found itself representing greater local control, more privatization, and less interference in schooling while also being accused of being the most powerful national force in British school politics. Secretary of State for Education, the Right Honorable Kenneth Baker, MP, commands top billing with his plan (a) to design a national curriculum and national testing, (b) to allow any public (government) school to "opt out" of the local school system, creating a nationally funded and independently controlled set of "grant maintained" schools, (c) to devolve greater authority to schools, and (d) to direct aid to children in private and parochial schools. During the 1987 British elections that returned Thatcher to power for an unprecedented third consecutive term, with a healthy 104-vote majority in the House of Commons, education became the key issue in Britain, and still is.

It seems, then, that to enforce a neoconservative ideology, politicians may ignore a central tenet of free-market life: that government intervention into the affairs of education retards choice and competition. Instead Reagan and Thatcher find education an important force in national development, international competition, and local choice. They also find it a national soapbox for preaching conservative beliefs.

GOVERNMENT OWNERSHIP OF SCHOOLS

If the government must support education for economic and social reasons, must it own and operate schools as well?

While perhaps only a few ultra-Rightists would insist on a strict separation of government and education, most neoconservatives acknowledge the vital contribution of schooling to society and realize the abiding interest of the state in promoting high-quality education. Friedman (1962) justifies government support as essential in preparing the young for democratic participation, literacy, numeracy, worthwhile employment, and the learning of civic virtues (respect for others and private property). He calls this the "neighborhood effect," the degree to which education benefits everyone in society, not just pupils and their families (p. 155). Or as E. G. West (1970) explains, "The social benefits of education are not confined to the 'educatee' but spread to society as a whole, most noticeably in the form of reduced crime and more 'social cohesion' " (p. 31).

But the need to foster education does not necessarily mean also to own and to control it. Thus, according to the New Right view, government may wish to guarantee food to everyone but not take over all food production, distribution, and sales. Rather, the state can give a needy family money or a food grant (stamps) and allow the family to determine what to buy and from whom. This preserves the competitive food market and gives greater choice to consumers, rich and poor.

In recent years, a number of schemes have attempted to introduce market forces into education by "privatizing" schooling—that is, by acknowledging the legitimate interest of the state in promoting and supporting education but allowing families choice "inside or outside the system." The darling of the New Right is "vouchers," chits from government to families, allowing them to "buy" education on the "open market." Again, according to Friedman (1975): "The voucher plan would produce a much wider range to alternatives. In the first place, choice among public schools themselves would be enormously increased. The size of public schools would be set by the number of customers it attracted, not by geographical boundaries" (p. 381; see also Hanushek, 1986).

Arthur Seldon, in *The Riddle of the Voucher* (1986), argues that vouchers overcome many of the problems of government ownership of schooling that lead to dissatisfaction, stifled creativity, and loss of identity for participants. He explains:

> The century-old attempt to run schools by the political process has failed to satisfy pupils, parents, and industry. The change *from politicization to commercialization* will be disturbing in the early years, although not as much as the educational establishment fears or asserts. But it will also be invigorating, liberating, innovative, and above all, creative. The new educators will be avid to embrace the new technologies and to satisfy the consumers in families and industry. (p. 87; italics added)

Short of the direct "voucherization of education," which has run into serious political opposition in both the United States and Britain, a number of other programs have emerged that attempt to separate the necessary government funding of schools from the undesirable government ownership of them. Most obviously, government support for private schools fulfills the goals of conservative policymakers, since these schools, by their very existence, offer alternatives, provide competition, and produce good (perhaps "better") results. (See the controversial findings of Coleman, Hoffer, & Kilgore, 1982; Coleman & Hoffer, 1987, and a critique of their findings by Willms, 1983.) A number of schemes have been devised for providing "parochiaid," some indirect (tax benefits, transportation, textbooks). Three more direct forms are tuition tax credits, tuition transfers, and local option vouchers.

Tuition Tax Credits/Deductions

Public aid to private and parochial schools has sparked interest in such schemes as "tuition tax credits" and "deductions." Such proposals are financial devices to aid families in using a nongovernment (or government) school, thus enhancing their options and getting public funds to families in the nonpublic sector. James and Levin (1983) explain:

> If the proposal [for tax credits or deductions] were enacted, it would encourage family choice and, many advocates argue, foster greater competition and excellence in education. Tuition tax credits would also shift some of the emphasis of public policy away from the public schools, an institution presently besieged by declining enrollments, economic retrenchment, and eroding public confidence. (p. 4)

Minnesota has such a law. Parents may deduct school-related costs from their state income taxes for "tuition, textbooks, and transportation," whether their children are in public or private schools. The law, furthermore, was found constitutional under the First Amendment in *Mueller* v. *Allen* (103 S. Ct. 3062; 1983) because the law "defrays certain school costs regardless of the type of school children attend—secular or religious; it does not advance (or inhibit) religion; and it avoids religious entanglement because money goes to parents rather than to schools" (Jones, 1985, pp. 256–257).

Tuition Transfers

A number of states have used "tuitioning out" as a device for enhancing choice, particularly in areas where no appropriate, accessible public school is available. First, for example, in the upper tier of rural New England, communities pay full tuition for children to attend private academies if a local public high school is unavailable. In some cases, parents may send their youngsters to schools across state lines, say, between Vermont and New Hampshire. Second, in finding an appropriate "placement" for special-education handicapped children, local districts often pay full tuition for pupils to attend special private (sometimes residential) schools—under, for example, the Education of All Handicapped Children Act (P.L. 94-142), especially if no suitable public school program is available.

In Britain, too, children may attend school in any school district (or local education authority, LEA, as it is called) if they can gain admission; the "home LEA" must pay students' tuition to the "receiving LEA," thus knocking down geographical barriers to parental choice and interdistrict competition. Now, nearly 20 percent of all British children attend religiously sponsored schools ("voluntary aided schools") with full tuition costs paid by the local (public) school authorities. The first education initiative of the Thatcher administration in 1981 was the Assisted Places Scheme, whereby some 25,000 needy but able children annually receive national scholarships to attend Britain's most prestigious independent schools at a total yearly cost of £35 million. Without the doctrine of church/state separation so prominent in the United States, Britain, with its Church of England, has no qualms about extending aid to a variety of "confessional" and independent schools (Roman Catholic, Anglican, Jewish), thus directly funding these schools without also "owning" them.

Chapter 1 Vouchers (Local Option Vouchers)

Between the creation of Title I/Chapter 1 in 1965 by President Lyndon B. Johnson and the 1985 Supreme Court ruling in *Aguilar* v. *Felton* (84/238/ 239, 105 S. Court, 3232), children in parochial schools received direct remedial help on the premises from public school teachers assigned to the federal program. However, on July 1, 1985, the Court ruled that bringing public employees into parochial schools was an illegal "entanglement" of church and state under the First Amendment "establishment" clause.

Thus children entitled to Chapter 1 help, who happened to select a denominational school, found that they had to lose time traveling "off site" to nearby, or not so nearby, public schools, neutral sites like libraries or fire houses, or to a mobile van pulled up to the schoolyard at an annual cost to the taxpayers of between $60,000 and $110,000 each per year. Research indicated that about 40 percent of eligible private school students were losing vital services, simply because they exercised their constitutional right to practice their religion (Vitullo-Martin & Cooper, 1987).

At this point, the Reagan administration and a group of conservative Republicans called the "Wednesday Group" proposed somewhat similar plans for limited Chapter 1 compensatory education vouchers to families qualifying for remedial help under federal law. The administration's suggested "Investment in Human and Intellectual Capital Bill" would have permitted LEAs to issue Compensatory Education Certificates (Chapter 1 vouchers) to families of poor and underachieving students if, because of *Aguilar*, these children were not being served "off the premises" of the parochial school.

But even this tiny amount of private choice was regarded suspiciously by the Democratically controlled Congress. The alternative bill proposed by Representative Augustus Hawkins (D-CA) offered a meager $30 million to buy mobile vans for some of the 300,000 needy children attending nonpublic, sectarian schools. Thus, ironically, the Democrats, traditionally the political party of city dwellers, Catholics, and Jews, seemed uninterested in guaranteeing poor children in Catholic and Jewish schools a chance to get remedial help under Chapter 1 through means other than the ineffective, expensive "off-site" programs of *Aguilar*.

In sum, the New Right has considered ways of funding schools without getting into the business of operating them. While vouchers by any other name were politically unsellable—even by the "hard" Right in Britain in the early 1980s, under Education Secretary Sir Keith Joseph—a number of other ways to detach funding from control have been tried. Children in private schools in the United States, for example, receive federal services under Chapter 1, though much lessened after 1985, as well as other public help (tax-free status, free transportation in many places, Chapter 2 equipment and textbooks). Children in church schools and some independent schools in Britain, by way of contrast, receive full and equal services as part of the "voluntary aided" system and the Assisted Places Scheme. Minnesota gives families a constitutionally permissible break on state taxes for education costs of either public or private schools. In general, however, the New Right dream of freeing the public funding of education from the government's control of education in the United States has not gone very far, thanks mainly to the "conservative" public school lobby.

Britain presents an opposite and informative case. The Thatcher government sponsors legislation to encourage schools to "opt out" of the local system and go "independent," with the understanding that these schools will continue to receive full funding from the central government. Conceivably, but improbably, Britain could end up with all 27,500 of its "public" (state) schools being privately owned by their individual boards of governors but nationally funded at the current local level by the central government. The local school authority (district) would either wither or improve its services, according to this New Right scenario. Each school would be self-governing and, presumably, be more responsive and competitive— pressed onward to excellence by the local markets.

CREATING "COMPETITIVE" MARKETS

If the government has to fund and operate most schools, why not allow families to chose among a variety of state-run (public) schools and let these schools compete for students?

Public schools (in the United States, anyway) are here to stay. They involve 42 million students and nearly 3 million professionals. They cost the nation $282 billion—$1,170 per year for every man, woman, and child (National Center for Education Statistics, 1987). Given the sheer size and resources of the "system," New Right policy efforts have been directed primarily at introducing qualities of "privatization" into the public education: devices for increasing excellence, choice, and competition.

Devices of "Privatization"

The Effective Schools Movement

Left wing agrees with right wing on what makes an "effective" school, since this research hardly threatens the hegemony of the public schools. In fact, the remarkable effort to see "what works" (U.S. Department of Education, 1986; Purkey & Smith, 1985) has sparked a growing amount of research and development in educational circles, uniting liberal and conservative, private and public school leaders, in a common task. The neoconservatives may claim credit for calling attention to the problems of "mediocre" to failing schools, but the current government hardly has a monopoly on these complaints (see Silberman, 1970, for a liberal's view).

The Bennett administration has actively tried to improve schools by rewarding "outstanding" schools, teachers, and principals as a way of prodding the system without promulgating new, expensive federal programs. Particular attention has been paid to high performing schools— located, not in the center of privilege, but in the nation's "worst" neighborhoods and under the most depressed (and depressing) conditions. Jung and Kirst (1986), applying Theodore Roosevelt's phrase about the moral suasion of the presidency to this effort, called it the "bully pulpit." The Reagan strategy, in short, is to publicize what makes a good school good including strong leadership, high expectations, effective use of time, homework, tests, demands, discipline, and hard work!

As Walberg (1984) explains, "Improvements in effectiveness . . . are costly to educators not in money but in required institutional, technological, staff, and personal changes. . . . Without the incentives and the discipline of the marketplace, the creativity and energy of educators may not improve productivity but preserve tradition, [salary] and office" (p. 19).

The rising interest in quality, performance, excellence, and accountability has been a keynote of the conservative agenda, as U.S. leaders realize that real privatization is unlikely, and existing public schools must be made to work better. More money is not the answer, the New Right claims; more school leadership is.

Devolution of Authority

Another quality of the New Right effort in education is what has been called the "Devolution Revolution" (Cooper, 1988a; Caldwell, 1987). In both Britain and the United States, reformers argue that unless schools are held accountable and given the resources to do the job, improvement will not occur. As Stuart Sexton, a key policy analyst in Britain, has explained in *Our School—A Radical Policy* (1987):

> The only choice left is to devolve the system to the schools themselves, and to create a direct relationship between the suppliers of education, the schools and the teachers, and the consumers, the parents and their children. It is to create, as near as practicable, a "free market" in education. To use a popular word, it is in some sense to "privatize" the State education system.(p. 10)

The new education act in Britain specifically requires that all schools become self-managing. Statements in the bill "set out provisions for the annual determination by local education authorities of the financing of each county and voluntary school they maintain, and for delegating to school governing bodies the responsibility for important aspects of financial management and the appointment of staff" (Chapter III, Clauses 23–36). But school-site management is not new in Britain or the United States. A number of states, Florida and California, for example, have experimented with "self-management" or "school-site management" (Caldwell, 1987, p. 19; Murphy, Hallinger, & Peterson, 1986), as have several counties in Britain. What is most intriguing about the new legislation in Britain is that, perhaps, for the first time, a national government is *requiring* that all LEAs hand major financial controls over to individual schools.

Interestingly, the literature on both school-site management and "ef-

fective schools" extols strong administrators—those with sufficient autonomy to make their schools special and with high staff involvement in key
decisions. Purkey and Smith (1985) describe a model for creating an effective school, which includes strong school-site management:

> The staff of each school is given a considerable amount of responsibility
> and authority in determining the exact means by which they address
> the problem of increasing academic performance. This includes giving
> staff [note the inclusive word "staff," not simply principals] more au-
> thority over curriculum and instructional decisions and allocation of
> building resources. (p. 358)

Hence, if the government is to fund and control most of education,
the argument goes, it can at least give schools—principals, teachers, and
parents—some direct control over program, use of funds, staffing, and
admissions as a means of breaking up the bureaucracy, making schools
more responsive and adaptive to local needs, and improving quality.

Magnet Schools

Perhaps nothing has captured the imagination of the "free marketeers" quite like the concept of creating "magnet schools." They would be
unique schools within the public sector that have special themes "that
place a special emphasis on select programs" such as math/science/com-
puters, dance/drama/art/music/film, or vocational programs—for example,
auto repair, jewelry design, refrigeration repair, computer design. These
schools could compete for students, accept students across school attendance zones and in some cases across school district lines, and enjoy considerable autonomy in selecting special programs, recruiting staff and
students, and operating the schools.

Magnets, like devolution of control and "school effectiveness," seem
to appeal to policymakers across a political spectrum. Those on the Right
see magnets as allowing some selectivity and specialness, while liberals
point to the ability of magnets to bring black and white and lower- and
middle-class students together voluntarily. Many U.S. districts, in fact, are
using Super-Magnets, and Metro-Magnets (Cooper, 1987)—whole systems
of magnets across city districts—to attract white and middle-class children
out of the suburbs and private schools into inner-city schools. Again, like
excellence and devolution, magnet schools are no threat to the monopoly
of the public system, though the "elitist" tinge of magnets such as New
York City's Stuyvesant and Bronx High School of Science bothers some
egalitarians.

Yet, magnets seem a viable way to ensure that inner city schools
retain some white pupils and may be preferable to "forced busing" as a
solution to federal mandates to end racial segregation. Thus liberals, labor
unions, and other groups are willing to tolerate the slight levels of parental

choice and interschool competition as long as most magnets accept children who show an interest by a lottery or by low-to-high ability groups (16 percent reading above grade level, 16 percent reading below, and 68 percent at grade level). Hence magnets seem to ride the fence of being purely meritocratic or purely egalitarian. By 1986, some 1,850 school districts were using magnets to improve schools and extend choice; New York City, for example, has created a system of diverse programs in 91 out of its 113 high schools.

In all, then, a number of reforms have introduced some choice into the public schools, even though no one seems willing to "let the market run free." The pressure is still strong, however, to keep a standard program and limit choice by requiring students to attend schools in their "zone." Attempts to open up choice and free movement among schools are often resisted on grounds of fostering elitism and making rational planning difficult, since school leaders never know which schools and programs a family may select.

CONCLUSION

The New Right has been a powerful force in school reform in the 1980s. It has redefined the nature of schooling and reoriented the way we look at reform. Now, "choice" and "competition" in education are accepted—and so is a national concern about standards and performance. It is not that the Reagan administration has been brimming over with new ideas for federal programs; it has been quite content to let other groups lead the way while lending moral support and public relations enthusiasm. Magnet schools, school-based management, professional standards boards for teachers, merit pay, and relations with business have all developed, but these innovations are identified with particular states, private foundations, cities, and regions.

This low-key approach is in strong contrast to Britain where the Tories are aggressively restructuring the entire educational service around New Right beliefs: changing from local authorities as the controlling force to individual, self-governing schools; from funding primarily public/secular schools to sectarian and independent ones; and from a set type of schools—the "comprehensive"—to a range of schools with their own purposes (new City Technology Colleges, for example).

The 1980s in the United States, then, will best be remembered as a time of monumental rhetoric and a redefinition of the education debate—not a time of new initiatives and programs (Chubb & Moe, 1986). Education has definitely been upgraded in the national consciousness, and placed into the neoconservative framework of high performance, international competition, choice, and market forces. The Reagan administration appears to be most successful in changing schools when it works *within the public school system* through school effectiveness efforts, more school autonomy, and, most notably, magnet schools (Cooper, 1987).

Whether these efforts will lead to better schooling—the main question—is often tough to answer, since it depends on what one means by "better" and how soon one needs to know. The New Right has learned—like the New Left in the 1960s—just how hard it is to change the nature of schools, whether that means making them more egalitarian or more competitive. A third ideology, one that maintains the structure of the public school "system," is perhaps the most pervasive and cannot be changed short of an all-out education revolution, like that happening in Britain. The ultimate challenge of school reform, then, appears to be how to decentralize, deregulate, and even "privatize" education without greatly increasing the power of the central government. This dilemma—how to make sweeping national change without violating basic philosophy—was confronted so directly by Thatcher and was avoided so assiduously by Reagan in the 1980s.

NOTE

Author's Note: I appreciate Phoebe Cooper's assistance in writing this article.

REFERENCES

Boyd, W. L. (1987, March 18). Commentary: The rhetoric and symbolic politics of school reform: President Reagan's school reform agenda. *Education Week, 28,* 21.

Butts, R. F. (1978). *Public education in the U.S.: From revolution to reform.* New York: Holt, Rinehart & Winston.

Caldwell, B. J. (1978). *The promise of self-management for schools.* London: Institute for Economic Affairs, Education Unit.

Carnegie Forum on Education and the Economy. (1986). *A nation prepared: Teachers for the 21st century.* The Report of the Task Force on Teaching as a Profession. New York.

Center for Educational Statistics. (1987). *The condition of education.* Washington, DC: U.S. Department of Education.

Chubb, J. E., & Moe, T. M. (1986). No school is an island: Politics, markets and education. *Brookings Review, 4,* 11–27.

Clark, D. L., & Astuto, T. A. (1987). *Implications for educational research: A changing federal education policy.* Charlottesville, VA: UCEA Center for Policy Study.

Coleman, J. S., & Hoffer, T. (1987). *Public and private high schools: The impact of communities.* New York: Basic Books.

Coleman, J. S., Hoffer, T., & Kilgore, S. (1982). *High school achievement: Public, Catholic, and private schools compared.* New York: Basic Books.

Cooper, B.S. (1987). *Magnet schools.* London: Institute for Economic Affairs, Education Unit.

Cooper, B.S. (1988a). The devolution revolution in education. *Bulletin of the German International Institute for Pedagogical Research.* Frankfurt: University of Frankfurt.

Cooper, B.S. (1988b). The politics of privatization: Policymaking and private schools in U.S. and Great Britain. In W. L. Boyd & J. G. Cibulka (Eds.), *Private schools and public policy: International perspectives.* London: Falmer.

Dennison, S. R. (1984). *Choice in education: An analysis of the political economy of private education.* London: Institute of Economic Affairs, Hobart Paperback no. 19.

Doyle, D. P., & Hartle, T. W. (1983, December 6). President Reagan goes to school: The Reagan administration's 1st three years with the department of education. *AEI Policy Week,* 7–21.

Finn, C. E., Jr. (1987). Education that works: Make the schools compete. *Harvard Business Review, 65*(5), 63–68.

Friedman, M. (1962). *Capitalism and freedom:* Chapter 6. The role of government in education. Chicago: University of Chicago Press.

Friedman, M. (1973, September 23). The voucher plan. *New York Times Magazine.*

Friedman, M. (1975). *An economist's protest.* Glen Ridge, NJ: Thomas Hoctor.

Fund, J., & Wooster, M. (1983). An education in empire building. *Reason, 21,* 7–41.

Hanushek, E. A. (1986). The economics of schooling: Production and efficiency in public schools. *Journal of Economic Literature,* 1131—1174.

Hayek, F. A. (1960). *The constitution of liberty* (Chap. 24). London: Routledge & Kegan Paul.

Hillgate Group. (1987). *The reform of British education: From principle to practice.* London: Claridge Press.

James, T., & Levin, H. M. (Eds.) (1983). *Public dollars for private schools.* Philadelphia: Temple University Press.

Jones, T. H. (1985). *Introduction to school finance: Technique and social policy.* New York: Macmillan.

Jung, R. K., & Kirst, W. M. (1986). Beyond mutual adaptation into the bully pulpit: Recent research on the federal role in education. *Educational Administration Quarterly, 22*(3), 80–109.

Levin, H. M. (1983). Education choice and the pain of democracy. In T. James & H. M. Levin (Eds.), *Public dollars for private schools.* Philadelphia: Temple University Press.

Mill, J. S. (1946). *On liberty.* London: Oxford University Press.

Murphy, J., Hallinger, P., & Peterson, K. D. (1986). *The administrative control of principals in effective schools.* Paper presented at the annual meeting of American Educational Research Association, San Francisco.

National Center for Education Statistics. (1987). *The condition of education.* Washington, DC.

National Governors' Association Center for Policy Research. (1986). *Time for results: The governors' 1991 report on education.* Washington, DC: National Governors' Association.

Purkey, S. C., & Smith, M. (1985). School reform: The district policy implications of the effective schools literature. *Elementary Schools Journal, 85*(3), 354–389.

Russell, B. (1955). J. S. Mill. *Proceedings of the British Academy, 41.*

Seldon, A. (1986). *The riddle of the voucher: An inquiry into obstacles to introducing choice and competition into state schools.* London: Institute of Economic Affairs, Hobart Paperback no. 21.

Sexton, S. (1987). *Our schools: A radical proposal.* London: Institute for Economic Affairs, Education Unit.

Silberman, C. E. (1970). *Crisis in the classroom: The remaking of American education.* New York: Random House.

Snider, W. (1987, January 24). The call for choice: Competition in the education marketplace. *Education Week,* p. C1.

U.S. Department of Education. (1986). *What works: Research about teaching and learning.* Washington, DC.

Vitullo-Martin, T., & Cooper, B. S. (1987). *The separation of church and child: The constitution and federal aid to religious schools.* Indianapolis: Hudson Institute.

Walberg, H. J. (1984, May). Improving the productivity of American schools. *Educational Leadership, 8,* 12–19.

West, E. G. (1970). *Education and the state.* London: Institute of Economic Affairs.

Willms, J. D. (1983). Do private schools produce higher levels of academic achievement? New evidence for the tuition tax credit debate. In T. James & H. M. Levin (Eds.), *Public dollars for private schools: The case for tuition tax credits* (pp. 223–234). Philadelphia: Temple University Press.

22

A Teacher Reports from Rochester: Choice Works Now!

Restructuring Schools for Greater Choice: The Rochester Initiative
ADAM URBANSKI

ADVOCATES OF TUITION tax credits and voucher schemes insist that they would go a long way toward curing what now ails public education. Parents would get more choice, and the competition would be healthy for the system. Unfortunately, not everything that sounds good is necessarily good and sound. Tuition tax credits and voucher schemes have been introduced in Congress many times since the early 1950s—without much success. They are a plan for *financing private schools, not for improving public ones.*

Why is this? Consider the effects of *allowing parents to write their children's tuition off their federal income taxes.* Some parents who currently see private schools as unaffordable would recalculate the costs, figuring in the tax credit, and enroll their children in private schools.

Which parents would these be? Certainly they would *not* be the parents of the students most "at risk" in the public schools—the poor and minority children. Instead, the children who would receive a federal subsidy to leave the public schools would be middle class.

This middle-class exodus would serve to erode the political base of support for improving the public schools. Why should parents whose children go to private schools support tax increases to improve the public ones? At a time when the federal government is slashing aid to public schools, the effect on schools in lower income areas would be devastating.

In fact, the public schools would be left to service the high-cost pupils, yet with dwindling resources to do so. The tuition tax credit plan would tip the scales against free public education. For inner-city children and millions of others, public schools would no longer represent the best hope for breaking out of the cycle of poverty and failure. Furthermore, those with learning problems, handicaps, and other special needs would still be locked into the public schools.

This tax subsidy to private schools would have other effects. Without representation through publicly elected school boards, taxpayers would have no control over decisions made by private and parochial schools, yet public tax dollars would be supporting their activities. Furthermore, private schools are not subject to the same federal and state regulations as public schools. They can be selective in admissions, expel unwanted students, and hire uncertified teachers. These critical differences should not be overlooked.

Like tuition tax credits, *voucher schemes* would constitute a means for public funding of private choices. In this case, each family would receive a voucher (which would be like a coupon good for x dollars worth of education) for each child. Each family would be free to spend their voucher at any public or private school, and would also be free to supplement their vouchers with cash out of their own pocket.

In the case of poor families, it is obvious that the voucher system would lock them into the cheapest (least profitable, and therefore *public)* schools, and thus the schools with the fewest resources per pupil. In the case of the parents who already send their children to expensive private schools, this program would simply have the effect of giving them a direct discount, which would be absorbed by some level of government (*public* financing of *private* schools). If we assume that the "market" for private education is efficiently cleared, then the very best schools would even be in a position to raise their tuition rates to get their share of the subsidy, since otherwise they might be flooded with new applicants at the economic margin, whose parents previously could not afford to send them there. The net effect, then, of a voucher system might be only to redistribute money into the pockets of private school owners.

More important, however, is the effect that vouchers would have on the middle classes. Because of the increasing profitability of private schools, more would open up, drawing those students at the margin away from the public schools. Thus, vouchers would create a two-tiered educational system: nonpublic schools for those who could afford them and pauper schools for the rest. This would be tantamount to an abandonment of efforts to improve the schooling of youngsters from economically or educationally disadvantaged backgrounds. Since most youngsters in this nation will continue to be served by public schools, we should do all that we can to improve them.

Are public schools salvageable? All of the recent education reforms reports, implicitly or explicitly, answer the question with a resounding "Yes!" Virtually all surveys of public attitudes toward public education indicate that the taxpayers would be willing to pay more for public education if, and only if, they had reason to believe that such an increase in investment would yield improved results.

This sounds like a reasonable posture. Given adequate resources, it ought to be possible to improve public schools while also offering greater choice among public schools for parents, teachers, and students. Unlike tuition tax credits and voucher proposals, the public school choice option would not undermine the public schools, nor would it drain resources away from them. Competition among public schools would be much more fair and much more productive than competition between public schools and private schools. In fact, greater choice within the public school system could constitute a mechanism for renewal and the enhancement of quality in public education in the United States.

Some choice within the public school system already exists, but parents of public school students want their choice and influence in public schools expanded. In the 1986 Gallup poll of "The Public's Attitudes toward the Public Schools," 71 percent of parents responded that they wanted that right. In a 1987 Louis Harris survey done for the Metropolitan Life company, we learn that only one-quarter of all parents surveyed, given a choice, would think seriously about choosing a different school.

Both parents and teachers see the potential for beneficial results as well as some undesirable effects of a system of choice between schools. The majority of both parents and teachers said that "having a choice of schools would mean that a child could go to the school best suited for his or her needs," that "competition between schools to attract students would force schools to improve" and that "having a choice between schools would raise the involvement of parents in their child's education."

But a majority also believe that "richer children would end up at better schools and poorer children would end up at others," that "some schools would be unpopular and children going there would lose out," and that "having a choice between schools would mean that a school would lose its identity with the local community."

For choice to be real, however, there must be real differences among the schools. That means that we should strive to alter the current school dynamics and to diversify the options now available. The current system fails to take into account the societal changes that have occurred.

Today's schools were designed nearly a century ago, at a time when the factory system and mass production were the predominant organizational models. In such a system, students are seen as the "product," and teachers are treated more like hired hands than autonomous professionals. This assembly line approach to educating our children results in too many "recalls" and is unsuitable for the changing needs of an ever more complex society. It promotes sameness and bland uniformity that makes choice—for parents, students, or teachers—difficult to implement. If all schools offer the same curriculum, all classrooms are arranged with desks in straight aisles, and all teachers are directed to cover prescribed items in a prescribed manner, then what is left for students or parents to choose? We must first permit—even better, *encourage*—different teaching approaches, with an awareness of the reality that students have different learning styles.

Arguing that "a geographical change is not an educational cure," American Federation of Teachers (AFT) President Albert Shanker often points out appropriately that choice is not the issue at all; rather, it is quality. According to this view, *choice is not an end in itself* but, rather, a helpful dynamic that could promote the reforming and improvement of public education. It need not be perceived as a safety valve (an opportunity for some individuals to escape their inadequate lot in life). Instead, choice should be a routine and normal mode of exercising the right to fit a school to one's educational needs by choosing the school that offers the best options. By this logic, Shanker's question is one that merits attention: *How do we restructure schools from unexamined tradition to reflective practice, as well as from compulsion to choice in the school attended?*

This is not a new idea. The notion of giving parents a choice of public schools is predicated on two pillars of the American system—equal opportunity and open market competition. The nation's governors called for it in their education reform report entitled *Time for Results* (1986). So did the Carnegie Task Force on Teaching as a Profession in *A Nation Prepared* (1986). The Committee for Economic Development echoed the call for schools of choice in their report entitled *Investing in Our Children* (1985). And several thousand schools of choice in districts across the country are thriving and yielding impressive results. Schools that have to compete for students are less likely to become complacent and more apt to adjust and improve what they have to offer. Schools of choice would stimulate parental involvement and reinforce the equity agenda that is in progress now in many districts. Schools of choice could then become laboratories of change and innovation, while the students and their parents could vote on a school's success or failure with their feet.

Yes, teachers and administrators would be challenged more than ever before. But the built-in system of incentives and disincentives would reward some schools and send a strong message to others. Not surprisingly, schools that do not have to compete for "clients" exhibit many of the characteristics of monopolies. Because of geography or other arbitrary guidelines, neither parents nor students have much choice. This significantly limits their ability to affect the school, heightens their sense of frustration, and often leads to resignation and apathy. It is a tragic but not uncommon cycle that can and should be broken.

Schools that must compete with others are also more likely to develop their own sense of cohesiveness, uniqueness, and shared purpose—the kind of school ethos that makes schools more effective. The resulting teamwork also creates an appropriate context for the emergence of collegiality and shared governance. It dovetails with the teacher empowerment movement. It would be unthinkable, for example, to put schools in such a competitive mode while retaining the dictatorial top-down management system that now characterizes most schools. With their very survival at stake, teachers could not afford to leave all decision making to the school principal; they would have to become more involved in decisions affecting their schools and their programs. Working together, teachers and school administrators would seek greater control over their own schools, and that could lead to significant improvements. For example, getting the central office off the backs of practitioners would provide a welcome relief in a profession plagued by too many mandates and too much long-distance decision making. Because realism is proportional to the proximity of the decision maker to the problem, successful efforts to improve education are most likely to occur at the school level.

Theoretically, "chosen" schools should be more productive for both students and professional staff. Selection of a school is more conducive to students having a positive learning attitude, especially at the secondary level, when students are given enough of a voice in the decision to give them psychological "ownership" of their school. In addition, teachers are likely to gain interest in the effectiveness and attractiveness of their school if the stakes are retention of program and "saleability" to consumers. It is possible that system participants would care more about *quality* if their organization's survival (and thus their jobs) depended on attracting students year after year. Thus, a districtwide schools-of-choice plan would force unsuccessful schools to change.

In the Rochester City School District, choice within the public school system was introduced during the late 1960s and early 1970s, not so much for educational reasons but as a means for voluntary desegregation of schools. Today, these alternative schools are thriving, and new schools of choice have been and are being added.

Elementary school students can choose intensive foreign language study in the Language Connection magnet and in the Primary Approach to Language (PAL) program; or they can concentrate on sciences in the Computech, Biology, and Natural Science magnet or the Science, Computers, and Technology magnet. Middle school students can choose between the Natural Science magnet at Charlotte Middle School, the Discovery magnet at Douglass Middle School, the Tech-Prep magnet at Jefferson Middle School, the Bilingual Language Academy or the School of the Arts at Monroe Middle School, the Liberal Arts magnet at Nathaniel Rochester Community School, or the Science, Computers, and Technology magnet at Nathaniel Rochester Community School.

At the high school level, students can select a nontraditional learning environment at School without Walls; a state-of-the-art Edison Technical and Occupational Educational Center; the Bioscience Academy, Business Magnet, or Communication Arts Magnet at Franklin High School; the Science and Technology Magnet or the Academy of Excellence at Wilson High School; or the Law and Government Magnet at Marshall High School.

Rochester's School without Walls is a good example of the benefits that school of choice can offer. Since 1971 the school has embodied innovations now promulgated by education reformists: team teaching, cooperative learning, community service, independent learning, self-discipline, emphasis on critical thinking skills. There are no bells at School without Walls, and the subject matter is treated with an interdisciplinary emphasis. Parents and students join the teachers and the teaching principal at the weekly staff meetings. In a model that serves as an alternative to bureaucratic hierarchy, all stakeholders are involved in planning and decision making.

In an effort to lower the walls between the school and the community, students at School without Walls are required to use community resources and to work with community professionals. Throughout the years, students at School without Walls have participated in overseas foreign exchange programs; served internships at local theaters, newspapers, and radio and television stations; and served as members of boards of directors of local civic and social organizations.

The results yielded by the School without Walls are spectacular: Approximately 80 percent of its graduates continue their education at colleges and universities; 90 percent of those who go to college are accepted by the college of their first choice. More important, the morale and level of satisfaction is extremely high—for teachers as well as for students.

Teachers and students at School without Walls attribute the improved environment to the choice factor. "Choice gives you a special reason to be here," they say. "You choose what you learn and you learn at your own pace," one student pointed out. Even teachers get to choose what to teach: "When I first got here," one teacher remembered, "I asked them 'Which courses will I be assigned to teach?' They said, 'What do you want to teach?' I was stunned. Nobody ever asked me to make such a choice before." That teacher designed an entire curriculum around the theme of jazz.

Rochester City School District's Board of Education now plans to expand the schools-of-choice system significantly. For example, the district's School of the Arts will eventually become a Metropolitan School of the Arts. In time, other magnet schools may follow suit. In a community in which a metropolitan school system would be quite unlikely in the near future, this transformation of selected urban schools into magnets for suburban students as well is quite intriguing. Conceivably, virtually every Rochester high school could become a "theme school." This might eliminate the nonacademic track that now plagues so many students in urban comprehensive high schools.

Beginning in September 1988, all of Rochester's secondary schools will be schools of choice and will provide options to many more parents and students. In an environment that emphasizes innovation and equity, this dynamic can help to revitalize our schools. In the age of teacher empowerment, it can also help to empower the clients. Through a schools-of-choice policy that allows secondary school students to select their school, 70 percent of the Rochester school district's students received their first choice of middle schools or high schools. Although the district controls admissions to ensure racial and academic balance, the intent of the choice plan is to get schools to compete with each other and thus improve.

To help parents and students make informed choices, the district hosted informational citywide meetings and recruitment fairs, arranged for open houses at the schools, sent letters to homes of students, and published informational literature. Because the transition occurred at the same time that the district changed its secondary schools from one school (grades 7–12) to separate middle schools (grades 6–8) and high schools (grades 9–12), the teachers' union negotiated with the district a staffing agreement that, in addition to seniority criteria, emphasizes choice as well as racial and programmatic balance.

The most important dynamic complementing the district's schools-of-choice movement is the school-based planning agreement negotiated in the 1987–1990 contract. Perhaps the most promising and the most important are the negotiated "agreements to agree," where the contractual language merely establishes the outside parameters while intentionally omitting the details. The specifics are now being developed—with substantial input from teachers, school administrators, parents, and others. This will promote the notion of choice very significantly because, at every school in the Rochester City School District, a team of stakeholders will make many of the decisions that, until now, were made at the central office or by the school principal alone.

Representatives of teachers, school administrators, parents, and (at the secondary level) students will make decisions through group consensus. Enjoying equal voice and not relegated to merely advisory roles, each school-based planning committee will decide on such matters as the school budget allocation, scheduling of school activities, procedures, instructional goals, and ways to measure academic progress. The group will even have the ability to seek waivers from school board policies and/or contractual provisions to accommodate their joint decisions.

Schools of choice will provide an important framework for a comprehensive effort to restructure schools by reforming teaching. The cornerstone of that effort is the career-in-teaching plan—an attempt to transform the single-level teaching occupation into a four-tiered profession.

1. *Intern teachers* are new practitioners without prior teaching experience. As is already the case in Rochester, interns teach under the guidance of more experienced mentor teachers.

2. *Resident teacher* status can be earned by those teachers who have successfully completed a year of internship but have not yet achieved tenure or received their permanent certification to teach.

3. *Professional teacher* status is conferred only on those who have earned their permanent teaching certification (which now requires a master's degree).

4. *Lead teachers* will be selected on a voluntary and competitive basis by a panel that includes other teachers. They will teach at least half-time and work also as *mentors* or as *consultants* (who will select textbooks, write curricula, plan staff development programs, and direct other instruction-related tasks), or as *demonstration teachers* (who will model teaching with an open-door policy). Lead teachers will have at least ten years of experience, work for up to 11 months, and receive a salary differential. They will work with at-risk students, teach in remedial and/or enrichment programs, serve as adjunct professors in local teacher education schools, and perform other duties that might be required of instructional leaders and expert practitioners.

Unlike merit pay schemes that purport to be career ladder programs, our career-in-teaching plan incorporates the peer review concept and offers additional professional options to those who qualify. Lead teachers would achieve higher status and more pay in exchange for accepting more responsibilities and working a longer school day or year. To ensure that they would not be perceived by fellow teachers as "snitches in administrative training," lead teachers would make themselves ineligible for administrative appointments within their district.

Although the career-in-teaching plan is a logical step in the drive to transform the teaching occupation into a genuine profession, it also incorporates a feature that attacks head on a major obstacle to effective student learning: the need to match at-risk students and the toughest teaching assignments with those teachers who are best equipped to accept them— that is, the experienced and expert lead teachers.

Under the current structure and existing practices, the most difficult assignments and the most challenging students often fall by default to the least experienced and most vulnerable teachers. The veteran teachers can choose to avoid such assignments—largely as a result of negotiated seniority rules. There is probably a correlation between that dynamic and the fact that 7 out of every 10 beginning teachers leave the classroom before their tenth year of teaching.

The newly negotiated 3-year agreement in Rochester raised starting teachers' pay by 52.4 percent (from $18,983 in 1986–1987 to $28,935 in 1989–1990). Top pay for lead teachers will be nearly $70,000 in the third year of the contract. The pact also calls for shared governance through a school-based planning process. Teachers will play a major role in making decisions about the instructional program and other school dynamics. They will even participate in decisions about filling vacancies for staff positions in their schools. No longer will seniority be the strict determinant for voluntary interschool transfers. Indeed, the school-based planning team at each school will screen all applications, interview all applicants, and select the candidate who best fits the ethos and the needs of that school. This form of expanded choice—rather than strict adherence to blanket rules—will go hand in hand with the schools-of-choice system districtwide.

Even more important than the specific provision of the Rochester contract is the spirit of the settlement. Achieved through a process best described as *principled negotiations,* the agreement is based on trust, mutual respect, and labor–management collaboration. Union and management share a joint commitment to these notions:

1. That *excellence* without *equity* is not worth pursuing
2. That *unionism* and *professionalism* are complementary and not mutually exclusive
3. That there is no reason not to use the collective-bargaining process to build a genuine profession for teachers
4. That all stakeholders in public education should have greater choices
5. That teacher *empowerment* must be accompanied by teacher *accountability*
6. That since *accountability* means assuming *responsibility* for the decisions and choices made, teachers must not be locked out of the decision-making process if they are to be held accountable for results

Although students, teachers, and parents in Rochester's public schools will enjoy more options, the schools-of-choice plan defines the parameters of those choices. These guidelines will ensure racial balance and curricular goals and will also provide an important component of diversity and accountability.

The challenge for education reform is not merely to shore up a failing system designed for the needs of the past century. It is not a question of simply doing harder what we do now. Instead, it is a question of finding new and more effective ways to better educate more students.

Admittedly, the jury is still out on the Rochester experiment. If student performance improves, others may decide that investing in teachers may be a model for breaking the cycle of failure—especially in urban public schools. But if there is no evidence of appreciable improvements in student learning, then the public may very understandably conclude that they can get today's lousy results without additional investments—so why throw good money after bad?

Lest the reader think that the Rochester way is the only alternative, let me say that the issue of choice in public education need not be framed as an either/or question. Instead of asking "Should we have choice or no choice?" we should ask "Could we offer to all our constituents *more* choices than they now have?" We can and we should.

Public schools can best be improved if we seek to *empower all those who are directly affected by them*. We cannot empower them unless they can be involved in making important decisions. That makes choice an indispensable part of any agenda for restructuring our educational system. But choice should not be restricted merely to choosing among similar failing schools. Because there are no quick fixes or ready answers, we should first unshackle the teachers, parents, and students to design better teaching and learning environments. They should be permitted to challenge even the most basic traditional assumptions—that one building means one school, that students learn best in 47-minute segments, that learning is passive, that *teaching* means *telling*.

Parents and students should have more choices, but *meaningful choice* will be possible only when schools become *centers of inquiry*, where students are workers and teachers remain learners. This can be achieved, eventually, *if we trust teachers* to design more effective learning environments for their students. That means doing what we now do differently, rather than doing the same things longer or harder. It also means recognizing the fact that the problem with today's schools is *not* that they are no longer the same as they once were. The problem with today's schools is that they are *precisely* what they always were. That is problematic because change is inevitable, but growth is not. Schools cannot afford to fail to grow and meet the demands of a changing environment.

We are at a pivotal juncture. Do we merely tinker with the status quo, or are we instead willing to restructure our schools significantly—even if it means taking risks and abandoning traditionally held postures? If we choose the former, we will continue to get the dismal results that prompted the cry for reform. The latter can offer hope for a much improved teaching and learning environment for our children.

The education reform movement raised our aspirations. Increasingly, there will be a willingness to take risks and to try different and better ways to fulfill our mission. Increasingly, we will focus on potential solutions rather than on past problems. Risking failure is a risk worth taking because so much is at stake.

REFERENCES

Carnegie Forum on Education and the Economy's Task Force on Teaching as a Profession. (1986). *A nation prepared: Teachers for the 21st century*. New York.

Committee for Economic Development. (1985) *Investing in our children: Business and the public schools*. Washington, DC: Research and Policy Committee.

Gallup, Alec M. (1986, September). The 18th annual Gallup poll of the public's attitudes toward the public schools. *Phi Delta Kappan*, pp 56–57.

Louis Harris and Associates. (1987). *The Metropolitan Life survey of the American teacher, 1987: Strengthening links between home and school,* pp. 8, 56–58.

The National Governors' Association. (1986). *Time for results: The governors' 1991 report on education.* Washington, DC.

Creating Better Choices *within* Schools: The Role of Teachers

28   What to Do with *Problem* Teachers   370
Managerial Responses to Poor Performance
EDWIN M. BRIDGES

Urbanski ended Unit Five by asserting that if public choice is to be real, there must be real differentiation. He used that as a jumping off point for a discussion of the role of theme schools in Rochester. What he did not say, however, was that if choice does not succeed in improving the quality of each school in the district, the political will to pass the necessary budget (i.e., tax) increases will soon erode.

Although some claim that a system of public choice would indirectly result in better schools, the authors in Unit Six believe that teachers have a powerful and direct role in improving schools, if the system is reoriented to support them in this effort.

Before we discuss ways to change the system to enhance teacher efforts at improving the quality of public schools, we must recognize that there are two conflicting metaphors of the role of a teacher—that of the lower level bureaucrat following the orders of the administration, and that of the empowered professional. Unsurprisingly, administrators tend to assume the former model, whereas teachers prefer the latter. Unfortunately, this lack of agreement about basic assumptions all too often leads to political stalemate and confrontation.

In Chapter 23, Conley shows a way out of this dilemma by providing us with a new metaphor in the middle ground. By examining the nature of teachers' work and recent managerial strategies, she comes up with the new metaphor of the teacher as a constrained decision maker. She uses this "constrained decision-maker"model to analyze the appropriate level of participation. By differentiating between participative influence and participative authority, she may have helped to bridge the gap between labor and management alluded to earlier with the bureaucrat and professional models.

Conley then argues that the most appropriate form of evaluation system for a constrained decision maker would be skill-oriented, would promote risk taking, and would be developmental rather than remedial. This last point is of particular interest because if we expect teachers to make a big difference in improving the quality of public schools, we should evaluate them in a way that encourages their professional development instead of holding them to minimum standards.

Chapters 24 and 25 concern the early professional development of teachers. In Chapter 24, Richard Schwab discusses the experimental five-year program at the University of New Hampshire. The program was set up in 1974 with the aim of training "teacher leaders" with a broad-based liberal arts undergraduate degree, an intense year-long program of graduate courses, and an internship for the entire year. This allows the student to decide not to take the graduate phase of the program and still have an alternative choice of career, and allows greater selectivity of students at the completion of the undergraduate phase.

In Chapter 25, Wagner picks up at the point when a teacher has actually begun teaching, but before he or she has received final permanent certification. She thoughtfully raises a number of issues relevant to the design of programs to assist these new teachers, and points out that the assessment of new teachers prior to certification needs to be done very carefully.

What can be done to help the experienced teacher? In Chapter 26, Shanker discusses the need to improve the working conditions of all teachers—to improve the physical quality of the environment, provide adequate supplies, and reduce the class sizes to more managable levels. Unfortunately, he doubts that enough resources will be found to make a noticeable dent in these monumental problems.

So what can be done? Shanker argues that the tightening up that characterized the first wave of reform "locks our schools into well-worn paths of mediocrity and failure for far too many of our young people." His answer involves restructuring the schools to provide teachers (1) enough flexibility to match students with appropriate learning experiences, (2) new technology like computers and videotape, (3) top-notch candidates to fill the staff shortages, and (4) a paraprofessional support staff.

Earlier in his chapter, Shanker points out some of the benefits to be derived from solving these problems. "We want [our youngsters] to be able to think, to evaluate information, to be able to express themselves with fluency and clarity, to be able to defend a point of view with cogency and force." In Chapter 27, Sykes provocatively suggests that the problem may be that teachers' styles need examining if we are to have students with the kinds of characteristics Shanker advocates. He laments the failure of the effective schools literature to move beyond management issues to a discussion of the job itself.

Based upon his opinion that "the quality of teaching does matter, that the evidence of a uniform, beige pedagogy is worrisome, and that approaches to school management that ignore teaching quality are inadequate," Sykes advocates a strategy of evaluation based on professional judgment, a strategy of engaging students based not only on the quality of results but also on the quality of the learning experience itself. He implies that teachers who make students enjoy *learning will have more of a long-term impact on those students.*

Sykes also points out that "Creative teaching is risky. Opening teaching to scrutiny is risky. And innovation is risky." He concludes by suggesting a number of structural arrangements to support norms of collegiality, experimentation, *and* deliberation.

If inspired teaching is inherently risky, then how should administrators deal with a problem case? This is the topic that Bridges addresses in Chapter 28. Bridges suggests that administrators' responses can be broadly lumped together into two categories—tolera-tion and confrontation. *He further subdivides these into a number of categories, placing them along a continuum ranging from "ig-nore" to "dismiss." More interestingly, Bridges makes the case for both* administrator *and* teacher responsibility *for recognizing the existence of the problem and working together to solve it.*

In summary, this unit provides a number of thoughtful approaches to changes that might be made in the way we train, sup-port, *and* evaluate teachers *in the classroom. If we are to implement successful quality-enhancing reform programs, teachers will be in the front lines, so the way we deal with them is crucial to the success of the overall reform movement.*

23

A Metaphor for Teaching: Beyond the Bureaucratic–Professional Dichotomy

Reforming Paper Pushers and Avoiding Free Agents: The Teacher as a Constrained Decision Maker
SHARON C. CONLEY

In the early 1980s, when the current education reform movement began, the assumption emerged that schools could achieve quality education by using bureaucratic strategies to reduce uncertainty in the school and in the classroom (Bacharach & Conley, in press). More recent reports, however, take into account the uncertain nature of teachers' work and the ineffectiveness of these bureaucratic measures (Carnegie Forum, 1986; Darling-Hammond, 1986; Frymier, 1987; Glickman, 1987; Holmes Group, 1986; Timar & Kirp, 1987). Specifically, second-wave reform proponents recommend allocating greater autonomy to teachers, increasing their influence in school and district decision making, and enhancing their professional knowledge and skills (Carnegie Forum, 1986). This article examines the problem of maintaining an effective balance between the bureaucratic and professional models of school management in the context of teachers as constrained decision makers.

TEACHERS AS DECISION MAKERS

The need for teachers to make numerous on-the-spot decisions and deal with uncertainty arises from three primary sources. First, the needs of students are variable and constantly changing (Doyle, 1986; Griffin, 1985; Jackson, 1968; Lieberman & Miller, 1978; Lortie, 1975; Williams, 1987). Second, unlike professionals in such occupational settings as medicine and law, teachers do not have the luxury of serving clients' needs individually. Teachers must operate in the context of a highly interactive group (Berliner, 1983; Doyle, 1986; Shedd, Malanowski, & Conley, 1986). Finally, the goals and purposes assigned to teachers are multiple, ambiguous, and often conflicting (Lampert, 1985; Lieberman & Miller, 1984; Griffin, 1985; Schlechty & Joslin, 1984).

Elsewhere, I have, with my coauthors, described a framework that attempts to capture some of the complexities of teaching by classifying teachers' decisions according to three teaching roles (instruction, counseling, and management) and three functions (planning, implementation, and evaluation) (Bacharach, Conley, & Shedd, 1987). Together, these roles and functions identify critical decision areas in teaching. More specifically, teachers make decisions about increasing the academic achievement of students, meeting the personal "counseling" needs of individual students, and managing groups of students. Similarly, teachers' decision making involves not only planning activities but also taking action and evaluating the consequences of action. Indeed, the process of combining different roles and functions constitutes the most demanding and difficult aspect of teaching (Kerchner & Mitchell, 1986; Shedd & Malanowski, 1985).

These observations help us appreciate why professional conceptions of teaching have enjoyed considerable popularity in the second wave of reform. If teachers constantly have to deal with uncertainty and make numerous decisions, it is extremely difficult for anyone except the teacher to plan and coordinate all of these separate decisions. Yet this is precisely what those who hold a bureaucratic conception of teaching hope to accomplish. In the bureaucratic model, "teachers' work is supervised by superiors whose job it is to make sure that teachers implement the curriculum and procedures of the school district" (Darling-Hammond, 1986, p. 532).

The bureaucratic model focuses on simplifying and routinizing the work of teachers, thereby reducing the decisions teachers have to make.

In such a conception, the teacher becomes a mere technician, implementing routine solutions to clear and predictable problems. This bureaucratic model requires teachers to use techniques based on research on "effective" teaching to solve classroom problems, but it ignores aspects of the classroom and students that are uncertain or indeterminate (Bacharach et al., 1987). In this context, teachers must rely heavily on external sources for what they teach and "view themselves as ciphers for other people's expert knowledge" (Elmore, 1987, pp. 72–73).

The professional model, in contrast, treats uncertainty as a given in professional practice (Schon, 1983; Fenstermacher, 1987) and emphasizes strategies that help the professional deal with daily uncertainty. The professional model assumes that the teacher is a decision maker who creatively adapts knowledge to unique and varied problem situations, expands skills beyond "textbook knowledge," and continuously refines professional judgment, initiative, and decision making.

Those who adopt the professional model assume that, although experts may identify basic decisions in teaching, they cannot totally delineate the teacher's creative integration and adaptation of decisions in response to problems. Indeed, because the problems teachers face do not have prescribed solutions, teachers are in the position of risking failure or success in decision making.

MANAGERIAL STRATEGIES FOR EDUCATION REFORM: THE SEARCH FOR A MIDDLE GROUND

The underlying assumptions of the bureaucratic and professional models go far toward explaining many of the reform debates of the past five years. The early reform strategies attempted to reduce uncertainty and thus implicitly bureaucratize teacher's work. Merit pay and career ladders illustrate this point.

Merit pay proposals encouraged administrators to generate, in Tayloristic fashion, "objective" indicators of teachers' performance. In doing so, administrators and policymakers implicitly assumed that teaching activities could be prescribed and delineated by management. In subjecting teaching to detailed specification, merit pay proponents attempted to achieve greater bureaucratic control over teacher's work.

When enthusiasm for merit pay began to dwindle in the mid-1980s, career ladders were heralded as a viable alternative. Career ladder proponents claimed that such plans would rectify the "flat" structure of teaching, provide teachers greater opportunities to develop skills, and help schools and districts make better use of teacher's skills. However, like merit pay, many career ladders ignored the reality of the uncertainty teachers encounter in their work in delineating tasks for teachers and linking detailed job descriptions to each hierarchical level. In one plan, for example, teachers could lose their career ladder status for "refusing to do the duties" prescribed at the next level (Tennessee Education Association, 1984). Consequently, many career ladders did not fulfill their original intent and became a variation of the bureaucratic answer to school reform.

Teachers and school officials recognized immediately the inherent discrepancy between bureaucratic reform prescriptions and the realities of teaching (Frymier, 1987; Rosenholtz, 1986). In many instances, they responded to reform initiatives by circumventing restrictive regulations but, all too often, in ways that could undermine effective school structures and work processes (Timar & Kirp, 1987). For example, many career ladder programs established uniform bureaucratic criteria; therefore, on the day of the evaluation, teachers presented a facade that their work was just as uniform and bureaucratic as expected.

Weick (1976) has maintained that schools are loosely coupled systems. While this metaphor has been useful, the first wave of reform proved clearly that schools could use such mechanisms as career ladders and merit pay to become very tight bureaucracies. The problem is not that school structures are loosely coupled but, rather, that teachers' activities (i.e., roles and functions) are loosely coupled, that is, dominated by uncertainty and unpredictability.

In this context, the first wave of reform tried to impose tightly coupled structures on what we know to be loosely coupled work activities. For reform efforts to be successful, they must overcome what is often viewed as an inherent contradiction. That is, while teachers face uncertainty and unpredictability in their daily work, they also carry out this work in a school organization to which they are accountable. If we fail to go beyond this contradiction, we will be constantly beset by the conflict apparent in the first wave of reform—the conflict between the structure of the school organization and the nature of teachers' work.

These observations emphasize the basic incompatibility between the bureaucratic solutions of the early reform movement and the complexity (more specifically, the uncertainty) that teachers encounter in their daily work activities. If we begin with the premise that teachers are critical to school improvement, then we must attend to two critical areas. First, we must examine teachers' professional preparation, that is, how teachers are prepared prior to their recruitment. The report of the Holmes Group (1986) dealt with this area in some detail. The second area, teachers' professional development following their recruitment, has received much less attention. Both the Carnegie Forum (1986) and the Holmes Group (1986) discussed it but not in great detail. To date, no clear focus or goal for teacher development exists.

When addressing the development of professionals who work in an organization, we must keep two goals in mind. First, professionals need to be confident about making daily decisions in a context of uncertainty.

Furthermore, in making these decisions, teachers must weigh risks and alternatives (Lampert, 1985). Individual teachers who do not weigh alternative decisions but instead repeat routines in a reflexive, not reflective, manner cannot be considered developed professionals regardless of the credentials they hold. Second, a developed professional considers alternative decisions within the normative framework of the organization, specifically, within the broad parameters of the organizations' goals and procedures. In this view, the teacher neither follows blindly (i.e., pushes paper) nor totally ignores organizational precedent and context (i.e., acts as an individual free agent).

Figure 23.1 illustrates a continuum of metaphors with the two roles of teacher as paper pusher and individual free agent at the extremes and the role of constrained decision maker occupying the middle. Neither the metaphor of teachers as paper pushers or as individual free agents is consistent with the reality of the professional teacher working in the school. The view of the teacher as paper pusher makes the teacher no more than a bureaucratic extension of the organization as seen, for example, in the teacher-proof curriculum heralded as the direction of the future. Another example is those who see the future of schools as collections of PCs with teachers replaced by floppy disks.

At the other extreme, teachers are metaphorically considered to be individual free agents who are granted the autonomy to act independently in the classroom. An example may be found in some of the "open" schools that emerged in the 1960s and early 1970s (Hoyle, 1986), where teachers' expression of their own values and idiosyncratic interests were seen as appropriate classroom activities.

Between these two extremes is the view of the teacher as a constrained decision maker. The constrained decision maker deals with uncertainty by weighing alternatives and taking creative risks, while at the same time being aware that he or she is operating within a specific organizational context characterized by goals, norms, precedent, and colleagues. A central goal for the next wave of reform is to develop teachers professionally as constrained decision makers, avoiding the rhetorical extremes implied in the metaphors of teachers as paper pushers or individual free agents. The notion of teachers as constrained decision makers has direct implications for three critical areas of school improvement: job design, teacher evaluation, and systems of participation.

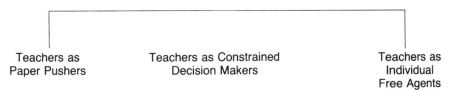

| Teachers as Paper Pushers | Teachers as Constrained Decision Makers | Teachers as Individual Free Agents |

Figure 23.1   Continuum of Teaching Metaphors

Job Design

How can teachers' jobs be designed to be consistent with the image of teachers as constrained decision makers? Those who view teachers as paper pushers would insist that we design jobs according to scientific management principles, specifying detailed steps and procedures to be followed in carrying out the work. On the other hand, those who view teachers as individual free agents suggest that we leave teaching to be conducted "behind classroom doors."

Genuine job design implies creating a work environment that facilitates constrained decision making. For example, Hackman and Oldham (1980) developed a job design model for occupations in general, which is also very useful for dealing with professional occupations (Conley, 1983). The model specifies that five critical job characteristics lead to greater skill utilization and internal motivation of employees: autonomy, skill variety, task identity, task significance, and feedback. Implicit in the Hackman and Oldham model are both dimensions of constrained decision making. Autonomy, skill variety, and task identity allow the professional to cope with uncertainty and process knowledge to facilitate decision making, while task significance and feedback imply constraint mechanisms assuring that the professional operates within the broad normative framework of the organization.

The authors define *autonomy* as the discretion employees have to carry out their work activities. In education, discretion ensures that teachers can deal with classroom uncertainty and take risks. Thus this dimension of job design would ensure that teachers have the flexibility they need to weigh alternatives and make decisions. *Skill variety* is the degree to which employees use a variety of skills and abilities in carrying out their work. As discussed earlier, the work of teaching demands a variety of decision-making skills on the part of teachers, for example, the need to instruct, manage group behavior, and deal with the needs of individual students simultaneously. Job design should enhance, not constrain, skill variety. This characteristic thus directly addresses the issue of task specification and deskilling, which is all too often inherent in detailed job descriptions (Apple, 1987).

Task identity is the degree to which the job involves completion of a "whole task." In education, teachers must be able to "see tasks through" from beginning to end, weighing alternatives that are often needed for taking creative risks necessitated by uncertainty. Jobs should be designed to avoid the fragmentation that we often find advocated by those who metaphorically think of teachers as paper pushers who must be controlled through detailed job descriptions.

While these three aspects of the model deal with teachers' ability to make decisions and take risks, the final two dimensions provide a context of constraint. *Task significance* is the extent to which work activities are viewed as significant to the organization or society as a whole. While task significance can be viewed as a "psychic reward" (Lortie, 1975), it can also be viewed as an implicit organizational constraint that can deter teachers from acting as individual free agents. The more significant the task, the more visibility it has in the organization and the more cautious teachers may be in their decision making and their willingness to take risks. Job design, then, can help make the work of teaching important to the organization as a whole, assuring that teachers operate within organizational constraints. *Feedback* is the degree to which the job itself and, to a lesser extent, supervisors and co-workers, provide professionals with direct and clear information about their job performance. In education, through peer review, supervisory communication, and student achievement, feedback also becomes a source of constraint. Taken together, task significance and feedback assure that teachers develop professionally as constrained decision makers, not simply as individual free agents operating behind the closed doors of their classrooms.

My description of Hackman and Oldham's (1980) model illustrates how job design may be used to avoid the metaphorical extremes of teachers as paper pushers or as free agents. This logically leads to the second critical question of how to evaluate teachers.

Teacher Evaluation

What kind of evaluation system works best for the constrained decision maker? Those who view teachers as paper pushers simply want to evaluate teachers' output—"counting" the number of papers that teachers produce. "New style" merit pay, which links teacher pay to measures of student achievement, is an example of this approach (Bacharach, Lipsky, & Shedd, 1984; Murnane & Cohen, 1986).

At the other extreme, those who view teachers as free agents argue that teaching cannot be evaluated. In this view, effective teaching is an "art" that is dependent on the idiosyncrasies of the free agent and, as an art form, cannot be analyzed or described.

Evaluation systems for the constrained decision maker must place a primary emphasis on evaluating decision-making skills. To the degree that teacher evaluation systems are structured around decision-making skills, teachers, as constrained decision makers, will have a basis for establishing consistent critique and dialogue concerning their professional development. For the constrained decision maker, an evaluation system must accomplish three tasks. First, it must help create a work environment in which the professional teacher can evaluate alternatives, make decisions, and take creative risks. Many evaluation systems inhibit risk taking and decision making because they specify tasks instead of skills. To evaluate on the basis of tasks is to deprofessionalize teaching and to fail to assure those being evaluated that they will be afforded feedback and opportunities for professional growth.

Second, evaluation systems for constrained decision makers should be developmental rather than remedial. Remedial evaluation systems focus on setting and enforcing minimum standards of performance for teachers, while developmental evaluation systems concentrate on setting "targets" for teacher performance. Goal-oriented, they specify skills that all teachers are expected to develop. Such systems assume that the primary purpose of personnel evaluation in schools is to assure the continued growth of all professional teachers.

Finally, an evaluation system for constrained decision makers must assure that teachers become self-monitoring through peer review. Peer review encourages teachers, as constrained decision makers, to assume responsibility for enhancing the professional growth of their colleagues. Indeed, peer assistance is a component of many career ladder programs around the country. However, these plans must also incorporate the first two components of evaluation systems. If mentor teachers simply assure that beginning teachers perform prescribed tasks and activities, or focus only on remediating teacher "deficiencies," it will not matter how many mentor teachers there are. Evaluations will be little more than perfunctory "paper pushing" rather than sources of meaningful feedback.

I have attempted to show how teacher evaluation might be structured to achieve a middle ground between the metaphorical views of the teacher as paper pusher and the teacher as an independent free agent. On one hand, in school organizations, evaluation systems are a source of constraint. Specifically, through peer review, evaluation systems can help assure that teachers become self-monitoring. On the other hand, to the degree that evaluation systems are designed to enhance the teacher's decision-making skills, they can also assure that teachers maximize independent judgment and initiative.

Participation

What kind of participation system can be used for the constrained decision maker? Those who metaphorically view teachers as paper pushers maintain that teachers should not be involved in decision making or that participation can be used as a manipulation tactic to gain teacher acceptance of decisions that have already been made (Conley, Schmidle, & Shedd, in press). At the other extreme, those who view teachers as independent free agents maintain that teacher empowerment alone will solve education's problems. The critical question is how to design a system of participation that allows teachers to broaden their decision making beyond the confines of their immediate classrooms without threatening the legitimate authority structure of schools and school districts.

It is critical to make a distinction between decision-making influence and decision-making authority. *Authority* connotes whether an organization member has the final voice in the decision-making process. *Influence* is broader in scope than authority because it connotes informal power (Bacharach & Lawler, 1980). While authority is zero-sum in nature (e.g., one has authority to make a decision or one does not), conceivably all organization members may exercise influence on decisions. Thus, in the context of teacher participation, it should be possible to increase teachers' influence on school decisions without necessarily altering the authority structure of the school or school district.

Teacher decision-making teams can be used to illustrate this point. Malanowski, Kennedy, and Kachris (1986) describe a "professional analysis team" program that was implemented in a school district in New York. The program trained small school-based groups of teachers in problem-solving techniques. The groups met twice per month over a one-year period to work on problems identified through various data gathering and analysis techniques. Moreover, the teams were implemented "without changing the locus of final authority." Thus, while teachers analyzed problems and developed change proposals, administrators retained the final authority for program approval. "This is an essential element [of the teams] because it lessens fear of loss of managerial control and prevents the loss of role and activity coordination, which are legitimate managerial concerns" (Malanowski, Kennedy, & Kachris, 1986).

Thus one way of increasing teacher participation is to involve teachers in school and district problem analysis and development of solutions. Only the decision to implement solutions requires final authority. Accordingly, teachers can increase their influence on many phases of decision making, with administrators still retaining final authority for implementation decisions. This illustration serves to sensitize us to the middle ground between those who maintain that teachers should have little input into decisions beyond their own classrooms and those who would "empower" teachers through completely restructuring the authority structure of the school.

BEYOND THE RHETORIC OF LABOR AND MANAGEMENT

I began this chapter by stating that the initial phase of the current reform movement was based on a bureaucratic conception of teachers' work. The assumption was that to "reform" public education, someone, whether a policymaker, state legislator, or administrator, had to determine new and more effective ways of controlling teachers, thereby reducing their uncertainty. The second phase of reform has begun to take into account the uncertain nature of teachers' work and to deal with teachers as professional decision makers. These two phases of reform have introduced two polarities in school management, one based on a metaphorical view of teachers as paper pushers and the other on teachers as "free agents." This dichotomy underlies many of the administrative changes that have been debated throughout the last five years of the reform movement.

It would be all too easy to maintain that, while management views teachers as paper pushers, labor's view of teachers (specifically, the view of teachers' unions) is that of free agents. These accusations have been implicitly tossed back and forth during the past five years of reform. In reality, however, these diametrically opposed positions reflect more of an exercise in polemics than real positions. Most school managers recognize that teachers are professionals who must cope with uncertainty and cannot simply be reduced to paper pushers. Likewise, few teachers' union leaders maintain that teachers should be left to operate as free agents. The problem faced by the past reform movement was that our logic was limited by our metaphors.

In proposing the metaphor of teachers as constrained decision makers, and in illustrating the implications of this metaphor for job design, evaluation, and participation, I have tried to define a realistic middle ground for which the next wave of reform should strive. Unless we begin to strike a middle ground based on management's recognition of teachers as professional decision makers and teachers' recognition that they are accountable to the organizations in which they work, many of our reforms will come to naught.

NOTE

Author's Note: I gratefully acknowledge the assistance of Samuel B. Bacharach in preparing this manuscript. Michael Sacken, Jo Ann Hurley, and Margy Diggs also provided helpful comments and editorial assistance.

REFERENCES

Apple, M. W. (1987). Will the social context allow a tomorrow for "tomorrow's teachers"? *Teachers College Record, 88*(3), 330–337.

Bacharach, S. B., & Conley, S. C. (In press). Uncertainty and decision making in teaching: Implications for managing line professionals. In T. J. Sergiovanni and J. H. Moore (Eds.), *Schooling for tomorrow: Directing reforms to issues that count.* Boston: Allyn and Bacon.

Bacharach, S. B., Conley, S. C., & Shedd, J. B. (1987). A developmental framework for evaluating teachers as decision-makers. *Journal of Personnel Evaluation, 1,* 181–194.

Bacharach, S. B., & Lawler, E. E. (1980). *Power and politics in organizations: The social psychology of conflict, coalitions and bargaining.* San Francisco: Jossey-Bass.

Bacharach, S. B., Lipsky, D. B., & Shedd, J. B. (1984). *Merit pay and its alternatives.* Ithaca, NY: Organizational Analysis and Practice.

Berliner, D. (1983). The executive functions of teaching. *Instructor, 93*(2), 28–40.

Carnegie Forum on Education and the Economy's Task Force on Teaching as a Profession. (1986). *A nation prepared: Teachers for the 21st century.* New York.

Conley, S. C. (1983). *The relationships among expectations, perceived job characteristics and work outcomes.* Unpublished doctoral dissertation, University of Michigan, Ann Arbor.

Conley, S. C., Schmidle, T., & Shedd, J. B. Teacher participation in the management of school systems. *Teachers College Record, 90*(2), 259–280.

Darling-Hammond, L. (1986). A proposal for evaluation in the teaching profession. *Elementary School Journal, 86*(4), 531–551.

Doyle, W. (1986). Classroom organization and management. In M. C. Wittrock (Ed.), *Handbook of research on teaching* (pp. 392–431). New York: Macmillan.

Elmore, R. F. (1987). Reform and the culture of authority in schools. *Educational Administration Quarterly, 23*(4), 60–78.

Fenstermacher, G. D. (1987, Fall). A reply to my critics. *Educational Theory, 37,* 413–421.

Frymier, J. (1987, September). Bureaucracy and the neutering of teachers. *Phi Delta Kappan, 69*(1), 9–14.

Glickman, C. D. (1987, October). Unlocking school reform: Uncertainty as a condition of professionalism. *Phi Delta Kappan, 69*(2), 120–122.

Griffin, G. (1985). The school as a workplace and the master teacher concept. *Elementary School Journal, 86*(1), 1–16.

Hackman, J. R., & Oldham, G. (1980). *Work redesign.* Reading, MA: Addison-Wesley.

The Holmes Group. (1986). *Tomorrow's teachers: A report of the Holmes Group.* East Lansing, MI.

Hoyle, E. (1986). *The politics of school management.* London: Hodder & Stoughton.

Jackson, P. (1968). *Life in classrooms.* New York: Holt, Rinehart & Winston.

Kerchner, C. T., & Mitchell, D. E. (1986). Teaching reform and union reform. *Elementary School Journal, 86*(4), 449–470.

Lampert, M. (1985, May). How do teachers manage to teach: Perspectives on problems in practice. *Harvard Educational Review, 55,* 178–194.

Lieberman, A., & Miller, L. (1984). *Teachers, their world and their work: Implications for school improvement.* Alexandria, VA: Association for Supervision and Curriculum Development.

Lortie, D. (1975). *Schoolteacher: A sociological study.* Chicago: University of Chicago Press.

Malanowski, R. M., Kennedy, V., & Kachris, P. (1986). *Professional analysis teams in schools: A case study.* Paper presented at the annual meeting of the American Educational Research Association, San Francisco.

Murnane, R. J., & Cohen, D. K. (1986). Merit pay and the evaluation problem: Why some merit pay plans fail and a few survive. *Harvard Educational Review, 56*(1), 1–17.

Rosenholtz, S. J. (1986, March). Career ladders and merit pay: Capricious fads or fundamental reforms? *Elementary School Journal, 86*(4), 513–529.

Schlechty, P. C., & Joslin, A. W. (1984, Fall). Images of schools. *Teachers College Record, 86*(1), 156–170.

Schon, D. A. (1983). *The reflective practitioner: How professionals think in action.* New York: Basic Books.

Shedd, J. B., & Malanowski, R. M. (1985). *From the front of the classroom: A study of the work of teachers.* Ithaca, NY: Organizational Analysis and Practice.

Shedd, J. B., Malanowski, R. M., & Conley, S. C. (1986). *Teachers as decision-makers.* Paper presented at the annual meeting of the American Educational Research Association, San Francisco.

Tennessee Education Association. (1984, June 15). *TEA News,* p. 14.

Timar, T. B., & Kirp, D. L. (1987). Educational reform and institutional competence. *Harvard Educational Review, 57*(3), 308–330.

Weick, K. (1976). Educational organizations as loosely coupled systems. *Administrative Science Quarterly, 21*(1), 1–19.

Williams, L. R. (1987). Teaching from a multicultural perspective: Some thoughts on uses of diversity. In F. S. Bolin & J. M. Falk (Eds.), *Teacher renewal: Professional issues, personal choices.* New York: Teachers College Press.

24

Preparing Education Students to Be Better Teachers

Reforming Teacher Education: Lessons Learned from a Five-Year Program
RICHARD L. SCHWAB

THE REFORM MOVEMENT is now more than five years old. During this time we have been exposed to an extensive list of must-do's in order for the movement to achieve the lofty goals outlined in the many reform reports. One of the more frequently mentioned is, "We must do a better job of preparing teachers before they enter the profession." The list of must-do's to prepare better teachers in pre-service programs is extensive. While several reports focused on this issue, *Tomorrow's Teachers* by the Holmes Group (1986) and *A Nation Prepared: Teachers for the 21st Century* by the Carnegie Forum on Education and the Economy (1986) received the most attention and sparked the most debate.

Although these reports were written by different groups, they share similar views on key issues relating to preservice teacher education. First, both agree that programs must attract the best and brightest students. These students should have the necessary academic and interpersonal skills to develop into effective classroom teachers and eventually be able to move up a hierarchical career ladder and assume additional responsibilities. These responsibilities include curriculum design and evaluation, peer supervision, and participation in school-based decision making about what is best for students.

The second area of agreement is that teacher education programs cannot prepare such teachers unless those prospective teachers enter their preparation programs with certain "basics." Two of these basics are a broad-based background in general education and an academic major in a discipline from the arts and sciences. In order to satisfy this requirement, preservice teacher preparation should take place in an extended undergraduate program or at the graduate level.

Many universities that prepare teachers have spent a great deal of energy debating these issues, but few have abandoned the undergraduate program in favor of extended or graduate-level programs. One reason for this reluctance to change is that many teacher educators argue that little or no research exists to support the contention that such programs prepare better teachers. It is also argued that moving teacher preparation to the graduate level will discourage all but financially able students from pursuing teaching as a career (see, for example, Howey & Zimpher, 1986; Cherry-Wilkinson, 1988). To date, arguments for and against moving in this direction have been based on conjecture, logic, or philosophical beliefs. Empirical evidence is lacking because there are few institutions that have successfully abandoned undergraduate programs in education in favor of extended or graduate programs. Universities have also been reluctant to change the way they prepare teachers because there are few concrete examples of programs that have successfully implemented the recommendations of the Holmes Group and the Carnegie Commission.

One program that offers both a concrete example of success and empirical evidence in favor of an extended program is the Five-Year Teacher Education Program at the University of New Hampshire (UNH). The UNH program, established in 1974, is an integrated program that begins at the undergraduate level and extends into a fifth year. All students must complete broad-based general education requirements and an academic major outside of education. The five-year program culminates in a master's degree and certification at either the elementary or the secondary level.

Many of the goals identified in the Holmes and Carnegie reports have been achieved in the UNH program. First, this program has attracted academically able students who are highly suitable for teaching. Despite competing for students with other programs in the immediate area that require less time for certification, enrollments have increased steadily. At the same time students' academic qualifications increased dramatically when UNH switched from a four- to a five-year program, and they have remained high (Andrew, 1986).

Students who complete the program have been actively recruited by school districts. Each year since 1975, 90 percent have received teaching positions. This level has stayed constant even through the reduction-in-force periods during the 1970s and early 1980s. Graduates also defy the trend of leaving the profession early. Follow-up research has shown that 75 percent of program graduates are still teaching after five years, a considerably higher figure than is currently being reported in teacher retention studies (Andrew, 1983, 1986).

The five-year program has also responded to the need to prepare teachers for leadership positions within schools. Michael Andrew, who designed the original five-year program, envisioned that graduates would become so-called teacher-leaders (Andrew, 1974). The *teacher-leader* was described by Andrew as a person who was "first an expert in classroom instruction but was also able to grow into leadership roles in curriculum development, curriculum decision making, and improvement of instruction of peers and beginning teachers" (Andrew, 1986, p. 2). Andrew argued that to produce such teacher-leaders, the program had to be challenging enough to attract the most able students. Currently, graduates of the five-year program are teacher-leaders within local schools who are active as cooperating teachers in the internship program and as researchers who present papers at professional meetings, publish journal articles, participate in grant-writing activities, and run workshops for other teachers.

Because the program has graduated teachers who are academically able, highly suitable for teaching, and committed to the profession, it has been identified as a lighthouse program by many people interested in extending teacher education beyond the normal four years. The five-year program has been featured in *Newsweek* as a model, identified in the National Commission on Excellence in Teacher Education (1985) report *A Call for Change in Teacher Education* as an innovative program and has received more than two hundred inquiries from universities interested in learning more about the program.

Most of the interest in our program has centered on recruiting and selecting students, clinical experiences, staffing needs, program development, and success of our graduates. This chapter will share insights into these areas based on experiences over the past 14 years and on research conducted by faculty members on various aspects of the program. It does not address all issues discussed in the Carnegie or Holmes reports, or everything we have grappled with or developed within the program. Instead it offers what experience has shown us are the most critical issues that others moving to extended programs should consider. Discussion of these critical issues will be presented as nine "lessons learned" in later sections.

It is hoped that the discussion in this chapter, rather than merely being a showcase for this program, will help those implementing new programs to learn from our successes and failures. Every institution needs to develop its own program based on the philosophical orientation of the institution and the available resources. The information presented will, it is hoped, encourage institutions to move beyond the debate stage and begin to plan and implement their own programs.

Before moving to the lessons learned section, a brief description of the five-year Teacher Education Program is necessary to understand the context of the issues. For those who are interested, more discussion of the philosophical basis and a more complete description of the program can be found in articles by Andrew (1974, 1981, 1983, 1986), Corcoran and Andrew (1988), and Oja (1988).

THE UNIVERSITY OF NEW HAMPSHIRE FIVE-YEAR TEACHER EDUCATION PROGRAM

Phase One

The integrated undergraduate–graduate teacher education program at the University of New Hampshire can be divided into three phases. Phase 1 includes the completion of the normal degree requirements in one of several colleges at the university. Although each college has its own degree requirements for a major field of study, all students must complete the following general education requirements:

1. One course in writing skills (must be taken during the student's first year)
2. One course in quantitative reasoning (must be taken during the first year)
3. Three courses in biological science, physical science, or technology, with no more than two courses in one area
4. One course in historical perspectives
5. One course in foreign culture
6. One course in fine arts
7. Two courses in social science or philosophical perspectives
8. One course in the works of literature and ideas

Students planning to teach at the secondary level must complete a major in the field in which they plan to be certified. Students planning to become elementary teachers usually major in a field that would be taught at the elementary level or in a field related to education, such as psychology.

Phase Two

The second phase of the preservice program consists of professional coursework. All students aspiring to enter the five-year program must first take Education 500: Exploring Teaching. As the title suggests, Exploring Teaching is a survey course that allows students to experience the real life of a classroom before committing themselves to a career. Students in Exploring Teaching spend a minimum of five hours a week for the semester (a total of at least 65 hours) working in a local school classroom assisting a cooperating teacher. The field-based part of this course requires active participation in classroom activities rather than passive observation. In addition to the fieldwork, students attend a weekly seminar to discuss experiences in the field, required readings, and a range of topics from effective teaching strategies to teaching as a career choice. Course requirements are fairly standardized for all sections and include weekly journal writing and a final self-assessment paper, which becomes part of the student's permanent file. In addition to the student's self-evaluation, cooperating teachers and the university seminar leader complete a standard evaluation and write a qualitative statement about the individual's performance in the seminar and in the field. Students cannot be accepted into the teacher education program without successful completion of this course.

Students who successfully complete Exploring Teaching are eligible to take education courses required for certification during their junior and senior year. These courses fall under the general areas of educational philosophy, curriculum design and instructional methods, educational structure and change, and human learning and development. Within these broad categories, students have several options so that advisors and students can meet individual interests and needs. Students seeking elementary certification are required to complete additional coursework in methods of teaching reading, mathematics, science, and social studies. It is important to note that students are aware that taking the courses and doing well in them is not sufficient evidence for admission into the five-year program. In fact, many marginal students who have completed enough courses to qualify for a minor area of concentration at the undergraduate level have nevertheless been denied admission to the five-year program.

In the fall of their senior year, students apply to the graduate part of the five-year program. Admission is based on performance in Exploring Teaching, undergraduate grade point average, verbal and analytical scores on the Graduate Record Examination (GRE), letters of recommendation, performance letters from education professors teaching the professional courses, and the applicant's personal statement.

Phase Three

The third phase of the preservice program is the graduate component. This phase includes 30 credits of graduate coursework, including a year-long internship and a culminating experience. At least 12 of the credits required for graduation must be in a concentration that is designed by the student with his or her advisor. The concentration provides students with an area of expertise, which is important when they begin to move toward teacher-leader status. Typical concentrations for elementary majors are curriculum development, math instruction, and reading and writing. At the secondary level, students may choose similar areas or may choose from work in their subject field. Students have the option of completing their concentration in one of the departments from arts and sciences. Students doing their concentration within arts and sciences receive a master of arts of teaching (M.A.T.) degree, while those concentrating within the education department receive a master of education degree (M.Ed.).

The focal point of the preservice teacher education program is a year-long, highly supervised internship. Interns spend a year working with cooperating teachers in local schools, attend weekly seminars, are visited at least 12 times during the year by university supervisors, and have weekly writing assignments designed to encourage them to become reflective teachers. Students earn 12 graduate credits for the internship.

Once the concentration, internship, and electives are finished, students must complete a culminating experience. Students choose from several options an experience that best suits their immediate needs and/or future aspirations. Among the options are a traditional master's-level research thesis, an oral defense of thesis statements written by the student, and a practical project in a school setting.

During the 14 years that this program has been in existence, we have experimented with many different approaches to selecting students, integrating professional coursework, and structuring the clinical experiences. The next section presents the lessons learned from these experiences and from research that has evolved during this period.

LESSONS LEARNED

Lesson 1. Requiring candidates to have an undergraduate degree in a field other than education allows them to select teaching as a career by choice rather than default.

A longitudinal study that examined reasons for pursuing a career in teaching via the UNH five-year program found that the desire to provide an important social service, enjoyment of working with children, and the love of subject matter were the top three reasons for both males and females. Although the importance of the social service motivation and working with children is similar to results from other studies, love of subject scored higher than in many previous studies (Andrew, 1983). Students who enter the five-year program have the opportunity to pursue a subject that interests them without giving it up to major in education. They have both time to think about how they want to use their major and experience in schools (Education 500: Exploring Teaching). Consequently, they have several options. They can pursue graduate study in their subject area, apply for a job after completing their undergraduate degree, or pursue teaching having a general idea of what the profession is like. Not only are these students better prepared because of their solid academic background, but they are also more committed to teaching because they have made an informed decision based on experience and reflection.

Lesson 2. Entrance requirements must be rigorous, and multiple sources of information are needed to screen students prior to accepting them into an extended program.

The success of this program is directly related to the quality of the students who are drawn into the program. Fortunately, success breeds success, and student demand for admission to the program is high. There are two parts to the lesson we have learned in selecting students for our program. The first is that self-selection is the best screening mechanism. Historically, about 40 percent of students decide not to pursue teaching as a career after the completion of Exploring Teaching. Some of these students never intended to teach. Others decide that the profession is not for them at this point in their life. The remaining students are counseled out by cooperating teachers and/or university seminar leaders. The important point is that students can choose career alternatives early in their college career, which allows them to pursue other options.

The second part of this lesson is that multiple sources of information are important for making decisions on admission to the program for the remaining students who apply to the program. Students' GRE scores, grade point averages, and letters of recommendation are important pieces of information about basic academic ability. However, our most important information comes from subjective judgments made by experienced educators during Education 500: Exploring Teaching. Cooperating teachers and university seminar leaders are expected to provide information and make judgments about an individual's performance in the classroom. They are also asked to make professional judgments about the student's potential to succeed in the program. Although many teacher preparation programs are reluctant to make subjective professional judgments about a student's potential to become a teacher-leader, we depend on it. Cooperating teacher recommendations, university supervisor evaluations, and the student's self-analysis paper are expected to help those screening applicants to answer such questions as: Does this student demonstrate enthusiasm and a love of learning? Is he or she dedicated to helping children and adolescents achieve their potential? Is he or she dedicated to giving all students equal opportunity to learn, regardless of sex, ethnic or racial background, disability, or socioeconomic level? Is he or she able to make appropriate decisions on his or her feet in the classroom? Does he or she work well with colleagues? Is he or she able to reflect upon his or her teaching to determine what works, what doesn't, and how the teaching can be improved? These are tough assessments to make, but they have been found to be crucial in screening preservice candidates.

Once the application and supporting materials have been assembled, the student's credentials are reviewed by a committee of education faculty, who make recommendations to the graduate school as to who should be admitted. Although the selection process is rigorous and time-consuming, we have found that many problems with internship placement and graduate coursework can be avoided by keeping the standards for admission high and retaining direct control of the admission process within the program.

Lesson 3. A year-long internship is essential.

The year-long internship is the heart of the Five-Year Teacher Education Program. The internship is much more than just a place to practice methods introduced in college courses. It is used to introduce new skills and concepts about teaching. It is also a place in which students grow into reflective teachers capable of analyzing their own teaching with careful guidance and supervision. In the case of the UNH program, many of the traditional methodology courses have been abandoned in favor of teaching the necessary skills in a classroom context (Andrew, 1986). They have been abandoned because research has shown that teachers do not perceive them as valuable and because teaching methodology in the actual classroom environment gives interns the opportunity to see the need and the applicability of methods instruction. Since much of the traditional methodology coursework is not completed prior to entering the classroom, cooperating teachers play an active role in assisting the intern in mastery of technical skills. Identifying cooperating teachers who share the philosophical orientation of the program is therefore paramount.

Corcoran and Andrew (1988) have identified five areas of concern that evolve for interns during the internship year: immersion, adjustment, expansion, analysis, and autonomy. Involvement with these areas usually happens sequentially and has formed the basis for the curriculum that has evolved for that year.

Immersion begins in late August when interns attend the teacher orientation and workshops that precede the start of school. During this time interns are consumed by the responsibilities of being in school all day, learning names of students and other teachers, learning classroom rules and routines, and becoming comfortable in building a working relationship with the cooperating teacher. Some interns can stay in this phase as long as 10 weeks before they are ready to communicate openly and honestly.

Adjustment usually begins around mid-October, when interns begin to come to grips with what they know and what they do not know. They also are able to see what aspects of teaching are easy for them and which are more difficult. The biggest areas of concern during this time are planning, classroom control, and discipline. This phase is when interns first begin to look at themselves with some objectivity.

Expansion is the phase when interns begin to look at the classroom as a whole. Until this time interns have focused on pieces of life in the classroom—planning single lessons, assuming responsibility for one reading group, designing assessment procedures for individual projects. In this phase interns are ready to try new teaching approaches, visit other schools to expand their horizons, and generally experiment. This highly intense period usually runs from November to sometime in January. It is the time when students form important frameworks for future inquiry when they assume a full-time job.

Analysis usually comes in mid-January, after the student returns from semester break. It is a time when many interns feel they are ready to begin a full-time job and question whether they can really learn more than they already know. Many of the friends with whom they finished undergraduate school are now working and have begun to be independent. At the same time, the interns are financially and emotionally drained. They begin to question whether teaching is for them. Fortunately, this occurs when interns are just realizing the effect they have had on students. This aspect usually ends with interns reaffirming the reasons they originally entered teaching. New energy is evident as they move toward obtaining their own classroom in the next year. This is an important, enlightened perspective that can only be achieved in a program where the preservice teacher has the time to reflect and act on cumulative experiences.

Autonomy is the final aspect of the internship. At this time interns are excited about trying all their new ideas without the cooperating teacher and university supervisor looking over their shoulder. They express interest in being left alone to plan, execute, and evaluate their lessons. They realize how much they know but also how much there is still to learn. A real example of the energy that is created at this time can be seen by the fact that more then half of the interns choose to stay in their placements until the end of the school year in late June, although the university requires only that they go to the end of the semester in early May.

Because of the amount of material interns must master and the different phases of development that occur, it is unrealistic to assume that anything less than a full year's internship is necessary. The year-long internship provides the opportunity for such growth, but whether or not growth occurs depends on the quality of the internship experience.

Lesson 4. Good internship experiences require a great deal of work on the part of the intern, cooperating teacher, and university supervisor.

Good internship experiences do not just happen. Three major studies have explored what makes an effective internship (Corcoran, 1981; Corcoran & Andrew, 1988; Oja & Ham, 1988). The results of these studies have indicated that the most successful internships occur when there is a close working relationship with the university supervisor and cooperating teacher, proper placement, and competent supervision.

The competence of the cooperating teacher is critical to success of the internship. Teachers welcome working with interns because it gives them an extra pair of hands for a full year. Oja (1988) found that teachers also welcome interns because they consider it their professional responsibility to introduce new people into the field. But despite the large number of teachers who express interest in having interns, identifying and providing training and support for those who will make good cooperating teachers is a time-consuming job. At UNH a full-time faculty member is released from two courses to act as director of field experiences. Typical responsibilities of the director of field experiences include: identifying new cooperating teachers, conducting training sessions and semester-long graduate courses in supervision for cooperating teachers, counseling prospective interns, and acting as ombudsman and trouble-shooter for the inevitable problems that arise in field placements.

The second prerequisite for a good internship is matching the individual student with the proper placement. Every school, teacher, and intern is different. To help make the best match occur, the placement process begins in the fall prior to the internship year. Prospective interns meet with the director of field placement in large-group orientation sessions and then in follow-up individual conferences. Starting in January, prospective interns are steered toward placement options that the director feels will fit the individual's needs. The schools and prospective interns then assume responsibility for site selection. Interns prepare brief resumes and go through an interview with prospective cooperating teachers and the building principal. Part of the interview process usually entails students spending part of the school day with the teacher. Both interns and cooperating teachers are urged to interview several people before deciding who will work with whom. Despite this complex process, several of these matches do not work out when the internship begins in the following fall. These situations are easily resolved, however, because placements can be made until October and there is still a good part of a school year remaining. This luxury does not exist in programs that depend on one semester of student teaching.

The third condition for a good internship experience is competent university supervision. Interns are supervised by both cooperating teachers and university supervisors. University supervisors normally visit the intern on at least 12 occasions and direct a weekly seminar for interns. In addition to working with the intern, the supervisor is expected to be a resource and support person for the cooperating teacher. Initiating and maintaining rapport with school personnel is part of this responsibility. Because of the intensity of the supervisory requirements, faculty members are given one course equivalent for every six interns they supervise. (A normal teaching load for full-time faculty is five courses a year.)

Lesson 5. Cluster placements, combined with training programs for cooperating teachers, are important for better education and for effective use of university resources.

Over the 14 years this program has been in place, we have tried several methods of internship placement. These have ranged from splitting the placement site between Europe and New Hampshire, to placements in interns' home towns so they could save money by living with parents, to placement with the best possible teacher no matter where that teacher was geographically located, to paid internships that had students assuming full responsibility for all classes. We have settled on making the majority of our placements in cluster sites where several interns work in the same building and/or district. These sites resemble professional development centers, as suggested in the Holmes and Carnegie reports. Most teachers in cluster sites have participated in supervisory training programs taught by a university professor with expertise in supervision. Training programs include both workshops and graduate-level courses specifically designed for cooperating teachers. Cooperating teachers, the building principal, and the university supervisor also meet on a regular basis to discuss issues relating to teaching, the internship, and supervision.

Research by Oja (1988), who studied two cluster sites over a two-year period, and practical experience have taught us that cluster sites are beneficial, for several reasons. First, the university supervisor and other university personnel are able to provide more technical support for cooperating teachers. This support can be provided by such activities as holding individual conferences, running seminars for the cooperating teachers, and providing journal articles on issues of interest to cooperating teachers. If the university supervisor can help the cooperating teacher do a better job, then the internship experience is greatly enhanced.

A second advantage of placing interns in cluster sites is that cooperating teachers have the support of a group of other teachers and principals, who can work through the university supervisor to effect change in the five-year program. This changes the traditional role of the university supervisor. Instead of being the outside person who monitors the internship experience, the supervisor becomes more of an expert resource person to help with problem solving and technical support. In turn, the cooperating teachers feel a greater sense of professionalism because they have a voice in decision making.

Lesson 6. A high reliance on intensive field-based courses places greater demands on university faculty.

Despite the fact that the university supervisor's teaching load is relatively light in terms of numbers of students, it is not light in responsibility. Directing the seminar, monitoring the writing assignments, and visiting the field sites all require much more time and effort than teaching a traditional graduate course. This is particularly true if the intern is having problems, if the cooperating teacher is not able to provide the quality of supervision that is necessary, and/or if the field site is a considerable distance from the university. Teaching the other field-based courses that students are required to take is also more time-consuming and demanding than teaching traditional courses.

It is important that all faculty assume responsibility for teaching at least one field-based course or section of internship supervision. Not only is this good for keeping faculty in touch with the real world of schools, but it also reinforces the concept of the importance of the field experiences to the integrity of the program. Additionally, requiring all faculty to assume responsibility for one field-based course underscores their central importance and prevents heavy reliance on adjunct faculty and graduate assistants. In summary, if a program faculty professes to value field experiences, then everyone must pitch in.

One way many faculty have made the most of their field placements is to dovetail them with research interests. Many faculty members who teach field-based courses have worked with cooperating teachers and students to conduct field-based research. As a result of these studies, faculty members have coauthored research presentations and journal articles with both interns and cooperating teachers. Such studies have included research on Logo and learning in elementary classrooms (Kull, 1988; Kull & Carter, 1985), collaborative supervision and adult development (Bloomquist, Bornstein, Fink, Michaud, Oja, & Smulyan, 1985), five-year program design issues and stages of intern development (Andrew, 1981, 1983; Corcoran, 1981; Corcoran & Andrew, 1988).

Lesson 7. It is crucial to develop social support networks for the interns, cooperating teachers, and university supervisors.

Research on occupational stress in the teaching profession has identified several factors that can help reduce stress in teaching. A major factor in controlling job stress is the presence of an effective collegial social support network (Schwab, Jackson, & Schuler, 1986; Jackson, Schwab, & Schuler, 1986). This network of people serves as: technical support (helping with issues relating to education), technical challenge (challenging the individual to think of new ideas relating to teaching that contribute to personal growth), emotional support (providing emotional comfort), emotional challenge (confronting the individual in humane ways when his or her behaviors are inappropriate), active listeners (paying attention to what individuals are saying and helping them clarify what they are feeling), and people who share similar values, beliefs, and perceptions of reality (Pines, Aronson, & Kafry, 1981). Although support networks can also emanate from administration or from people outside the organization, research has found that support provided by co-workers is the most crucial (Schwab et al., 1986).

Part of the success of the UNH program can be attributed to the fact that all of the major groups of individuals involved in the internship process have a formal collegial support groups that meets on a regular basis. These groups are also empowered to make decisions that directly affect their positions.

The university supervisors meet on a biweekly basis to discuss issues relating to the supervision of the internship. The agenda of these meetings are set by the supervisors and the director of field experiences. These meetings can be instructional, for information sharing, or focused on helping a supervisor solve a difficult supervisory problem. This group also makes policy relating to the internship. For example, this group spent two years designing, field testing, and revising the evaluation system for the internship experience (Kull & Mercier, 1986).

The interns' support group is based in the weekly seminar. Part of each weekly seminar is dedicated to solving or discussing issues relating to each individual intern's situation. Interns are also placed in peer support dyads. Dyads participate in such activities as videotaping each other while teaching, conducting peer evaluation of each other's teaching, and visiting other schools to observe master teachers. These activities are strictly designed to be supportive and are not used in summative assessments of interns.

A major advantage of having cluster sites is that it facilitates the establishment of in-house support groups for cooperating teachers. Cooperating teachers in cluster placements meet on a regular basis with the site coordinator. Research by Oja (1988) indicates that when cooperating teachers spent more time interacting with each other about supervision and teaching, it contributes to their professional growth as well as to that of the interns. Oja also found that cooperating teachers were more likely to hold the university responsible for making changes that improve the five-year program if they have a formalized support group.

Lesson 8. Finding financial support for interns is a constant battle that must be fought.

One of the most pressing problems created by the five-year program is the additional financial burden placed on the intern. We have worked hard to address this problem but have not solved it. The first effort we have made is to get our students a fair share of the regular graduate student financial aid. Because the admission standards are high and externally defensible, our students have successfully secured scholarships open to all graduate students. It is not unusual to see more than half of the scholarships offered to graduate students at the university going to our students.

Second, with the help of private-sector businesses within the state, we have initiated a scholarship fund to fund New Hampshire students during the internship year. The scholarship has a broad-based appeal to the business community. First, all money goes directly to graduate students who work in schools where the companies conduct business. Second, all monies go to students without any part going to the university in overhead. Third, such scholarships are seen as one way private-sector businesses can provide the kind of partnerships discussed in the various reform reports. Currently we have raised enough endowment money to provide seven students with Excellence in Teaching scholarships that give them a flat grant of $2,000 to help offset costs of the internship year.

The third area for funding support, and the most difficult to develop and nurture, is the paid internship. Since the program started in 1974, several efforts have been undertaken to develop paid internships. Currently slightly less than one-third of our internships are paid. In a paid internship a district provides a stipend for the intern to assume more responsibility earlier than might normally be expected, or to perform extra duties such as coaching or home tutoring. The paid internship can benefit both parties. The district gets assistance it needs in the classroom, and the intern gets a stipend while completing certification and master's degree requirement's. Unfortunately, the requirements discussed here for a good internship sometimes conflict with the needs of the district paying for the internship. For example, interns may not have access to good cooperating teachers in the departments where the school district needs the interns' help the most. The other problem with having school districts pay for the internship year is that internships are one of the first items to go when districts have to cut back budgets. It has taken time for our program to develop paid internship sites, and adding more good sites remains a priority for the program.

Lesson 9. None of the previous lessons apply unless the central administration of the university and the people responsible for implementing the program make some basic commitments to each other.

Fourteen years ago, the University of New Hampshire made a commitment to the five-year program. The commitment was based on an understanding that improving the quality of teacher education would call for bold changes. These changes involved risks, and they also meant that preservice teacher education would cost the university more money to turn out fewer teachers. The university also had to make a commitment to give the education department enough time to institute the program and experiment with different approaches to preparing teachers. In turn, the education department had to make a commitment to develop a program that was rigorous yet flexible enough to attract the best students. The department also had to make a commitment to work closely with practicing teachers and local schools to develop and implement the program.

Unless those who wish to implement extended programs make these commitments, instituting an effective program is impossible.

SUMMARY

Those involved in teacher education have been debating the merits of the reforms suggested in the Holmes and Carnegie reports for more than two years. Although debate is important, it is time to take action so that the types of teachers envisioned by these reports will be in our classrooms when we begin the next decade. The Five-Year Teacher Education Program at the University of New Hampshire is not a panacea, but it does offer those who are considering a move in this direction insights based on research and experience.

REFERENCES

Andrew, M. D. (1974). *Teacher leadership: A model for change.* Washington, DC: Association of Teacher Educators. (ERIC Document Reproduction Service No. ED 096 288.)

Andrew, M. D. (1981). A five-year teacher education program: Successes and challenges. *Journal of Teacher Education, 32*(3), 41–43.

Andrew, M. D. (1983). The characteristics of students in a five-year teacher education program. *Journal of Teacher Education, 34*(1), 20–23.

Andrew, M. D. (1986). Restructuring teacher education: The University of New Hampshire's five-year program. In T. J. Lasley (Ed)., *The dynamics of change in teacher education* (Vol. 1). Background papers from the National Commission on Excellence in Teacher Education. (AACTE-ERIC Teacher Education Monograph No. 5.)

Bloomquist, R., Bornstein, S., Fink, G., Michaud, R., Oja, S. N., & Smulyan, L. (1985). *Action research on change in schools: The relationship between teacher morale/ job satisfaction and organizational changes in a junior high school.* Durham, NH: Collaborative Research Office. (ERIC Document Reproduction Service No. ED 269 873.)

Carnegie Forum on Education and the Economy. (1986). *A nation prepared: Teachers for the 21st century.* New York.

Cherry-Wilkinson, L. (1988). Prospects for graduate preparation of teachers. In A. Woolfolk (Ed.), *Beyond the debate: Research perspectives on the graduate preparation of teachers.* Englewood, NJ: Prentice-Hall.

Corcoran, E. (1981). Transition shock: The beginning teacher's paradox. *Journal of Teacher Education, 32*(3), 19–24.

Corcoran, E., & Andrew, M. (1988). A full year internship: An example of school/ university collaboration. *Journal of Teacher Education, 39*(3), 17–35.

Holmes Group. (1986). *Tomorrow's teachers: A report of the Holmes Group.* East Lansing, MI.

Howey, K. R., & Zimpher, N. L. (1986). The current debate on teacher preparation. *Journal of Teacher Education, 37*(5), 41–49.

Jackson, S. E., Schwab, R. L., & Schuler, R. A. (1986). Toward an understanding of the burnout phenomenon. *Journal of Applied Psychology, 71*(4), 630–639.

Kull, J. A. (1988). Children learning logo: A collaborative, qualitative study in the first grade. *Journal of Research in Childhood Education, 3*(1).

Kull, J. A., & Carter, J. S. (1985). *Rapping in the first grade classroom.* Paper presented at the World Logo Conference, Cambridge, Massachusetts.

Kull, J. A., & Mercier, M. (1986). *Evaluating pre-service teaching interns.* Paper presented at the annual meeting of the Northeast Educational Research Association, Kerhonkson, New York.

National Commission on Excellence in Teacher Education. (1985). *A call for change in teacher education.* Washington, DC: American Association of Colleges for Teacher Education.

Oja, S. N. (1988). *A collaborative approach to leadership in supervision.* Final report to the Office of Educational Research and Improvement. Washington, DC: U.S. Department of Education.

Oja, S. N., & Ham, M. C. (1988). *Keys to successful collaboration: The role of the university researcher on a collaborative action research team.* Manuscript submitted for publication.

Pines, A., Aronson, E., & Kafry. (1981). *Burnout: From tedium to personal growth.* New York: Free Press.

Schwab, R. L., Jackson, S. E., & Schuler, R. A. (1986). Educator burnout: Sources and consequences. *Educational Research Quarterly, 10*(3), 14–29.

25

Starting a Career in the Classroom

Emerging Public Policy Issues in the
Support and Assessment of New
Classroom Teachers
LAURA A. WAGNER

THE TEACHING CAREER has recently been the subject of considerable public policy discussion, focused primarily upon (1) demographic
shifts affecting teacher supply and demand (Guthrie, 1987; Cagampang,
Guthrie, & Kirst, 1986; Hodgkinson, 1985); (2) the academic background
and preparation of K–12 classroom teachers (Lanier & Little, 1986; Schlechty,
1985); and (3) analysis of the teacher's role, salary, working conditions,
and opportunities for career advancement (Boyer, 1988; Odden, 1987).

The purpose of this analysis is to describe two of the public policy
issues emerging in this discussion and their implications for future developments. These particular issues arose in the course of a year-long seminar
conducted in 1987–1988 by the California State Department of Education,
in cooperation with the Commission on Teacher Credentialing and a group
of faculty members in the Graduate School of Education, Stanford University. Over 200 teachers, administrators, college and university faculty,
and other educators participated in the deliberations. In brief, the central
issues discussed were as follows:

- New teacher assessment and support programs should be viewed as part
  of the larger agenda to restructure the teaching occupation. Otherwise,
  they run the risk of becoming an isolated categorical initiative.
- In the current political climate, staff development assistance for new
  teachers in the form of additional resources will be provided only in

exchange for greater accountability, defined at the induction level as candidate-based demonstrations of competence for teaching as part of a professional licensure decision. We currently know much more about the crucial elements for supporting new teachers than about how to mount the comprehensive formative and summative assessments implied by proposals to move to a candidate-based credentialing system (California State Department of Education, in press).

THE RESOURCE–ACCOUNTABILITY EXCHANGE

Teacher licensure reform and induction needs were embedded in many of the commissioned reports calling for the restructuring of the teaching occupation (e.g., the Carnegie, Holmes, American Association of Colleges of Teacher Education (AACTE), American Federation of Teachers (AFT), National Education Association (NEA), and California Commission on the Teaching Profession reports). Calls to professionalize the occupation are in response to the historic definition of the teaching career path as organized around labor, art, and craft models (Kerchner & Mitchell, 1988). These concerns are reflected in the working conditions of many teachers, where bargained agreements view teaching primarily as a technical skill and where a majority of teachers still do not participate in central professional activities, including staff selection, budgeting, professional development, evaluation, and a host of student standards and policy issues (Boyer, 1988).

The lack of support for new teachers, the availability of more lucrative and higher status jobs elsewhere, and the absence of any individually based accountability mechanism for ensuring teacher mastery of knowledge and skills all weaken teaching's claim to be a profession and encourage exit from the occupation and rapid turnover. This is particularly problematic in the sunbelt states of the Southeast and Southwest, where there is an increasing demand for classroom teachers (Grissmer & Kirby, 1987). The Policy Analysis for California Education (PACE) research group predicts that the state will need between 77,300 and 85,000 additional K–12 teachers by 1989–1990 and between 159,700 and 183,400 by 1994–1995 to allow for both enrollment growth and attrition (Guthrie & Kirst, 1988).

New teacher induction programs are particularly appropriate to help address the developmental needs of new teachers. Historically we have assumed that a teacher's education is largely complete once the initial hurdle of licensure has been cleared. This contrasts with other professions, such as nursing, accounting, and law, where an individual's relative newness in the profession is recognized, and new professionals receive the supervision of more experienced peers, take responsibility for fewer clients, and are expected to grow into their role. By contrast, we frequently give our newest teachers the same teaching load as their more experienced colleagues, with as many students and extracurricular assignments as are given to the ten-year veteran. In fact, research indicates that the newest teachers often have the toughest assignments, in the worst classrooms, with inadequate curriculum materials and supplies, and little opportunity either to vent their frustrations or to learn from their peers (McLaughlin, 1986).

Support services for novice teachers serve simultaneously as continued training for the individual, as an institutional service to help schools organizationally receive new teachers, and as a safeguard for the public. Such programs typically include opportunities for participants to be supervised in their initial teaching role, to get feedback on their teaching strengths and weaknesses, and increasingly to inform the state's decision to grant them a full professional license. Taxpayers and policymakers are linking resources for induction programs to stronger measures of teacher accountability. Candidate-based assessment for licensure was proposed in a number of the commissioned reports and featured in our seminar discussions as one approach to strengthening the teaching occupation and putting it more on a par with other professions that require prospective practitioners to demonstrate knowledge and the ability to use knowledge in performance settings as a prerequisite for earning a license.

Candidate-based assessment means that prospective practitioners are individually tested for licensure; if deficient, they are either given additional assistance to help them along the route to full professional status or are counseled out of the occupation. This contrasts with a *program approval* approach to licensure, which assumes that program graduates have mastered the requisite professional knowledge if the preparation program itself has been "approved." In a candidate-based approach, novices are asked instead to demonstrate their knowledge and skill directly on some form of assessment, typically a range of measures that are designed to document knowledge and skill in teaching and serve either formative or summative purposes, or both. The formation component is particularly important in teaching, where a growing body of research literature documents the differences in teaching knowledge held by expert and novice teachers in their own subject area (Berliner, 1988; Leinhardt & Greeno, 1986; Pecheone, Garon, Forgione, & Abeles, 1988).

A number of states, including California, have connected the desire to move to a candidate-based assessment system with a commitment to provide a support system for beginning teachers. Such a system constitutes an exchange relationship that reflects the dual policy priorities of improving teacher preparation, compensation, and working conditions while also increasing teacher accountability. Salaries constitute the largest part of school budgets, and in the current fiscal climate state legislatures are increasingly reluctant to augment teacher salaries without concomitant demonstrations of competence.

These parallel efforts, then—one to provide a range of services for new teachers during their early, induction years and the other to link the award of the professional teaching credential to successful practice during induction—are being implemented in at least 11 states (Goertz, 1986). More are likely to follow as teachers seeking competitive salaries lobby in state legislatures committed to more accountability in return for greater resources.

PROTOTYPE PROGRAMS TO SUPPORT NEW TEACHERS

Several state-supported programs underway in California are providing evidence of the forms new-teacher support can take and the ways a candidate-based assessment system might inform teacher licensure. The New Teacher Retention Project in Inner City Schools is sponsored by the California State University chancellor's office and the state department of education, working with San Diego State University and the San Diego Unified School District, and with Hayward State University and the Oakland Unified School District. This pilot program is intended to increase the retention of new inner-city classroom teachers. Although the program is relatively small, early data suggest that new teachers in these settings are staying in the profession.

In a second initiative, 768 first- and second-year teachers are participating in an evaluation study of new-teacher assessment and support. Under the direction of the state education and teacher licensing departments, 15 pilot programs are being implemented to identify the kinds of specific state policies needed to ensure the retention and effectiveness of new teachers. The 15 funded projects involve individual school districts working alone; districts sharing governance with colleges, universities, and teachers' organizations; and large consortia composed of school districts, county offices of education, and institutions of higher education. An assessment component is analyzing the role of formative and summative assessments of new teachers in improving their initial teaching performance, and whether and how such assessments should be used as one requirement for state certification. An evaluation will document the success of the program in increasing teacher retention, effectiveness, satisfaction, collegiality, and commitment to the profession.

A number of other initiatives, sponsored by colleges, universities, and large school districts around California already support new teachers through site-level programs, telecommunications, college and university seminars, and staff development programs targeted specifically to the needs of the new teachers. The seminar series identified a number of elements crucial to the success of these programs and to the reform of teacher credentialing practices. Each of these areas is summarized next.

1. *The design of a new teacher support program needs to be built around the defined purposes of the program and involve those most directly affected—teachers, administrators, and college and university faculty.* Any of the following purposes might be encouraged in a program for new teachers, including: orientation to district and school, psychological support, teaching assistance, expansion of subject matter and pedagogical skills, evaluation for staff development or employment, identification with the teaching profession, and increased professional colleagueship (Wise et al., 1987). Where purposes are in part specified (e.g., by legislation), opportunity needs to be given for local elaboration to reflect local priorities, existing support services, and unique features of the local environment.

2. *Connections to other initiatives, including teacher recruitment, selection, staff development, teacher evaluation, and school improvement need to be established, preferably early in the design, to increase the chances for later institutionalization.* Even if the new-teacher support program is intended only to help new teachers during the initial survival stage, it is important that the people and perspectives of those involved in other efforts be incorporated in the design to promote a sense of ownership and the likelihood of later institutionalization.

3. *Teachers should be selected for the support program on the basis of program purposes, design, and new teachers' needs.* All teachers working in new situations can benefit from induction support, but a new-teacher support program cannot be everything to all people. Experience suggests that when different kinds of new teachers are included in a support program, consideration should be given to modifying the program content, duration, and level of support and supervision to reflect prior teaching experience, levels of teaching proficiency, and continuing need for the support.

4. *A variety of individuals from different organizations are qualified to work with new teachers, although they need training for the role.* Experienced teachers, mentors, college faculty, and school and district administrators are likely candidates to provide support for new teachers. In particular, school principals have a pivotal role in setting the tone for new teacher support, both in the assignments given new teachers and in providing resources for staff development and school improvement. Many of them will have taught elementary and/or secondary school themselves. However, they will likely need orientation and training for their support roles—training that reflects adult learning needs. Adults learn best when they are presented with meaningful experiences in the course of real work, when training builds upon those experiences and anticipates that they will be differentially motivated by particular learning experiences (Krupp, 1987).

5. *Support services for new teachers are likely to be variants on three dominant approaches. These are: personal support, professional consulting, and seminars and coursework.* Regardless of the approach or provider (typically a district or postsecondary institution), support systems should be designed to provide

assistance that is context-specific and, as much as possible, based on the individual needs of the new teachers.

Initially, most new teachers will want to be paired with an experienced teacher in their own building, preferably in their subject area or grade level, to help with the first difficult weeks. Over time, teacher needs will change, and local programs need to be designed to accommodate different teacher learning needs. At differential rates, new teachers will need opportunities to learn more about their subject matter and how to teach it, how students learn and how instruction should be modified to reflect individual differences, the norms of schools as organizations, and their own roles as members of the teaching occupation.

Induction into the profession implies the development of a set of values and mores about good teaching. To develop these norms, new teachers and their more experienced colleagues need opportunities to talk about teaching, share their individual conceptions of teaching, and build understanding and commitment to the profession.

The relationship between new teachers and their support personnel is a key variable in the success of the new teacher and the support program (Ward, 1988). If the support is provided by other teachers, new teachers and their support partners need to be in close proximity. Opportunities need to be provided for new teachers to observe both one another and their more experienced colleagues. If the support is provided by the university, faculty must be able to work at the new teacher's school site on a regular basis.

The forms of support should match the anticipated goals. This means that the program should be designed toward specific outcomes. Thus, although a before-school orientation is useful, it is unlikely to develop new knowledge and skill unless the orientation sessions are part of an ongoing staff development program. Similarly, if collegiality is a goal of the new teacher support system, time and opportunity must be provided for teachers to work together (McDonald, 1980).

6. *Seminars and college and university coursework for new teachers needs to be practical.* Higher education plays an important role in new-teacher support and can be crucial in helping new teachers make the transition from student/student teacher to classroom teacher of record and teaching professional. The demands of the new classroom, however, make it important that coursework offered for teachers during their first year be extremely practical. Where coursework is theoretical, it needs to be offered either during a second year or over a two-year period, because first-year teachers are simply attending to too many other issues at the outset of their career (Ward, 1988).

7. *Time and compensation need to be provided for new teachers and their support personnel to work together.* Regardless of the design, new-teacher support programs require resources. Curricular, instructional, and man-

agement skills are developed through opportunities to practice them with more experienced others—mentors, faculty, and school administrators. Both the experienced teacher and the novice need time for this work, and the time needs to be recognized. There are a variety of ways to provide this recognition, including salary compensation, released time, reduced teaching loads, reduced additional responsibilities, ceremonies of recognition, and other rewards. A compensation package that new teachers and other faculty regard as meaningful should be collaboratively developed.

One caution about released time: A little goes a long way. Both evaluation data and informal reports from the New Teacher Retention Project in Inner City Schools document that neither new teachers nor their administrators want large amounts of released time (Morey, 1988). An initial requirement for 20 percent released time has been relaxed in favor of more flexible scheduling of time for new teachers to work with faculty and mentors. Released time is expensive; new teachers are burdened when they are required to prepare extensive lesson plans; they don't want to be out of their own classrooms for extended periods; and substitutes are difficult to find. (During 1988-1989, we are experimenting with 5 to 20 days of released time per year in various settings.)

8. *A formative assessment component is a critical part of any teacher support program and may be linked to teacher evaluation.* The formative assessment side of a teacher support program is crucial. Depending on the program's purposes, formative assessment may be used to design individual or staff development plans for general program revision. The success of the formative component depends in large part on the extent to which teachers and their advisors trust its accuracy, fairness, and utility. Some of the better systems provide frequent feedback to new teachers about their teaching, opportunities for novices to learn new subject matter and practice new instructional strategies, assessments of teaching performance with diverse student groups, and resources for individualized professional development programs tied to school improvement activities.

Some districts may elect to tie formative assessment to teacher evaluation and employment decisions. Poway, California, has such a system. There is considerable debate about whether the same individual can both formatively and summatively assess a new teacher. Regardless of who conducts the evaluation, the evaluation system itself needs to be developed collaboratively with teachers, related directly to identified instructional goals, and linked to staff development (McLaughlin & Pfeiffer, 1988). Those who are evaluating the new teacher need to be trained for that role, and the criteria on which the new teacher is to be evaluated need to be collaboratively defined. As one personnel director put it, "A teacher evaluation system should provide no surprises."

9. *Monetary and human resources, site leadership, and flexibility in program*

design are essential for implementation and a key to institutionalizing a new-teacher support system. An overwhelming majority of respondents in a study of new-teacher support programs in the Southeast reported insufficient funding as the major program weakness. Respondents also cited inadequate compensation for mentors, faculty, and university staff working on new-teacher induction (Hawk & Robards, 1987). Educational systems need to plan and budget for new-teacher induction, not assume that it can be supported without resources. Nevertheless, a local system to recognize and support the developmental status of the new teacher need not be costly. Pilot programs with existing mentor teachers, telephone hotlines to answer personal and professional questions, and before-school orientations can provide important services for new teachers and set the stage for a larger initiative.

At the same time, new-teacher support must be an explicit initiative if it is to be successful. Site administrative support is key here, as is design flexibility, so the program can be refined over time.

10. *The development of support systems for new teachers needs to be encouraged not as separate categorical programs but as part of a local staff development system.* Ironically, to define its goals and develop a constituency, an educational initiative is most frequently defined as a *program*. In the process, the program takes on a life of its own, develops a categorical constituency, and then is only reluctantly institutionalized into the system. (Witness the uneasy incorporation of special-population strategies into the mainstream of the educational program.) New teachers are just entering the system, and whatever efforts we support on their behalf need to help them become part of the whole enterprise, rather than a categorical class.

Staff development also has a larger mission than simply improving the individual new teacher's skills. The findings of the CPEC State Staff Development Policy Study illuminate the need for staff development to be broadened from the categorical definitions of in-service courses and after-school seminars to become part of the everyday fabric of teachers' work on curriculum and instruction (Little & Geritz, 1987).

Staff development is also an important vehicle for encouraging teacher professionalism. As noted by Kanthak and Mitchell (1988),

> The goals of individual teacher accountability and the creation of professional standards throughout the occupation remain strong, but they are now balanced by a new set of goals. Direct investment in teacher staff development over the last three decades has been stimulated by the need to reform school programs and curricular structures, not simply to improve the performance of individual teachers. Professionalism means accepting responsibilities for leadership with the school and district as well as competence in the classroom.

THE DIFFICULTIES AND POTENTIALS OF A NEW-TEACHER ASSESSMENT SYSTEM

Increased professional accountability within a more collegial, professional environment is the other side of the teacher support equation. Key to the development of proposals for new teacher support are parallel calls to make teacher preparation and assessments for the credential more rigorous.

Assessment for licensure during a teacher induction program is a complex matter. The high-stakes nature of licensure assessment requires that strict standards of equity and fairness be observed and that the teaching context not condition performance (Wise et al., 1987). Licensure is a public protection, a quality control assurance that guarantees the public that an individual meets minimal expectations for performing in an occupation. Although data can and should be drawn from naturalistic settings (as in a medical or architectural residency), licensure requirements need to include a combination of state standardized measures and applied performance tests, along with observational data and recommendations from individuals who work with the new teacher (Darling-Hammond & Wise, 1985).

Standardized tests have historically been used in teacher licensure because of their statistical ability to document levels of psychometric validity and reliability and their ease of administration. We have created a mystique surrounding many tests of basic skills because we have the capacity to measure them. However, a central component of efforts to define a more comprehensive candidate-based assessment process is recognition that individual knowledge, skills, attributes, and abilities need to be demonstrated through performance in teaching, in addition to, or in lieu of, completion of coursework or standardized pencil-and-paper tests.

Building such a system is difficult. Although we think we know what good teaching looks like, we do not have a consensus on the complexity of its measurement. How would such a system be organized? First and foremost, it would have both formative and summative components, junctures at which individuals would receive information about their performance and be encouraged either to continue with professional development or to consider an alternative career. Second, a comprehensive teacher assessment system would have multiple measures, rather than one or two tests on which individuals must achieve a designated passing score in order to teach. Third, such a system would inform both teacher education and the credentialing process (Wise et al., 1987).

The California New Teacher Project is examining these issues, many of which are being analyzed in evaluation and assessment work being conducted by the Southwest Regional Educational Laboratory (SWRL) and the Far West Regional Educational Laboratory (FWL). Important work is also being done in Minnesota by the Rand group, as well as by the Connecticut State Department of Education, the states participating in the

Southern Regional Educational Board consortium, and the Interstate New Teacher Assessment and Support Consortium. The challenges of creating a valid and reliable assessment system for licensing beginning teachers are many, particularly when the goal is to ensure that licensed teachers have not only a grasp of the subject matter they will teach, but also the knowledge and skill required to teach effectively (Shulman, 1988; Millman, 1988). Other critical issues that must be addressed in a teacher assessment system include the need to:

- Define the knowledge, skill, and expectations of documenting teaching demonstration in straightforward yet nontrivial ways.
- Provide candidates with adequate opportunities to master the knowledge and skills on the measures prior to licensure assessment.
- Ensure that the assessments themselves do not differentially affect one group of candidates over another.
- Require a combination of measures—for example, site-based, naturalistic observations of teaching along with standardized measures of knowledge and simulations of ability to teach.
- Include a diagnostic component to inform staff development decisions (California State Department of Education, in press).

We can expect individual states to take different approaches to candidate-based assessment for teacher licensure. Reflecting different environments, curricula, instructional priorities, and values in teaching, approaches to licensure assessment will necessarily differ. For instance, in states of any size, performance assessments would necessarily have to be conducted locally because of the cost. Opinion is divided about whether the individuals who provide the staff development support for new teachers can, in an unbiased fashion, also participate in their summative evaluation (Griffin & Millies, 1987). In states like Oklahoma, the new teacher is supported and evaluated by the same people; in other settings, the support and assessment components are kept strictly separate. The current evaluation study in California is experimenting with both approaches. Regardless of who conducts the assessment, states should anticipate an increased cost if performance assessments are to be included: States currently conducting on-site assessments estimate the costs at $500 to $2,600 per teacher (Brooks, 1987).

SUMMARY

Do new teachers need special staff development and assessment assistance during their first year or early years in teaching? If so, what kinds of assistance work best for what kinds of individuals in what kinds of settings?

Can such assistance have an impact on teacher retention, effectiveness, satisfaction, professionalism, and commitment to staff development? Does it truly inform the credentialing process? Should it? How much should new-teacher assessment and support reasonably cost? Who should pay?

These are some of the central questions being asked and answered in evaluations of teacher induction programs around the United States. Extant research suggests that new teachers teach better if they are provided with the resources to teach fewer students; have access to various curricular, instructional, and management resources; and have opportunities to work with one another and with experienced teacher role models (Fox & Singletary, 1986; Schlechty, 1985; Ward, 1988). But should states pay for these services? Are there real benefits of broadening the scope of the licensure assessment, so we are not relying solely on a single standardized measure?

These questions do not lend themselves well to quick answers, as it will take time to track new teacher retention, satisfactions, effectiveness, and commitment to the career. The development of the performance assessments will also be costly and time-consuming as we ensure that they measure performance equitably, without penalizing some candidates. Nevertheless, both the support and the assessment components in these ventures hold real promise. The support components recognize that teachers, like other professionals, need to grow into their role. The assessment components reflect another feature of professionalism—self-monitoring of those who practice the profession. Taken together, new teacher support and assessment can make a real contribution to the development of the profession as a whole. They can do so, however, only if given time and resources to develop, and if the other elements of professionalism—decision-making discretion, competitive compensation, and career opportunity— are also advanced.

REFERENCES

Berliner, D. (1988, June). *Proceedings of the National Governors' Association Symposium on New Teacher Assessment*, Boulder, Colorado.

Boyer, Ernest. (1988). *Teacher involvement in decision-making: A state by state profile.* Washington, DC: Carnegie Foundation.

Brooks, D. M. (Ed.). (1987). *Teacher induction: A new beginning.* Papers from the National Commission on the Induction Process. Reston, VA: Association of Teacher Educators.

Cagampang, H. H., Guthrie, J., & Kirst, M. (1986). Teacher supply and demand in California: Is the reserve pool a realistic source of supply? *Policy Analysis for California Education (PACE).* Berkeley: University of California Press.

California State Department of Education. (In press). *New teachers for California: Proceedings of the 1987–88 Seminar Series*, Sacramento, California.

Darling-Hammond, L., & Wise, A. (1985). Beyond standardization: State standards and school improvement. *Elementary School Journal, 85,* 315–336.

Fox, S. M., & Singletary, T. J. (1986). Deductions about supportive induction. *Journal of Teacher Education, 37,* 12–15.

Goertz, M. (1986). *State educational standards: A 50-state survey.* Princeton, NJ: Educational Testing Service.

Griffin, G. A., & Millies, S. (1987). *The first years of teaching: Background papers and a proposal.* Chicago: University of Illinois at Chicago, in cooperation with the Illinois State Board of Education.

Grissmer, D. W., & Kirby, S. N. (1987). *Teacher attrition: The uphill climb to staff the nation's schools.* Santa Monica, CA: Rand Corporation, Center for the Study of the Teaching Profession.

Guthrie, J. W. (1987). Professionalizing teaching in California. *Policy Analysis for California Education. (PACE)* Berkeley: University of California Press.

Guthrie, J. W., & Kirst, M. W. (1986, 1988). Conditions of education in California. *Policy Analysis For California Education (PACE).* Berkeley: University of California Press.

Hawk, P., & Robards, S. (1987). Statewide teacher induction programs. In D. M. Brooks (Ed.), *Teacher induction: A new beginning.* Papers from the National Commission on the Induction Process. Reston, VA: Association of Teacher Educators.

Hodgkinson, H. L. (1985). *All one system: Demographics of education, kindergarten through graduate school.* Washington, DC: Institute for Educational Leadership.

Kanthak, L. M., & Mitchell, D. E. (1988). *Staff development programs in California.* Far West Laboratory Policy Briefs, No. 7, San Francisco.

Kerchner, C. T., & Mitchell, D. E. (1988). *The changing idea of a teachers' union.* Philadelphia: Falmer.

Krupp, J. A. (1987). Understanding and motivating personnel in the second half of life. *Journal of Education, 169,* 20–46.

Lanier, J., & Little, J. (1986). Teacher education. In M. C. Wittrock (Ed.), *Handbook of research on teaching* (3rd ed.) (pp. 527–569). New York: Macmillan.

Leinhardt, G., & Greeno, J. G. (1986). The cognitive skill of teaching. *Journal of Educational Psychology, 78*(2), 75–95.

Little, J., & Geritz, W. (1987). *Staff development in California: Public and personal investments, program patterns and policy choices.* San Francisco: Far West Laboratory for Educational Research and Development.

McDonald, F. (1980). The problems of beginning teachers: A crisis in training (Vol. 1). *Study of induction programs for beginning teachers.* Princeton, NJ: Educational Testing Service.

McLaughlin, M. W., & Pfeiffer, S. (1988). *Teacher evaluation: Learning for improvement and accountability.* New York: Teachers College Press.

McDonald, M. W., Pfeiffer, S., Swanson-Owens, D., & Yee, S. (1986). Why teachers won't teach. *Phi Delta Kappan, 67,* 420–425.

Millman, J. (1988). *Proceedings of the Interstate Consortium on New Teacher Assessment and Support.* Boulder, CO: Education Commission of the States.

Morey, A., Dean, School of Education, San Diego State University. (1988, July 26). Personal communication, San Diego, California.

Odden, A. (1987). Education reform and services to poor students: Can the two policies be compatible? *Policy Analysis for California Education (PACE)*. Berkeley: University of California Press.

Pecheone, R., Garon, J., Forgione, P., & Abeles, S. (1988). A comprehensive approach to teacher assessment: Examples from math and science. *This year in school science*. Washington, DC: American Association for the Advancement of Science.

Schlechty, P. C. (1985). A framework for evaluating induction into teaching. *Journal of Teacher Education, 36*(1), 37–42.

Shulman, L. S. (1988, September). *Use of portfolios in TAP: Proceedings of Seminar III*. Hartford, CT: Interstate Consortium on New Teacher Assessment and Support.

Ward, B. A. (1986). State and district structures to support initial year of teaching programs. In G. Griffin, (Ed.), *The first years of teaching: Background papers and a proposal* (pp. 1–14). Chicago: Illinois State Board of Education.

Ward, B. A. (1988). *Preliminary findings on an evaluation of new teacher retention program in inner city schools*. Los Angeles: Southwestern Regional Educational Laboratory.

Wise, A. E., et al. (1987, January). *Effective teacher selection: From recruitment to retention*. Santa Monica, CA: Rand Corporation.

Wise, A., Darling-Hammond, L., Berry, B., & Klein, S. (1987). *Licensing teachers: Design for a teaching profession*. Santa Monica, CA: Rand Corporation.

26

The *Conditions* of Teaching: Flexibility and Authority in the Classroom

Reforming the Reform Movement
ALBERT SHANKER

I<small>N ITS</small> S<small>EPTEMBER</small> 1987 issues, the *Phi Delta Kappan* published the eighteenth annual Gallup Poll of the public's attitudes toward public schools. Some of the results were offered as a referendum on the success of the school reform movement that began with the appearance of *A Nation at Risk* in 1983. Did people think that schools had improved in the last five years? The answers were not encouraging. Only one in four questioned thought that education had gotten better.

But even if the public perception were accurate, would that be a fair evaluation of the reform movement? Many changes put in place have been called "reforms," but exactly what is it that they are supposed to achieve? Will we be getting something significantly better or just a spruced-up version of the old system?

What we have mainly seen so far has been a spate of state-level initiatives aimed at tightening up the looseness that crept into our schools in the freewheeling sixties and seventies. The message of this first round of reform was that students would no longer be allowed to graduate without taking solid academic courses. They would no longer be allowed to elect to "study" comic books or TV sitcoms instead of Dickens or Shakespeare. They would also have to measure up on basic competency tests, particularly in arithmetic and reading. Staying power would no longer be the main requirement for graduation; and in some places, even athletes—stars and scrubs alike—would be benched by bad report cards.

A parallel effort was made to shape up the teaching staff. Significant gains were made in salary levels aimed at improving recruitment and retention. In addition, states and communities that had once hired teachers solely on the basis of academic credits decided to try to find out if college diplomas meant anything and if teachers actually knew at least the basics of what they were supposedly trying to teach their students. In some states, veteran as well as beginning teachers were tested—in most cases on basic writing skills and on elementary level reading and arithmetic. Reform often meant demonstrating to taxpayers that they were getting at least some minimum value for their education tax dollar in their school staff.

Legislatures also tightened up the schoolhouse rule book. A wave of increased regulation, sometimes literally in massive tomes, cascaded from state capitals specifying what should be taught and when and from exactly what textbooks. Ironically, school systems, in the name of reform, thus adopted with a vengeance the highly centralized management style that industry was abandoning as reactionary and counter-productive.

Test teachers as well as students. Set tougher graduation and basic competency requirements. Mandate solid and clearly defined curriculums. But what is the likely impact of this "tightening up" process? Certainly it would be an improvement over what we had in 1983. In fact, success of this version of reform would mean going back to "the good old days," to the kind of schools that my generation knew in the forties and early fifties, which served many students quite well. But it also would mean going back to schools that had drop-out rates of up to 70 percent, to a time when a relatively small minority managed to earn a high school diploma, even though family structures were far more supportive than they are today.

Undoubtedly, many able youngsters who have been too casual about their education will respond positively to greater demands, but we can also easily imagine how other kids, who cannot function in the current system, will react to even tougher standards. Tightening the current system probably means a better education for some students but increased frustration and failure for many others who, before reform, might have put in enough seat-time to get a diploma.

A look into the demographic crystal ball reveals other stumbling blocks down the road for efforts to save public education by rejuvenating the current system. Projections for the next five to seven years point to a major turnover in the teaching profession—replacing half of the nation's 2.2 million teachers, at least 200,000 new teachers each year. California alone, according to state education superintendent Bill Honig, will have to find at least 100,000 new teachers in the next five years. Putting it another way, just to retain current staff levels, our schools will have to recruit and retain about 23 percent of each college graduating class for the next seven years! Is it reasonable or even desirable to expect that one institution in our society should be able to secure such a huge share of the nation's talent pool?

But the question is moot because nowhere near that number of undergraduates show an interest in teaching. Back in 1983, only 4 percent of all college students said that they were preparing to become teachers. This year, after all the reform measures and publicity about improving our schools, this figure had risen to 6 percent, hardly within shouting range of the target number that our schools need. The picture looks even bleaker when we consider that the avowed aim of many reformers is to staff our schools with only the most highly qualified talent, which means that we would be faced with the hopeless task of recruiting close to half of the top half of every year's graduating class.

But how on earth did we manage to staff our schools in the good old days? Might the current reform movement learn something from the tactics of the past? The truth is that our schools were never very competitive and, over the years, benefited from social problems that often literally forced top-notch talent into the classroom. For example, traditionally, the largest pool of highly qualified personnel for our schools were women, who, for many generations, had few other career options. But a quick glance at the breakdown of college degrees awarded in recent years would show an immense shift of women into fields once closed to them—medicine, law, accounting, management, and computer technology. In the 1984–85 academic year, for example, 105,319 women received bachelor's degrees in business and management compared to 66,897 in education. This breakdown of economic and professional barriers has been a boon to women but a disaster for our schools.

Our schools gained another windfall from the great depression of the 1930s. Widespread unemployment made teaching attractive to many of the best and brightest. Competition for jobs—any job—was intense; as the hard times dragged on, many of the most highly qualified candidates waited years for an appointment and, when it came, eagerly accepted it. Schools were in the rare position of being able to pick and choose.

Years later, the selective service system provided another source of teaching talent. Many able young men were excused from military service by offering to teach in difficult-to-staff schools. They chose to struggle in the classrooms of our crumbling inner cities instead of fighting in the jungles of Vietnam.

But selective service has ended; there are many other career opportunities for educated people, and the economic and social barriers that once existed for women have been removed. Our schools will no longer get a "leg up" in recruitment from social problems. Perhaps for the first time in their history, they will have to face other employers in head-on competition for the available talent.

We need to ask ourselves how successful our reform initiatives will be in helping our schools meet this challenge. Consider the traditional strategies that employers use to recruit and retain staff. The first rule of the game, if you want top-level personnel, is to offer competitive salaries, equal to or more than the person you want to hire could get somewhere else. According to a recent national survey, "the average teacher *with a master's degree and 15 years' experience* (my emphasis) now makes $26,704" a year. This, remember, is the level achieved after five years of reform effort. In the decade before *A Nation at Risk*, teachers' salaries actually declined in terms of purchasing power.

Furthermore, are computer companies and accounting firms around the country promising new recruits fresh out of college (with a B.A., not an M.A.) that they'll be able to make over $26,000 in fifteen years? More likely, they're offering top candidates close to that or more as a starting salary.

Our schools need to add several thousand dollars to each teacher's salary to begin to bridge the gap between the education "industry" and the private sector. However, it takes only quick calculations to demonstrate that this is not likely to happen. Since we have 2.2 million teachers, every thousand dollar increase means a $2.2 billion increase in the nationwide education budget. If we took an average competitive professional salary to be about $35,000, and added pension and social security costs, we would face a staggering $30 billion beyond what we now spend for education. The largest federal education program, Chapter 1, has an annual budget of about $3 billion. Therefore, when we speak of increases to make teachers' salaries competitive with other professions, we're talking about a huge sum that is unlikely to be allocated to just one item in the overall education budget.

But even with substantial salary increases, schools will find it difficult to compete with the private sector, particularly in shortage areas like math and science. It's unlikely that corporate giants will allow themselves to come up short in the scramble for chemists, physicists, and computer experts. An illustration comes from the recent news report that business schools of prestigious universities were finding it difficult to fill all openings as faculty members hired in the 1950s retired, given the recruiting among both new college graduates and faculty by banks and other financial organizations.

Here's the bottom line: Though the reform movement has brought about significant and long-delayed improvements in teachers' salaries, it is unlikely that the new levels alone will offer sufficient incentives to enable us to restaff our schools as they are now structured with the caliber and quantity of candidates that we need for the twenty-first century.

But what if our schools significantly improve working conditions as well as raise salaries? Of course, a great deal can be done in this area, which, inevitably, brings us back to money. School plants in many places need to be repaired, cleaned up, and made into civilized workplaces. Supplies need to be provided in sufficient quality and quantity. Teachers shouldn't continue to subsidize school systems out of their own pockets by supporting underfunded (or, more likely, nonfunded) programs or by making up the shortfall of basic equipment and supplies.

The magnitude of the problem can be seen by looking at the item near the top of almost every teacher's personal agenda for change—class size. We've generally agreed that we don't want our youngsters to graduate from high school just knowing how to take multiple-choice tests, proficient only in filling in the right box or in checking the right square. We want them to be able to think, to evaluate information, to be able to express themselves with fluency and clarity, to be able to defend a point of view with cogency and force. But these skills can only be acquired by frequent writing—not just by putting words on paper but by writing and rewriting with extensive and thoughtful feedback from teachers who have the time to read and reflect on their students' work, who do individual coaching to clarify thoughts and suggest alternate ways to express and support ideas.

But what's the real world like? The average high school teacher has five classes a day with 30 to 35 students in each—a total of at least 150 papers to read and grade for each writing assignment. If he or she spends just five minutes reading each paper and another five minutes making comments, the total time expended adds up to at least 25 hours of work—for one assignment! Added to the enormous amount of normal preparation time needed for daily lessons, an effective, continuing writing program is simply impossible.

Any reduction in class size would be welcome, but a 20 percent cut applied to the example above would still mean 20 hours of work instead of 25 for each writing assignment, a significant decline but still a crushing burden. And, remember, we're still talking about *minimum* time on task. How much would it take to do an optimum job? In short, a substantial reform of class size would still leave us with slightly better but essentially not very good working conditions, and, most important, probably no significant change in education quality.

Again, arithmetic is fate. The numbers just don't add up for such an improvement. A 20 percent cut in class size would mean an equal increase in staff and education budget—a huge and utterly unrealistic increase for one item. And if, by some magic, the money were there, it is unlikely that we could begin to find that number of extra teachers because of the demographic facts of life I have already pointed out. The traditional reform approach won't even be able to recreate the "good" schools of the past.

Though a great deal of the tightening up so far has been a welcome corrective to the excesses of the recent past, it also has reinforced some of the worst characteristics of our education system. In the name of reform, we've had strengthened bureaucracies empowered to enforce rigid curriculums and mandated basic skills tests, which, in the classroom, translates into more of what we've had before—lots of drill work and rote information processing from the teachers' lessons to the students' notebook and on to the periodic test.

Last spring, the *Washington Post* (May 4, 1987) reported the impact of "reform" in action, the implementation of a new systemwide basic skills test in the District of Columbia's schools. In a junior high school, students in the grades to be tested spent time "every school day since September" preparing for the exam," and, weeks before the test date, they "slogged through worn copies of the old test, answering multiple-choice questions on spelling, science, arithmetic and the always-knotty reading passages."

Call it reform, but it's suspiciously like the old system intensified, with a cramped and circumscribed vision of education. The system that many people are trying to spruce up in the name of reform locks our schools into well-worn paths of mediocrity and failure for far too many of our young people. It's a system that those with an eye exclusively on basic skills test scores can live with. Significantly, however, according to the Gallup poll that I referred to earlier, the greatest disapproval of the changes of the last five years came from inner-city, minority parents, whose children have been the most poorly educated. Perhaps the message is that many parents see the crucial difference between cosmetic change and real reform.

There's no doubt that we can improve basic skills test scores with large doses of student prepping and sufficient fudging of statistics. But exactly what will we thereby accomplish? Will young people have been engaged in their own education so that they're motivated and able to learn on their own? Will they have developed analytical powers to come to grips with important ideas? Will they have acquired the power of verbal and written communication so that they can express themselves with clarity and cogency? The truth is that these are not the usual by-products of an education in multiple-choice, test-taking strategies.

But there's another reform movement with another vision gaining momentum throughout the country. In an already much-quoted passage, the landmark Carnegie report, *A Nation Prepared* (1986), spoke of the need to educate "the vast majority" of our students "with achievement levels long thought possible for only the privileged few." It's an awesome challenge, but our national survival is at issue. And it's clearly a challenge that cannot be met by trying, like some of our reformers, to fine-tune the current system that regularly fails to reach anywhere from 40 to 60 percent of our young people.

Though there are models here and there that can teach us some valuable lessons about how to proceed, the reforms that we need largely involve moving into uncharted territory. The time is ripe for bold departures. But whatever is done needs to be based on several fundamental principles:

1. Schools must be restructured to give teachers the greatest possible flexibility in matching the student with the appropriate learning experience. We can't continue to expect the vast majority of pupils to do their best while spending most of their school time passively listening to an adult talk at them. Our drop-out and failure rates are proof of this. Students need to be directly and actively engaged in their own education—in small groups, in individual projects, in peer tutoring, and in one-on-one coaching sessions with teachers where written work can be effectively critiqued. We also need to break down the rigidity of our academic calendar. Some students who lack the discipline to tackle a whole semester's work might find success in mini-courses. Perhaps all five-year-olds are not ready for school in September. Some might do better if they started with another group in November or January and didn't have to compete with students who might be as much as eight to ten months older.

2. This increased flexibility needs to be complemented by a vastly expanded use of technology. Blackboard and chalk may be basic, but they can't be the end-all of our teaching tools as they are in too many of our classrooms. It's foolish for a teacher to lecture on the flora and fauna of the Galapagos Islands when the material can be more vividly and effectively presented by film or videotape. Computers may have been oversold in some areas, but we still haven't begun to tap the full potential of their real use in individualized learning.

3. We must solve the crisis in staffing our schools. In a recent report, Rand Corporation researchers warned that teacher attrition rates may soon reach their highest levels in 25 years. As I've argued, traditional strategies won't be able to cope with the magnitude of the problem. We need professional-level salaries as well as professional workplaces. As of now, the responsibilities of the 30-year veteran are exactly the same as those of the first-year beginner. There's almost no way to grow within the profession. We can't expect to recruit top-notch candidates to go into our classrooms unless we offer them the challenge and opportunity to exercise their creativity and judgment, the chance to control their working lives, the stimulation of frequent exchanges with their peers and a sense of being part of a vital intellectual community.

4. Such options will be possible, not only with a flexible school structure, but with an extensive and varied support staff. In a restructured school, teachers will need to be able to call on paraprofessionals, undergraduate "interns," and/or peer tutors. Our schools will need to form alliances with private industry that can "lend-out" short-term staff, particularly in such shortage areas as math and the sciences. We will have to explore a variety of staffing strategies if we want to break away from the rigidity of the prevailing system.

School improvement has been near the top of the national agenda for nearly five years with widespread support at all levels of society. But the latest Gallup poll should serve as a warning that the patience of the taxpayer has its limits. Most citizens are not impressed with what has been done in the name of reform. Attempting to fulfill our aspirations within the present structure can only lead to further disillusionment and perhaps, ultimately, to the abandonment of our current system of public education.

But a second wave of reform with far-reaching, revolutionary implications and vast potential has already begun. Communities like Rochester, New York; Hammond, Indiana; Toledo, Ohio; and Dade County, Florida, have taken the first bold strides to restructure the teaching profession and remake our schools. Second-wave measures are not panaceas. We will see mistakes and false starts. But such measures are thoughtful challenges to the old rules and restraints. They are not commitments to bringing back the dubious good old days but commitments to creating something that we've never had before—schools that work for all our children.

27

Creative Teaching: Evaluating the Learning *Process* Instead of Just the *Outcome*

Inspired Teaching: The Missing Element in "Effective Schools"
GARY SYKES

Hᴇʀᴇ ɪs ᴀ ᴘᴜᴢᴢʟᴇ. In almost every recent account of "good" or "successful" or "effective" schools, the observer or analyst eventually admits that whatever else is going on, the quality of teaching is unremarkable. Drop-out rates may be down, test scores up, kids, teachers, and parents satisfied, but the teaching itself most often appears flat, unimaginative, and uniform. There are exceptions to be sure, but whether the observer is Sara Lightfoot (1983), Joan Lipsitz (1984), Theodore Sizer (1984), or Michael Rutter et al. (1979), there comes a point when each reluctantly comments on the teaching itself. The schools they visit may be good, the principals dynamic, the curriculums rich, the culture strong, the expectations high, but . . .

But the teaching does not stand out.

Large-scale studies of schooling tend to confirm the impressions of these and other observers. John Goodlad's 1984 study, for example, contains dispiriting evidence drawn from a large sample of schools. Both Goodlad and Kenneth Sirotnik (1983) found at elementary and secondary levels, and with little variation across or within schools that,

- teachers "outtalk" students by a 3:1 ratio;
- teachers provide little corrective feedback to students;
- teachers devote little time to questioning of any sort and almost no time to open questions that call for complex cognitive and emotional responses;
- whole-class instruction predominates, with almost no independent, small-group, or cooperative work by students;
- emotions rarely appear in classrooms;
- there is little praise, enthusiasm, or intensity of any sort. Classrooms are emotionally neutral, affectless places.

Summarizing this data, Sirotnik writes,

> Consider again the model classroom picture presented here: a lot of teacher talk and a lot of student listening, unless students are responding to teachers' questions or working on written assignments; almost invariably closed and factual questions; little corrective feedback and no guidance; and predominantly total class instructional configurations and traditional activities—all in a virtually affectless environment. It is but a short inferential leap to suggest that we are implicitly teaching dependence upon authority; linear thinking; social apathy; passive involvement, and hand-off learning. This so-called "hidden curriculum" is disturbingly apparent. (p. 29)

Now place this description next to an observation: The "effective schools" research from which factors for school management are derived is entirely silent on the question of teaching. The emphasis is on "instructional leadership," high expectations, clear objectives, test–curriculum alignment, coordination of instruction, and the like. These are all crucially important matters, but I want to point out that there is no conception within this literature of what constitutes good teaching or good learning.

Here, then, is our situation. We identify successful schools within which much teaching is pedestrian and uninspired. And we create a management literature on schooling that leaves out the core activity of the organization. Does this strike anyone as peculiar?

This tendency has a parallel within the literature on teaching itself. There the emphasis rests on classroom management and on generic teaching skills that tend to ignore subject matter and responsiveness to individual students. What seems peculiar from one angle, however, is quite understandable from another. These approaches serve well the needs and interests of school administrators and school teachers respectively. Both have strong needs for predictability and control in their work environments.

Teachers daily confront dozens of fractious students all of whom may not be fascinated with the school curriculum. The first and continuing imperative of teaching is to establish and maintain an orderly classroom—to set up rules and routines that support predictable patterns of behavior. Only within an orderly environment can teaching proceed. The enemy is disruption, and the precious resource is time. Teachers seize on methods that increase their efficiency in managing students in large groups.

School principals likewise are under pressure to produce. They are responsible for aggregate results—test scores, drop-out rates, advanced placement, college attendance, and school climate. They must ensure that instruction is coordinated across grade levels and that what is tested corresponds to what is taught. But their span of control is long, and they are generalists managing the work of specialists. They have neither the time nor the expertise to monitor the work of individual teachers. They require broad and efficient control strategies to manage the work of the organization. The effective schools research provides a cognitive map of schooling that directs attention to a manageable set of factors. Not surprisingly, then, the most popular and prevalent approaches to school improvement help solve the most pressing problems faced by teachers and administrators.

Is there a problem here? If these approaches result in orderly classrooms and higher test scores, do we care what the teaching looks like? I want to make the case that the quality of teaching does matter, that the evidence of a uniform, beige pedagogy is worrisome, and that approaches to school management that ignore teaching quality are inadequate.

My argument concerns the nature of means and ends in education, the relation of teaching to learning. The twin claims are that, in practice,

- we cannot justify teaching solely on the basis of its outcomes; but,
- we cannot justify teaching absent *some* evidence that it has produced a desirable outcome.

These assertions have significance for how we evaluate teaching, how we manage schools, and how we seek to improve them. But each claim first requires some defense.

Consider the case of a teacher or a school principal who seeks credit for improvements on test scores or other educational outcome indicators. Without the opportunity to judge the means used, we cannot give a whole-hearted endorsement. Any educational acts, methods, or systems have multiple consequences for students; not all of them can be measured simply and accurately. Teachers must consider the social effects of their instructional strategies, must balance what is good for the individual with what is necessary in the group, must provide opportunities to acquire basic skills, cultural literacy, *and* higher-order thinking, must attend to the emotional lives of students, and must create a learning community that teaches civic virtues—tolerance, fairness, justice, and empathy.

Teaching is a complex activity that requires constant decision making about means and ends. Judging teaching largely on one or two outcomes ignores too much of to what ends teachers must attend, while avoiding necessary judgments about means. An unrelieved diet of drilling on test-related exercises, for example, might produce higher scores but quench the spirit of learning.

There is a further complication. Teachers must worry not only about what kinds of learning occur, and how much, but also about *who* learns. Teaching inevitably must distribute opportunities to learn, but attention to aggregate outcomes often conceals distributional effects. Averages may rise, but not all students benefit equally. Those at the bottom of the distribution may be learning little. Pressures to produce results may impel teachers to concentrate on students most likely to learn, not on those most in need of special attention.

Ends cannot justify means in education because the interplay of means and ends is so complex. But as a practical matter, we must evaluate teaching on the basis of results because teaching is an instrumental activity aimed at producing learning. We would find it peculiar if a principal or teacher claimed to be doing wonderful things with children but was indifferent to their learning and could produce no evidence of it. This seems self-evident in a results-oriented culture such as ours, yet in two respects this perspective on teaching may be shortsighted.

First, state-of-the-art practice in a field may not guarantee results because knowledge connecting means to ends is imperfect and incomplete. Incompetence in the form of incorrect decisions and inadequate skill may produce poor results, but poor results may also be caused by lack of knowledge and an inability to control important contingencies affecting the outcome. In these latter cases, the practitioner cannot be held responsible. The brain surgeon may rightfully claim that the operation was a "success" (i.e., that the decision to operate was justified and that he or she skillfully employed the latest techniques) even though the patient died. Standards for best practice based on professional judgment are necessary even if they cannot guarantee results. With respect to such standards, a judgment about the practice becomes the appropriate measure, not reference to results alone.

Second, there are valued human activities in which we treat the outcome as incidental, concentrating instead on the quality of experience within the activity itself. Play is the classic example. Play fosters human growth and development, but that is not its raison d'être. Children and adults engage in play for the intrinsic pleasure of the experience. John Dewey reminds us that we must not sacrifice the playful aspects of learning to results-oriented methods. Must education have an aim? asked fellow philosopher R. S. Peters, and he thought not.

Other philosophers have disagreed, but Dewey's thought is valuable in returning us to the immediacies of experience. We do care that schools and classrooms be humane and welcoming, and that school life be joyful, meaningful, and fulfilling. After all, children attend by law; they have no choice. Educators have a basic responsibility to provide for school *lives* as well as for school *learning*. Here as elsewhere, Dewey sought to overcome dichotomy and dualism: Within pleasurable activity, the distinction between work and play dissolves; such solvent experience, he argued, is the ideal toward which education should tend.

But we also care about how school experiences live on in children and with what consequences for their future lives. If we rely on rational-technical modes to pursue knowledge and skill, we can pursue other purposes only through mutual engagement with children in pleasurable and interesting activities. We cherish and seek to nourish such qualities as curiosity, creativity, and love of learning. But as the saying goes, these dispositions are "caught, not taught." Teachers convey and exemplify such qualities as much through their personhood as through their formal lessons. We should not be surprised, then, when research reveals that teachers think about their work in terms of activities, not results. All things considered, this is a wise and sensible orientation to teaching.

To judge teaching solely by its results is a mistake, yet results serve as teaching's anchor and compass. Teachers sail a sea of intense, vivid experiences with children. Their workdays and lives are emotionally demanding and fraught with uncertainty. A teacher's aims and objectives, purposes, and intentions help direct his or her planning. A teacher's actual achievements, in the form of systematic and anecdotal evidence of student learning, help to modify and guide subsequent teaching.

Return now to the original puzzle, the relative absence of inspired and adventuresome teaching in our schools. Historians (e.g., Cuban, 1984; Cohen, 1987) have explored why this should be the case, indicating a range of factors. But I want to suggest that a contributing reason is a preoccupation with the results of instruction and a corresponding lack of attention to teaching itself. At first glance, this appears a peculiar indictment. After all, the point of teaching is to produce learning.

Recall, though, the arguments just made. As a practical matter we cannot ground judgments about teaching in results alone because we cannot fully specify nor accurately measure the outcomes of teaching, nor can we compare in a common scale of value the learning costs and benefits of particular strategies of instruction. As a professional matter, we can only employ best practices that reflect the current state of knowledge, however imperfect. And as a philosophical matter, we must value teaching for its intrinsic qualities, its contribution to communities of learning and to the lives of children.

The import of this argument is not that we should abandon testing and other devices to assess the outcomes of teaching. But standardized testing leads to standardized teaching, which cannot be healthy for children's growth and development. The implication is, rather, that we must fashion a public, appreciative framework for educational quality that conjoins attention to results with attention to teaching itself. We must begin to develop ways and means, process and language, to directly assess the quality of teaching and to persuade important publics that such methods are necessary and legitimate.

I propose that we supplement the prevailing emphasis on management by results with the creation of professional subcultures within schools based on *norms of conduct* and *standards of practice.* By norms of conduct I mean a range of moral and aesthetic judgments governing the role responsibilities of teachers. By standards of practice I mean the technical and procedural rules and guidelines that direct instruction. Such norms and standards can rise only out of dialogue and reflection based on the close observation of teaching. To create such norms and standards will require changes in what the public regards as evidence of good schools, in how administrators approach the management of teaching, and in the responsibilities teachers assume.

These are not minor adjustments. They will require time, inventiveness, and the conviction that it is necessary to move in a new direction toward schools that value teaching in explicit and thorough-going ways. Three questions that I can only begin to explore serve as starting points:

- What should be the form and substance of norms and standards for teaching?
- Through what practices should teachers and administrators begin to develop explicit norms and standards?
- What structural arrangements are necessary to support such practices?

Administrators have a crucial role both in interpreting teaching to the public and in creating professional subcultures that in turn generate norms and standards. Goals, results, and planning are the traditional tools of management, but these are insufficient. School administrators must also establish expectations and provide resources for frequent, regular observation of teaching by teachers, for ongoing deliberation about teaching, curriculum, evaluation, and learning, and for teacher writing about these matters. Teachers should regularly engage in the production of curricular materials and in critique of each others' handiwork. There should be video and audio tape equipment throughout schools, not only for student lessons, but to assist in the assessment of teaching itself.

Unlike many other professions, teaching leaves few traces: no precedents and decisions, no medical write-ups, no architectural or engineering feats. Consequently, there are few traditions of critical reflection on teaching, few codifications of the wisdom of practice. The starting point for an appreciation of teaching must be with the activity itself, but this means making teaching visible and accessible.

In every school, all teachers should spend some of their time trying out new practices, and some teachers should spend all of their time this way. This should be one hallmark of a teaching culture in schools, a commitment to practical inquiry and experimentation. We are not approaching that millennium in education when teachers may rely on settled practices and standard technologies in their work. They must become involved in efforts to invent new practices, to develop new materials, and to study children's development in collaboration with colleagues and with the support of administrators.

Teaching cultures need not be unique to individual schools, however. Promising programs and practices originate in many locales and should be available for scrutiny and trial. It must become a professional responsibility to stay abreast of developments in the field, to identify and try out approaches and materials developed elsewhere. Administrators should encourage and provide opportunity for teachers to identify and evaluate new materials, instructional strategies, and programs.

Creative teaching is risky. Opening teaching to scrutiny is risky. And innovation is risky. Teachers must experiment with activities unfamiliar to themselves and to their students. They must open their classrooms to observation and learn to become articulate about their practice. And they must reckon the costs of increased experimentation, collegiality, and openness. Departures from the norm may provoke uneasiness among students, may cause disruptions, may threaten a teacher's control, may provoke disapproval from other teachers and administrators. Consequently, adventuresome teaching must be explicitly encouraged, rewarded, even expected, because powerful tendencies within schools press toward routine practices. Trust is critically important as is understanding within the community. Teachers cannot heedlessly experiment with children; they must approach new practices responsibly and inform and educate parents about their work.

There are a number of structural arrangements that might support norms of collegiality, experimentation, and deliberation, and practices of observation, constructive criticism, and development. A supervised induction for new teachers provides a valuable occasion for clarifying and transmitting norms and standards. Formal residencies can include requirements to demonstrate skill in employing a range of instructional techniques, including, for example, simulations, small group work, collaborative goal structures, discovery learning, and other innovative approaches. Regular classroom observation would be necessary as well, with mentor teachers taking on such responsibilities. Such residencies have value, not only for inducting newcomers, but for encouraging experienced teachers to become explicit about teaching practice.

A related structural support is the opportunity for teachers to assume advanced roles and responsibilities within schools. There must be ways to recognize teacher experience and expertise and to involve teachers in a variety of professional and leadership roles within schools. Such arrangements are already underway in many states and districts, going by names such as *career ladders, differentiated staffing,* and *mentor, master,* or *lead teachers.* These experiments are valuable but begin to suggest dangers in introducing bureaucratic ranks into the teaching profession. In the future, I believe light formalization will best serve, with teachers rotating through positions that are not permanent. Again, this approach requires skillful and flexible management to create such opportunities and to welcome the emergence of teacher leadership rather than regard it as a threat to management prerogatives.

A third promising arrangement is some form of association between schools and universities to create clinical settings for teacher education, to encourage collaborative inquiry, to establish status-enhancing adjunct positions for master teachers, and to join theory to practice in creating teaching norms and standards.

These suggestions regarding structure, practices, and the content of standards can only begin to suggest practical steps toward schools that value inspired teaching. Most of us believe that great teachers are "naturals"—gifted individuals born to be teachers. We think of a Marva Collins, a Sylvia Ashton-Warner. There are such people, to be sure, but we can systematically cultivate adventuresome teaching among many more teachers if we so choose. Phillip Schlechty is fond of saying that teachers know what is *expected* by what is *inspected* and what is *respected*. We have tended to inspect results alone and have failed to respect superb teaching. I can only hope that, in the future, one distinguishing characteristic of "successful" schools will be the presence of strong teaching—passionate, inspired, creative, idiosyncratic—nurtured within a strong professional subculture that takes pride in explicit norms and standards for teaching.

REFERENCES

Cohen, D. K. (1987). Educational technology, policy, and practice. *Educational Evaluation and Policy Analysis, 9*(2), 153–170.

Cuban, L. (1984). *How teachers taught.* New York: Longman.

Goodlad, J. (1984). *A place called school: Prospects for the future.* New York: McGraw-Hill.

Lightfoot, S. L. (1983). *The good high school.* New York: Basic Books.

Lipsitz, J. (1984). *Successful schools for young adolescents.* New Brunswick: Transaction Books.

Rutter, M., Maugham, R., Mortimore, P., & Ouston, J. (1979). *Fifteen thousand hours.* Cambridge, MA: Harvard University Press.

Sirotnik, K. (1983). What you see is what you get: Consistency, persistency, and mediocrity in classrooms. *Harvard Education Review, 53*(1), 16–31.

Sizer, T. (1984). *Horace's compromise.* Boston: Houghton Mifflin.

28

What to Do with
Problem Teachers

Managerial Responses to
Poor Performance
EDWIN M. BRIDGES

P OOR PERFORMANCE IS a problem facing all organizations and all professions, including the teaching profession. In a study of the Fortune 500 companies, the flagships of American business and industry, 97 percent of the administrators responding to a recent survey indicated that they were currently supervising an ineffective subordinate (Stoeberl & Schnied-erjans, 1981). This problem is felt at all levels of management in these companies and is on the increase. Doctors and lawyers, as well as industrial chiefs, have incompetents in their midst. Malpractice suits plague the medical profession (King, 1977), and lawyers are charged with ineffectively representing their clients (Burger, 1968; Finer, 1973). Poor performers are also to be found in the nation's classrooms, and the number of students who are being taught by these ineffective teachers exceeds the total combined public school enrollments of our 14 smallest states (Bridges, 1986). Clearly, incompetence is a pervasive and serious problem.

Educational reformers, whether from the first or the second wave, offer solutions to this problem that reflect little, if any, first-hand understanding of the realities of the workplace. These reformers are oblivious to the universal nature of the problem and are ignorant of how educational administrators actually deal with poor performers. Accordingly, the recommendations of these reformers rest more on conviction and philosophical persuasion than on a careful study of what is happening and why.

Unlike those of these first- and second-wave reformers, my diagnosis and prescription are based on a five-year study of how school administrators actually deal with the problem of poor performance in the classroom. Moreover, my treatment of the problem centers on the inner workings of local school districts and attempts to reach a level of concreteness generally missing in both the first and the second wave of educational reforms.

With this context in mind, let us now examine in somewhat greater detail how administrators in educational institutions deal with ineffective teachers. Managerial responses fall into two general classes: *tolerance,* the more common response, and *confrontation.* Within each class there are several different responses to the poor performer; these various responses are arrayed along the continuum depicted in Figure 28.1. As we shall see, these managerial responses seldom lead to improvement in the ineffective teacher's performance; the underlying reasons for this lack of improvement suggest an organizational response that offers the possibility for greater success.

TOLERATING THE POOR PERFORMER

School administrators exhibit their inclination to tolerate the ineffective teacher's performance in five ways. They may *ignore* what is happening

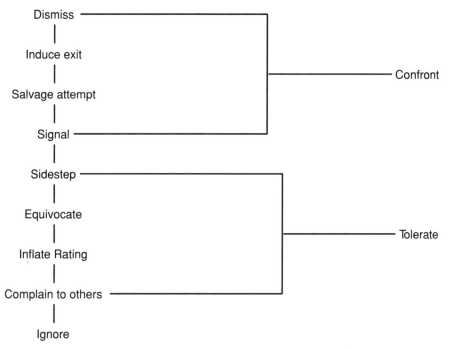

Figure 28.1   Steps in Tolerating and Confronting the Poor Performer

The discussion of "Tolerating the Poor Performer" is a summary of the research reported in *The Incompetent Teacher* (Bridges, 1986).

by looking the other way or by convincing themselves that the problem is not really that serious. Alternatively, administrators may *complain* to significant others (e.g., friends, colleagues, or superiors) that the teacher really does not belong in the classroom; griping becomes a substitute for forthright action. Despite the complaints and the recognition that a problem exists, the administrator may *inflate the rating* of the poor performer in the mistaken belief that this action will act as positive reinforcement and thereby improve the teacher's performance. When this response fails, the administrator begins to *equivocate* by using double-talk, a form of verbal Novocaine, to deaden the sting of criticism.

If the problem persists and parents start to complain vehemently about what is happening to their children, administrators seek ways to *sidestep* the problems created by these parental complaints (Bridges, 1986). In an effort to skirt these problems and to shield the teacher from parental criticism, school administrators use several types of escape hatches. Transferring the teacher to another school is a favorite escape hatch. When trying to find a new home for the poor performer, administrators look for schools where parents are unlikely to complain, schools attended by minority children and those of low socioeconomic status. School administrators refer to this practice as "the dance of the lemons." Another escape hatch is a teaching assignment that removes the teacher from continuing contact with the same group of students (e.g., as a roving substitute or a member of the home-teaching staff). A third type of escape hatch entails reassignment of the poor performer to a nonteaching position (e.g., school bus driver, custodian, or clerk). Sidestepping, ignoring, complaining, inflating evaluations, and equivocating all represent tolerant responses because they share a common feature—failure to confront teachers about their poor performance in the classroom.

CONFRONTING THE POOR PERFORMER

If these various escape hatches are closed and administrators are unable to use them to sidestep the problems created by the poor performer, they will confront the teacher about his or her difficulties in the classroom. When administrators decide to confront the poor performer, their actions usually progress through the following stages (Bridges, 1986). First, the administrator *signals* that a problem exists by formally issuing a rating of "needs to improve" or "unsatisfactory." This signal is generally accompanied by an attempt to *salvage* the teacher. These salvage attempts involve a period of unmuted criticism, where straight talk replaces double talk and equivocation. In addition, the administrator spells out what the teacher must do to improve his or her performance and provides the teacher with limited assistance to overcome the deficiencies that have been noted. This assistance typically includes opportunities to visit the classes of exceptional teachers and to attend workshops on a variety of topics, such as assertive discipline.

When the salvage attempt fails, administrators turn their attention to how to get rid of the poor performer. The way administrators choose to attain this goal depends on the employment status of the teacher. If the teacher has tenure, what the Chinese call the "iron rice bowl," administrators are inclined to *induce* the teacher to resign or to request an early retirement.

These induced exits typically involve four distinctive actions by administrators (Bridges, 1986). First, they exert a great deal of pressure on the teacher by increasing the flow of negative communications, using threat and intimidation, issuing formal notices of deficiency, and declaring the intention to institute dismissal proceedings if the teacher does not improve his or her performance. Second, the administrator negotiates with the teacher in an effort to learn what obstacles stand in the way of the teacher's departure and to reach agreement about the terms of the separation. Third, the administrator works behind the scenes to secure the cooperation of the teacher's union in persuading the teacher to leave quietly. This cooperation is forthcoming only after the union has become convinced that the teacher is incompetent and has been treated fairly by the administration. Fourth, the administration offers inducements to the poor performer in exchange for his or her resignation or early retirement. These inducements commonly include one or more of the following: medical coverage for a fixed period of time, employment in the district as a consultant for a period up to five years, a cash settlement, employment as a substitute teacher in the district for 30 to 45 days per year, and paid leave for the remainder of the school year.

If the administration fails to induce the exit or the teacher has probationary status and is not entitled to due process, administrators move toward dismissal. This is an extremely rare event. For example, in the state of California fewer than 0.6 percent of the teachers were dismissed for incompetence over the two-year period spanning September 1, 1982, through the spring of 1984. The vast majority of the teachers who were dismissed did not have tenure. Tenured teachers, by a margin of 20 to 1, were induced to resign, not dismissed.

RESPONSES OF THE POOR PERFORMER

How the poor-performing teacher responds to the administrator depends to a large extent on the way in which the administrator chooses to deal with the problem of poor performance. If the administrator tolerates the substandard performance by ignoring the problem, complaining about it, inflating the poor performer's ratings, or equivocating, the teacher *ignores the problem* simply because he or she believes there is no problem. If administrators decide to sidestep the problem when parental complaints surface, the teacher typically *gripes* about the new assignment and exhibits similar performance problems in a different setting.

When the administrator begins to confront the problem, the teacher reacts quite strongly. Criticism initially begets *denial* that a problem exists. Teachers who finally acknowledge that they are having difficulties *blame* them on circumstances beyond their control—students who do not care, impossible working conditions, and uncooperative parents. In the face of continued criticism, the teacher may *attack* the source of the criticism and accuse administrators of unprofessional conduct, unfairness, and having unreasonable expectations. At the point where the administrator undertakes a salvage attempt, specifies what the teacher should be doing to improve, and prescribes assistance, the teacher's poor performance *persists.* If improvement occurs, it is hardly dramatic, simply enough to avert dismissal for incompetence.

When the teacher's performance fails to improve, the administrator presses for an induced exit or dismissal. Teachers under fire generally *leave;* however, their reactions to what is happening vary. Some are angry and embittered while others are relieved and even grateful for having been extricated from a painful situation. Their reactions depend to an extent on whether they perceive that the administration has made a good-faith attempt to provide assistance and treated them with dignity during the process. As we have seen, relatively few teachers are likely to experience such reactions because fewer than 1 percent a year are dismissed or induced to leave. The net result is a substandard education for more than two million students each year.

THE DIAGNOSIS AND A POSSIBLE CURE

The preceding analysis highlights several major problems. One is the reluctance of administrators to confront poor-performing teachers unless there are numerous complaints from parents, while another is the failure of teachers to improve much, if any, even when they are confronted. Conceivably, both problems stem from the same root—the unwillingness of individuals, whether administrators or teachers, to own the problem and to acknowledge partial, if not full, responsibility for doing something constructive about it. Both parties go to great lengths to find reasons for doing little, if anything, to solve the problem. The cure for this underlying ailment may lie in creating conditions within school organizations that are conducive to admitting that a problem exists and assuming responsibility for solving it.

A starting point for creating these conditions is to define norms within the organization that explicitly underscore the importance of "personal responsibility as the key to professional growth through evaluation." A set of norms that are congruent with this view should be reflected in the philosophy of evaluation and the associated operating procedures. The following example illustrates how the norms of personal responsibility as a key to professional growth through evaluation can be institutionalized within an educational organization.

Philosophy of Teacher Evaluation

Teaching is a noble, but demanding, occupation. In order for teachers to maintain a high level of professional performance under these conditions, they must assume personal responsibility for their own performance, growth, and development. The exercise of this responsibility is admittedly difficult and is likely to occur only when administrators exhibit genuine concern for the teacher's welfare and facilitate the teacher's effort to assume personal responsibility. In those rare instances when an overriding concern for the teacher's welfare runs contrary to the best interests of the school and the students, administrators will assume the responsibility if the teacher is unable or unwilling to do so.

POLICIES AND PROCEDURES

Teacher evaluation is to be implemented in two distinct stages.

Stage 1
During this stage no teacher, except under grossly unusual circumstances, will receive a negative evaluation or a needs-to-improve designation. Moreover, during stage 1 no written record will be kept of what has transpired; the responsibilities of administrators and teachers during this period are as follows.

Administrators. In this stage the administrator is to function as an ally who nudges teachers and facilitates their efforts to assume personal responsibility for their own professional performance, growth, and development. More specifically:

1. The administrator *nudges* by calling problems that the teacher may be having, but may not be recognizing, to the teacher's attention in a casual but friendly manner and offering whatever assistance the teacher deems useful or necessary.
2. The administrator *facilitates* by providing assistance whenever it is feasible to do so. This assistance may take a variety of forms, including (a)

altering the teacher's working conditions, (b) providing access to individuals who are capable and interested in working with the teacher, (c) supplying access to personal counseling for dealing with crisis situations and personal problems, and (d) providing access to therapy for treating specific disorders like alcoholism or drug abuse.

Teachers. During stage 1 the teacher is expected to respond as someone would to an individual who is perceived to be acting in the teacher's best interests. Specifically:

1. The teacher should acknowledge that he or she has a problem for which he or she is fully or partially responsible, to accept the responsibility for (a) understanding what the nature of the problem is; (b) figuring out why it may be occurring; and (c) deciding what should be done to eliminate the problem, including what assistance is desired.
2. The teacher should face reality—that is, confront the possibility that the problem may or may not have been satisfactorily resolved; that the problem, if not resolved, may be serious enough to raise doubts about the wisdom of the teacher's decision to be a teacher; and that the course of action that may be in the best interests of the teacher and the district is for the teacher to pursue another line of work with assistance from the district.

Stage 2
If the problem persists and the situation seriously impairs the school and/or the students, the administrator will assume primary responsibility for dealing with the teacher's problem. However, before entering this stage, the administrator will indicate to the teacher that he or she seems to have reached the point where the teacher must make a choice. Should the teacher be given one more opportunity to exercise responsibility for solving the problem, or should the administrator become more directive in attempting to resolve it? If the teacher chooses to forego the opportunity, the administrator will do one or more of the following in sequential order as the situation warrants: (a) issue a needs-to-improve and/or an unsatisfactory evaluation of the teacher's performance; (b) prescribe a program of remediation; (c) evaluate the teacher to see if sufficient improvement has occurred to warrant continued employment in the district as a teacher; (d) issue a notice of the intent to dismiss if the person does not improve within a specified period of time; and (e) recommend dismissal if the person fails to improve.

CONCLUSION

The responses to unsatisfactory performance in elementary and secondary schools are ineffective. Managers typically tolerate the poor performance.

The poor performers, even when they are confronted, rarely improve; if they do, their performance remains marginal at best. Underlying the ineffective responses of both teachers and administrators is the unwillingness to own the problem and to assume responsibility for solving it. If administrators are to overcome their reluctance to let teachers know when they are in difficulty, and if teachers are to own the problem and seek to solve it, new norms for teacher evaluation must be created. These norms should be grounded in the belief that "personal responsibility is the key to professional growth through evaluation."

On its surface the proposal seems to emphasize the teacher's, not the administrator's, personal responsibility. Such is not the case. Under this proposal, administrators, once they have called a problem to the attention of the teacher, must face the possibility that the teacher's difficulties are due to an unreasonable set of organizational demands, unfavorable working conditions, and insufficient resources. Moreover, the administrator has the responsibility to make a concerted effort to alter these factors.

Implementation of a new philosophy and a set of operating procedures for carrying out teacher evaluation, such as the ones discussed in this proposal, will not be straightforward. As with any organizational change that entails a restructuring of beliefs and behavior, administrators will need to consult with teachers in seeking answers to questions like the following:

1. What conditions need to be present, which are not now, if these changes are to be implemented?
2. What obstacles stand in the way of these changes being implemented? How might we remove these obstacles?
3. If the new philosophy and set of operating procedures were implemented, what do we fear might happen? If these things did happen, how serious would they be? If they are serious, how might we prevent these unwelcome consequences from occurring?

The proper way of judging this proposal for restructuring teacher evaluation to promote personal responsibility is not whether it is flawless, but whether it produces more beneficial and less harmful consequences than current practices. Given the woeful state of what is now happening, the proposal warrants a trial. The risk is small, and the possibility for substantial rewards is great. The two million students who are being shortchanged by the shopworn philosophy and practices of the past deserve a chance for a better fate.

REFERENCES

Bridges, E. (1986). *The incompetent teacher.* New York: Falmer.
Burger, W. (1968, January). A sick profession? *Tulsa Law Journal*, 5:1–12.

Finer, J. (1973, July). Ineffective assistance of counsel. *Cornell Law Review, 58*:1077–1120.

King, J. (1977). *The law of medical malpractice.* St. Paul, MN: West.

Stoeberl, P., & Schniederjans, M. (1981, February). The ineffective subordinate: A management survey. *Personnel Administrator, 26*:72–76.

What Hath Reform Wrought?

Unlike previous units, this one probably raises more questions than it answers. If thinkers and policymakers in education are to make intelligent choices, they need to reflect on the results of the past five years and two waves of reform. Although the mobilization of public interest (and, to a somewhat lesser extent, resources) has been nothing short of impressive, there are a few gaps.

One of the biggest gaps is the lack of empirical evidence that the changes already implemented are having any substantial effect on student learning. In Chapter 29, Koretz asks about the link between the "lax" educational practices of the 1960s and 1970s and the decline in standardized test scores. The other half of that question is whether the new postreform "tautness" has had anything to do with the recent rise in test scores.

One of his more interesting examples concerns the fallacy of assuming that simple rises in aggregate test scores mean better performance. If raising minimum graduation requirements has had the effect of increasing the dropout rate (as some claim), then the absence of test scores for the low-performing dropouts would certainly tend to raise aggregate scores even if the remaining students scored exactly the same as before. In sum, Koretz provides strong arguments that the evaluation issue is not as simple as it may seem, and that we need new and more precise ways of evaluating the success or failure of our educational policies and programs.

This need to take a closer look is supported by Glasman and Glasman (Chapter 30), who take a broader view, asking what role(s) the evaluation process has played in the reform movement. They argue that initially evaluation was instrumental in creating a climate for change. After that, policymakers often used evaluation as a policy instrument for actually effecting change. By mandating that schools be evaluated regularly, states have put evaluation issues under the spotlight.

This process of developing evaluative instruments can go too far, Wise warns, especially if the process is developed to such a degree that judgment is removed from it. In Chapter 31, taking stock of the latest half-decade of reform, Wise asks if reform has rescued schools from, or accelerated their movement toward, a bureaucratized, centralized, hyperrationalized hell. He suggests that it is still an open question whether local administrators and school board members will "decide whether they prefer state-oriented control, with its emphasis on producing standardized results through regulated teaching, or client-oriented control, with its emphasis on meeting the educational needs of student clients through professional teaching." Wise asks questions about the effect that "legislated learning" has on teachers' sense of ethical conflict and guilt. Should they follow the state mandates and "teach to the test," or should they teach what long experience has convinced them is best for their students' long-term development? Such moral dilemmas seem a natural outgrowth of such degrading devices as "teacher-proof" or "administrator-proof" curricula.

Pushing this theme of moral dilemmas even further in Chapter 32, Soltis draws a parallel between the current situation of the reform movement and that of the Catholic Church in the sixteenth century. He suggests that if the changes are to be powerful enough to be lasting, there will have to be a change in the basic mind set about the legitimate role of teachers within our educational system. In other words, reform within the current system is not enough. *Instead, just as there was a reformation in the sixteenth century viewpoint about the absolute authority of the clergy, today we need a* reformation in the way we conceptualize teaching. *Whether or not this is true, Soltis's metaphor is provocative because it spurs us to ask fundamental questions about the role of education in society.*

Indeed, in the concluding chapter, Bacharach expresses the hope that the themes of reform in this book will cause educators and policymakers to engage in some thoughtful reflections about five basic questions:

1. *Who (and at what level) are the important reform actors, and what are their most appropriate roles?*
2. *Should we strive for the same excellent education for everybody, or should we tailor an education to a particular child's needs? Put differently, should we strive for equality of* opportunity *or for equality of* results?
3. *How do we redefine the goals of education to prepare students for the realities of the twenty-first century?*
4. *Should education be distributed in a market fashion, with parents free to choose a "product" for their children, or would this result in more inequality?*
5. *Should we reconceptualize the role of the teacher, and if so, what structural changes are appropriate?*

29
Educational Practices and Test Scores: The Search for the Missing Link

Educational Practices, Trends in Achievement, and the Potential of the Reform Movement
DANIEL KORETZ

Hᴏᴡ ᴍᴜᴄʜ ᴏꜰ ᴀ positive effect can we reasonably expect from recent educational reforms? Many policymakers hold the optimistic expectation that the reforms will create an improvement in performance similar in size and pervasiveness to the test-score decline of the 1960s and 1970s; they see the current nationwide rise in test scores as evidence that such an improvement is already underway. A careful assessment of recent achievement trends, however, suggests taking a far more cautious view of the reform movement's potential and effects to date.

Bad news about the achievement of American students—the sizable decline of test scores in the 1960s and 1970s and the typically mediocre ranking of American performance in international comparisons of achievement—provided much of the impetus for the reform movement. Many educators saw the reforms as well-tailored responses to the underlying causes of this bad news. For example, increases in course work requirements have been a cornerstone of the reform movement (Education Commission of the States, 1985; Goertz, 1986) in part because of the common view—voiced, for example, in *A Nation at Risk* (National Commission on Excellence in Education, 1983)—that lax course work requirements contributed to the test-score decline.

As a logical concomitant, these same educators assume the effectiveness of the reforms. After all, if we can identify and correct the educational factors that were the keys to the decline, is it not reasonable to expect that the result will be an improvement in performance as large and pervasive as the decline? This presumption of effectiveness has been bolstered by the concurrence between the onset of the reform movement and the reversal of the decline in the test scores of high school students. However, this concurrence is largely coincidental.

To assess the reasonableness of this widespread, if often tacit, model of the reforms, it is necessary to answer two distinct questions. First, what is the link between educational practices and the achievement decline of the 1960s and 1970s? Second, what is the connection between the recent wave of reforms and the current widespread rise in test scores?

EDUCATIONAL POLICIES AND THE ACHIEVEMENT DECLINE

Explaining the achievement decline of the 1960s and 1970s has long been something of a cottage industry, and the many posited explanations are remarkably diverse (see, for example, Wharton, 1976). While the commonly cited explanations include many educational factors, they also include a diversity of noneducational factors such as demographic trends, trends in drug use, and trends in exposure to radioactive fallout.

Neither the abundance of posited causes nor the possibility that some causes might be noneducational has had much apparent impact on the reform movement. Much of the debate about reforms appears to be predicated on an implicit view—never empirically substantiated—that a relatively small number of educational factors can account for much of the decline. The warning of the Advisory Panel on the Scholastic Aptitude Test Score Decline (1977) that it is unreasonable to think of the decline as the result of a few causes—or to expect that it could ever be fully explained—has seemingly had little effect on the debate about reform.

A recent assessment of more than two dozen possible causes of the achievement trends (Koretz, 1987) revealed how little basis there is for attributing the achievement decline to a handful of educational variables. Perhaps most important, there is little doubt that a sizable portion of the decline of the 1960s and 1970s stemmed from noneducational causes. Changes in family composition and in the ethnic composition of the school-age population, for example, both made significant contributions to the aggregate drop in test scores. That noneducational causes can be identified should not be surprising given the characteristics of the test score trends. For example, the decline was remarkably pervasive, affecting almost all grades, all subject areas, all regions of the country, students at all levels of achievement, Catholic as well as public schools in the United States, and even Canadian schools. It is difficult to formulate a mix of educational factors that alone would produce such a degree of uniformity.

Second, some of the widely accepted educational explanations of the achievement decline don't weather close scrutiny. For example, while few can argue that course work requirements have indeed been lax in many jurisdictions, state requirements were, in fact, stable between 1974 and 1980 (National Association of Secondary School Principals, 1975, 1980) and therefore could not have contributed directly to the latter half of the decline among senior high students. Similarly, the widely heralded drop in the SAT scores of potential teachers—first noted after 1972—occurred too late to have contributed to the decline. (Earlier changes in these two factors theoretically could have been important; but in both cases, there are no data indicating whether earlier changes occurred.)

It is worth noting—although it is less germane to expectations of the educational reform movement—that some of the noneducational factors often credited in the public debate as contributors to the decline also played little role. The growing proportion of children in single-parent households is a striking example. Although cross-sectional research on this point is inconsistent, some studies indicate that children from such households score significantly below other children in elementary school (Hethering-ton, Camara, & Featherman, 1984; Milne, Myers, Ellman, & Ginsburg, 1983; Scott-Jones, 1984). Even if one accepts those findings, however, the proportion of students directly affected by this change in household composition during the years of declining test scores was so small it could have had only a negligible effect on aggregate test scores nationwide.

Third, data about many of the commonly posited causes of the achievement decline are inadequate or lacking altogether, leaving their possible contributions a matter of speculation. Systematic data about local graduation requirements, for example, are not available, and data about students' attitudes and motivation are sketchy at best.

Finally, the individual contributions of specific factors (both educational and other) to the decline, when they can be gauged at all, generally appear small, relative to the total drop in scores. A decline in homework, for example, is often cited—probably correctly—as a contributor to the decline, but the average time spent on homework by high school seniors declined by less than 10 percent, or about *25 minutes per week*, during the 1970s (Fetters, Brown, & Owings, n.d.). Given research on the impact of homework (e.g., Keith, 1982), we would not expect a 10 percent drop to have a major effect on aggregate scores. Similarly, trends in family composition (particularly, average birth order and the average number of children) have sometimes been cited as especially important determinants of test score trends by the minority of observers who focus on noneducational explanations (for example, Schrag, 1986; Zajonc, 1986). The best studies, however, attribute only 4 percent to 25 percent of the decline in scores to changes in these variables, and even those estimates are almost certainly exaggerated because of inadequate controls for background factors that are strongly confounded with family composition (Koretz, 1987).

EDUCATIONAL POLICIES AND THE RECENT RISE OF TEST SCORES

Many of those concerned about education tacitly assume that known educational factors explain the achievement decline; in contrast, they voice frequently and explicitly the view that such variables explain the subsequent upturn. Secretary Bennett, for example, has for years interpreted changes in average SAT scores as a barometer of the effectiveness of the reform movement. In September 1985, he greeted an announcement of an increase in average SAT scores with the comment: "Bravo! We begin to see here the impact of the reform movement of the past several years" (Richburg, 1985).

The evidence, however, points to a very different conclusion: Whatever effects the reform movement has had—positive or negative—on average test scores, it cannot account for the end of the long decline in scores or the onset of the subsequent rise. Given the time needed to implement reforms, the long duration of schooling, and the cumulative nature of achievement, it is clearly unreasonable to expect the reforms to have large effects on test scores almost immediately after they were formally adopted. Even apart from the inevitable lag between adoption and impact, however, the adoption of the recent reforms occurred years too late to have caused the turnaround in test scores.

Across a wide variety of tests, the decline in test scores generally ended within a few years of the birth cohorts of 1962 and 1963—that is, with the cohorts that entered school in the late 1960s (Koretz, 1986). The improvement in test scores first became apparent in the middle elementary grades in the mid-1970s and slowly moved into the higher grades as these cohorts passed through school. (Trends in performance in the early elementary grades are hard to interpret in this respect because there was

never a significant decline in those grades.) The rise was typically unin-
terrupted thereafter, with each succeeding cohort out-scoring that which
preceded it.[1]

The misconception that the end of the achievement decline was roughly
contemporaneous with the reform movement thus stems from the coin-
cidence that the birth cohort of 1963 reached age 17 (the modal age for
grade 12) in 1980. In keeping with the cohort pattern just described, 1980
was the first time in many years that average SAT scores did not fall; in
1981, SAT scores began an initially erratic rise, and by the time the reform
movement was fully underway, the rise in scores had become unmistakable.[2] If the debate about educational achievement had focused less exclusively on the performance of high school students, the fact that this
concurrence was substantially coincidental would have been apparent.

Relative gains of minority students and certain other low-achieving
groups have recently gained considerable attention, but these too began
too early to have been initiated by the reform movement. Indeed, one of
the most striking and consistent of these trends, the gains of black students
relative to their nonminority peers, appears to have begun at least a half
decade earlier than the overall rise in scores—that is, with the students
who entered school in the early 1960s. Two policy changes that affected
the early schooling of the cohorts of black students responsible for the
initial years of gains, and that could plausibly account for a portion of
the improvement, were the rapid desegregation of the early 1960s and the
implementation of compensatory education programs.[3] Still, a substantial
share of those relative gains remain unexplained.

Not only do some of the causes of the current rise in scores antedate
the reform movement, but some are apparently noneducational as well.
For example, the fertility-related changes in household composition that
contributed to the decline in scores have since reversed direction and probably aided the rise in scores. A decline in certain types of drug use might
have facilitated the rise in scores in the higher grades, although it probably
had no role in the lower grades and occurred too late to have initiated the
rise in the lower grades. A widespread, marked drop in the exposure of
children to environmental lead—apparently an effect of the reduced sale
of leaded gasoline—might also have contributed to the rise in scores (Koretz, 1987, pp. 73–76; detailed analysis of data on exposure and cognitive
effects, but no analysis of test score trends per se, can be found in Environmental Protection Agency, 1986).

PLACING EDUCATIONAL POLICIES AND REFORM
IN PERSPECTIVE

The reform movement is sometimes cast as counterpoint to the supposed
dissolution and foolishness in educational practices of the 1960s and 1970s,

but the data suggest a more temperate appraisal of those decades. One can certainly identify policies of those years that were undesirable or even foolish, and some—for example, a watering-down of secondary school course content—might well have contributed to the achievement decline. Nonetheless, given the timing of test score trends, the cohort pattern shown by the recent rise in scores, and the cumulative nature of achievement, it is also reasonable to look among the policies of those years for factors that helped to raise scores, particularly in the elementary grades and in schools serving certain minority students. It is plausible, for example, that the policies of the 1970s simultaneously helped improve performance in the elementary grades while prolonging the decline in the secondary grades. Moreover, even the undesirable policies of those years can be blamed for only a portion of the achievement decline, since a substantial share of the blame lies with noneducational factors beyond the influence of schools.

More important, the recent achievement trends also suggest that the policy changes of the past few years warrant more cautious appraisal and more modest expectations than they have generated in many quarters. The recent reforms should be seen as an experiment rather than as a well-tailored response to past achievement trends and their causes. If much of the achievement decline really could be attributed to a handful of powerful educational policies contemporaneous with the decline, then it would make sense to reform education by undoing those policies. However, this did not happen. Thus we need other rationales for selecting among policies and setting realistic expectations for them.

If we turned for ideas about educational reform, not to presumptions about what went wrong in the 1960s and 1970s, but rather to research and past experiences with educational innovations, would we arrive at a menu similar to the policy changes of this decade? The answer is, of course, open to debate, but I believe the mix would be substantially different. On the one hand, some elements of the recent reform movement are certainly hard to argue against. There can be little argument, for example, that graduation requirements in many states have been too lax for many students (though the appropriateness of stiffer standards for certain low-achieving students is clearly still arguable). At the same time, copious research casts doubt on some of the central thrusts of the reform movement, such as the reliance on top-down, centrally imposed policy changes, the often uncritical reliance on standardized tests as both an achievement measure and a goad to improved performance, and the use of fixed cutoff scores on tests as gateway criteria (e.g., Fredericksen, 1984; Green, 1981; Madaus, 1985; McLaughlin, 1987; Wise, 1988). Presumptions about the causes of recent achievement trends have allowed some observers to ignore these questions, but in fact, we have no justification for doing so.

Even when research and experience show a particular reform to be desirable, we should usually maintain modest expectations about its potential impact. Decades of research and experience indicate that the aggregate effects of educational changes are typically small compared to the variance of test scores. In addition, simple arithmetic indicates that some of the central reforms should have modest effects. For example, *A Nation at Risk* calls for a new requirement of three years of high school mathematics. This is certainly a reasonable recommendation given the wholesale failure American education has shown in the teaching of mathematics (see, e.g., Koretz, 1986). But how much of an impact should we expect? Nationally representative data (National Center for Education Statistics, 1984) indicate that nearly half of all graduates already exceeded that requirement, and the mean increase in course work required for all students to meet it would be a bit over one semester. In other words, the requirement would add an additional 6 percent to the prior average of 10.4 years of often ineffective mathematics instruction—marginal change, from which it is unreasonable to expect more than a marginal impact.

If the reforms are an experiment and if their effects are debatable and probably modest at best, the need for careful monitoring and evaluation is clear. The fallaciousness of using simple trends in aggregate test scores as a surrogate for evaluation—an error in which the secretary of education has all too many companions—should be obvious. Here again, a careful analysis of test score trends removes a spurious justification for ignoring what has long been known. In addition, analysis of the trends indicates some specific ways in which aggregate trends in scores are likely to be a biased substitute for real evaluation.

In most instances, aggregate trends are likely to offer an overly optimistic estimate of the reforms' effects, for two reasons. First, the fact that scores are rising need not indicate anything at all about the reforms' effects. Given the cohort pattern shown by the current rise in scores, it is likely that scores in the upper grades would have continued rising for several years even in the absence of the reforms, as the cohorts that raised scores in earlier grades move through the secondary grades. Moreover, if gains continued in the lower grades as well, that improvement could reflect the continued influence of the changes underway before the reforms that were responsible for initiating the national rise in scores. Only evidence that trends have been *deflected* upward, not simply continuing the rise, constitutes real evidence that the reforms are working.

Second, given that one of the cornerstones of the reform movement is a vastly increased emphasis on testing, teaching to test will certainly increase. Regardless of whether this change is desirable in terms of instruction, it will almost certainly alter the validity of tests—that is, the relationships between scores and the broader domains of achievement from which tests sample—and will therefore bias assessments of trends upward.

At the same time, simple trends in test scores will provide downwardly biased estimates of educational initiatives in certain circumstances. Perhaps most important, initiatives that succeed in decreasing the dropout rate will deflect test score trends downward, making the package of policies implemented in those jurisdictions seem less effective. In addition, in jurisdictions in which certain demographic trends—such as the growth in the minority share of the school-aged population—are particularly pronounced, trends in test scores will be less favorable than they otherwise would be.

A final and critical uncertainty about the effects of the reform movement concerns its effects on low-achieving students. The question of whether reforms tailored to average students will help low-achieving students and potential dropouts or further discourage them has been frequently and bitterly debated since the reform movement began, but there is little solid evidence available to resolve the issue. The fact that certain minority groups are greatly overrepresented among these students at risk, and that we cannot fully explain their recent gains, underscores the need for caution in addressing this question. If we cannot identify some of the key variables that facilitated their improvement, we should be extremely cautious in designing policy changes lest these gains be eroded rather than augmented. Rather than imposing changes with false certainty about their effects, we need to encourage innovation and experimentation—much of it bottom-up—and meticulously monitor the effects of both centrally imposed reforms and local innovations on the achievement of students at risk of failure.

NOTES

Author's Note: This article reflects work done while I was with the Congressional Budget Office, United States Congress. The opinions expressed here are solely mine, however, and do not represent an official position of the Congressional Budget Office.

1. Despite certain assertions to the contrary, the stability of average SAT scores for the past several years does not contradict this generalization. The proportion of high school graduates taking the SAT has been rising sharply in recent years. This trend probably made the test-taking group less selective and therefore made the trend in average scores considerably less favorable than it would have been in the absence of decreasing selectivity bias (see Koretz, 1987, p. 19).

2. The years given here are school years (that is, the date at school entry in the autumn) and are therefore one year earlier than those used by the College Board and other organizations that focus on the date at graduation.

3. For quantitative estimates of the possible contribution of Title I (now Chapter I) to the relative gains of minority students, see Koretz, 1987, pp. 94–95. These estimates take into account the apparently short duration of Title I's effects but do not consider the possible additional impact of state-sponsored compensatory education programs.

REFERENCES

Advisory Panel on the Scholastic Aptitude Test Score Decline. (1977). *On further examination.* New York: College Entrance Examination Board.

Education Commission of the States. (1985, September). *Changes in minimum high school graduation requirements—1980 to 1985.* Unpublished manuscript.

Environmental Protection Agency. (1986). *Air quality criteria for lead.* Research Triangle Park, NC: EPA, Environmental Criteria and Assessment Office.

Fetters, W., Brown, G. H., & Owings, J. A. (n.d.). *High school seniors: A comparative study of the classes of 1972 and 1980.* Washington, DC: U.S. Department of Education, National Center for Education Statistics.

Fredericksen, N. (1984). The real test bias: Influences of testing on teaching and learning. *American Psychologist, 39*(3), 193–202.

Goertz, M. E. (1986). *State educational standards: A 50-state survey.* Princeton, NJ: Educational Testing Service.

Green, B. F. (1981). A primer of testing. *American Psychologist, 36*(10), 1001–1011.

Hetherington, E. M., Camara, K. A., & Featherman, D. A. (1984). Achievement and intellectual functioning of children in one-parent households. In J. T. Spence (Ed.), *Achievement and achievement motives: Psychological and sociological approaches.* San Francisco: Freeman.

Keith, T. Z. (1982). Time spent on homework and high school grades: A large-sample path analysis. *Journal of Educational Psychology, 74*, 248–253.

Koretz, D. (1986). *Trends in educational achievement.* Washington, DC: Congressional Budget Office.

Koretz, D. (1987). *Educational achievement: Explanations and implications of recent trends.* Washington, DC: Congressional Budget Office.

Madaus, G. F. (1985). Public policy and the testing profession: You've never had it so good? *Educational Measurement: Issues and Practice, 4*(4), 5–11.

McLaughlin, M. (1987). Learning from experience: Lessons from policy implementation. *Educational Evaluation and Policy Analysis, 9*(2), 171–178.

Milne, A., Myers, D., Ellman, F., & Ginsburg, A. (1983). *Single parents, working mothers and the educational achievement of elementary school age children.* Unpublished manuscript. Washington, DC: Decision Resources.

National Association of Secondary School Principals. (1975). *Graduation requirements.* Reston, VA.

National Association of Secondary School Principals. (1980). *Graduation requirements, 1980.* Reston VA.

National Center for Education Statistics. (1984, February). More coursework in the new basics is needed to meet standards of the National Commission of Excellence in Education. *Bulletin.*

National Commission on Excellence in Education. (1983). *A nation risk: The imperative for educational reform.* Washington, DC: U. S. Department of Education.

Richburg, K. (1985, September 24). SAT scores rise for fourth year: Minority students post highest gains in college entrance exam. *Washington Post,* p. A-6.

Scott-Jones, D. (1984). Family influences on cognitive development and school achievement. In E. W. Gordon (Ed.), *Review of research in education.* Vol. 11 (pp. 259–304). Washington, DC: American Educational Research Association.

Schrag, P. (1986, October 4). Why Johnny can't . . . (I): What the test scores really mean. *The Nation,* cover and pp. 311–314.

Wharton, Y. L. (1976). *List of hypotheses advanced to explain the SAT score decline.* New York: College Entrance Examination Board.

Wise, A. (1988). Legislated learning revisited. *Phi Delta Kappan, 69*(5), 328–333.

Zajonc, R. B. (1986). The decline and rise of Scholastic Aptitude scores: A prediction derived from the confluence model. *American Psychologist, 41*(8), 862–863.

30

Evaluation: Catalyst for or Response to Change?

Educational Reform and Evaluation

NAFTALY S. GLASMAN

LYNETTE DIAMOND GLASMAN

T HE REFORM MOVEMENT of the 1980s springs out of damning critiques of American schools. These evaluations have come, not from employees of school districts or from state departments of education, but from other sources—national and state commissions, university people, and "think tanks." They criticize not only the educational system's products (e.g., low student test scores, uninformed graduates), but also the system's means for pursuing those outcomes (e.g., incompetent and inadequately trained teachers, watered-down curricula). While it is probably an exaggeration to argue that the reform movement has been fueled solely by these evaluations, it is an undeniable fact that the issue of educational quality has become a major concern of American society within the last few years.

In this essay, we provide examples of two types of evaluation that, we believe, serve two different but interrelated purposes of the reform movement. The first contributes to creating a climate for change. The second contributes to actually changing public policy.

CREATING CLIMATE FOR CHANGE

A crucial prerequisite for educational reform is a climate conducive to change—fundamental attitudes pervading a community or nation about the need for change. But how can this prerequisite be identified? We submit that published evaluations are such indicators. In this section, we provide examples of evaluations from commissions and study groups that, we believe, identified and further helped create a climate that welcomed large-scale changes in education. The extent to which these evaluations actually did shape the reform movement remains to be analyzed.

An early example of an evaluation that documented a change in climate was the preamble of the federal 1981 Consolidation and Improvement Act. This critiqued some dimensions of education, in addition to other domestic programs, and demanded change. Since the federal government has only limited authority over education, it had to begin by creating a climate conducive to change in educational policymaking at the state and local levels.

We believe that the 1981 act was a significant part of changing the climate. Until its passage, the Reagan administration had actually been seeking to *decrease* federal involvement in education. Although the 1981 act did little to change education substantively, it allowed Congress to block the administration's efforts to reduce federal funding to education (Darling-Hammond & Marks, 1983). Department of Education officials interpreted the passage of this act as a green light to initiate pleas and demands for educational reform (Clark & Astuto, 1986; Whitt, Clark, & Astuto, 1986).

The climate developed further—not only encouraging change in public education but demanding it. Several evaluation reports published in 1983 by commissions, university researchers, and other study groups crystallized the national consensus for change (Boyer, 1983; Business–Higher Education Forum, 1983; College Board Educational Equality Project, 1983; Education Commission, 1983; Goodlad, 1983; National Commission, 1983). Of particular note was the report titled *A Nation At Risk*, submitted to Secretary of Education Terrell H. Bell by the National Commission on Excellence in Education (1983).

This document described schools as mediocre, noncompetitive, and in desperate need of reform, demanding changes in education in strong, unequivocal language. The report presented 13 indicators of educational system outcomes that the commission believed had put the nation "at risk." All of these indicators were associated with student academic achievement. They compared America's past academic achievements with its present ones and compared the nation's academic achievement to those of other nations. This study also pinpointed possible causes for the decline in achievement.

Other evaluations published in 1983 prompted numerous debates about directions that changes in education ought to take. Some of these debates reflected ideological differences, pitting educational equity against educational excellence. Other debates focused on the content of the curriculum, the actual amount of time students spend engaged in learning, teacher training, work conditions, and teacher compensation. As these topics were debated, questions came up about whose responsibility it was to initiate the various changes (Altbach, Kelly, & Weis, 1985; Chelimsky, 1987; Stedman & Smith, 1983; United States Department of Education, 1984). Only some of the debates discussed the possible and misunderstood connections between desired changes in education and findings of educational research (Elmore & McLaughlin, 1988; Finn, 1988; Glass, 1987; Shavelson & Berliner, 1988; Smith, 1986; United States Department of Education, 1986).

There is no empirical evidence that climate-related evaluations contributed directly to increased allocations to education (Knapp, 1987; Tsang & Levin, 1983). In fact, William Bennett, as outgoing secretary of education, claimed in *A Nation At Risk II* (United States Department of Education, 1988) that increased financial support was not the solution. Despite being ranked number one in the world in per-pupil expenditure, the United States lags behind other Western nations in science and mathematics achievement.

Bennett inherited from Terrell Bell, and Shirley Hufstedler before him, an election debt to educators—more federal financial support. Bennett has not denied that schools need funding to enact various reforms, but he has repeatedly stated that education is a local responsibility; its funding must come from state legislatures.

The *Nation at Risk II* highlights improvement in areas over which the federal government has no policymaking authority. Presumably, this makes Bennett's tenure in office appear successful. But the report admits "The nation is still at risk" and does not claim that the situation has significantly improved. Bennett claims that he and his department have distributed to schools in great measure, not money, but questions and opinions. He may be right.

Several educational issues remain high on the national agenda in 1988, a testimony to the enduring climate that has nurtured educational reform. Student academic requirements, school curriculum, and proposals for teacher competency testing are still receiving full national attention.

We doubt that climate-related evaluation efforts have used or offered evidence of high scientific value. We also doubt these evaluations would have even been undertaken had it not been for frustrated citizens and for visionary leaders who understood their feelings. These leaders have possessed only limited policymaking authority, but they exercised their "symbolic leadership" (Bolman & Deal, 1984, chap. 9) to create a climate that virtually demanded new policies.

The climate-related evaluations created a sense of crisis. Their findings were shocking, even frightening; they commanded attention. They bred debates that, we believe, facilitated a variety of changes. Leaders have used these evaluation reports to set agendas for policymakers (Ginsberg & Wimpelberg, 1987) and to pressure policymaking authorities to pursue these agendas.

EVALUATION AND POLICY CHANGES

Large-scale reforms require the enactment of policies. Many public policies enacted in the 1980s consist of new educational directions, standards, and requirements. These policies address what students ought to study, what curriculum should include, what teachers need to know, when testing should occur, and a variety of other topics. But what evidence is there that these policies reflect actual educational change? We submit that educational policies that include requirements for evaluating educational practice are indicative of changes in policies. This section provides examples of evaluations required by public policies, primarily at the state level.

Only one year after the publication of *A Nation At Risk* (National Commission, 1983), the Education Commission of the States had already counted 275 state-level task forces evaluating numerous aspects of education and recommending approval of a variety of new educational policies. The majority of these recommendations focused heavily on required evaluations of educational practice (United States Department of Education, 1984). By mid-1984, for example, 48 states were studying high school graduation requirements; 35 of them had approved changes. A total of 21 states were evaluating textbooks and instructional materials; 17 had approved changes. A total of 24 states had approved changes in master-teacher or career-ladder programs; 6 had initialed related statewide or pilot programs.

In all of these policy areas, a central ingredient of proposed changes was the requirement to evaluate. In the area of graduation requirements, the courses that students are supposed to take have to be evaluated. In the area of textbook requirements, the instructional material covered has to be evaluated. In the area of teacher advancement requirements, teacher performance has to be evaluated. Few, if any, of these requirements are identical to those used during the 1970s.

The number of state-level task forces engaged in evaluating education has increased since 1984, and so has the number of educational policies enacted that require evaluation (Glass, 1987; Smith, 1986; United States Department of Education, 1986). State-level agencies have found themselves under pressure to evaluate, particularly in areas for which they already possess legal authority to do so.

Some states have also established task forces to evaluate areas of education over which the state has limited authority. One example is California and Texas task forces created to deal with some aspects of curriculum (Kerchner, 1986; Plank, 1986). Other examples include teacher training, where universities possess much of the decision-making authorities, and teacher compensation, where the school districts decide. Evaluations done in these areas resemble those that were climate-related more than those that were policy-related.

As a result of the policy-related state-level initiatives, local school districts have made policy changes, too. Local educational authorities have emphasized student achievement in their required evaluations of district-wide instructional goals, student promotion policies, and student graduation requirements (Cuban, 1984; Knoffler, 1987). They have also made more visible and systematic evaluations of educational programs and textbook selection. Evaluation staff (rather than line) units have been established in many districts (Stufflebeam, 1985). Most of these school district-level activities use the legal authority already granted to local educational authorities.

During the reform of the 1980s, evaluation in connection with policy has occurred mainly at the state level, less at the local school district level, and still less at either the federal or the school levels. For example, evaluation requirements in the 1980s have been built into Title I, Title III, and Title IV-c of the Elementary and Secondary Education Act, originally passed in 1965. Evaluation requirements have also been instituted at the school site level in teacher evaluations and student achievement-based instructional goals (Glasman, 1986, chaps. 8, 10, 12; Glasman & Nevo, 1988, chaps. 7, 8, 10).

We doubt that policy-related evaluations have used or offered evidence high in scientific value. We also doubt that these evaluations would have taken place had it not been for leaders who understood that they must enact new educational policies or be replaced. These leaders may have had policy answers before they pinpointed either policy questions or concomitant evaluation questions (Chelimsky, 1987; Glasman, 1987); but once they called for the evaluation questions, they targeted education domains for policy enactment. These policies forced some issues on the administrators at the policy-implementation level.

TOWARD INTEGRATION

Instances of evaluation indicate the existence of change. In this essay, we have provided examples of two such interrelated linkages: published evaluations and changes in the climate about education and evaluation requirements built into public mandates and changes in educational policies. It could be contended that evaluation breeds change, so that the publications have helped shape attitudes, and the requirements have helped institutionalize policies. But it could also be contended that the reverse is true—namely, that an orientation to change has brought about evaluation at these levels.

Our examples have included two fundamental elements: collecting information and judging the worth of that information. In the educational reform movement of the 1980s, evaluation has consisted of two elements: (a) the shaping of judgment by the information and (b) the shaping of the information by judgment—a two-way activity that is not unfamiliar to behavioral and social scientists.

In all of our examples, a central issue has been authority. The authority to evaluate is linked to the authority to initiate changes. Those authorized to collect information about the educational climate, and to render judgment about the worth of the information, were closely associated with those authorized to change that climate. Similar associations were noted between those authorized to evaluate policies and those authorized to change them.

We have not discussed perhaps the most central aspects of a reform in education—namely, changes in what teachers and students do in school. If we had extended our essay to include these changes, would we have linked them to some evaluations that teachers and students do themselves? Perhaps so, but we do not have such evidence.

What we do have is some evidence of teachers' feelings about the reform. In one of the most recent national surveys, *Report Card on School Reform* (Carnegie Commission, 1988), teachers expressed both positive and negative opinions about the last five years of educational reform. Of the 13,500 teachers surveyed, 2 out of 3 said that their student's mathematics, reading, and writing achievements have improved. A total of 3 out of 4 agreed that learning goals have become more clearly defined and that more is now expected of students. But only 1 out of 4 said that their own morale increased. In fact, 1 out of 4 reported "no change," and 2 out of 4 said that their morale has actually *declined*. A total of 50 percent gave an overall C to the reform movement, 29 percent gave it a B, and 13 percent gave it a D. Which students had their achievement scores increase? Which teachers helped clarify learning goals and set higher expectations for students? And what do teachers mean when they give an overall grade to the educational reform of the 1980s? These and similar questions need to be tackled before more definitive evaluative statements can be made about the educational reform movement.

REFERENCES

Altbach, P. G., Kelly, G. P., & Weis., L. (Eds.). (1985). *Excellence in education*. Buffalo: Prometheus.

Bolman, L. G., & Deal, T. E. (1984). *Modern approaches to understanding and managing organizations.* San Francisco: Jossey-Bass.

Boyer, E. L. (1983). *High school: A report on secondary education in America.* New York: Harper & Row.

Business–Higher Education Forum. (1983). *America's competitive challenge: The need for a national response.* Washington, D.C.

Carnegie Commission on the Advancement of Teaching. (1988). *Report card on school reform.* Washington, DC.

Chelimsky, E. (1987). What have we learned about the politics of program evaluation? *Educational Evaluation and Policy Analysis, 9*(3), 199–214.

Clark, D. L., & Astuto, T. A. (1986, January). *The significance and permanence of changes in federal educational policy 1980–1988.* Bloomington, IN: UCEA, Policy Studies Center.

College Board Educational Equity Project. (1983). *Academic preparation for college: What students need to know and be able to do.* New York.

Cuban, L. (1984). Transforming the frog into a prince: Effective schools research, policy and practice at the district level. *Harvard Educational Review, 54*(2), 129–151.

Darling-Hammond, L., & Marks, E. L. (1983). *The new federalism in education.* Santa Monica, CA: Rand Corporation.

Education Commission of the States Task Force on Education for Economic Growth. (1983). *Action for excellence.* Denver, CO.

Elmore, R. F., & McLaughlin, M. W. (1988). *Steady work* (R-3574-NIE/RC). Santa Monica, CA: Rand Corporation.

Finn, C. E., Jr. (1988). What ails education research. *Educational Researcher, 17*(1), 5–9, 12–14.

Ginsberg, R., & Wimpelberg, R. K. (1987). Educational change by commission: Attempting "trickle down" reform. *Educational Evaluation and Policy Analysis, 9*(4), 344–360.

Glasman, N. S. (1986). *Evaluation-based leadership.* Albany: State University of New York.

Glasman, N. S. (1987). Evaluation in the context of policymaking. *Educational Evaluation and Policy Analysis, 9*(3), 215–218.

Glasman, N. S., & Nevo, D. (1988). *Evaluation in decision making.* Boston: Kluwer Academic.

Glass, G. V. (1987). What works: Politics and research. *Educational Researcher, 16*(3), 5–10.

Goodlad, J. (1983). *A place called school: Prospects for the future.* New York: McGraw-Hill.

Kerchner, C. (1986). Selling an education culture in lotusland. *Politics of Education Bulletin, 13*(2), 9–12.

Knapp, M. S. (1987). Educational improvement under the education block grant. *Educational Evaluation and Policy Analysis, 9*(4), 283–299.

Knoffler, S. J. (1987). Assessing the impact of a state's decision to move from minimum competency testing toward higher level testing for graduation. *Educational Evaluation and Policy Analysis, 9*(4), 325–336.

National Commission on Excellence in Education. (1983). *A nation at risk: The imperative for educational reform.* Washington, DC: U.S. Government Printing Office.

Plank, D. N. (1986). The ayes of Texas: Rhetoric reality and school reform. *Politics of Education Bulletin, 13*(2), 13–16.

Shavelson, R. J., & Berliner, D. C. (1988). Erosion of the education research infrastructure: A reply to Finn. *Educational Researcher, 17*(1), 9–12.

Smith, M. S. (1986). What works works! *Educational Researcher, 15*(4), 290–330.

Stedman, L. C., & Smith, M. S. (1983). Recent reform proposals for American education. *Contemporary Education Review, 2*(2), 85–104.

Stufflebeam, D. L. (1985). Coping with the point-of-entry problem in evaluating projects. In N. S. Glasman (Ed.), Evaluation as a management tool. *Studies in Educational Evaluation, 2*(2), 123–130.

Tsang, M., & Levin, H. M. (1983). The impact of intergovernmental grants on educational expenditure. *Review of Educational Research, 53*(3), 329–368.

United States Department of Education. (1984). *The nation responds.* Washington, DC: U.S. Government Printing Office.

United States Department of Education. (1986). *What works.* Washington, DC: U.S. Government Printing Office.

United States Department of Education. (1988). *A nation at risk II.* Washington, DC: U.S. Government Printing Office.

Whitt, E. J., Clark, D. I., & Astuto, T. A. (1986, December). *An analysis of public support for the educational policy preferences of the Reagan administration.* Charlottesville, VA: UCEA, Policy Studies Center.

31
Overregulating
Our Schools

*Student Welfare in the
Era of School Reform:
Legislated Learning Revisited*
ARTHUR E. WISE

A DECADE AGO, I wrote *Legislated Learning: The Bureaucratization of the American Classroom*[1] to sound an alarm about the kind of educational world which legislation, centralization, and regulation were creating. It was a world characterized by standardized testing . . . not educational standards; teacher-proof curriculum . . . not curriculum reform; standardized teaching . . . not professional teaching; and management-by-the-numbers . . . not instructional leadership. It was a world where policy dominated, schools were bureaucratic, and students were processed. It was a world in which state government called the shots; state and local boards of education became irrelevant; teachers were told what, when, and how to teach; and administrators, caught in the cross-fire, could not figure out whether to follow their educational instincts . . . or the law.

It was a world where passive learners were fed basic skills in bite-sized chunks to be regurgitated on command before the next spartan fare would be served. It was a world where students were to be prepared not to challenge society but to take their place in it. It was a world curiously devoid of concern for individualism, individual freedom, creativity, analytical thinking, international competitiveness, and the twenty-first century.

It was an educational world which could best be described by sociological jargon: bureaucratization, centralization, rationalization, hyperrationalization.

A decade later, including a half-decade of "reform," where are we? Specifically, did reform rescue America's schools from this bureaucratic fate? Did it launch them on a course which will help them prepare well-educated citizens to face the future? Or did reform accelerate the arrival of bureaucratic hell?

Our answer must begin with a closer look at "reform." While politicians and educational politicians may like to characterize reform as moving America's schools along a certain path from failure to success, the truth is different. No common vision (dare we say, theory and/or philosophy of education?) has guided reform. And we must always distinguish between the rhetoric of reform (which may or may not be implemented) and the reality of reform (which may or may not reflect the rhetoric). Moreover, while reform is dated to 1983 *(A Nation at Risk)*, much relevant legislative activity preceded it, and much "reform" has yet to happen. The picture is, needless to say, complicated.

Two trends are evident in the last decade. One trend, representing a long-term distrust of boards of education and educators, is the continuation of state efforts to consolidate control over local school districts and local educators. The second trend, representing the assertion of power by educators and some policymakers, returns to the classical conservative view that educational decisions, like other political and economic decisions, are best made closest to the people being served. Advancing the trend toward state-oriented control are most "education governors" and legislators, some Reagan administration "conservatives," and others who champion the incorporation of dubious scientific management schemes into state education policy. Advancing the trend toward client-oriented control are some elected officials, the teachers' organizations, and parents and others who believe that schoolchildren are not standardized in their cognitive and affective needs and interests.

In the middle are local school administrators who gain bureaucratic influence under state law as they lose the discretion to uphold important educational values. On the sidelines are local school board members who are "seriously concerned about state-level intrusiveness but have not yet developed a strong response that would make them partners in educational improvement."[2]

The future will be determined by local administrators and board members who must decide whether they prefer state-oriented control, with its emphasis on producing standardized results through regulated teaching, or client-oriented control, with its emphasis on meeting the educational needs of student clients through professional teaching.

TIGHTENING STATE-ORIENTED CONTROL

The central message of *Legislated Learning* was that while equal educational opportunity can be advanced by regulation, the quality of education is less susceptible to regulation. Problems of inequity in the allocation of educational opportunities, resources, and programs can be solved by central mandate. They may, because of self-interest and parochialism, be otherwise insoluble. On the other hand, problems in educational quality cannot easily be solved by edict. Indeed, central mandates to improve educational quality often, paradoxically, *reduce* the quality of education.

By mandating educational outcomes through standardized tests, content through curriculum alignment, and teaching methods through teacher evaluation criteria, mandates set in motion a chain of events which alter educational ends and means. In effect, mandates say to many elementary school teachers: Don't teach everything, just teach the basics; don't teach reading, just teach reading skills; don't teach real reading skills, just teach tested reading skills; don't teach writing skills, just teach them to fill-in-the-blanks; don't teach them to think, just teach them the right answer.

The standardized test would set the educational objectives for the teacher. Curriculum alignment would ensure that the teacher would cover the material to be tested. The teacher would prepare plans and reports to inform bureaucratic superiors that the material was being covered. Evaluators would observe and inspect to make sure that teachers were using the proper methods. And, finally, the external test would demonstrate whether or not the teacher had properly executed his or her duties.

How do teachers respond to this conception of their work?[3] Teachers worry about standardized tests as an appraisal mechanism; they worry that multiple-choice tests cannot assess all that they teach . . . and should teach. They worry that the results of tests are used to contravene their judgment about what students know and should know. They worry that the tests do not match their conception of the curriculum.

Teachers worry that tests do alter the real curriculum. Some effects are obvious. Testing takes time; preparation for testing takes even more time. Testing takes time away from *real* teaching.

Less obvious are the distortions introduced into the curriculum. Some teachers begin to emphasize the content that they know will appear on the test. They begin to teach in a format that will prepare students to deal with the content as it will be tested. Some even teach items that will appear on the test. Meanwhile, the rest of the curriculum is deemphasized.

The result for teachers is ethical conflict and guilt. If teachers follow their own instincts about what to do in their classrooms, they are violating the policies which they are supposed to be following. And their students may perform less well on the external examinations. On the other hand, if they follow the policies, they worry that they are shortchanging their students even as their students perform better on the examinations. As a result of this ethical conflict, many teachers become disengaged from their work. While some leave the field, others adopt coping strategies designed to meet the letter of the law. And guilt is the near certain result, because teachers know that as the test scores rise, the quality of education is deteriorating. And so it is that legislated learning, an effort to regulate the schools into improvement, has the opposite effect.

McCloskey, Provenzo, Cohn, and Kottkamp set out to test some of the assumptions which policies make and found a number of contradictions.[4] Among their findings: Teachers questioned scientific management when the solutions it proposed had little correlation with the reality of classrooms; in the face of mandated universal performance criteria, teachers reported needing autonomy to deal with the variation in student ability and accomplishment; teachers realized that the demands of increased compliance would never lead to recognition of them as professionals; teachers found that the demand that they systematize their work, a fact physically manifested in the growth of paperwork, distracted them from the primary tasks of teaching; and teachers found that standardized curriculum and standardized methods of evaluating teachers and students did not fit the heterogeneity of their classrooms. Teachers found that efforts to regulate educational quality through the enforcement of uniform standards had the effect of reducing equity by preventing them from accommodating differences among students.

Many of the effects are traceable to 1970s legislation and regulation which mandated scientific management to promote educational accountability—Planning-Programming-Budgeting Systems (PPBS), Competency-Based Education (CBE), minimum competency testing, learner verification, test-based instructional management, and more. During the 1980s, new forms of scientific management for education have emerged which reinforce these effects, some with considerable potency.

Concern over the performance of teachers and concern over teaching methods has led a number of states to mandate uniform approaches to teacher evaluation. On a regular schedule, evaluators (generally administrators) are supposed to inspect the performance of teachers by observing them teach. Evaluators use a state-developed checklist of approved teacher behaviors. Teachers get points for acting out the approved teaching behaviors. The more approved teaching behaviors the teacher exhibits in the period during which the evaluator is present, the higher his or her score.

State officials, in preparing the checklist, approve certain behaviors. These are behaviors which have purportedly been found to produce student achievement on standardized tests of basic skills. The process by which narrow research findings are translated into general prescriptions for performance is conceptually wrong and empirically indefensible, but that is no barrier to state officials' use of "science" to buttress their positions.[5] In any case, teachers are encouraged to teach in the approved manner. Many teachers are troubled that the approved teaching behaviors are not appropriate to their subjects, their students, and their understanding of sound educational practice. Their consternation is justified.[6]

Earlier innovations mandated content, leaving method to the teacher's discretion; teacher evaluation criteria mandate method. The combination is potent; teacher-proof teaching is just about guaranteed.

But it is not only the behavior of the teacher that is regulated by the new teacher evaluation procedures. Local administrators have no discretion either. State officials seek to assure a high degree of reliability in evaluation—to ensure that administrators will judge the same behavior in the same way. State officials, therefore, create an instrument which requires little judgment on the part of the administrator. They then require administrators to undergo training in the use of the instrument. The goal is to make sure that the administrator knows and records an approved behavior when he or she sees it. Teaching is not only teacher-proof but also administrator-proof. Teacher *evaluation,* an inherently judgmental activity, is no longer subject to judgment. Many administrators worry that the approved teacher behaviors have little if anything to do with effective teaching in their schools. Still they must evaluate teachers by-the-numbers.

Another innovation of the 1980s is curriculum alignment, making sure that what is tested is taught, ensuring congruence among objectives, textbooks, and tests. Many school districts found that their curricula did not necessarily cover the material which was being tested by their state's minimum competency tests. Districts have been reviewing their curriculums and choice of textbooks to create a closer fit with items on the state tests. By realigning their curricula, districts can improve their students' performance on state tests. This close tracking of the curriculum has been described as the latest accountability model.[7]

Looming on the horizon is yet another force for centralization, regulation, indeed nationalization. That is, of course, the proposed legislative expansion of the National Assessment of Educational Progress (NAEP). A national commission appointed by the secretary of education has called for an expansion of NAEP to permit state-by-state comparisons. This change would treat each state as the significant educational unit producing test scores and would allow each state to compare its performance with those of other states. Treating the state as the unit is a dramatic departure, for in the past states were more like "holding companies," setting broad policies for numerous, diverse local school districts. Several consequences follow. The states will need to agree among themselves about what should be tested, and, effectively, what should be taught. The Council of Chief State School Officers has already begun a federally funded project to build the consensus.

The increased visibility of state average test score performance will concentrate state-level attention on the subjects covered by the test. States will compete with each other to improve performance on the tests. State officials will increase efforts to regulate district educational practices since the state's average test score is the product of district activity. And a new impetus to legislated learning will have been launched.

In sum, the trend toward state-oriented control has continued, even intensified. Early efforts directed attention to the objectives of education by mandating the basics. Attention was concentrated by mandating outcomes in the form of minimum competency testing and other forms of statewide testing. When these mandates proved not to be potent enough (policymakers could not be sure what went on behind the classroom door), curriculum was mandated, and inspectors stepped inside the classroom door. Because there are not enough inspectors to monitor constantly, the regulators look forward to the day when they can use computers to track the attainment of every objective by every student every day.[8]

PROMOTING CLIENT-ORIENTED CONTROL

My purpose in writing *Legislated Learning* was to signal the dual need to strengthen professional and local control of education in the interest of making schools more responsive to their clientele. The expansion of central control was occurring at the expense of professional control and local control. In a profound sense, it does not matter who controls education so long as every young citizen is fully prepared to exercise the rights and duties of citizenship in the American, democratic, free-enterprise tradition. So long as constitutional rights are protected, the question of who should control education is pragmatic. Central control is to be deplored not because it represents a shift in power. Power ebbs and flows among the three branches of government and the three levels of government. Rather, central control is to be deplored because, under the technology available for managing schools, it reduces the responsiveness of schools to their clientele, and, as a result, reduces the quality of education.

Teachers were the first to notice the decline in the quality of education produced by regulation. Teachers realized that, because they were not trusted, conditions were being forced upon them that caused them to treat students poorly. Standardized teaching meant ignoring the needs and interests of students. The solution that they seized upon was to assume responsibility for the quality of the teaching force. Teachers were joined by some policymakers who were persuaded that exercising control over the quality of teaching personnel would alleviate the need for exercising day-to-day control over the quality of teaching practice. It was time to make teaching a profession.

The argument for professionalism in teaching is similar to the arguments that have led to the transformation of other occupations into professions. *The primary rationale is a need for quality control over a process in which the service provider, in a largely private transaction, provides important services to a client who inevitably knows less than the service provider.*

The question then is: How can the state, the client, and the profession be assured that the appropriate services—those that best serve the client's needs—are being delivered?

The appropriateness of instruction, like the appropriateness of other professional services, must be determined by context. Because students are not standardized in their needs, stages of development, preconceptions, or learning styles, a given stimulus does not produce a predictable response. A teacher must make decisions based on knowledge of the student, of the subject matter, and of pedagogy in order to produce the right conditions for learning. *Necessarily, appropriate instructional decisions must be made at the point of service delivery. Therefore, the quality of services delivered inevitably depends upon the capacity of the teacher to make appropriate decisions.*

The problem of teaching is not unique. It shares in common with other professions the reality that high-quality service cannot be prescribed in advance of the professional–client interaction. High-quality service results only when the professional is prepared to apply general knowledge to the specific needs of the client.

The professions have created an arrangement with the state, in which they have sought and been granted the right and the obligation to control the quality of members of their profession. As the bargain is struck, professions have intensified their educational requirements and installed testing procedures which are designed to assure the public and themselves that new members are qualified to practice and should be licensed to practice. In this way, the professions seek to assure the public and themselves of a high quality of service by individual members. The bargain has been struck by medicine and law and increasingly by architecture, accounting, and engineering—all occupations which require discretion and judgment in meeting the unique needs of clients.

Some may wonder about the relevance of the experiences of other professions to teaching. After all, public school teaching takes place exclusively in a nonprofit, bureaucratic, publicly accountable setting. Most members of other professions operate in a market setting, where client choice and profit play a role. *These major differences, however, do not vitiate the commonality that knowledgeable professionals must make decisions on behalf of less knowledgeable clients in settings where no "higher authority" (except professional ethics) is present.*

In the last year, a number of developments suggest that the idea of a teaching profession is taking root:

• About 100 of the nation's leading schools of education have joined forces under the banner of the Holmes Group, with a commitment to preparing teachers who can teach professionally.

- The National Board for Professional Teaching Standards has come into being, with a commitment to establish professional certification standards for teachers. Meanwhile, a number of states have established state boards for professional teaching standards.
- The major teachers' organizations have successfully negotiated contracts which change the roles and responsibilities of teachers, and have begun to insist that all classrooms be staffed by fully qualified teachers.
- School-based school reform projects which restructure roles and responsibilities in schools are flourishing. At least four networks nurture these "grassroots" endeavors—Theodore Sizer's Coalition of Essential Schools; John Goodlad's National Network for Educational Renewal; the National Education Association's Mastery in Learning Project, and the American Federation of Teachers' Research-into-Practice Practitioners Network.

These efforts are intended to define, transmit, and enforce improved standards of practice.

MAKING CLIENT-ORIENTED CONTROL REAL

Whether these efforts to professionalize teaching will flourish or wither depends upon several factors. In the first place, parents will have to judge that the quality of education their children receive under client-oriented control is superior to that which they receive under state-oriented control. But before the fruits of teacher professionalism will be visible, the orchard will have to be tended to maturity. That will take time and will require that school boards and school administrators ally themselves with teacher professionalism, currently the major force respecting client-oriented control. Local officials will have to resist the seductive and powerful forces favoring state-oriented control.

If client-oriented control is to take hold, school administrators will have to move away from the middle. They will have to become champions of educational values, not implementers of state-imposed curriculum alignment and teacher evaluation procedures. They will have to exercise the kind of instructional leadership which will allow and oblige teachers to meet the needs and interests of students in their schools. They will have to stand firm in the face of bureaucratic interference which results in the uniform processing of students.

But professional teachers and professional administrators cannot, indeed should not, go it alone. The public schools, like the military, must be accountable to the public. The public authority to which public schools should be accountable is the local school board. Local school boards must be the arbiters of the collective interest of their clientele. They must make sure that the professional staff they assemble meet the needs of their students. Locally elected officials must represent the public interest—or state officials will continue to fill the leadership vacuum. Local school boards must move off the sidelines and onto the playing field.

On the state and national level, leaders, including opinion leaders, will determine the climate within which the control issue will be resolved. Educators and parents might take heart from the recent warning about the expansion of NAEP by the National Academy of Education, perhaps the most prestigious group in education:

> *We must be ever mindful of what NAEP is and is not. We are concerned that the results of future assessments may begin to exercise an influence on our schools that exceeds their scope and true merit.*
>
> Even the best of current efforts within NAEP only provides a view of children's command of basic academic knowledge and skills in mathematics, reading, and writing.
>
> The Academy Committee is concerned lest the narrowness of NAEP may have a distorted impact on our schools. When test results become the arbiter of future choices, a subtle shift occurs in which fallible and partial indicators of academic achievement are transformed into major goals of schooling.
>
> At root here is a fundamental dilemma. Those personal qualities that we hold dear—resilience and courage in the face of stress, a sense of craft in our work, a commitment to justice and caring in our social relationships, a dedication to advancing the public good in our communal life—are exceedingly difficult to assess. And so, unfortunately, we are apt to measure what we can, and eventually come to value what is measured over what is left unmeasured. The shift is subtle, and occurs gradually. It first invades our language and then slowly begins to dominate our thinking. It is all around us, and we too are a part of it. In neither academic nor popular discourse about schools does one find nowadays much reference to the important human qualities noted above. The language of academic achievement tests has become the primary rhetoric of schooling.

Educators and parents might take heart from these stirring words . . . but they could be wrong. The National Academy of Education's concern about state-by-state comparisons of average test scores has not stopped the U.S. Education Department from moving ahead to implement an expanded NAEP.[9]

All of which is to say that the jury is still out on who will control America's classrooms and on how well students' interests will be served. It would be ironic—but perhaps not surprising—if the most lasting effects on education of the Reagan era were a big push toward central management of education, a further diminution in the power of local officials, and increasing unresponsiveness of the schools to their clientele. Americans must depend upon educators to remind them of the conservative idea that decisions should generally be made closest to the people being served.

NOTES

This chapter is adapted with permission from "Student Welfare in the Era of School Reform: Legislated Learning Revisited," *Phi Delta Kappan,* Vol. 69, No. 5, pp. 328–333.

1. Wise, Arthur E. *Legislated learning: The bureaucratization of the American classroom.* Berkeley: University of California Press, 1979.

2. *School Boards: Strengthening Grassroots Leadership.* Washington, DC: Institute for Educational Leadership, November 1986.

3. Darling-Hammond, Linda, & Wise, Arthur E. Beyond standardization: State standards and school improvement. *Elementary School Journal, 85* (3): January 1985.

4. McCloskey, Gary N., Provenzo, Eugene F., Jr., Cohn, Marilyn M., & Kottkamp, Robert B. *A profession at risk: Legislated learning as a disincentive to teaching.* Washington, DC: Office of Educational Research and Improvement, U.S. Department of Education, March 1987.

5. Shulman, Lee S. Those who understand: Knowledge growth in teaching. *Educational Researcher,* February 1986, p. 13.

6. Darling-Hammond, Linda. Valuing teachers: The making of a profession. *Teachers College Record, 87*(2): Winter 1985.

7. *Education Week, 7*(8), October 28, 1987, pp. 1, 26.

8. Ibid.

9. *The nation's report card: Improving the assessment of student achievement.* Cambridge, MA: National Academy of Education, Harvard Graduate School of Education, 1987.

32

What Next? A Metaphor for the Next Wave

Reform or Reformation?
JONAS F. SOLTIS

WE ALL KNOW that American education has been in an extended period of reform since 1983 and that the end is not yet in sight. We are not quite as clear as we might be, however, about the nature of the reforms already called for, currently being instituted, and yet to be proposed. The journals buzz with talk of a second reform wave following upon the first, of curriculum and standards reform differing from professional and teacher education reform, of the need for bottom-up reform to replace top-down reform, of school organization and management reform as the key to implementing all other reforms, and many other such reflective characterizations of the diversity of the reform movement. In this short essay, I would like to provide some philosophical and historical perspective on the idea of reform itself rather than deal with any specific reforms so that we can see more clearly what is at stake in the current attempts to reform American education.

What is a reform? What is a reformation? How may reforms make a reformation? In dealing with these questions, I am going to assume a shared cultural literacy among my readers that some recent critics of American education deny exists. Perhaps the best known historical example of reforms and reformation was the Protestant Reformation of the sixteenth century. Reforms were then proposed within the Catholic Church to correct corrupt practices, not to make basic changes; but somehow a reformation

410

occurred, and a new form of religion, Protestantism, emerged. This historical example, however dim it may be in the minds of my readers, will serve us well as a backdrop against which to view crucial aspects of the current educational reform movement in America. It will also help me to argue that the possibility of a real reformation rests squarely upon our ability and willingness to reconceptualize the role and authority of teachers.[1] Reforms ordinarily are proposed to repair, improve, or redirect an institution, not to change it in radical ways. Reformers, as opposed to revolutionaries, accept the basic form and purpose of the institution in question. They seek to right imbalances, excise ineffective or corrupt practices, and bring about whatever adjustments or changes seem needed to improve what they perceive as a bad or deteriorating situation. So it was in the sixteenth century with regard to the church. So it seems to be now, near the close of the twentieth century, with regard to education in American.

Many have perceived the American educational system as flawed, unable to deliver a high-quality education for all. These same individuals have accused American schools of putting the nation at risk, of neglecting the basics, of graduating cultural illiterates, of protecting incompetent teachers, of lowering standards, and more. Think of the many recent reforms aimed at correcting these perceived shortcomings. Here are a few:

—Perception: Students are allowed to graduate from high school barely literate and with little or no math and science in their programs.
—Reform: Raise literacy, promotion, and graduation standards and require more units of math and science for graduation.
—Perception: Some schoolteachers cannot spell or read beyond grade school level.
—Reform: Require minimum competency tests for teachers.
—Perception: The best and brightest of our college graduates choose better-paying occupations over teaching careers.
—Reform: Raise teachers' salaries to a competitive level and provide alternative paths for entry into the profession.

Add to these reforms others aimed at increasing the length of the school year, providing merit pay and career ladders to motivate teachers, raising the quality of textbooks, giving teachers more say in curriculum decision making, and reforming teacher education. In the aggregate these provide a good sample of *reforms,* that is, efforts aimed at adjusting the system and providing incremental adaptive changes and improvements— but not the makings of a *reformation*—or so it seems.

What is the key feature of a reformation? What happened in the sixteenth century to produce the Protestant Reformation and not just a series of reforms of the Catholic Church? In bare-bones terms, a radical shift occurred in the mind-set of a significantly large number of people to create a new institution. The Christian mind-set for more than 1,000 years took as axiomatic that God's relationship to the individual was strictly mediated through the office of the clergy. The new mind-set gave the individual a direct line to God by way of conscience and a personal interpretation of scriptures. Of course, the Protestant world still contained churches and clergy. Protestant churches would be sanctuaries for the worshipping faithful, but there would be no *Church* that served as the last and final word on God's meanings and actions. Thus a fundamental change occurred that still left many of the surface features of Christianity intact. Nonetheless, it was a real reformation, not just a set of reforms.

The parallel is obviously imperfect, but think of teachers in today's schools who cannot directly use their own judgment in many educational matters but must go through duly constituted authority and a hierarchy, not unlike that in the early Church, made up of curriculum specialists, principals, supervisors, superintendents, and school boards. The system is tightly ordered and controlled. If system problems are perceived, educational reforms are instituted to improve the system and increase the effectiveness of people engaged in it. Teachers are rarely consulted or given the power to create and institute their own reforms. Almost everything in classrooms and schools has to be approved and supervised by authorities. Reforms are authority driven, not teacher driven. Certainly, such reforms can lead to perceptibly higher standards and even to demonstrably better results. The current system is not hopeless. There is no doubt that we can achieve improvement as we have at other times in this century, while operating within the dominant mind-set and educational structure of contemporary America.

But are there any chances of a re-formation of this mind-set given the nature of the current reform movement? And what might a reformation of American education look like if it happened? Would there be observable radical changes, or would most of the surface features of the system remain intact?

Before suggesting answers to these questions, let me make a few observations. I agreed to contribute to this symposium because I genuinely feel that history doesn't just happen to people. Instead people, whether knowingly or unconsciously, often have a chance to shape their own histories. This possibility increases when people become conscious of the options that open up various individual and collective choices. But these options need to be recognized to be consciously acted upon. I also believe that we stand at a juncture in the evolution of the practice of teaching when a genuine reformation is possible. If it is to happen, this reformation of American education will require a basic shift in mind-set regarding the authority of teachers.

There has been much talk these days about empowering teachers. This concept is on the right track. Clearly, reforms aimed at giving teachers more say in curriculum matters, more control over schooling, and even sharing authority in personnel decisions are important reforms. As reforms, however, they assume that the system has gotten out of balance with too much top-down and not enough bottom-up exercise of power. Such reforms seek to right the balance of, but not to change, the basic mind-set.

On the other hand, some of those who talk about empowering teachers hint of an expanded role where teachers are included in such things as the collegial governance of schools, peer review, a mutually supportive teaching environment, and the self-regulation of the profession. Powerful forces work to block these dreams from ever becoming realities. The most insidious forces would make these changes in teacher role *reforms* instead of the outgrowth of a *re-formation* in the way we perceive the educational authority of teachers.

I believe, however, that a reformation is possible. It will require a mind-shift to a trust in the teacher's benevolence, professional judgment, wisdom, and skill. It will shift the locus of educational decision-making authority clearly toward teachers, not as single-classroom, autonomous individuals, but as responsible colleagues collectively sharing and executing a public trust. Parents, state legislatures and educational agencies, school boards, and superintendents still will create broad educational policies and provide the climate and resources for schools and their teachers to carry them out. But in a genuine reformation, it will have to be the teachers who have the real authority to educate in the best way their collective wisdom dictates. Teachers will choose the materials they judge most educative. They will schedule and distribute their students and resources in ways that they judge provide the richest educational environments. They will assess and govern themselves. They will teach. And we and our children and their children will be the benefactors.

During this period of sustained educational reform in the waning years of the twentieth century, there is a chance—just a chance—that we will have a reformation. Many will wait for history to happen. Some will work to shape it. Only the educational historian in the twenty-first century will know if we went through just one more period of reform or had a genuine reformation. Let us pray.

NOTES

1. When I first proposed this Reformation analogy [to the editor of this symposium], he brashly asked, "Who is the modern Martin Luther?" Without hesitation, I answered, "Albert Shanker, of course." Instead of nailing theses to the church door, Shanker writes a weekly column whose underlying consistent theme might be characterized in Marxian revolutionary terms as "Teachers of Amer-

ica, unite and govern yourselves. You have nothing to lose but your chains!"
Shanker has the clearest vision of what a reformation in American education led
by teachers would require; and, like Luther, he is still trying to bring it about by
acting within the system.

33

Putting It All Together

*Education Reform: Making Sense
of It All*
SAMUEL B. BACHARACH

IN THE HANDS of reformers, words are elusive. Metaphors become facts, facts become assumptions, and assumptions are rarely explicated and almost never discussed. Similar terms are used in debating dissimilar constructs and radically different positions. The resultant debates lead to a dialogue that is at best frustrating and at worst polarizing. Unfortunately, the current education reform movement has been conducted in this way, leading many to wonder what lies beneath the rhetoric. This book presents the same problem the reform movement has presented to educators and the public: What is the thematic unity of the reform movement, as expressed in the various authors' concerns? Where are their points of similarity and dissimilarity? How are their constructs alike and how are they different? Put simply, this book presents a traditional dilemma for its editor: How do you see both the forest and the trees at the same time? This integrative concluding chapter will concern itself with five critical themes that may prove useful in unraveling the current reform movement. Each theme corresponds to one of the units in the volume, starting with Unit Two.

THEME I: WHO AND AT WHAT LEVEL ARE THE IMPORTANT REFORM ACTORS, AND WHAT ARE THEIR MOST APPROPRIATE ROLES?

The current reform movement, more than any other period in history, has raised fundamental questions about the role of government in education. Working down from the federal level to the individual level, Unit Two considers the effect of past, present, and future involvement by the important actors in the reform process. The need for appropriate cooperation between the various levels and participants in the reform movement was dramatized by comparing education reform to the planning and construction of a skyscraper, with its need for the involvement of many different kinds of people, from bricklayers to financiers. Sorting out the most appropriate amount and kind of participation from each level is the focus of this first theme.

At the federal level, the Reagan administration came into power with a promise that it would decrease the role of the federal government in education and eliminate the Department of Education. As Boyd points out in Chapter 4, the approach was in sharp contrast to the efforts of previous administrations. Beginning with Lyndon Johnson's presidency, the role of the federal government in education was expanded. In spite of this recent history, the Reagan administration began by denying that there was an important federal role to be played in education (Cooper, Chapter 21; Boyd, Chapter 4). Soon after embarking on this path, however, the administration began to suffer from what has been called "the Toyota problem" (Boyd, Chapter 4). Specifically, the Reagan administration began to realize that education is crucial to the ability of the United States to compete successfully in the new international economy.

Caught between its ideological commitment to decreasing the federal role in education and the pragmatic reality of the increasing economic importance of education, the Reagan administration established the "bully pulpit" as its primary mechanism for resolving this contradiction. The administration embarked on a course that Boyd refers to as "efforts to reform education without half trying." Through the use of reports, commissions, and much rhetoric, the administration began to place pressure on the states to assume responsibility for the emergent reform. Soon afterwards, various governors and state legislatures began their own agenda for school reform.

The Reagan administration succeeded in pulling off a classic hat trick: The administration did nothing, the states took on the responsibility, and the administration took all the credit. Specifically, as some of the chapters in this book point out, while establishing itself as a catalyst of education reform and appearing to show leadership, the Reagan administration has skirted any real fiscal and policy responsibility. At the same time, the administration put pressure on the states to assume responsibility for educational change. By doing so, the administration appears to have decentralized education. In the hands of many state governors and legislatures, however, education policymaking simply became centralized to the state level (Honig, Chapter 5; Passow, Chapter 1).

During the first wave of reform, the states used this new authority to set minimum standards and goals, measure achievement of those goals by massive standardized testing, and persuade school districts to align their curricula so as to induce higher student scores on these standardized tests.

Unfortunately, as Koretz (Chapter 29) and Wise (Chapter 31) point out, these techniques were not without problems. Koretz points to the lack of evidence that the widely publicized decrease in standardized test scores actually was caused by overly loose curricula. He also questions whether the recent increase in test scores has been caused by tightened-up standards, or whether other, coincidental factors were involved. Until our measurement techniques have improved, we are not likely to find the answers.

On the other hand, Wise suggests that to the extent that the process is working well, it may be making things worse. Teachers feel obligated to "teach to the test," ignoring important individual differences in their attempt to get higher merit pay by cramming in more facts for their students to regurgitate at test time. Unfortunately, this leaves little time for reflective teaching and learning or for student understanding and development.

Fortunately, some state leaders seem to be learning these lessons. Some state governments now recognize that the state role should be to set goals, measure performance, and coordinate resources, while letting local districts and communities decide how best to achieve these goals, and granting teachers the autonomy and flexibility to implement the state and local plan (Honig, Chapter 5). There seems to be a growing consensus that the states may set pie-in-the-sky goals, but the *implementation* of those goals can only occur from and at the local level.

Within the local level, there are many different interest groups, each pursuing its own agenda under the rubric of reform. *Local school boards* have control of the purse strings but are being shut out of the consideration of site-based reforms (Muth and Azumi, Chapter 6). Can this paradox continue over the long term?

Large numbers of *teachers* are now formally organized, with interesting implications for their clout in the local school district. Teachers now talk about reform in terms like "teacher empowerment" and "participative decision making." Shedd suggests that their increased bargaining power will likely result in contracts with more shared decision making. To the extent that teachers become involved in goal setting, they are more likely to accept those goals and work toward them in the classroom.

Marburger, in Chapter 7, makes a very convincing case for the need for greater *parental* involvement in their children's education. He presents some ideas for encouraging that involvement and concludes that school-based management is the "best mechanism available to involve parents in the affairs of the schools."

In general, during the first wave, the Reagan administration's bully pulpit tended to pull up the policymaking authority and responsibility from the local to the state level. To some extent, the second wave can be viewed as a reaction to that process, pulling authority and responsibility back down to the local level, where teachers, administrators, school boards, and parents can all implement that amorphous blob called "reform." This parallels the talk about whether the reform movement should be *top-down* or *bottom-up*. The reform movement is doomed to acrimonious failure if the participants see it as a zero-sum power struggle between higher and lower level participants. Just as architects, financiers, and masons must all work harmoniously to build a skyscraper, so federal, state, and local education reformists must integrate their efforts to *empower the overall reform process*, rather than just their own faction or level.

THEME II: EXCELLENCE OR EQUITY? (EQUALITY OF OPPORTUNITY OR EQUALITY OF RESULTS?)

The tension between *equity* and *excellence* in education is a reflection of a tension between two basic societal values. Equity is concerned with the assurance that all individuals in society be given an opportunity to succeed. Excellence is concerned with the assurance that there will be an adequate pool of well-trained individuals to control society's vital functions. Thus, excellence implies that the "best" students reach their full potential. Although on the surface it would appear that equity and excellence do not imply a zero-sum game, they are rooted in different social philosophies.

Excellence (as currently defined) is based on a rationalistic/functionalist model that assumes that unless our society, as a competitive nation-state, creates a core of skilled and constantly self-improving individuals, it will fail to compete successfully in the world market. Indeed, some view the emergent interest in excellence as driven by the demise of the U.S. monopoly of world markets. The excellence movement believes that unless students are held to high standards and compete for grades, are placed in the "best" schools, and are rewarded for competence, the United States will lose its competitive edge. At its heart, excellence advocates hold fast to the basic capitalist values of reward and sanction, competition and choice, and character and accomplishment.

Equity, on the other hand, implies that the goal of education is to prepare *all* individuals intellectually and socially for economic and social survival. The proponents of equity take into consideration the inherent inequality to which certain social groups are subjugated and view schools as playing a vital ameliorating role.

Many of the chapters in this book express a concern that the current reform movement, with its primary focus on excellence, fails to recognize the special needs of specific groups of students. Medina (Chapter 15) criticizes reform efforts that impose a "single standard of excellence, an undeniably white and middle class standard," without addressing equity

issues, Hispanic interests and the "dilemma of educating even larger numbers of minority children." Shanker (Chapter 26) wonders about the effect
of tougher standards on children "who cannot function in the current
system" and will come to expect "increased frustration and failure." Boyer
(Chapter 3) questions if "the reform movement [will] reach all students,
not just the privileged few?"

Ironically, Monk and Haller (Chapter 14) worry that in their zeal to
improve both equity *and* excellence, state bureaucrats tend to favor large
schools at the expense of smaller rural ones. They point to research that
questions the conventional wisdom about the inherent superiority of larger
school districts in providing a wider curriculum to students at lower per-
pupil cost. Perhaps more ominous are the undemocratic methods that these
state bureaucrats use to "persuade" small rural schools to consolidate, and
the negative impact on the socialization of the children in the new larger
school systems. Might not the unique needs of small communities be getting lost in the drive for ever-larger "units of accountability"?

Both Kirst (Chapter 2) and Metz (Chapter 12) advocate programs
related to the differentiated needs of students, needs that are based on (or
rooted in) external social and economic conditions that have negative impacts on educational achievement. Kirst, realizing that reform proposals
generally benefit the top two-thirds of students, proposes that schools
coordinate community resources to aid the other one-third. The bottom
one-third "needs drastic change in the current delivery system and an
overall attack on out-of-school influences that inhibit school attainment."

The 1960s and 1970s were periods when liberal ideology dominated
domestic policy. The role of government (federal, in particular) was greatly
expanded, as were funds and control, in efforts to narrow the differences
between schools. It was a period in which the primary mission of education
focused on achieving equity and increasing educational opportunities for
the economically disadvantaged. The 1980s, on the other hand, has been
a decade during which conservatism has reemerged. Excellence has begun
to replace equity as a major rallying cry for American education. As Apple
(Chapter 13) laments:

> No longer is education seen as part of a social alliance which combines
> many minority groups, women, teachers, administrators, government
> officials, and progressively inclined legislators who act together to pro-
> pose social democratic policies for schools (e.g., expanding educational
> opportunities, developing special programs in bilingual and multicul-
> tural education and for the handicapped, and so on). A new alliance
> has been formed, one that has increasing power in educational and
> social policy. This power bloc combines industry with the New Right.

Unfortunately, all too often equity and excellence are seen as mutually
exclusive. Although conceptually this may not be true, pragmatically it

may well be the case. In a society with limited resources, the expansion of programs to achieve excellence may necessitate (or be used as an excuse for) the elimination of programs that aspire toward equity. Indeed, as some of the contributors here have maintained, the early phases of the reform movement were not focused on questions of equity. As Hawley points out in Chapter 17, "Wave 1 policies and initiatives paid little attention to students who were physically, mentally, or environmentally handicapped, and federal spending for programs serving such children declined."

Many conservatives currently dominating the education reform movement claim that American education's failures, in recent years, have been due to the prioritization of equity at the expense of excellence. For example, the Heritage Foundation has stated:

> The most damaging blows to Science and Mathematics education have come from Washington. For the past 20 years, federal mandates have favored "disadvantaged" pupils at the expense of those who have the highest potential to contribute positively to society. . . . By catering to the demands of special interest groups—racial minorities, the handicapped, women, and non-English-speaking students—America's public schools have successfully competed for government funds, but have done so at the expense of education as a whole. (Pincus, 1985)

It appears at times that the advocates of excellence and the advocates of equity are talking past each other. The problem for the advocates of equity in education is how to achieve equity without appearing to support socialism; the problem for the advocates of excellence in education is how to achieve excellence without appearing to support social Darwinism. The apparent conflict between equity and excellence is essentially a confusion concerning the means and ends of education. Equity might be better viewed as a *means* for delivering education, with excellence cast as the ultimate *goal* of American education. In a democratic society, educational policy must deal with issues of both equity and excellence. Thus, a series of questions emerges regarding these dual goals:

- Should equity imply equal treatment, sameness for all, standardization?
- What differences among individuals should be accommodated or compensated for in the educational curriculum?
- Does such accommodation of different individual characteristics result in higher achievement, or does it lead instead to tracking, lowered expectations, and lowered opportunity?
- To what degree should the educational system intervene in the individual's life beyond the school in order to ensure success in the school?
- Does *excellence* imply that education will accommodate only the cream of the crop, and does it therefore support perpetual second-class citizenship for others?

- Or do competition and choice force educational quality for all to rise?
- Does the call for high standards in a standardized curriculum represent equal opportunity or discriminatory elitism for a privileged few?

THEME III: REDEFINING GOOD EDUCATION FOR A NEW CENTURY

A basic principle of any organizational change is that it must be goal-directed. Therefore, reform can only be evaluated in the context of a specific definition of *education* (Hawley, Chapter 17). One might think that *reform* implies a specificity of goals and directions, and that reformers have conceptually delineated and empirically operationalized what they mean. Logically, reform is seen as an antecedent condition necessary for the consequent condition: quality education. Unfortunately, while there has been much discussion about the antecedent reform issues, most reformers have failed to specify what is meant by a "good education." Beyond measures of student achievement and measures of teacher performance, the current reform movement has yet to struggle with the problem of defining this crucial concern.

Between 1893 and 1918, contrasting views of education emerged. One view, set forth in 1893 by the NEA's Committee of Ten (Cuban, Chapter 11), prescribed a detailed four-year curriculum of five major subject areas: languages (including English), mathematics, history, natural history (including biology, geology, and astronomy), and the physical sciences. The board was concerned with teaching the skills of observation, memory, expression, and reasoning to develop mental discipline and intellectual prowess. An opposing view was set forth in 1918 in *The Cardinal Principles of Secondary Education*, which posited that the purpose of education is to "develop in each individual the knowledge, interests, ideals, habits, and powers whereby he will find his place and use that place to shape both himself and society toward even nobler ends" (p. 7)

So, in the broadest sense, *education* can be divided into three categories: values, knowledge, and analytical techniques. *Values* include such concerns as citizenship and individual responsibility. *Knowledge* encompasses the learning of specific content (facts). *Analytical techniques* imply teaching students to learn by developing students' abilities to think critically, analyze problems, and reach solutions, irrespective of the empirical referent of the problem. Even many decades ago, then, there were several different ways of prioritizing these categories, reflecting the changing coalitions of public consensus (Cuban, Chapter 11).

Today, even more than the early 1900s, one of the major obstacles to education reform is the tendency to see values, knowledge, and analytical techniques as mutually exclusive. But if the goal of education is the creation of an informed, reflective, and active citizenry, then the educational system must integrate all three of these functions. An individual with a complete education should be able to select a problem based on his or her values, understand it fully, analyze the problem on the basis of its factual context, and develop a solution to the problem based on his or her problem-solving capabilities.

Another issue that is dealt with implicitly in each author's definition of *education* is the question of whether education should be more responsive to the workplace or to civil society. Honig, in Chapter 5, takes a middle ground, maintaining that "schools have a responsibility to prepare students for the workplace . . . [and] to encourage students as citizens."

Employers, concerned primarily with productivity, claim that knowledge and techniques are the essential ingredients of a high-quality education. In this context many (e.g., Apple, Chapter 13) have argued that the current reform movement, with its emphasis on training students in standard techniques and routinized knowledge, has become no more than the servant of corporations and public bureaucracies. Civil society, on the other hand (concerned with the individual as citizen, not employee), places primary emphasis on the importance of values.

Most of the chapters in this book maintain that a successful education gives students the tools they need to succeed both in the workplace and in civil society. This view implies that all three categories of education—values, analytical techniques, and knowledge—should be the goal of the educational system. The problem is that the educational system that may best fulfill any one or two of these goals may not be the educational system that can accomplish all three goals simultaneously. So, if one accepts such an all-encompassing notion of educational goals, the first problem for education reform is how to structure organizations that can achieve these different (and, at times, seemingly mutually exclusive) goals.

This may have seemed difficult to reformers at the turn of this century, but today each category is much more complicated than before. First, *values* used to be taught largely at home, with the extended family present as role models. Now, with the prevalence of broken or two-income nuclear families, the schools are left to teach values to children from diverse cultural backgrounds, and with little or no reinforcement from other institutions like the family.

Second, there has been an *explosion of new facts*, with the total amount of knowledge more than doubling every decade. This has meant that if students are to succeed professionally, they must *focus* their energies on a narrow specialty, and they must do so earlier than ever. This factor tends to crowd out general studies and prevent students from becoming well-rounded.

Finally, powerful new ways of thinking about the world have resulted in a proliferation of new *analytical techniques*. More than ever before, the real advances in thinking have come from people applying the latest techniques across different disciplines. This means that it is often necessary to learn new analytical techniques from fields in which one has little or no background. Teaching calculus to college statistics students who have not taken high school geometry is one example of this: Although they don't need to know geometry to understand statistics, they *do* need to know calculus, which in turn is more difficult to learn without any background in geometry.

These are some of the issues dealt with in Unit Four. Robert Reich (Chapter 16) discusses the types of traits that working people will need in order to survive in the economic world of the twenty-first century. He claims that Americans either will have to learn to live with Third World wages or else they will have to learn to produce high-quality, customized products or services for the ever-richer world market. To achieve this, our educational system must prepare our work force for more than the routinized, assembly-line jobs for which it now prepares them. In short, we now need workers who can be creative, innovative, and flexible.

Hawley (Chapter 17) laments the fact that today's schools are not designed for today's demographic realities (such as one-parent families), and that in trying to cram enough facts into kids so that they can pass standardized tests, teachers pay inadequate attention to the development of problem-solving and decision-making skills. Hawley links the two issues by claiming that the development of higher order skills appears to be strongly linked to the levels of cognitive demand placed on children during their social experiences outside of school.

Why is our society having difficulty educating the masses of students to be thinkers instead of mere fact regurgitators or trivia buffs? Is the problem that parents fail to demand enough from their children? Or is it perhaps instead that the structure of the school and the social system are set up to *penalize* those students who do respond to the demands placed on them at school. Bishop points out that employers rarely look at a student's high school transcript before deciding whether or not to hire that student, or how much to pay him or her. Therefore, students who do not have the desire or the money to go to an elite college have little incentive to do more than pass. In fact, there is a strong *social disincentive to working hard,* since the grading system is a fixed-sum game in which the high-achieving student is only hurting his or her best friends.

Looking at it from a different perspective, Futrell (Chapter 19) suggests that defining education purely in terms of the national *economic* interest may succeed in getting funds but may result in an unfortunate neglect of those aspects of education that are *intrinsically valuable,* such as civic responsibility, morality, and an aesthetic appreciation of music, literature, and art. Given that the economy and the culture are becoming more *global,* a narrow educational nationalism may not be appropriate for the future. Futrell implores us to seek "an education . . . that prepares them not only for a life of *work* but for a life of *worth.* . . ."

THEME IV: TOWARD AN EDUCATION MARKETPLACE—CHOICE OR GREATER INEQUALITY?

Before discussing this first prescriptive remedy, a quick review of the common ground that we have uncovered is in order. The first theme of this concluding chapter dealt with the difficulty of sorting out the appropriate roles for each level of government and group of participants (i.e., each interest group) in the educational system of the future. The second dealt with the recurring tension inherent in a system that attempts to achieve excellent results across an extremely diverse body of students. The third theme discussed the apparently contradictory needs for increasing specialization; a broad-based curriculum; and aesthetic, social, and creative skills in the current mass-produced system, which was designed to turn out good assembly-line workers. In other words, how can we change the system to better serve both college-bound and non-college-bound students. As Cuban (Chapter 11) suggests, perhaps it is finally time to question the basic structure of the comprehensive high school.

The underlying thread in these three themes is *the attempt to satisfy very diverse constituencies in a way that does not shortchange any of them.* This seems appropriate in our increasingly fragmented but still thoroughly pluralist process. At the heart of all the arguments is the belief that the *structures of public education*, both governmental and nongovernmental, need reforming in order to better serve *all* of its constituencies.

In Chapter 21, Cooper summarizes this issue in three questions:

1. What is the fundamental interest of the government, particularly at the federal level, in education—if any?
2. If the government must support education for economic and social reasons, why must it also own and operate schools as well?
3. If the government must fund and operate schools, why not allow families to choose from among a variety of state-run [public] schools and let these schools compete for students?

In answering these basic questions, Cooper emphasizes a limited role for government and a maximum role for the free local marketplace as a mechanism for assuring quality education. He sees tuition tax credits, tuition transfers, vouchers, and the like as a way to ensure the responsiveness of the educational system. On the other hand, critics from the left, like Apple (Chapter 13), oppose such a direction, claiming that it would be inevitably discriminatory in that higher income people would have access to better choices.

Because it seems to be so hard for our public school system simultaneously to teach *values, knowledge,* and *analytical techniques,* it may be only natural for schools to specialize a bit. Rather than trying to be all things to all people, schools should aim at a certain type of clientele—that is, at students who have a narrower range of needs from and expectations about school. Kerchner (Chapter 20) suggests that this would be a natural outgrowth of the predominant social values of this era. The neoconservative ideology that has been so successfully sold to the U.S. public lionizes *competition* and *choice*. Why shouldn't the public schools each develop a more distinct *service* and compete with other public schools for parent and student choice (Cooper, Chapter 21; Kerchner, Chapter 20)? One of the interesting side effects of such a transformation would be a new vision of school administrators as *public entrepreneurs*, while they and the other participants would tend to feel more like *owners* than cogs in a bureaucratic machine.

A good example of the benefits of this approach can be seen from the enthusiasm of Rochester, New York, teachers for the grand experiment in public choice that is now taking place there (Urbanski, Chapter 22). These staunch defenders of the public school system are crying out for market-style competition *within* that system in much the same way that Mikhail Gorbachev is crying for market reforms within the publicly run Soviet economy. Urbanski believes that the taxpayers will send more resources to schools *if and only if* they believe they are getting better results. Implicit in his argument is the sense that "better results" may mean different things to different "clients"—hence the need for *greater differentiation* between public schools, even those within the same system.

In effect, advocates and opponents of public choice are arguing about the appropriate roles of the participants in the educational process, as discussed under Theme I. Implicit in that debate over centralization are three primary policy questions:

1. Who will hold the focal responsibility for educational policy?
2. How do we ensure that our schools are responsive to the demands of the public and the needs of the nation?
3. From what level should reform be implemented?

When the question of centralization is broken down into these component parts, the stereotype of the left wing advocating centralization and the right wing advocating decentralization quickly falls apart. The right does see only minimal centralized government responsibility for school *financing*, but the right has also called for centralized quality control through core curricula and standardized teaching and student evaluation. The left, on the other hand, sees a greater fiscal role for the federal government, but maintains that the content of teaching and the criteria for evaluation should remain locally determined.

With respect to the second question, the left, on the one hand, opposes voucher systems because it maintains that they are inevitably discriminatory. On the other hand, in its pursuit of equity, the left suggests that schools must be responsive to the unique needs of different societal groups. The public choice option occupies an ambiguous middle ground, with the claim that it would not divert resources and the best students away from the public schools, while at the same time it would provide a structure of accountability in that failing schools would experience feedback in the form of declining enrollments.

With reference to the third question, both political camps agree with Passow (Chapter 1), who points out that "[s]hifting to the local district and the individual building as the unit for change and reform has proven, as has long been known, a complex and difficult process." The interesting thing is that both the right and the left seem to agree that successful reform can only occur on the local level. However, this leaves as problematic what the unit of analysis on the local level should be. Kirst (Chapter 2) maintains that: "The district is an important actor in local school reform. While education improvement occurs school site by school site, the appropriate unit for analyzing the local site improvement process is the school district, since the district can play several crucial and important roles in the site improvement process." Others in this book imply that the school should be the focal point of change. As we begin to accept that "the implementation of education reform is truly local and site-based" (Honig, Chapter 5), the question that emerges for all local officials is where best to begin this reform: with the students, the parents, the teachers, the classroom, the school, the district, the administration, or the school board. Whereas the first wave of the reform movement was concerned primarily with the role of the federal government versus the state government and localities, the second wave is beginning to confront the issue of inherent conflict between the district administration and the teachers and school-site leadership.

THEME V: RECONCEPTUALIZING THE ROLE OF THE TEACHER

The first wave of reform was implicitly guided by twin premises:

1. Achieving quality education depends on reducing uncertainty in the classroom.
2. Obtaining efficient schools depends on tightening bureaucratic controls and thereby making teacher behavior more predictable (and less uncertain) to administrators.

With these two premises, it was inevitable that the first wave of reform would emphasize merit pay, career ladders, and tight bureaucracies, based on the assumption that *standardization* would provide a mode of control that would enhance the quality of education. That is, *standardization was viewed as the best way to achieve higher standards.*

Unfortunately, as many of the chapters in this book point out, standardization as a mode of control may actually be the *least* effective way to achieve higher standards. As James Rundle points out in an unpublished paper, "Standardization as a Result of Education Reform," the effects of standardization on educational quality and on teachers are stated equivocally by some authors and hotly contested by others. The equivocators acknowledge that standards had slipped and that tightening of standards has probably been beneficial, but they doubt that current reform efforts will lead to substantial improvements in education (Boyd, Chapter 4; Boyer, Chapter 3; Shanker, Chapter 26; Kirst, Chapter 2).

The advocates of standardization claim that it is only through tighter control, routinized coursework, and rigid teacher evaluation that we will achieve a more effective educational system. Indeed, to reinforce this claim, they point to improvements in test scores and increases in the amount of academic coursework (and homework) done by high school students, and claim that texts, curriculum, student assessment, and teacher evaluation have all improved (Honig, Chapter 5). Detractors claim that teachers are being deskilled and demoralized by increasingly rigid requirements imposed from above, and that state mandates have worsened the climate of distrust (Passow, Chapter 1; Apple, Chapter 13; Hawley, Chapter 17), prevented teachers from responding flexibly to the varied needs of their students, and probably increased the dropout rate. (Hawley, Chapter 17; Metz, Chapter 12; Koretz, Chapter 29; Medina, Chapter 15).

The standardization issues fall into two categories:

1. The direct effects on the quality of teaching and the professionalization of teachers
2. The indirect effects on students, especially on disadvantaged students

During the more recent reform efforts, debate has raged over teacher empowerment, teacher discretion, and teacher professionalism (Futrell, Chapter 19). Some have argued that the recent reform efforts have deprofessionalized teaching through standardized specifications of teaching methods and evaluations. The argument is made that through the loss of discretion teachers are being deskilled (Apple, Chapter 13; Futrell, Chapter 19; Passow, Chapter 1; Shanker, Chapter 26).

Clearly, there is emerging tension between teacher discretion and administrative authority. Conley (Chapter 23) maintains that this implies a tension between two conflicting models of school management, the *bureaucratic* and the *professional*. She argues that the issue is how to achieve a middle ground between these two models. The bureaucratic model "treats teachers as technicians" and leads to attempts to reduce uncertainty, specify tasks in detail, and create "teacher-proof" curricula. Conley argues that these strategies, which characterized the first wave of reform, are incompatible with the complexity and uncertainty inherent in teaching.

On the other hand, the professional model "takes uncertainty as a given" and emphasizes the need for teachers to exercise professional judgment, initiative, and decision making. Teachers cannot, however, be free agents. They must therefore be "constrained decision makers," having influence but not authority over the policies that affect their work in the classroom. Conley advocates higher participation levels for teachers, improved professional preparation, and developmental (not remedial) evaluation systems.

Boyer (Chapter 3) agrees that teachers need more involvement in "key professional decisions," but also believes that the "K–12 curriculum lacks quality and coherence" and has strong opinions about what curricula should include, implying that he would favor some form of standardization. For both Boyer and Conley, the issue is not whether there will be standardization of curricula and teaching methods, but how much discretion teachers will be given and how much of a voice they will have in setting organizational constraints on that discretion.

Shedd (Chapter 8) reaches the same conclusion from a different perspective—that of teacher unions adapting collective bargaining to an environment in which there is no practical distinction between employer policies and working conditions. The cornerstone of the emerging system of collective bargaining in public education, he suggests, is the structuring of teachers' participation in school and district decision making. Like Conley and Boyer, Shedd develops an argument that foresees a different approach to school management.

At the heart of the standardization issue is evaluation (Glasman and Glasman, Chapter 30). The first wave of reform is widely viewed as placing an overreliance on standardized evaluation of teachers and students. Many fear that teachers will "teach to the test," emphasizing routine knowledge rather than creative thinking and problem-solving techniques (Shanker, Chapter 26). Sykes (Chapter 27) maintains that it is standardized evaluation and testing that have resulted in such unimaginative teaching. The problem for evaluation is how to achieve the quality control that is ensured by standardized testing while at the same time not stifling the creativity and experimentation that are so crucial in successfully teaching a diverse body of students. This takes us full circle back to the equity-versus-excellence argument.

Standardization has often been viewed as being unresponsive to the special needs of minorities and students at risk. As Metz argues in Chapter 12, if schools are going to help disadvantaged students, teachers need "skills in responding to students' life experiences, purpose, and perspectives." To the degree that standardization inhibits these efforts, an argument can be made that standardization only provides an illusion of equality and an obstacle to equity. Misplaced standardization may result in the most frustrating form of inequity—equal treatment of unequals.

In truth, we have come full circle; how we manage our schools will depend on what we expect our schools to accomplish. This circularity would suggest that maybe the time has come for a serious debate about the purpose of education. Until we clarify this issue (and stop sweeping it under the rug), we will inevitably be caught in the Sisyphean trap of rolling our stone of reform up the hill, only to have it roll back down. Only when we critically examine the goals of our educational system will we be able to strategically structure our schools and their functions to achieve these goals. An organization that is uncertain of its goals is incapable of strategic reform.

SOLTIS'S MISSING BOX: THE QUESTION OF REVOLUTION

Jonas Soltis (Chapter 32) offers an intriguing description when he discusses the current debate in education as "reform versus reformation." To date, he sees our efforts as those of well-intended reformers, but he sees our hopes as resting with the ambitions and goals of a reformation. By *reform*, Soltis primarily means incremental adjustments in the system within the given structure, purpose, and normative framework of our educational institutions. By *reformation*, he means change that is brought about by challenging the fundamental purposes of education.

Illustrating the differences between reform and reformation, Soltis discusses the need to expand the teacher's role in decision making. The movement from top-down to bottom-up management is seen by Soltis as indicative of a step toward reformation. If such distinctions can be accepted, many of the chapters in this book imply that the movement from the first wave of reform toward the second wave is in fact a movement away from reform and toward reformation.

What Soltis did *not* say was that the public choice advocates would probably claim that there needs to be a corresponding devolution of authority to *parents* as well. Although this need not conflict with the goals of teacher empowerment, it seems that one of the basic premises of the public choice argument is that *parents are qualified to make basic choices about the nature of their children's education.* This seems to be parallel to Martin Luther's conception of the role of prayer and conscience among lay Christians.

But Soltis forgot to stretch his historical metaphor back in time. Before the Protestants engaged in reformation of the Catholic Church, early Christianity emerged as a revolution in relation to Judaism. The debate between Peter and Paul was a debate between those who would reform Judaism and those who maintained that Judaism had to be revolutionized. Therefore, if we take Soltis's historical metaphor as a serious guiding tool, we must ask ourselves whether current activity in education will lead to reform, reformation, or revolution.

Reform, obviously . . .
Reformation, maybe . . .
Revolution, I doubt it. . . .

The bully pulpit has been effective, but even it must face the limits of the real world.

REFERENCE

Pincus, F. L. (1985). From equity to excellence: The rebirth of educational conservatism. In B. Gross & R. Gross (Eds.), *The great school debate.* New York: Simon & Schuster.

Index